Windows
Malware Analysis
Accelerated

with Memory Dumps

Dmitry Vostokov
Software Diagnostics Services

Published by OpenTask, Republic of Ireland

OpenTask books and magazines are available through booksellers and distributors worldwide. For further information or comments send requests to press@opentask.com.

A CIP catalogue record for this book is available from the British Library.

ISBN-l3: 978-1-908043-44-3 (Paperback)

First printing, 2013

Contents

Introduction

Hello Everyone, my name is Dmitry Vostokov and I teach this training course.

The main audience of this training are technical support and escalation engineers who analyze memory dumps from complex software environments using WinDbg debugger from Debugging Tools for Windows and need to check for possible malware presence in cases of abnormal software behavior. Software engineers, quality assurance and software maintenance engineers, security researchers and malware analysts who have never used this WinDbg debugger for analysis of computer memory may find this training useful as well as they learn how familiar malware detection and analysis concepts map into WinDbg commands. The ability to read assembly language has some advantages but not strictly necessary.

Our primary goal is to learn malware memory dump analysis in accelerated fashion. In other accelerated courses we first reviewed absolutely essential fundamentals necessary for memory dump analysis. Here we decided to review them as needed and start with analysis after a few introductory slides. During this course we learn how to analyze different types of memory dumps such as process, kernel and complete or physical memory. Kernel minidumps will not be covered in this training because they are similar to kernel memory dumps with much less information saved available for analysis and we need to be very lucky to find traces of malware in minidumps. Also this training about memory dump analysis and not about memory dump collection methods, tricks and tips although I provide you a reference for memory acquisition during this training.

Training Principles

- Talk only about what I can show

- Lots of pictures

- Original content and examples

For me there were many training formats to consider for this training and I decided that the best way is to concentrate on exercises and explain concepts as necessary because the main audience should be familiar with WinDbg already.

This course is split into 2 parts: user space process memory analysis and kernel and complete or physical space analysis. To facilitate more questions and answers we split training into 4 one-hour sessions and also added another two-hour session 20 days later for those who can't attend but anyone from you are welcome to attend and send me questions in the mean time so I could improve this training and may be add additional material.

Malware and Victimware

Typical scenarios when we want to check for possible malware presence:

⊚ System or application abnormal behavior

⊚ Controlled crash dumps during or after tracing and monitoring

Because this course is primarily targeted to support engineers there are typical scenarios when we want to check for possible malware presence. First, there are typical situations when we have abnormal software behaviour such as crashes, hangs, CPU spikes, memory leaks. All these can result not only from unintentional software defects or complex component interaction but also from malware mistakes and could also result from intentional shutdown of processes and systems (some sort of denial-of-service attacks). The second scenario is when we proactively seek memory dump analysis or analyze memory dumps as supplemental artifacts to accompany software traces and logs. Note that malware may be completely transparent to observed software behavior that can be the same as without malware.

Pattern-Oriented Approach

- How malware can be written

- How can we see that in a dump file

- Using WinDbg as a support tool

Here we outline our approach based on the main audience of this training. From our analysis of how malware can be written we show through practical exercises how we can see that in memory dump files using WinDbg debugger from Debugging Tools for Windows. This tool is a primary support tool for analysis of computer memory in Windows software support teams.

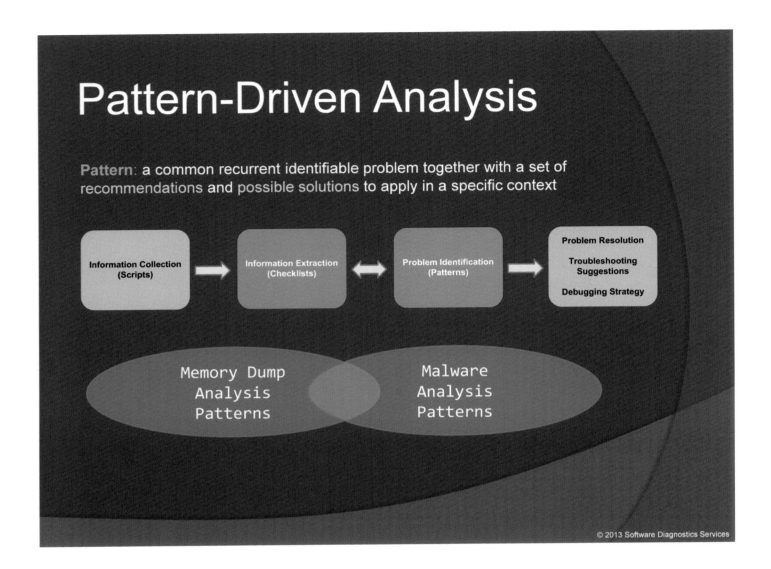

A few words about logs, checklists, and patterns. Memory dump analysis is usually an analysis of a text for presence of patterns. We run commands, they output text and then we look at that textual output and when we find something suspicious we execute more commands. Here checklists can be very useful. We provide a checklist by the end of this training. In some cases (such as complete memory dumps) it is benefitial to collect information into one log file by running several commands at once (like a script) and then do the first-order analysis. We will do that during our complete memory dump analysis exercise. Malware analysis patterns are patterns of intentional abnormal structure and behaviour. Because signs of non-intentional behaviour and intentional non-malicious behaviour such as value-adding hooking and code patching may be the same as intentional malicious behaviour such patterns may overlap with memory dump analysis patterns.

Practice Exercises

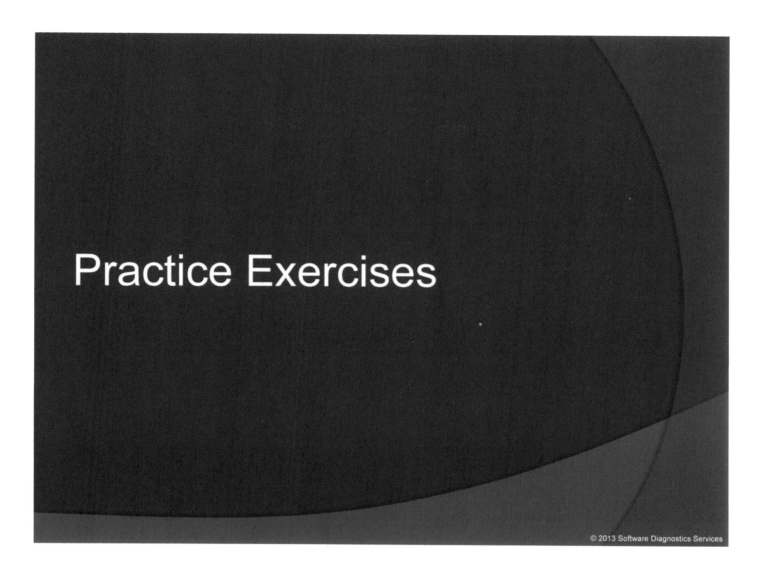

Now we come to practice. The goal is to show you important commands and how their output helps in recognizing malware analysis patterns.

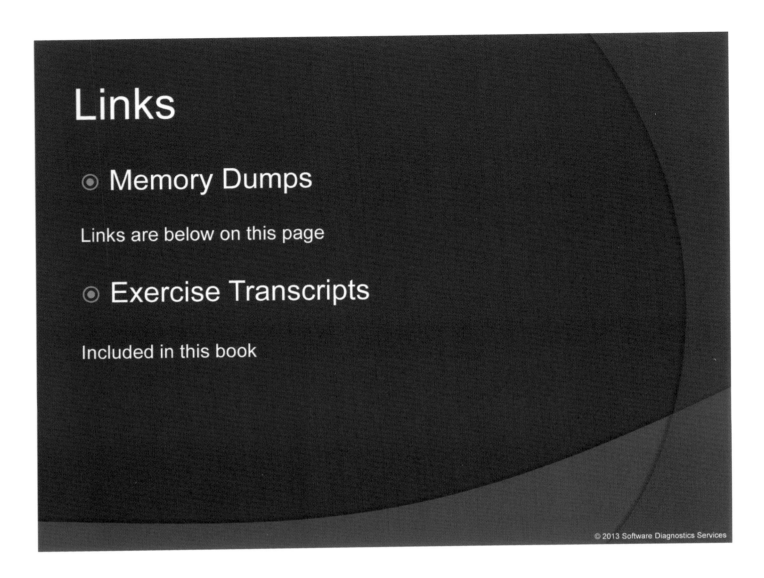

http://www.dumpanalysis.com/Training/AWMA/AWMA-Dumps-Part1.zip
http://www.dumpanalysis.com/Training/AWMA/AWMA-Dumps-Part2.zip
http://www.dumpanalysis.com/Training/AWMA/AWMA-Dumps-Part3.zip
http://www.dumpanalysis.com/Training/AWMA/AWMA-Dumps-Part4.zip
http://www.dumpanalysis.com/Training/AWMA/InjectionResidue.zip

Exercise 0

- **Goal:** Install Debugging Tools for Windows and learn how to set up symbols correctly

- **Patterns:** Incorrect Stack Trace

- \AWMA-Dumps\Exercise-0-Download-Setup-WinDbg.pdf

Here I assume you already prepared the environment and skip this exercise.

Exercise 0: Download, setup and verify your WinDbg installation

Goal: Install Debugging Tools for Windows and learn how to set up symbols correctly.

Patterns: Incorrect Stack Trace

1.   Download and install the latest version of Debugging Tools for Windows (x86 or x64 or both) using links from WinDbg.org

2.   Choose Complete option during installation

3.   Launch WinDbg from Windows Kits \ Debugging Tools for Windows (X64) or Debugging Tools for Windows (X86)

4.   Open \AWMA-Dumps\Processes\notepad.DMP

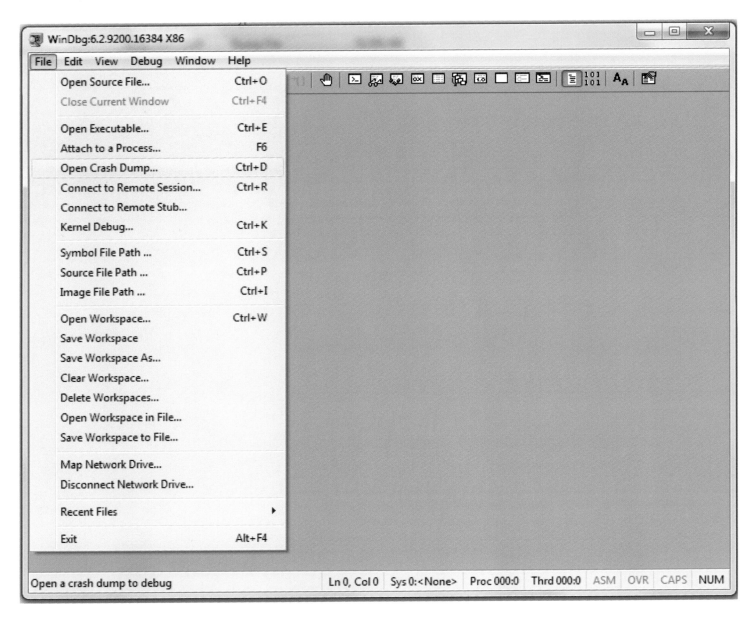

5.   If you are presented with this dialog say No:

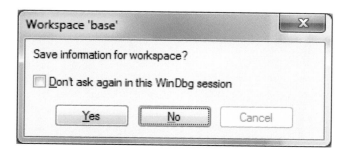

6.   You get the dump file loaded:

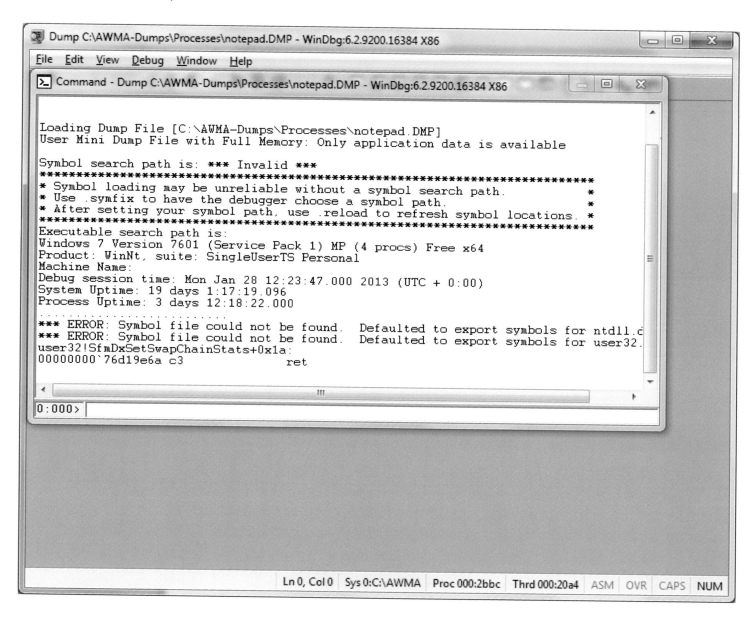

7. Type the command **.symfix c:\mss** to set a path to download symbol files from Microsoft symbol file server (use ENTER to execute commands after typing):

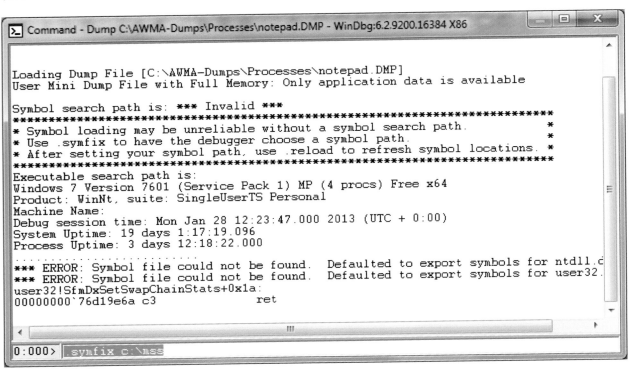

8. Type **.reload** command to download them if necessary

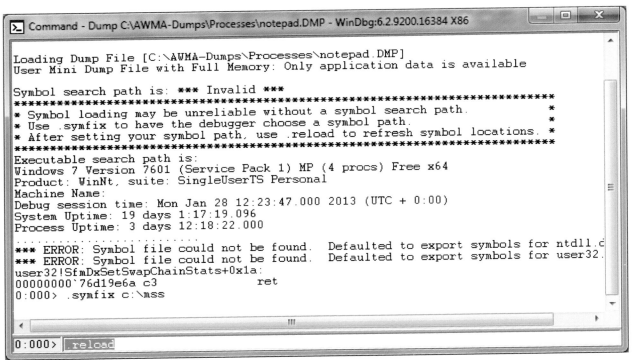

9.   Type **k** command to verify the correctness of stack trace:

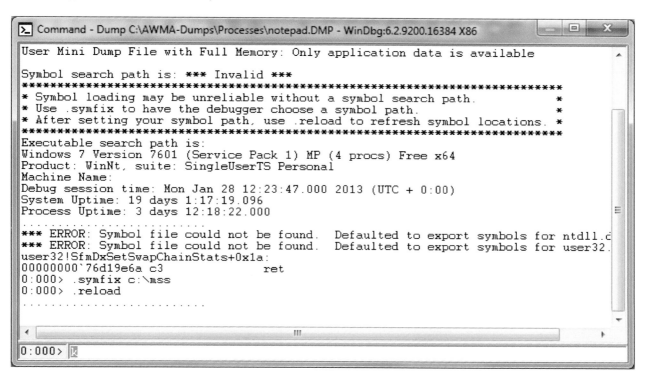

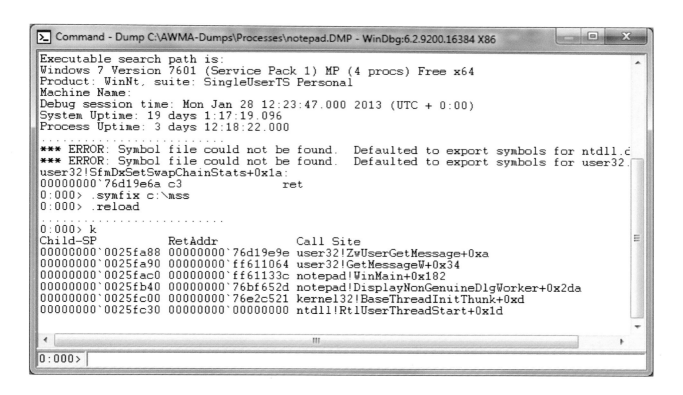

10. The output of command shoud be this:

```
0:000> k
Child-SP          RetAddr           Call Site
00000000`0025fa88 00000000`76d19e9e user32!ZwUserGetMessage+0xa
00000000`0025fa90 00000000`ff611064 user32!GetMessageW+0x34
00000000`0025fac0 00000000`ff61133c notepad!WinMain+0x182
00000000`0025fb40 00000000`76bf652d notepad!DisplayNonGenuineDlgWorker+0x2da
00000000`0025fc00 00000000`76e2c521 kernel32!BaseThreadInitThunk+0xd
00000000`0025fc30 00000000`00000000 ntdll!RtlUserThreadStart+0x1d
```

If it has one of these forms below then your symbol files were not set up correctly (*coloring is mine*) - **Incorrect Stack Trace** pattern (from memory dump analysis pattern catalog):

```
0:000> k
Child-SP          RetAddr           Call Site
00000000`0025fa88 00000000`76d19e9e user32!SfmDxSetSwapChainStats+0x1a
*** ERROR: Module load completed but symbols could not be loaded for notepad.exe
00000000`0025fa90 00000000`ff611064 user32!GetMessageW+0x2a
00000000`0025fac0 00000000`ff61133c notepad+0x1064
*** ERROR: Symbol file could not be found.  Defaulted to export symbols for kernel32.dll -
00000000`0025fb40 00000000`76bf652d notepad+0x133c
*** ERROR: Symbol file could not be found.  Defaulted to export symbols for ntdll.dll -
00000000`0025fc00 00000000`76e2c521 kernel32!BaseThreadInitThunk+0xd
00000000`0025fc30 00000000`00000000 ntdll!RtlUserThreadStart+0x21
```

```
0:000> k
Child-SP          RetAddr           Call Site
00000000`0025fa88 00000000`76d19e9e user32!SfmDxSetSwapChainStats+0x1a
00000000`0025fa90 00000000`ff611064 user32!GetMessageW+0x2a
00000000`0025fac0 00000000`ff61133c notepad+0x1064
00000000`0025fb40 00000000`76bf652d notepad+0x133c
00000000`0025fc00 00000000`76e2c521 kernel32!BaseThreadInitThunk+0xd
00000000`0025fc30 00000000`00000000 ntdll!RtlUserThreadStart+0x21
```

11. To avoid possible confusion and glitches we recommend exiting WinDbg after each exercise.

If you are presented with this dialog choose No:

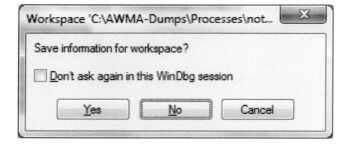

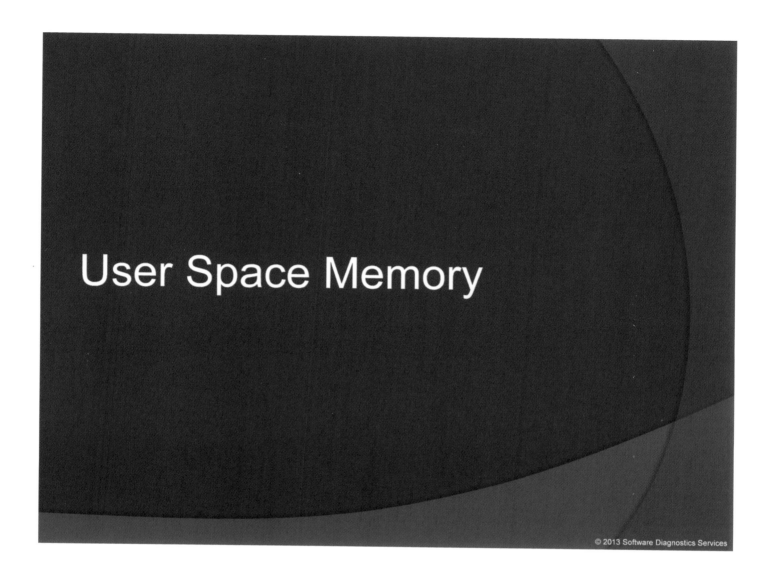

All exercises were modelled on real-life examples using specially constructed applications. All process dumps were saved from Windows Vista and Windows 7 systems running on real hardware.

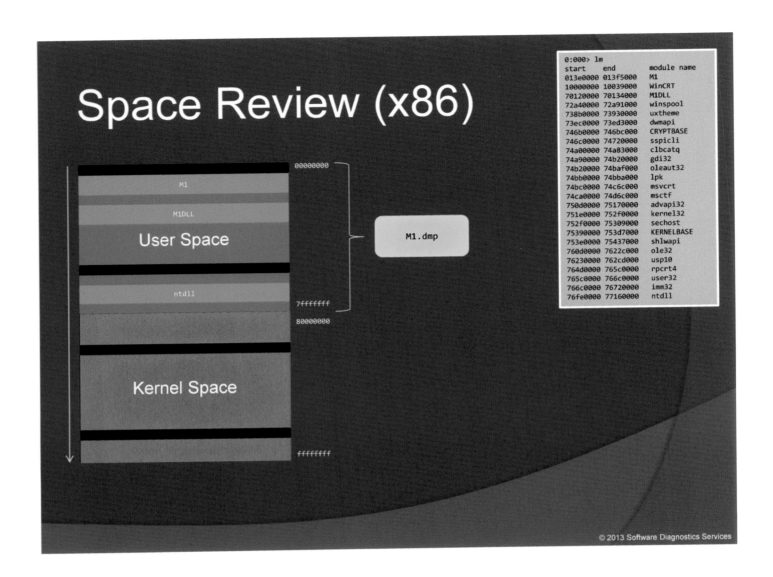

Space Review (x86)

```
0:000> lm
start    end        module name
013e0000 013f5000   M1
10000000 10039000   WinCRT
70120000 70134000   M1DLL
72a40000 72a91000   winspool
738b0000 73930000   uxtheme
73ec0000 73ed3000   dwmapi
746b0000 746bc000   CRYPTBASE
746c0000 74720000   sspicli
74a00000 74a83000   clbcatq
74a90000 74b20000   gdi32
74b20000 74baf000   oleaut32
74bb0000 74bba000   lpk
74bc0000 74c6c000   msvcrt
74ca0000 74d6c000   msctf
750d0000 75170000   advapi32
751e0000 752f0000   kernel32
752f0000 75309000   sechost
75390000 753d7000   KERNELBASE
753e0000 75437000   shlwapi
760d0000 7622c000   ole32
76230000 762cd000   usp10
764d0000 765c0000   rpcrt4
765c0000 766c0000   user32
766c0000 76720000   imm32
76fe0000 77160000   ntdll
```

Labels in diagram: M1, M1DLL, User Space, ntdll, Kernel Space, M1.dmp

Addresses: 00000000, 7fffffff, 80000000, ffffffff

Most of you are familiar with 32-bit process address space mapping especially if you attended or read Accelerated Windows Memory Dump Analysis course as most of you indicated when registering. So I just briefly repeat that when we run an application or service its executable file is loaded into memory and if it references other DLLs they are loaded too at some addresses in memory. There may be gaps between them like black regions on this picture. Some memory is also allocated for additional working regions needed for process execution. What kind of memory is of no importance to us when we look at a process memory dump. It usually has 2 GB range and we see addresses where modules are loaded by using **lm** command. When we save a dump all accessible memory including loaded modules are saved. The dump is usually much smaller than 2 GB unless we have a memory leak or application is memory demanding such as an in-memory database, for example. Please also note that we reversed the direction of the space diagram if you compare with Accelerated Windows Memory Dump Analysis training to keep the same direction we see in WinDbg such as when we have lower addresses on top and memory addresses increase down.

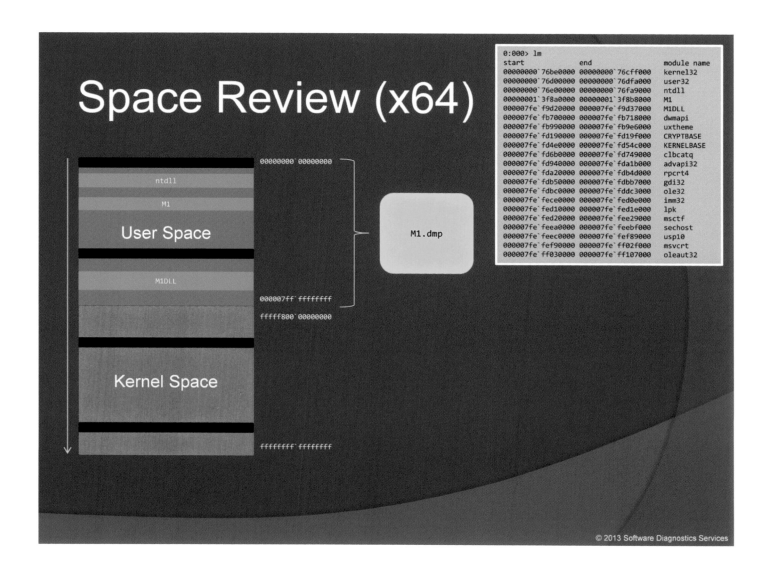

Here we provide a picture for a process space in 64-bit Windows. You see that user space is no longer restricted to 2 or 3 GB. Some DLLs are loaded in 2 GB address range as before but many others are loaded at higher addresses. We see that space distribution when we do a later exercise. But for now we first look at executable files and DLLs.

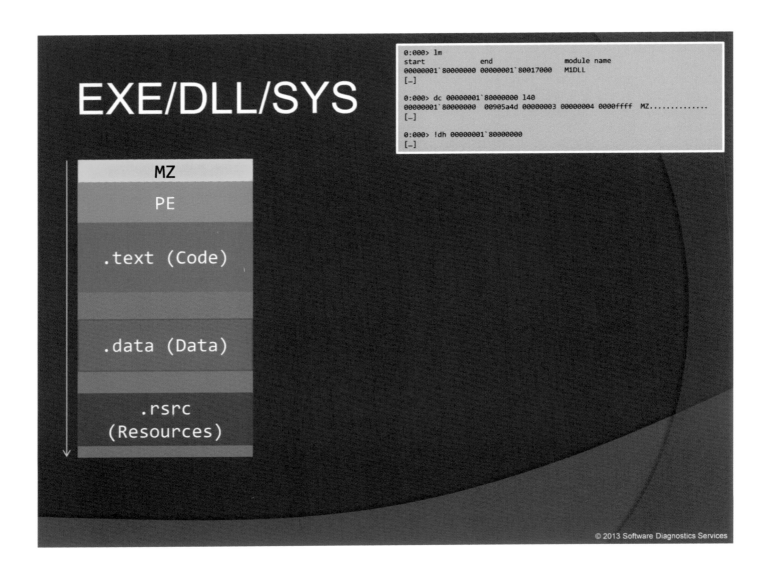

Executable files, DLLs and drivers (.SYS) all share the same format. The first comes old MS DOS header with MZ signature and then PE header or Portable Executable header that contains relative pointers or offsets to sections of code, data and resources such as localized strings and dialog descriptions. However, anything can be stored as a resource and we see that later in one of exercises.

Exercise M1A

- **Goal:** Look at module headers and version information before load

- **Patterns:** Unknown Module

- \AWMA-Dumps\Exercise-M1A.pdf

In addition to loading crash dumps in WinDbg we can also load an executable or a DLL file as a crash dump. We do this in our first exercise.

Goal: Look at module headers and version information before load.

Patterns: Unknown Module

1.   Launch WinDbg from Windows Kits \ Debugging Tools for Windows (X64) or Debugging Tools for Windows (X86)

2.   Open \AWMA-Dumps\Executables\M1.exe

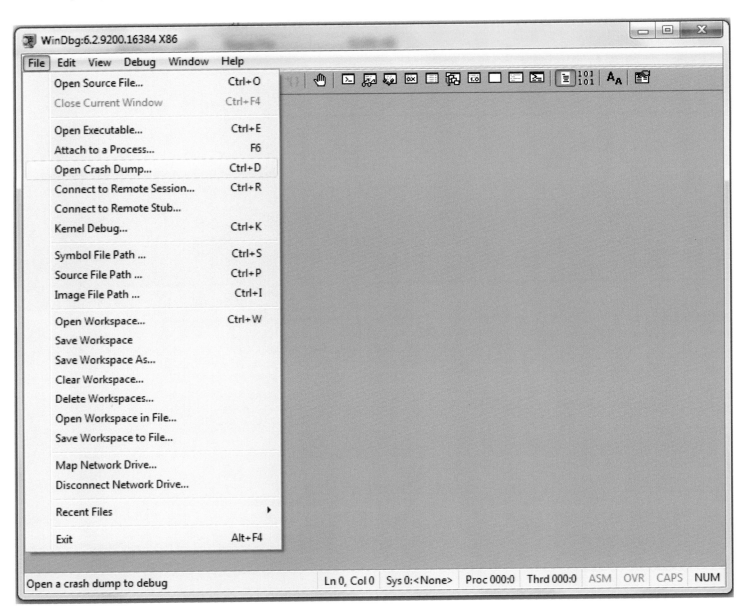

3. If you are presented with this dialog say No:

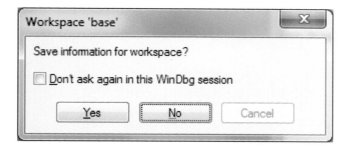

4. You get the EXE file loaded:

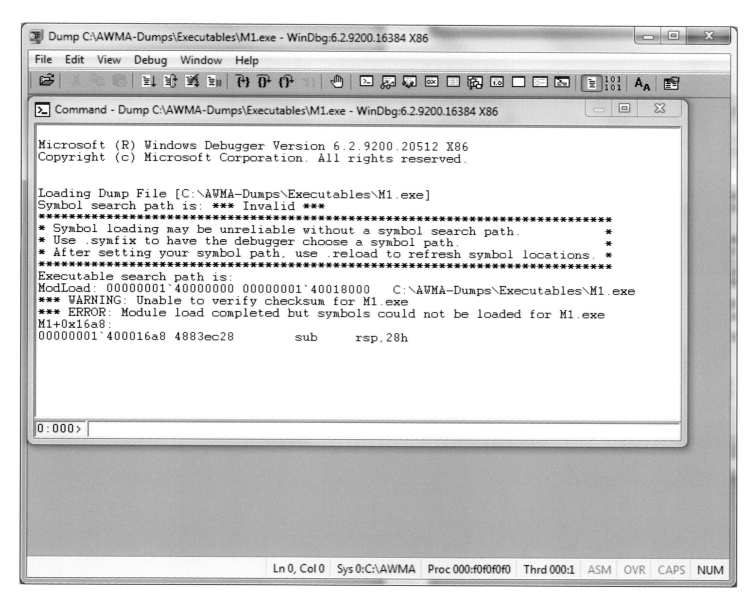

5. Symbols are not necessary here.

6.   Open a log file:

```
0:000> .logopen C:\AWMA-Dumps\M1A.log
Opened log file 'C:\AWMA-Dumps\M1A.log'
```

7.   **lmv** command lists module information:

```
0:000> lmv
start             end               module name
00000001`40000000 00000001`40018000  M1        C (no symbols)
    Loaded symbol image file: M1.exe
    Mapped memory image file: C:\AWMA-Dumps\Executables\M1.exe
    Image path: C:\AWMA-Dumps\Executables\M1.exe
    Image name: M1.exe
    Timestamp:        Mon Jan 28 15:24:45 2013 (5106983D)
    CheckSum:         00000000
    ImageSize:        00018000
    Translations:     0000.04b0 0000.04e4 0409.04b0 0409.04e4
```

Note module default load address.

8.   **!lmi** command gives a bit more information:

```
0:000> !lmi 00000001`40000000
Loaded Module Info: [00000001`40000000]
         Module: M1
   Base Address: 0000000140000000
     Image Name: M1.exe
   Machine Type: 34404 (X64)
     Time Stamp: 5106983d Mon Jan 28 15:24:45 2013
           Size: 18000
       CheckSum: 0
Characteristics: 22
Debug Data Dirs: Type  Size       VA  Pointer
         CODEVIEW    3b, e370,    cb70 RSDS - GUID: {3F1487A5-A6DC-4351-AD23-76FC12BB9482}
             Age: 1, Pdb: C:\Work\AWMA\M1\x64\Release\M1.pdb
                 ??    10, e3ac,    cbac [Data not mapped]
     Image Type: FILE     - Image read successfully from debugger.
                 M1.exe
    Symbol Type: NONE     - PDB not found from image path.
    Load Report: no symbols loaded
```

Note a reference to a PDB file. If left by a developer it might give some clues as we in other exercises.

9.   We dump the first kilobyte:

```
0:000> dc 00000001`40000000 L100
00000001`40000000  00905a4d 00000003 00000004 0000ffff  MZ..............
00000001`40000010  000000b8 00000000 00000040 00000000  ........@.......
00000001`40000020  00000000 00000000 00000000 00000000  ................
00000001`40000030  00000000 00000000 00000000 000000e8  ................
00000001`40000040  0eba1f0e cd09b400 4c01b821 685421cd  ........!..L.!Th
00000001`40000050  70207369 72676f72 63206d61 6f6e6e61  is program canno
00000001`40000060  65622074 6e757220 206e6920 20534f44  t be run in DOS
00000001`40000070  65646f6d 0a0d0d2e 00000024 00000000  mode....$.......
```

32

```
00000001`40000080    cb8e1818 98e0795c 98e0795c 98e0795c    ....\y..\y..\y..
00000001`40000090    982fbfad 98e0794e 982ebfad 98e07908    ../.Ny.......y..
00000001`400000a0    982dbfad 98e0795b 98e1795c 98e07903    ..-.[y..\y...y..
00000001`400000b0    98590ea0 98e07959 9833befe 98e0795e    ..Y.Yy....3.^y..
00000001`400000c0    9829befe 98e0795d 9877795c 98e0795d    ..).]y..\yw.]y..
00000001`400000d0    982cbefe 98e0795d 68636952 98e0795c    ..,.]y..Rich\y..
00000001`400000e0    00000000 00000000 00004550 00068664    .........PE..d...
00000001`400000f0    5106983d 00000000 00000000 002200f0    =..Q..........".
00000001`40000100    000b020b 00007400 0000d200 00000000    .....t..........
00000001`40000110    000016a8 00001000 40000000 00000001    ............@....
00000001`40000120    00001000 00000200 00000006 00000000    ................
00000001`40000130    00000006 00000000 00018000 00000400    ................
00000001`40000140    00000000 81600002 00100000 00000000    ......`.........
00000001`40000150    00001000 00000000 00100000 00000000    ................
00000001`40000160    00001000 00000000 00000000 00000010    ................
00000001`40000170    00000000 00000000 0000eaa4 0000003c    ..............<.
00000001`40000180    00015000 00001d68 00014000 0000078c    .P..h....@......
00000001`40000190    00000000 00000000 00017000 00000530    ..........p..0...
00000001`400001a0    00009320 00000038 00000000 00000000    ...8............
00000001`400001b0    00000000 00000000 00000000 00000000    ................
00000001`400001c0    0000e300 00000070 00000000 00000000    ....p...........
00000001`400001d0    00009000 000002a0 00000000 00000000    ................
00000001`400001e0    00000000 00000000 00000000 00000000    ................
00000001`400001f0    7865742e 00000074 0000731b 00001000    .text....s......
00000001`40000200    00007400 00000400 00000000 00000000    .t..............
00000001`40000210    00000000 60000020 6164722e 00006174    .... ..`.rdata..
00000001`40000220    00006366 00009000 00006400 00007800    fc.......d...x..
00000001`40000230    00000000 00000000 00000000 40000040    ............@..@
00000001`40000240    7461642e 00000061 00003900 00010000    .data....9......
00000001`40000250    00001400 0000dc00 00000000 00000000    ................
00000001`40000260    00000000 c0000040 6164702e 00006174    ....@....pdata..
00000001`40000270    0000078c 00014000 00000800 0000f000    ......@.........
00000001`40000280    00000000 00000000 00000000 40000040    ............@..@
00000001`40000290    7273722e 00000063 00001d68 00015000    .rsrc...h....P..
00000001`400002a0    00001e00 0000f800 00000000 00000000    ................
00000001`400002b0    00000000 40000040 6c65722e 0000636f    ....@..@.reloc..
00000001`400002c0    00000c52 00017000 00000e00 00011600    R....p..........
00000001`400002d0    00000000 00000000 00000000 42000040    ............@..B
00000001`400002e0    00000000 00000000 00000000 00000000    ................
00000001`400002f0    00000000 00000000 00000000 00000000    ................
00000001`40000300    00000000 00000000 00000000 00000000    ................
00000001`40000310    00000000 00000000 00000000 00000000    ................
00000001`40000320    00000000 00000000 00000000 00000000    ................
00000001`40000330    00000000 00000000 00000000 00000000    ................
00000001`40000340    00000000 00000000 00000000 00000000    ................
00000001`40000350    00000000 00000000 00000000 00000000    ................
00000001`40000360    00000000 00000000 00000000 00000000    ................
00000001`40000370    00000000 00000000 00000000 00000000    ................
00000001`40000380    00000000 00000000 00000000 00000000    ................
00000001`40000390    00000000 00000000 00000000 00000000    ................
00000001`400003a0    00000000 00000000 00000000 00000000    ................
00000001`400003b0    00000000 00000000 00000000 00000000    ................
00000001`400003c0    00000000 00000000 00000000 00000000    ................
00000001`400003d0    00000000 00000000 00000000 00000000    ................
00000001`400003e0    00000000 00000000 00000000 00000000    ................
00000001`400003f0    00000000 00000000 00000000 00000000    ................
```

10. **!dh** command dumps PE header:

```
0:000> !dh 00000001`40000000

File Type: EXECUTABLE IMAGE
FILE HEADER VALUES
    8664 machine (X64)
       6 number of sections
5106983D time date stamp Mon Jan 28 15:24:45 2013

       0 file pointer to symbol table
       0 number of symbols
      F0 size of optional header
      22 characteristics
            Executable
            App can handle >2gb addresses


OPTIONAL HEADER VALUES
     20B magic #
   11.00 linker version
    7400 size of code
    D200 size of initialized data
       0 size of uninitialized data
    16A8 address of entry point
    1000 base of code
         ----- new -----
0000000140000000 image base
    1000 section alignment
     200 file alignment
       2 subsystem (Windows GUI)
    6.00 operating system version
    0.00 image version
    6.00 subsystem version
   18000 size of image
     400 size of headers
       0 checksum
0000000000100000 size of stack reserve
0000000000001000 size of stack commit
0000000000100000 size of heap reserve
0000000000001000 size of heap commit
    8160 DLL characteristics
            High entropy VA supported
            Dynamic base
            NX compatible
            Terminal server aware
       0 [       0] address [size] of Export Directory
    EAA4 [      3C] address [size] of Import Directory
   15000 [    1D68] address [size] of Resource Directory
   14000 [     78C] address [size] of Exception Directory
       0 [       0] address [size] of Security Directory
   17000 [     530] address [size] of Base Relocation Directory
    9320 [      38] address [size] of Debug Directory
       0 [       0] address [size] of Description Directory
       0 [       0] address [size] of Special Directory
       0 [       0] address [size] of Thread Storage Directory
    E300 [      70] address [size] of Load Configuration Directory
       0 [       0] address [size] of Bound Import Directory
    9000 [     2A0] address [size] of Import Address Table Directory
       0 [       0] address [size] of Delay Import Directory
       0 [       0] address [size] of COR20 Header Directory
```

34

```
        0 [        0] address [size] of Reserved Directory


SECTION HEADER #1
   .text name
     731B virtual size
     1000 virtual address
     7400 size of raw data
      400 file pointer to raw data
        0 file pointer to relocation table
        0 file pointer to line numbers
        0 number of relocations
        0 number of line numbers
 60000020 flags
          Code
          (no align specified)
          Execute Read


SECTION HEADER #2
   .rdata name
     6366 virtual size
     9000 virtual address
     6400 size of raw data
     7800 file pointer to raw data
        0 file pointer to relocation table
        0 file pointer to line numbers
        0 number of relocations
        0 number of line numbers
 40000040 flags
          Initialized Data
          (no align specified)
          Read Only



Debug Directories(2)
        Type        Size    Address   Pointer
         cv          3b       e370     cb70    Format: RSDS, guid, 1,
C:\Work\AWMA\M1\x64\Release\M1.pdb
       (    12)      10       e3ac     cbac

SECTION HEADER #3
   .data name
     3900 virtual size
    10000 virtual address
     1400 size of raw data
     DC00 file pointer to raw data
        0 file pointer to relocation table
        0 file pointer to line numbers
        0 number of relocations
        0 number of line numbers
 C0000040 flags
          Initialized Data
          (no align specified)
          Read Write
```

```
SECTION HEADER #4
  .pdata name
     78C virtual size
   14000 virtual address
     800 size of raw data
    F000 file pointer to raw data
       0 file pointer to relocation table
       0 file pointer to line numbers
       0 number of relocations
       0 number of line numbers
40000040 flags
         Initialized Data
         (no align specified)
         Read Only

SECTION HEADER #5
  .rsrc name
    1D68 virtual size
   15000 virtual address
    1E00 size of raw data
    F800 file pointer to raw data
       0 file pointer to relocation table
       0 file pointer to line numbers
       0 number of relocations
       0 number of line numbers
40000040 flags
         Initialized Data
         (no align specified)
         Read Only

SECTION HEADER #6
  .reloc name
     C52 virtual size
   17000 virtual address
     E00 size of raw data
   11600 file pointer to raw data
       0 file pointer to relocation table
       0 file pointer to line numbers
       0 number of relocations
       0 number of line numbers
42000040 flags
         Initialized Data
         Discardable
         (no align specified)
         Read Only
```

Note Import Address Table and code .text section.

11.   Let's look at Import Address Table before dynamic linking takes place:

```
0:000> dps 00000001`40000000+9000 L2A0/8
00000001`40009000  00000000`0000ed80
00000001`40009008  00000000`0000f34a
00000001`40009010  00000000`0000f33a
00000001`40009018  00000000`0000f326
00000001`40009020  00000000`0000f316
00000001`40009028  00000000`0000f304
00000001`40009030  00000000`0000f2f4
00000001`40009038  00000000`0000f2e0
```

```
00000001`40009040    00000000`0000f2d0
00000001`40009048    00000000`0000f2c4
00000001`40009050    00000000`0000f2b2
00000001`40009058    00000000`0000f29c
00000001`40009060    00000000`0000f28e
00000001`40009068    00000000`0000f282
00000001`40009070    00000000`0000eee4
00000001`40009078    00000000`0000eef6
00000001`40009080    00000000`0000ef0a
00000001`40009088    00000000`0000ef26
00000001`40009090    00000000`0000ef36
00000001`40009098    00000000`0000ef46
00000001`400090a0    00000000`0000ef5c
00000001`400090a8    00000000`0000ef6c
00000001`400090b0    00000000`0000ef7c
00000001`400090b8    00000000`0000ef8a
00000001`400090c0    00000000`0000efa0
00000001`400090c8    00000000`0000efb2
00000001`400090d0    00000000`0000efc8
00000001`400090d8    00000000`0000efd8
00000001`400090e0    00000000`0000efe4
00000001`400090e8    00000000`0000effa
00000001`400090f0    00000000`0000f00c
00000001`400090f8    00000000`0000f01a
00000001`40009100    00000000`0000f042
00000001`40009108    00000000`0000f05a
00000001`40009110    00000000`0000f06c
00000001`40009118    00000000`0000f086
00000001`40009120    00000000`0000f09c
00000001`40009128    00000000`0000f0b6
00000001`40009130    00000000`0000f0d0
00000001`40009138    00000000`0000f0ea
00000001`40009140    00000000`0000f0fe
00000001`40009148    00000000`0000f118
00000001`40009150    00000000`0000f12c
00000001`40009158    00000000`0000f148
00000001`40009160    00000000`0000f166
00000001`40009168    00000000`0000f17a
00000001`40009170    00000000`0000f18e
00000001`40009178    00000000`0000f19a
00000001`40009180    00000000`0000f1a8
00000001`40009188    00000000`0000f1b6
00000001`40009190    00000000`0000f1c0
00000001`40009198    00000000`0000f1d4
00000001`400091a0    00000000`0000f1e2
00000001`400091a8    00000000`0000f1fa
00000001`400091b0    00000000`0000f212
00000001`400091b8    00000000`0000f21e
00000001`400091c0    00000000`0000f226
00000001`400091c8    00000000`0000f238
00000001`400091d0    00000000`0000f242
00000001`400091d8    00000000`0000f24e
00000001`400091e0    00000000`0000f25a
00000001`400091e8    00000000`0000f26c
00000001`400091f0    00000000`0000f358
00000001`400091f8    00000000`00000000
00000001`40009200    00000000`0000eecc
00000001`40009208    00000000`0000eeba
00000001`40009210    00000000`0000eeae
00000001`40009218    00000000`0000eea0
```

```
00000001`40009220  00000000`0000ee8e
00000001`40009228  00000000`0000ee7e
00000001`40009230  00000000`0000ee6c
00000001`40009238  00000000`0000ee5c
00000001`40009240  00000000`0000ee4e
00000001`40009248  00000000`0000ee3c
00000001`40009250  00000000`0000ee28
00000001`40009258  00000000`0000ee1a
00000001`40009260  00000000`0000ee0e
00000001`40009268  00000000`0000edfa
00000001`40009270  00000000`0000ede6
00000001`40009278  00000000`0000edce
00000001`40009280  00000000`0000edc0
00000001`40009288  00000000`0000edac
00000001`40009290  00000000`0000ed9e
00000001`40009298  00000000`00000000

0:000> dc 00000001`40000000+00000000`0000ed80 L100
00000001`4000ed80  6f4c03c6 694c6461 72617262 00005779  ..LoadLibraryW..
00000001`4000ed90  4e52454b 32334c45 6c6c642e 02330000  KERNEL32.dll..3.
00000001`4000eda0  64616f4c 69727453 0057676e 6f4c021e  LoadStringW...Lo
00000001`4000edb0  63416461 656c6563 6f746172 00577372  adAcceleratorsW.
00000001`4000edc0  65470175 73654d74 65676173 03410057  u.GetMessageW.A.
00000001`4000edd0  6e617254 74616c73 63634165 72656c65  TranslateAcceler
00000001`4000ede0  726f7461 03430057 6e617254 74616c73  atorW.C.Translat
00000001`4000edf0  73654d65 65676173 00b60000 70736944  eMessage....Disp
00000001`4000ee00  68637461 7373654d 57656761 02260000  atchMessageW..&.
00000001`4000ee10  64616f4c 6e6f6349 02240057 64616f4c  LoadIconW.$.Load
00000001`4000ee20  73727543 0057726f 6552028a 74736967  CursorW...Regist
00000001`4000ee30  6c437265 45737361 00005778 72430071  erClassExW..q.Cr
00000001`4000ee40  65746165 646e6957 7845776f 03240057  eateWindowExW.$.
00000001`4000ee50  776f6853 646e6957 0000776f 7055035b  ShowWindow..[.Up
00000001`4000ee60  65746164 646e6957 0000776f 694400b3  dateWindow....Di
00000001`4000ee70  676f6c61 50786f42 6d617261 00ad0057  alogBoxParamW...
00000001`4000ee80  74736544 57796f72 6f646e69 00a10077  DestroyWindow...
00000001`4000ee90  57666544 6f646e69 6f725077 00005763  DefWindowProcW..
00000001`4000eea0  6542000e 506e6967 746e6961 00ea0000  ..BeginPaint....
00000001`4000eeb0  50646e45 746e6961 02720000 74736f50  EndPaint..r.Post
00000001`4000eec0  74697551 7373654d 00656761 6e4500e8  QuitMessage...En
00000001`4000eed0  61694464 00676f6c 52455355 642e3233  dDialog.USER32.d
00000001`4000eee0  00006c6c 654701e9 6d6f4374 646e616d  ll....GetCommand
00000001`4000eef0  656e694c 03860057 65447349 67677562  LineW...IsDebugg
00000001`4000ef00  72507265 6e657365 038b0074 72507349  erPresent...IsPr
00000001`4000ef10  7365636f 46726f73 75746165 72506572  ocessorFeaturePr
00000001`4000ef20  6e657365 02700074 4c746547 45747361  esent.p.GetLastE
00000001`4000ef30  726f7272 05250000 4c746553 45747361  rror..%.SetLastE
00000001`4000ef40  726f7272 022e0000 43746547 65727275  rror....GetCurre
00000001`4000ef50  6854746e 64616572 00006449 6e450140  ntThreadId..@.En
00000001`4000ef60  65646f63 6e696f50 00726574 65440118  codePointer...De
00000001`4000ef70  65646f63 6e696f50 00726574 78450173  codePointer.s.Ex
00000001`4000ef80  72507469 7365636f 02860073 4d746547  itProcess...GetM
00000001`4000ef90  6c75646f 6e614865 45656c64 00005778  oduleHandleExW..
00000001`4000efa0  654702bc 6f725074 64644163 73736572  ..GetProcAddress
00000001`4000efb0  03ef0000 746c754d 74794269 576f5465  ....MultiByteToW
00000001`4000efc0  43656469 00726168 654702e4 64745374  ideChar...GetStd
00000001`4000efd0  646e6148 0000656c 72570601 46657469  Handle....WriteF
00000001`4000efe0  00656c69 65470283 646f4d74 46656c75  ile...GetModuleF
00000001`4000eff0  4e656c69 57656d61 02c10000 50746547  ileNameW....GetP
00000001`4000f000  65636f72 65487373 00007061 6547025e  rocessHeap..^.Ge
00000001`4000f010  6c694674 70795465 036f0065 74696e49  tFileType.o.Init
```

38

```
00000001`4000f020    696c6169 7243657a 63697469 65536c61    ializeCriticalSe
00000001`4000f030    6f697463 646e416e 6e697053 6e756f43    ctionAndSpinCoun
00000001`4000f040    011f0074 656c6544 72436574 63697469    t...DeleteCritic
00000001`4000f050    65536c61 6f697463 02de006e 53746547    alSection...GetS
00000001`4000f060    74726174 6e497075 00576f66 7551043f    tartupInfoW.?.Qu
00000001`4000f070    50797265 6f667265 6e616d72 6f436563    eryPerformanceCo
00000001`4000f080    65746e75 022a0072 43746547 65727275    unter.*.GetCurre
00000001`4000f090    7250746e 7365636f 00644973 654702fb    ntProcessId...Ge
00000001`4000f0a0    73795374 546d6574 41656d69 6c694673    tSystemTimeAsFil
00000001`4000f0b0    6d695465 02470065 45746547 7269766e    eTime.G.GetEnvir
00000001`4000f0c0    656d6e6f 7453746e 676e6972 00005773    onmentStringsW..
00000001`4000f0d0    724601bd 6e456565 6f726976 6e656d6e    ..FreeEnvironmen
00000001`4000f0e0    72745374 73676e69 04bb0057 436c7452    tStringsW...RtlC
00000001`4000f0f0    75747061 6f436572 7865746e 04c20074    aptureContext...
00000001`4000f100    4c6c7452 756b6f6f 6e754670 6f697463    RtlLookupFunctio
00000001`4000f110    746e456e 00007972 745204c9 7269566c    nEntry....RtlVir
00000001`4000f120    6c617574 69776e55 0000646e 6e5505a0    tualUnwind....Un
00000001`4000f130    646e6168 4564656c 70656378 6e6f6974    handledException
00000001`4000f140    746c6946 00007265 6553055f 686e5574    Filter.._.SetUnh
00000001`4000f150    6c646e61 78456465 74706563 466e6f69    andledExceptionF
00000001`4000f160    65746c69 02290072 43746547 65727275    ilter.).GetCurre
00000001`4000f170    7250746e 7365636f 057e0073 6d726554    ntProcess.~.Term
```

We see it contains function names that need to be imported from DLLs such as kernel32.dll and user32.dll.

12.   Close the log file:

```
0:000> .logclose
Closing open log file C:\AWMA-Dumps\M1A.log
```

13.   To avoid possible confusion and glitches we recommend exiting WinDbg after each exercise.

If you are presented with this dialog choose No:

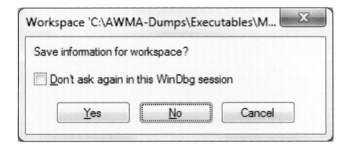

Dynamic Linking Design

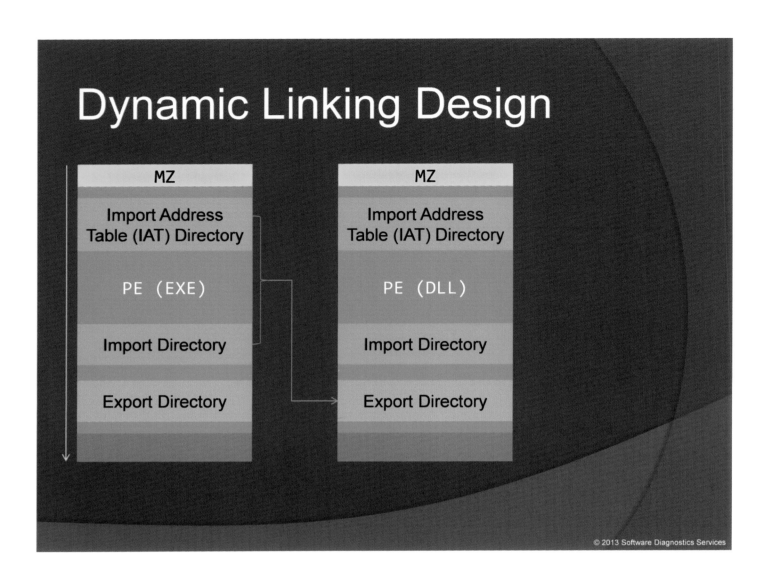

When a file such as an executable is loaded into memory a runtime OS linker checks if that module references other DLL files. Recall that DLL means Dynamic Link Library. This is basically a collection of code and data that can be shared among processes. In a PE header there is an Import Address Table that contains locations to store addresses of exported functions from another module. The same can also happen between DLLs, for example, user32.dll can reference ntdll.dll.

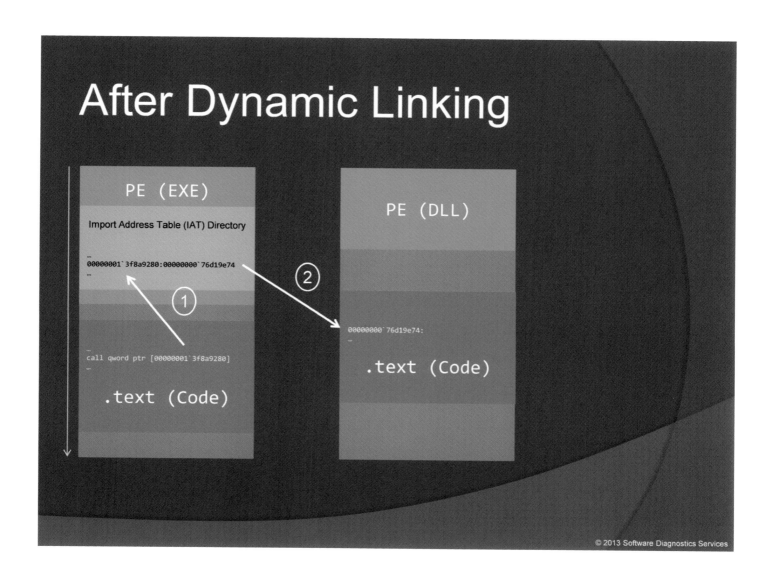

Linking changes Import Address Table directory by substituting each entry with a real address from another already loaded DLL module. Code that transfers execution to such addresses uses indirect addressing. It uses an address from Import Address Table that points to code in another module. We see that during one of exercises.

Exercise M1B

- **Goal:** Look at address map, module headers and version information after load, check IAT, check import library calls, check module integrity

- **Patterns:** Unknown Module

- \AWMA-Dumps\Exercise-M1B.pdf

Now in our next exercise we look at modules after dynamic linking had already completed and process memory was saved.

Goal: Look at address map, module headers and version information after load, check IAT, check import library calls, check module integrity.

Patterns: Unknown Module

1.   Launch WinDbg from Windows Kits \ Debugging Tools for Windows (X64) or Debugging Tools for Windows (X86)

2.   Open \AWMA-Dumps\Processes\M1.dmp

3.   If you are presented with this dialog say No:

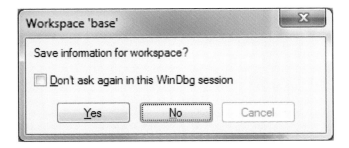

4.   You get the dump file loaded:

```
Microsoft (R) Windows Debugger Version 6.2.9200.20512 X86
Copyright (c) Microsoft Corporation. All rights reserved.


Loading Dump File [C:\AWMA-Dumps\Processes\M1.DMP]
User Mini Dump File with Full Memory: Only application data is available

Symbol search path is: *** Invalid ***
************************************************************************
* Symbol loading may be unreliable without a symbol search path.       *
* Use .symfix to have the debugger choose a symbol path.                *
* After setting your symbol path, use .reload to refresh symbol locations. *
************************************************************************
Executable search path is:
Windows 7 Version 7601 (Service Pack 1) MP (4 procs) Free x64
Product: WinNt, suite: SingleUserTS Personal
Machine Name:
Debug session time: Mon Jan 28 15:37:44.000 2013 (UTC + 0:00)
System Uptime: 19 days 4:31:16.182
Process Uptime: 0 days 0:00:14.000
....................
*** ERROR: Symbol file could not be found.  Defaulted to export symbols for ntdll.dll -
*** ERROR: Symbol file could not be found.  Defaulted to export symbols for user32.dll -
user32!SfmDxSetSwapChainStats+0x1a:
00000000`76d19e6a c3              ret
```

5.   Open a log file:

```
0:000> .logopen C:\AWMA-Dumps\M1B.log
Opened log file 'C:\AWMA-Dumps\M1B.log'
```

6.   Set up a link to Microsoft symbol server and reload symbols:

```
0:000> .symfix c:\mss

0:000> .reload
...................
```

7.   **lmt** command lists modules and their timestamps:

```
0:000> lmt
start             end                 module name
00000000`76be0000 00000000`76cff000  kernel32  Mon Aug 20 19:45:21 2012 (503285C1)
00000000`76d00000 00000000`76dfa000  user32    Sat Nov 20 13:15:29 2010 (4CE7C9F1)
00000000`76e00000 00000000`76fa9000  ntdll     Thu Nov 17 06:32:46 2011 (4EC4AA8E)
00000001`3f8a0000 00000001`3f8b8000  M1        Mon Jan 28 15:24:45 2013 (5106983D)
000007fe`f9d20000 000007fe`f9d37000  M1DLL     Mon Jan 28 15:24:48 2013 (51069840)
000007fe`fb700000 000007fe`fb718000  dwmapi    Tue Jul 14 02:28:07 2009 (4A5BDF27)
000007fe`fb990000 000007fe`fb9e6000  uxtheme   Tue Jul 14 02:34:11 2009 (4A5BE093)
000007fe`fd190000 000007fe`fd19f000  CRYPTBASE Tue Jul 14 02:29:53 2009 (4A5BDF91)
000007fe`fd4e0000 000007fe`fd54c000  KERNELBASE  Mon Aug 20 19:45:22 2012 (503285C2)
000007fe`fd6b0000 000007fe`fd749000  clbcatq   Tue Jul 14 02:26:18 2009 (4A5BDEBA)
000007fe`fd940000 000007fe`fda1b000  advapi32  Tue Jul 14 02:24:59 2009 (4A5BDE6B)
000007fe`fda20000 000007fe`fdb4d000  rpcrt4    Sat Nov 20 13:13:18 2010 (4CE7C96E)
000007fe`fdb50000 000007fe`fdbb7000  gdi32     Sat Nov 20 13:00:01 2010 (4CE7C651)
000007fe`fdbc0000 000007fe`fddc3000  ole32     Sat Nov 20 13:12:12 2010 (4CE7C92C)
000007fe`fece0000 000007fe`fed0e000  imm32     Tue Jul 14 02:28:32 2009 (4A5BDF40)
000007fe`fed10000 000007fe`fed1e000  lpk       Tue Jul 14 02:29:03 2009 (4A5BDF5F)
000007fe`fed20000 000007fe`fee29000  msctf     Tue Jul 14 02:30:18 2009 (4A5BDFAA)
000007fe`feea0000 000007fe`feebf000  sechost   Tue Jul 14 02:33:18 2009 (4A5BE05E)
000007fe`feec0000 000007fe`fef89000  usp10     Sat Nov 20 13:15:33 2010 (4CE7C9F5)
000007fe`fef90000 000007fe`ff02f000  msvcrt    Fri Dec 16 08:37:19 2011 (4EEB033F)
000007fe`ff030000 000007fe`ff107000  oleaut32  Sat Aug 27 06:21:44 2011 (4E587EE8)
```

Note the new module M1 load address.

8.   Let's look at the address map (note how many regions are of different type):

```
0:000> !address

Mapping file section regions...
Mapping module regions...
Mapping PEB regions...
Mapping TEB and stack regions...
Mapping heap regions...
Mapping page heap regions...
Mapping other regions...
Mapping stack trace database regions...
Mapping activation context regions...
```

```
           BaseAddress      EndAddress+1        RegionSize      Type       State           Protect              Usage
--------------------------------------------------------------------------------------------------------------------
+        0`00000000       0`00010000       0`00010000                 MEM_FREE    PAGE_NOACCESS          Free
+        0`00010000       0`00020000       0`00010000 MEM_MAPPED MEM_COMMIT  PAGE_READWRITE         Heap       [ID: 1; Handle:
0000000000010000; Type: Segment]
[…]
+        1`3f8a0000       1`3f8a1000       0`00001000 MEM_IMAGE  MEM_COMMIT  PAGE_READONLY          Image      [M1; "C:\AWMA\M1\x64\M1.exe"]
         1`3f8a1000       1`3f8a9000       0`00008000 MEM_IMAGE  MEM_COMMIT  PAGE_EXECUTE_READ      Image      [M1; "C:\AWMA\M1\x64\M1.exe"]
         1`3f8a9000       1`3f8b0000       0`00007000 MEM_IMAGE  MEM_COMMIT  PAGE_READONLY          Image      [M1; "C:\AWMA\M1\x64\M1.exe"]
         1`3f8b0000       1`3f8b4000       0`00004000 MEM_IMAGE  MEM_COMMIT  PAGE_READWRITE         Image      [M1; "C:\AWMA\M1\x64\M1.exe"]
         1`3f8b4000       1`3f8b8000       0`00004000 MEM_IMAGE  MEM_COMMIT  PAGE_READONLY          Image      [M1; "C:\AWMA\M1\x64\M1.exe"]
+        1`3f8b8000       7fe`f9d20000     7fd`ba468000                MEM_FREE    PAGE_NOACCESS          Free
+      7fe`f9d20000     7fe`f9d21000       0`00001000 MEM_IMAGE  MEM_COMMIT  PAGE_READONLY          Image      [M1DLL;
"C:\AWMA\M1\x64\M1DLL.dll"]
       7fe`f9d21000     7fe`f9d29000       0`00008000 MEM_IMAGE  MEM_COMMIT  PAGE_EXECUTE_READ      Image      [M1DLL;
"C:\AWMA\M1\x64\M1DLL.dll"]
       7fe`f9d29000     7fe`f9d30000       0`00007000 MEM_IMAGE  MEM_COMMIT  PAGE_READONLY          Image      [M1DLL;
"C:\AWMA\M1\x64\M1DLL.dll"]
       7fe`f9d30000     7fe`f9d34000       0`00004000 MEM_IMAGE  MEM_COMMIT  PAGE_READWRITE         Image      [M1DLL;
"C:\AWMA\M1\x64\M1DLL.dll"]
       7fe`f9d34000     7fe`f9d37000       0`00003000 MEM_IMAGE  MEM_COMMIT  PAGE_READONLY          Image      [M1DLL;
"C:\AWMA\M1\x64\M1DLL.dll"]
+      7fe`f9d37000     7fe`fb700000       0`019c9000                 MEM_FREE    PAGE_NOACCESS          Free
[…]
```

Note the first no access region highlighted in red. Its purpose is to catch NULL pointer access. Regions highlighted in blue belong to M1 module. The first read-only one belongs to MZ/PE header and the second one execute-read belongs to code section. Another command variant shows a summary:

```
0:000> !address -summary
```

```
--- Usage Summary --------------- RgnCount ----------- Total Size -------- %ofBusy %ofTotal
Free                                    45       7ff`fb89e000 (    8.000 Tb)          100.00%
<unknown>                               23         0`033f5000 (   51.957 Mb)  72.85%    0.00%
Image                                  124         0`00d88000 (   13.531 Mb)  18.97%    0.00%
Heap                                    11         0`00320000 (    3.125 Mb)   4.38%    0.00%
Other                                    9         0`001b2000 (    1.695 Mb)   2.38%    0.00%
Stack                                    3         0`00100000 (    1.000 Mb)   1.40%    0.00%
TEB                                      1         0`00002000 (    8.000 kb)   0.01%    0.00%
PEB                                      1         0`00001000 (    4.000 kb)   0.01%    0.00%


--- Type Summary (for busy) ------ RgnCount ----------- Total Size -------- %ofBusy %ofTotal
MEM_MAPPED                              23         0`02593000 (   37.574 Mb)  52.68%    0.00%
MEM_PRIVATE                             24         0`01436000 (   20.211 Mb)  28.34%    0.00%
MEM_IMAGE                              125         0`00d89000 (   13.535 Mb)  18.98%    0.00%


--- State Summary --------------- RgnCount ----------- Total Size -------- %ofBusy %ofTotal
MEM_FREE                                45       7ff`fb89e000 (    8.000 Tb)          100.00%
MEM_RESERVE                             14         0`025a2000 (   37.633 Mb)  52.77%    0.00%
MEM_COMMIT                             158         0`021b0000 (   33.688 Mb)  47.23%    0.00%


--- Protect Summary (for commit) - RgnCount ----------- Total Size -------- %ofBusy %ofTotal
PAGE_READONLY                           80         0`01783000 (   23.512 Mb)  32.97%    0.00%
PAGE_EXECUTE_READ                       21         0`008be000 (    8.742 Mb)  12.26%    0.00%
PAGE_READWRITE                          40         0`00153000 (    1.324 Mb)   1.86%    0.00%
PAGE_WRITECOPY                          16         0`0001a000 (  104.000 kb)   0.14%    0.00%
PAGE_READWRITE|PAGE_GUARD                1         0`00002000 (    8.000 kb)   0.01%    0.00%


--- Largest Region by Usage ----------- Base Address -------- Region Size ----------
Free                                    1`3f8b8000       7fd`ba468000 (    7.991 Tb)
<unknown>                               0`00c67000         0`01029000 (   16.160 Mb)
Image                                 7fe`fdbc1000         0`0017e000 (    1.492 Mb)
Heap                                    0`002f8000         0`000c8000 (  800.000 kb)
Other                                   0`00700000         0`00181000 (    1.504 Mb)
Stack                                   0`001c0000         0`000f9000 (  996.000 kb)
TEB                                   7ff`fffde000         0`00002000 (    8.000 kb)
PEB                                   7ff`fffd7000         0`00001000 (    4.000 kb)
```

9.   Let's dump M1 module header and see all these sections:

```
0:000> !dh 00000001`3f8a0000

File Type: EXECUTABLE IMAGE
FILE HEADER VALUES
    8664 machine (X64)
       6 number of sections
5106983D time date stamp Mon Jan 28 15:24:45 2013

       0 file pointer to symbol table
       0 number of symbols
      F0 size of optional header
      22 characteristics
            Executable
            App can handle >2gb addresses


OPTIONAL HEADER VALUES
     20B magic #
   11.00 linker version
    7400 size of code
    D200 size of initialized data
       0 size of uninitialized data
    16A8 address of entry point
    1000 base of code
         ----- new -----
000000013f8a0000 image base
    1000 section alignment
     200 file alignment
       2 subsystem (Windows GUI)
    6.00 operating system version
    0.00 image version
    6.00 subsystem version
   18000 size of image
     400 size of headers
       0 checksum
0000000000100000 size of stack reserve
0000000000001000 size of stack commit
0000000000100000 size of heap reserve
0000000000001000 size of heap commit
    8160  DLL characteristics
            High entropy VA supported
            Dynamic base
            NX compatible
            Terminal server aware
       0 [       0] address [size] of Export Directory
    EAA4 [      3C] address [size] of Import Directory
   15000 [    1D68] address [size] of Resource Directory
   14000 [     78C] address [size] of Exception Directory
       0 [       0] address [size] of Security Directory
   17000 [     530] address [size] of Base Relocation Directory
    9320 [      38] address [size] of Debug Directory
       0 [       0] address [size] of Description Directory
       0 [       0] address [size] of Special Directory
       0 [       0] address [size] of Thread Storage Directory
    E300 [      70] address [size] of Load Configuration Directory
       0 [       0] address [size] of Bound Import Directory
    9000 [     2A0] address [size] of Import Address Table Directory
       0 [       0] address [size] of Delay Import Directory
       0 [       0] address [size] of COR20 Header Directory
```

         0 [0] address [size] of Reserved Directory

SECTION HEADER #1
    .text name
    731B virtual size
    1000 virtual address
    7400 size of raw data
     400 file pointer to raw data
       0 file pointer to relocation table
       0 file pointer to line numbers
       0 number of relocations
       0 number of line numbers
60000020 flags
         Code
         (no align specified)
         Execute Read

SECTION HEADER #2
    .rdata name
    6366 virtual size
    9000 virtual address
    6400 size of raw data
    7800 file pointer to raw data
       0 file pointer to relocation table
       0 file pointer to line numbers
       0 number of relocations
       0 number of line numbers
40000040 flags
         Initialized Data
         (no align specified)
         Read Only

Debug Directories(2)
        Type   Size   Address   Pointer
        cv   3b   e370   cb70   Format: RSDS, guid, 1,
C:\Work\AWMA\M1\x64\Release\M1.pdb
        (12)   10   e3ac   cbac

SECTION HEADER #3
    .data name
    3900 virtual size
    10000 virtual address
    1400 size of raw data
    DC00 file pointer to raw data
       0 file pointer to relocation table
       0 file pointer to line numbers
       0 number of relocations
       0 number of line numbers
C0000040 flags
         Initialized Data
         (no align specified)
         Read Write

```
SECTION HEADER #4
   .pdata name
      78C virtual size
    14000 virtual address
      800 size of raw data
     F000 file pointer to raw data
        0 file pointer to relocation table
        0 file pointer to line numbers
        0 number of relocations
        0 number of line numbers
 40000040 flags
          Initialized Data
          (no align specified)
          Read Only

SECTION HEADER #5
   .rsrc name
     1D68 virtual size
    15000 virtual address
     1E00 size of raw data
     F800 file pointer to raw data
        0 file pointer to relocation table
        0 file pointer to line numbers
        0 number of relocations
        0 number of line numbers
 40000040 flags
          Initialized Data
          (no align specified)
          Read Only

SECTION HEADER #6
   .reloc name
      C52 virtual size
    17000 virtual address
      E00 size of raw data
    11600 file pointer to raw data
        0 file pointer to relocation table
        0 file pointer to line numbers
        0 number of relocations
        0 number of line numbers
 42000040 flags
          Initialized Data
          Discardable
          (no align specified)
          Read Only
```

10.   Now we look Import Address Table and compare with the previous exercise:

```
0:000> dps 00000001`3f8a0000+9000 L2A0/8
00000001`3f8a9000  00000000`76bf6f80 kernel32!LoadLibraryW
00000001`3f8a9008  00000000`76c02f10 kernel32!CloseHandleImplementation
00000001`3f8a9010  00000000`76bf3d40 kernel32!WriteConsoleW
00000001`3f8a9018  00000000`76beaf00 kernel32!SetFilePointerExStub
00000001`3f8a9020  00000000`76c2bce0 kernel32!SetStdHandleStub
00000001`3f8a9028  00000000`76c02df0 kernel32!GetConsoleMode
00000001`3f8a9030  00000000`76c205e0 kernel32!GetConsoleCP
00000001`3f8a9038  00000000`76be69f0 kernel32!FlushFileBuffersImplementation
00000001`3f8a9040  00000000`76c00d70 kernel32!LCMapStringWStub
00000001`3f8a9048  00000000`76e282d0 ntdll!RtlSizeHeap
```

```
00000001`3f8a9050  00000000`76bf9070  kernel32!GetStringTypeWStub
00000001`3f8a9058  00000000`76c03580  kernel32!WideCharToMultiByteStub
00000001`3f8a9060  00000000`76e33f20  ntdll!RtlReAllocateHeap
00000001`3f8a9068  00000000`76e533a0  ntdll!RtlAllocateHeap
00000001`3f8a9070  00000000`76bfc420  kernel32!GetCommandLineWStub
00000001`3f8a9078  00000000`76be8290  kernel32!IsDebuggerPresentStub
00000001`3f8a9080  00000000`76c2cc50  kernel32!IsProcessorFeaturePresent
00000001`3f8a9088  00000000`76c02d60  kernel32!GetLastErrorStub
00000001`3f8a9090  00000000`76c02d80  kernel32!SetLastError
00000001`3f8a9098  00000000`76bf3ee0  kernel32!GetCurrentThreadIdStub
00000001`3f8a90a0  00000000`76e33bd0  ntdll!RtlEncodePointer
00000001`3f8a90a8  00000000`76e29c50  ntdll!RtlDecodePointer
00000001`3f8a90b0  00000000`76e240f0  ntdll!RtlExitUserProcess
00000001`3f8a90b8  00000000`76beb780  kernel32!GetModuleHandleExWStub
00000001`3f8a90c0  00000000`76c03620  kernel32!GetProcAddressStub
00000001`3f8a90c8  00000000`76bf5b50  kernel32!MultiByteToWideCharStub
00000001`3f8a90d0  00000000`76bfd6f0  kernel32!GetStdHandleStub
00000001`3f8a90d8  00000000`76c03530  kernel32!WriteFileImplementation
00000001`3f8a90e0  00000000`76bf7700  kernel32!GetModuleFileNameWStub
00000001`3f8a90e8  00000000`76c02fe0  kernel32!GetProcessHeapStub
00000001`3f8a90f0  00000000`76c02d90  kernel32!GetFileTypeImplementation
00000001`3f8a90f8  00000000`76bf64e0  kernel32!InitializeCriticalSectionAndSpinCountStub
00000001`3f8a9100  00000000`76e25350  ntdll!RtlDeleteCriticalSection
00000001`3f8a9108  00000000`76bf8080  kernel32!GetStartupInfoWStub
00000001`3f8a9110  00000000`76bf6500  kernel32!QueryPerformanceCounterStub
00000001`3f8a9118  00000000`76bf5a50  kernel32!GetCurrentProcessIdStub
00000001`3f8a9120  00000000`76bf3f40  kernel32!GetSystemTimeAsFileTimeStub
00000001`3f8a9128  00000000`76bf6d20  kernel32!GetEnvironmentStringsWStub
00000001`3f8a9130  00000000`76bf6d00  kernel32!FreeEnvironmentStringsWStub
00000001`3f8a9138  00000000`76c2b6f0  kernel32!RtlCaptureContextStub
00000001`3f8a9140  00000000`76c2b610  kernel32!RtlLookupFunctionEntryStub
00000001`3f8a9148  00000000`76c2b5b0  kernel32!RtlVirtualUnwindStub
00000001`3f8a9150  00000000`76c79300  kernel32!UnhandledExceptionFilter
00000001`3f8a9158  00000000`76bf9b80  kernel32!SetUnhandledExceptionFilter
00000001`3f8a9160  00000000`76bf5cf0  kernel32!GetCurrentProcessStub
00000001`3f8a9168  00000000`76c2bca0  kernel32!TerminateProcessStub
00000001`3f8a9170  00000000`76bf7100  kernel32!TlsAllocStub
00000001`3f8a9178  00000000`76c02b80  kernel32!TlsGetValueStub
00000001`3f8a9180  00000000`76bf5cd0  kernel32!TlsSetValueStub
00000001`3f8a9188  00000000`76bf1590  kernel32!TlsFreeStub
00000001`3f8a9190  00000000`76c036c0  kernel32!GetModuleHandleWStub
00000001`3f8a9198  00000000`76c12d20  kernel32!RtlUnwindExStub
00000001`3f8a91a0  00000000`76e52fc0  ntdll!RtlEnterCriticalSection
00000001`3f8a91a8  00000000`76e53000  ntdll!RtlLeaveCriticalSection
00000001`3f8a91b0  00000000`76c03000  kernel32!HeapFree
00000001`3f8a91b8  00000000`76c02b20  kernel32!SleepStub
00000001`3f8a91c0  00000000`76bf9090  kernel32!IsValidCodePageStub
00000001`3f8a91c8  00000000`76bf6f90  kernel32!GetACPStub
00000001`3f8a91d0  00000000`76bfb520  kernel32!GetOEMCPStub
00000001`3f8a91d8  00000000`76bf6ce0  kernel32!GetCPInfoStub
00000001`3f8a91e0  00000000`76bf6640  kernel32!LoadLibraryExWStub
00000001`3f8a91e8  00000000`76beb760  kernel32!OutputDebugStringWStub
00000001`3f8a91f0  00000000`76bf1870  kernel32!CreateFileWImplementation
00000001`3f8a91f8  00000000`00000000
00000001`3f8a9200  00000000`76d250b0  user32!EndDialog
00000001`3f8a9208  00000000`76d07400  user32!PostQuitMessage
00000001`3f8a9210  00000000`76d16e30  user32!ZwUserEndPaint
00000001`3f8a9218  00000000`76d16e40  user32!NtUserBeginPaint
00000001`3f8a9220  00000000`76e2b0ac  ntdll!NtdllDefWindowProc_W
00000001`3f8a9228  00000000`76d0cbf0  user32!ZwUserDestroyWindow
```

```
00000001`3f8a9230  00000000`76d1d410  user32!DialogBoxParamW
00000001`3f8a9238  00000000`76d12790  user32!UpdateWindow
00000001`3f8a9240  00000000`76d11930  user32!NtUserShowWindow
00000001`3f8a9248  00000000`76d10810  user32!CreateWindowExW
00000001`3f8a9250  00000000`76d10e9c  user32!RegisterClassExW
00000001`3f8a9258  00000000`76d11498  user32!LoadCursorW
00000001`3f8a9260  00000000`76d114c0  user32!LoadIconW
00000001`3f8a9268  00000000`76d1991c  user32!DispatchMessageW
00000001`3f8a9270  00000000`76d196f0  user32!TranslateMessage
00000001`3f8a9278  00000000`76d19390  user32!TranslateAcceleratorW
00000001`3f8a9280  00000000`76d19e74  user32!GetMessageW
00000001`3f8a9288  00000000`76d0b080  user32!LoadAcceleratorsW
00000001`3f8a9290  00000000`76d0f99c  user32!LoadStringW
00000001`3f8a9298  00000000`00000000
```

Note that we have real addresses.

11.   Let's now check how imported functions are called. We now get stack trace for the current thread:

```
0:000> k
Child-SP          RetAddr           Call Site
00000000`002bfa38 00000000`76d19e9e user32!ZwUserGetMessage+0xa
*** WARNING: Unable to verify checksum for M1.exe
*** ERROR: Module load completed but symbols could not be loaded for M1.exe
00000000`002bfa40 00000001`3f8a10ac user32!GetMessageW+0x34
00000000`002bfa70 00000001`3f8a1638 M1+0x10ac
00000000`002bfae0 00000000`76bf652d M1+0x1638
00000000`002bfb20 00000000`76e2c521 kernel32!BaseThreadInitThunk+0xd
00000000`002bfb50 00000000`00000000 ntdll!RtlUserThreadStart+0x1d
```

We repeat this command to clear warning and error messages:

```
0:000> k
Child-SP          RetAddr           Call Site
00000000`002bfa38 00000000`76d19e9e user32!ZwUserGetMessage+0xa
00000000`002bfa40 00000001`3f8a10ac user32!GetMessageW+0x34
00000000`002bfa70 00000001`3f8a1638 M1+0x10ac
00000000`002bfae0 00000000`76bf652d M1+0x1638
00000000`002bfb20 00000000`76e2c521 kernel32!BaseThreadInitThunk+0xd
00000000`002bfb50 00000000`00000000 ntdll!RtlUserThreadStart+0x1d
```

Recall that a return address is a return address for the call site below so its backwards disassembly normally shows a call CPU instruction, this time we expect a call to GetMessageW:

```
0:000> ub 00000001`3f8a10ac
M1+0x1090:
00000001`3f8a1090 f4              hlt
00000001`3f8a1091 810000488944    add     dword ptr [rax],44894800h
00000001`3f8a1097 2420            and     al,20h
00000001`3f8a1099 4533c9          xor     r9d,r9d
00000001`3f8a109c 4533c0          xor     r8d,r8d
00000001`3f8a109f 33d2            xor     edx,edx
00000001`3f8a10a1 488d4c2428      lea     rcx,[rsp+28h]
00000001`3f8a10a6 ff15d4810000    call    qword ptr [M1+0x9280 (00000001`3f8a9280)]
```

Square brackets mean an indirect address. The value at memory address 00000001`3f8a9280 should contain an address to transfer execution:

```
0:000> dps 00000001`3f8a9280 L1
00000001`3f8a9280  00000000`76d19e74 user32!GetMessageW
```

Note that the address 00000001`3f8a9280 is inside Import Address Table above.

12.   Finally we check integrity of our M1 module:

```
0:000> !chkimg -v -d M1
Searching for module with expression: M1
Error for M1: Could not find image file for the module. Make sure binaries are included in the
symbol path.
```

WinDbg cannot find a module to compare what's inside a dump file. So we specify an executable search path:

```
0:000> .exepath+ C:\AWMA-Dumps\Executables\
Executable image search path is: C:\AWMA-Dumps\Executables\
Expanded Executable image search path is: c:\awma-dumps\executables\
```

```
0:000> !chkimg -v -d M1
Searching for module with expression: M1
Will apply relocation fixups to file used for comparison
Will ignore NOP/LOCK errors
Will ignore patched instructions
Image specific ignores will be applied
Comparison image path: C:\AWMA-Dumps\Executables\M1.exe
No range specified

Scanning section:    .text
Size: 29467
Range to scan: 13f8a1000-13f8a831b
Total bytes compared: 29467(100%)
Number of errors: 0
0 errors : M1
```

13.   Close the log file:

```
0:000> .logclose
Closing open log file C:\AWMA-Dumps\M1B.log
```

14.   To avoid possible confusion and glitches we recommend exiting WinDbg after each exercise.

If you are presented with this dialog choose No:

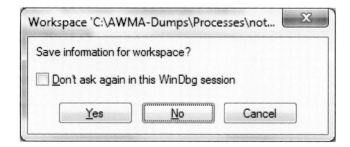

Packed Code and Data

- Less/No strings

- Less/No code signatures

- Less/No import functions

- Possibly different sections

Example: UPX

The sections and their names can be arbitrary. It is possible to have different name and even one or two sections only. At the end a module is just a binary that can be loaded at some memory address. It is even possible to write your own loader and linker. Code and data may also be packed. Here we look at a process dump file that contains packed modules. One module after compilation was packed by UPX packer and upon start a program loads it and also loads the same module but unpacked for comparison. Usually, if you search for strings in any normal module you find plenty of them. Obviously, you find less of them in a packed module although some fragments may survive (the so called **Pre-Obfuscation Residue** pattern). Every function usually have some standard signatures such as the so called function prologue and epilogue that have the same binary values. Also Import Address Table might be empty or contain a few specific functions and section names and attributes may be completely different as in the case of UPX (http://upx.sourceforge.net/).

Thread Raw Stack Data

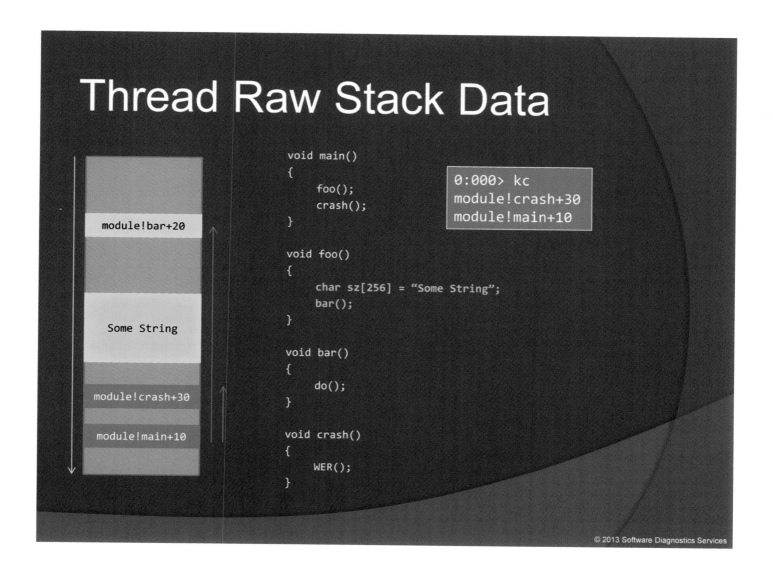

Please recall that each thread of execution has its own region in user space called a stack. We also call it a raw stack to differentiate from a stack trace. Every function call results in return address stored there. Sometimes such return addresses are overwritten by subsequent execution and sometimes they survive. We call this **Execution Residue** pattern. We can also see ASCII and UNICODE strings if survived there. After *crash()* function execution that calls exception processing code we see a stack trace but there is also surviving execution residue of *bar()* function because of a pre-allocated buffer. Please also note that a stack grows towards lower addresses during function calls as shown by blue arrows on the right to the raw stack box.

Exercise M2

- **Goal:** Diagnose packed and hidden modules and their execution residues

- **Patterns:** Packed Code, Hidden Module, Pre-Obfuscation Residue, Execution Residue, String Hint

- \AWMA-Dumps\Exercise-M2.pdf

Goal: Diagnose packed and hidden modules and their execution residues.

Patterns: Packed Code, Hidden Module, Pre-Obfuscation Residue, Execution Residue

1.   Launch WinDbg from Windows Kits \ Debugging Tools for Windows (X64) or Debugging Tools for Windows (X86)

2.   Open \AWMA-Dumps\Processes\M2.dmp

3.   If you are presented with this dialog say No:

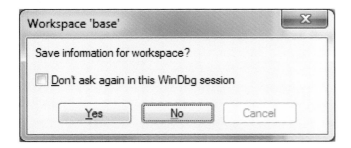

4.   You get the dump file loaded:

```
Microsoft (R) Windows Debugger Version 6.2.9200.20512 X86
Copyright (c) Microsoft Corporation. All rights reserved.


Loading Dump File [C:\AWMA-Dumps\Processes\M2.DMP]
User Mini Dump File with Full Memory: Only application data is available

Symbol search path is: *** Invalid ***
************************************************************************
* Symbol loading may be unreliable without a symbol search path.       *
* Use .symfix to have the debugger choose a symbol path.               *
* After setting your symbol path, use .reload to refresh symbol locations. *
************************************************************************
Executable search path is:
Windows 7 Version 7601 (Service Pack 1) MP (4 procs) Free x86 compatible
Product: WinNt, suite: SingleUserTS Personal
Machine Name:
Debug session time: Wed Jan 30 18:24:22.000 2013 (UTC + 0:00)
System Uptime: 21 days 7:17:59.279
Process Uptime: 0 days 0:00:28.000
.......
*** ERROR: Symbol file could not be found.  Defaulted to export symbols for ntdll.dll -
*** ERROR: Symbol file could not be found.  Defaulted to export symbols for KERNELBASE.dll -
eax=00000000 ebx=00000000 ecx=00000000 edx=00000000 esi=0045f9bc edi=00000000
eip=76fffd71 esp=0045f978 ebp=0045f9e0 iopl=0         nv up ei pl zr na pe nc
cs=0023  ss=002b  ds=002b  es=002b  fs=0053  gs=002b             efl=00000246
ntdll!ZwDelayExecution+0x15:
76fffd71 83c404          add     esp,4
```

5.   Open a log file:

```
0:000> .logopen C:\AWMA-Dumps\M2.log
Opened log file 'C:\AWMA-Dumps\M2.log'
```

6.   Set up a link to Microsoft symbol server and reload symbols:

```
0:000> .symfix c:\mss
```

```
0:000> .reload
....................
```

7.   Lists modules and their timestamps:

```
0:000> lmt
start    end      module name
012e0000 012ec000 M2         Wed Jan 30 18:23:18 2013 (51096516)
5ea70000 5eb46000 msvcr110   Tue Nov 06 03:35:42 2012 (5098858E)
60640000 60654000 calc3du    Wed Jan 30 16:21:24 2013 (51094884)
71610000 71627000 calc3d     Wed Jan 30 16:21:24 2013 (51094884)
751e0000 752f0000 kernel32   Mon Aug 20 18:40:01 2012 (50327671)
75390000 753d7000 KERNELBASE Mon Aug 20 18:40:02 2012 (50327672)
76fe0000 77160000 ntdll      Thu Nov 17 05:28:47 2011 (4EC49B8F)
```

Note some modules have approximately the same build timestamp and therefore can be related.

8.   Let's check headers for each module. We can use **!for_each_module** command to automate this task (here logs are useful):

```
0:000> !for_each_module !dh @#ModuleName
[…]

File Type: DLL
FILE HEADER VALUES
     14C machine (i386)
       5 number of sections
51094884 time date stamp Wed Jan 30 16:21:24 2013

       0 file pointer to symbol table
       0 number of symbols
      E0 size of optional header
    2102 characteristics
            Executable
            32 bit word machine
            DLL

OPTIONAL HEADER VALUES
     10B magic #
   11.00 linker version
    6400 size of code
    9800 size of initialized data
       0 size of uninitialized data
    1262 address of entry point
    1000 base of code
         ----- new -----
60640000 image base
```

```
    1000 section alignment
     200 file alignment
       2 subsystem (Windows GUI)
    6.00 operating system version
    0.00 image version
    6.00 subsystem version
   14000 size of image
     400 size of headers
       0 checksum
00100000 size of stack reserve
00001000 size of stack commit
00100000 size of heap reserve
00001000 size of heap commit
     140 DLL characteristics
            Dynamic base
            NX compatible
   C600 [      A9] address [size] of Export Directory
   C034 [      28] address [size] of Import Directory
  10000 [     1E0] address [size] of Resource Directory
      0 [       0] address [size] of Exception Directory
      0 [       0] address [size] of Security Directory
  11000 [     B80] address [size] of Base Relocation Directory
   8140 [      38] address [size] of Debug Directory
      0 [       0] address [size] of Description Directory
      0 [       0] address [size] of Special Directory
      0 [       0] address [size] of Thread Storage Directory
   BCA0 [      40] address [size] of Load Configuration Directory
      0 [       0] address [size] of Bound Import Directory
   8000 [     100] address [size] of Import Address Table Directory
      0 [       0] address [size] of Delay Import Directory
      0 [       0] address [size] of COR20 Header Directory
      0 [       0] address [size] of Reserved Directory


SECTION HEADER #1
   .text name
   6320 virtual size
   1000 virtual address
   6400 size of raw data
    400 file pointer to raw data
      0 file pointer to relocation table
      0 file pointer to line numbers
      0 number of relocations
      0 number of line numbers
60000020 flags
         Code
         (no align specified)
         Execute Read

SECTION HEADER #2
   .rdata name
   46A9 virtual size
   8000 virtual address
   4800 size of raw data
   6800 file pointer to raw data
      0 file pointer to relocation table
      0 file pointer to line numbers
      0 number of relocations
      0 number of line numbers
40000040 flags
```

```
        Initialized Data
        (no align specified)
        Read Only


Debug Directories(2)
        Type        Size      Address   Pointer
        cv          3b        bce8      a4e8      Format: RSDS, guid, 1,
C:\Work\AWMA\M2\Release\calc3d.pdb
        (    12)    10        bd24      a524

SECTION HEADER #3
    .data name
    2BF4 virtual size
    D000 virtual address
     E00 size of raw data
    B000 file pointer to raw data
       0 file pointer to relocation table
       0 file pointer to line numbers
       0 number of relocations
       0 number of line numbers
C0000040 flags
        Initialized Data
        (no align specified)
        Read Write


SECTION HEADER #4
    .rsrc name
     1E0 virtual size
   10000 virtual address
     200 size of raw data
    BE00 file pointer to raw data
       0 file pointer to relocation table
       0 file pointer to line numbers
       0 number of relocations
       0 number of line numbers
40000040 flags
        Initialized Data
        (no align specified)
        Read Only


SECTION HEADER #5
    .reloc name
    2106 virtual size
   11000 virtual address
    2200 size of raw data
    C000 file pointer to raw data
       0 file pointer to relocation table
       0 file pointer to line numbers
       0 number of relocations
       0 number of line numbers
42000040 flags
        Initialized Data
        Discardable
        (no align specified)
        Read Only
```

```
File Type: DLL
FILE HEADER VALUES
      14C machine (i386)
        3 number of sections
 51094884 time date stamp Wed Jan 30 16:21:24 2013

        0 file pointer to symbol table
        0 number of symbols
       E0 size of optional header
     2102 characteristics
             Executable
             32 bit word machine
             DLL

OPTIONAL HEADER VALUES
      10B magic #
    11.00 linker version
     6000 size of code
     1000 size of initialized data
     F000 size of uninitialized data
    15600 address of entry point
    10000 base of code
          ----- new -----
 71610000 image base
     1000 section alignment
      200 file alignment
        2 subsystem (Windows GUI)
     6.00 operating system version
     0.00 image version
     6.00 subsystem version
    17000 size of image
     1000 size of headers
        0 checksum
 00100000 size of stack reserve
 00001000 size of stack commit
 00100000 size of heap reserve
 00001000 size of heap commit
      140  DLL characteristics
             Dynamic base
             NX compatible
    16274 [        AC] address [size] of Export Directory
    161DC [        98] address [size] of Import Directory
    16000 [       1DC] address [size] of Resource Directory
        0 [         0] address [size] of Exception Directory
        0 [         0] address [size] of Security Directory
    16320 [        10] address [size] of Base Relocation Directory
        0 [         0] address [size] of Debug Directory
        0 [         0] address [size] of Description Directory
        0 [         0] address [size] of Special Directory
        0 [         0] address [size] of Thread Storage Directory
    157CC [        48] address [size] of Load Configuration Directory
        0 [         0] address [size] of Bound Import Directory
        0 [         0] address [size] of Import Address Table Directory
        0 [         0] address [size] of Delay Import Directory
        0 [         0] address [size] of COR20 Header Directory
        0 [         0] address [size] of Reserved Directory
```

```
SECTION HEADER #1
    UPX0 name
    F000 virtual size
    1000 virtual address
       0 size of raw data
       0 file pointer to raw data
       0 file pointer to relocation table
       0 file pointer to line numbers
       0 number of relocations
       0 number of line numbers
60000080 flags
         Uninitialized Data
         (no align specified)
         Execute Read

SECTION HEADER #2
    UPX1 name
    6000 virtual size
   10000 virtual address
    5A00 size of raw data
     400 file pointer to raw data
       0 file pointer to relocation table
       0 file pointer to line numbers
       0 number of relocations
       0 number of line numbers
60000040 flags
         Initialized Data
         (no align specified)
         Execute Read

SECTION HEADER #3
   .rsrc name
    1000 virtual size
   16000 virtual address
     400 size of raw data
    5E00 file pointer to raw data
       0 file pointer to relocation table
       0 file pointer to line numbers
       0 number of relocations
       0 number of line numbers
C0000040 flags
         Initialized Data
         (no align specified)
         Read Write
```

[...]

Note that we see calc3d.dll loaded at 71610000 and having empty Import Address Table and different section names UPX0 and UPX1.

9.   We now search UPX1 address range for ASCII strings (we can use **s-su** to search for UNICODE strings):

```
0:000> s-sa 71610000+10000 L6000
71624009   "GetCommandLineA"
7162401a   "GetCurrentThreadId"
7162402e   "IsDebuggerPresent"
71624041   "EncodePointer"
71624050   "DecodePointer"
7162405f   "IsProcessorFeaturePresent"
```

```
7162407a  "GetLastError"
71624088  "SetLastError"
71624096  "InterlockedIncrement"
716240ac  "InterlockedDecrement"
716240c2  "ExitProcess"
716240cf  "GetModuleHandleExW"
716240e3  "GetProcAddress"
716240f3  "MultiByteToWideChar"
71624108  "GetProcessHeap"
71624118  "GetStdHandle"
71624126  "GetFileType"
71624133  "InitializeCriticalSectionAndSpin"
71624153  "Count"
7162415a  "DeleteCriticalSection"
71624171  "GetStartupInfoW"
71624182  "GetModuleFileNameA"
71624196  "HeapFree"
716241a0  "QueryPerformanceCounter"
716241b9  "GetCurrentProcessId"
716241ce  "GetSystemTimeAsFileTime"
716241e7  "GetEnvironmentStringsW"
716241ff  "FreeEnvironmentStringsW"
71624218  "WideCharToMultiByte"
7162422d  "UnhandledExceptionFilter"
71624247  "SetUnhandledExceptionFilter"
71624264  "GetCurrentProcess"
71624277  "TerminateProcess"
71624289  "TlsAlloc"
71624293  "TlsGetValue"
716242a0  "TlsSetValue"
716242ad  "TlsFree"
716242b6  "GetModuleHandleW"
716242c8  "Sleep"
716242cf  "EnterCriticalSection"
716242e5  "LeaveCriticalSection"
716242fb  "IsValidCodePage"
7162430c  "GetACP"
71624314  "GetOEMCP"
7162431e  "GetCPInfo"
71624329  "WriteFile"
71624334  "GetModuleFileNameW"
71624348  "LoadLibraryExW"
71624358  "RtlUnwind"
71624363  "HeapAlloc"
7162436e  "HeapReAlloc"
7162437b  "GetStringTypeW"
7162438b  "OutputDebugStringW"
7162439f  "LoadLibraryW"
716243ad  "HeapSize"
716243b7  "LCMapStringW"
716243c5  "FlushFileBuffers"
716243d7  "GetConsoleCP"
716243e5  "GetConsoleMode"
716243f5  "SetStdHandle"
71624403  "SetFilePointerEx"
71624415  "WriteConsoleW"
71624424  "CloseHandle"
71624431  "CreateFileW"
[...]
71624ae4  ".text"
```

```
71624b0b  "`.rdata"
71624b33  "@.data"
71624b5c  ".rsrc"
71624b83  "@.reloc"
[...]
71624ce7  "o:\Work\AWMA\M2\ReleaseN"
71624d02  "\:c3d.pd"
[...]
7162502a  "ommand"
71625041  "IsDe"
71625049  "buggerP"
71625054  "Encodnmk"
[...]
```

10.   Now we check the number of threads and look at the current thread raw stack:

```
0:000> ~
.  0  Id: 233c.1254 Suspend: 0 Teb: 7efdd000 Unfrozen


0:000> k
ChildEBP RetAddr
0045f978 753a3bc8 ntdll!NtDelayExecution+0x15
0045f9e0 753a4498 KERNELBASE!SleepEx+0x65
0045f9f0 012e101e KERNELBASE!Sleep+0xf
WARNING: Stack unwind information not available. Following frames may be wrong.
0045fa38 751f33aa M2+0x101e
0045fa44 77019ef2 kernel32!BaseThreadInitThunk+0xe
0045fa84 77019ec5 ntdll!__RtlUserThreadStart+0x70
0045fa9c 00000000 ntdll!_RtlUserThreadStart+0x1b
```

To get raw stack region boundaries we use **!teb** command:

```
0:000> !teb
TEB at 7efdd000
    ExceptionList:        0045f9d0
    StackBase:            00460000
    StackLimit:           0045e000
    SubSystemTib:         00000000
    FiberData:            00001e00
    ArbitraryUserPointer: 00000000
    Self:                 7efdd000
    EnvironmentPointer:   00000000
    ClientId:             0000233c . 00001254
    RpcHandle:            00000000
    Tls Storage:          7efdd02c
    PEB Address:          7efde000
    LastErrorValue:       0
    LastStatusValue:      c0000139
    Count Owned Locks:    0
    HardErrorMode:        0
```

Now can dumps memory values with corresponding symbols using **dps** command:

```
0:000> dps 0045e000 00460000
0045e000  00000000
0045e004  00000000
0045e008  00000000
0045e00c  00000000
0045e010  00000000
[...]
0045eb80  00000000
0045eb84  00000000
0045eb88  0045ec18
0045eb8c  0045ebc4
0045eb90  753bea9e KERNELBASE!LCMapStringEx+0x130
0045eb94  00000000
0045eb98  00000200
0045eb9c  0045ee28
0045eba0  00000100
0045eba4  0045ec18
0045eba8  008a4498
0045ebac  7efb0222
0045ebb0  00000100
0045ebb4  0045ebe8
0045ebb8  753c0c6e KERNELBASE!WideCharToMultiByte+0x19f
0045ebbc  008a4498
0045ebc0  0045ec18
0045ebc4  0045ee18
0045ebc8  0045f2d0
0045ebcc  0045f3d0
0045ebd0  00000000
0045ebd4  00000100
0045ebd8  0045ec18
0045ebdc  0045ee28
0045ebe0  008a4498
0045ebe4  00000000
0045ebe8  0045f040
0045ebec  6064503b calc3du!fncalc3d+0x3fdb
0045ebf0  00000000
0045ebf4  00000000
0045ebf8  0045ec18
0045ebfc  00000001
0045ec00  0045f2d0
0045ec04  0045f040
0045ec08  6064504a calc3du!fncalc3d+0x3fea
0045ec0c  0045ee28
0045ec10  0000cccc
[...]
0045f964  0045f950
0045f968  7701c439 ntdll!LdrpLoadDll+0x635
0045f96c  0045fa28
0045f970  770571d5 ntdll!_except_handler4
0045f974  6db8e6f2
0045f978  76fffd71 ntdll!NtDelayExecution+0x15
0045f97c  753a3bc8 KERNELBASE!SleepEx+0x65
0045f980  00000000
0045f984  0045f9bc
0045f988  4f2ad6dc
0045f98c  00000000
0045f990  00000001
0045f994  00000000
```

```
0045f998    00000024
0045f99c    00000001
0045f9a0    00000000
0045f9a4    00000000
0045f9a8    00000000
0045f9ac    00000000
0045f9b0    00000000
0045f9b4    00000000
0045f9b8    00000000
0045f9bc    00000000
0045f9c0    80000000
0045f9c4    00000000
0045f9c8    0045f988
0045f9cc    001c001a
0045f9d0    0045fa28
0045f9d4    753c6fa0 KERNELBASE!_except_handler4
0045f9d8    3a53a6c4
0045f9dc    00000000
0045f9e0    0045f9f0
0045f9e4    753a4498 KERNELBASE!Sleep+0xf
0045f9e8    ffffffff
0045f9ec    00000000
0045f9f0    0045fa38
0045f9f4    012e101e M2+0x101e
0045f9f8    ffffffff
0045f9fc    012e1231 M2+0x1231
0045fa00    00000001
0045fa04    008c9660
0045fa08    008cbb78
0045fa0c    22fb0166
0045fa10    00000000
0045fa14    00000000
0045fa18    7efde000
0045fa1c    00000000
0045fa20    0045fa0c
0045fa24    000002c5
0045fa28    0045fa74
0045fa2c    012e17e9 M2+0x17e9
0045fa30    2390dab6
0045fa34    00000000
0045fa38    0045fa44
0045fa3c    751f33aa kernel32!BaseThreadInitThunk+0xe
0045fa40    7efde000
0045fa44    0045fa84
0045fa48    77019ef2 ntdll!__RtlUserThreadStart+0x70
0045fa4c    7efde000
0045fa50    1afddd0e
0045fa54    00000000
0045fa58    00000000
0045fa5c    7efde000
0045fa60    00000000
0045fa64    00000000
0045fa68    00000000
0045fa6c    0045fa50
0045fa70    00000000
0045fa74    ffffffff
0045fa78    770571d5 ntdll!_except_handler4
0045fa7c    6db8e2ba
0045fa80    00000000
0045fa84    0045fa9c
```

```
0045fa88   77019ec5 ntdll!_RtlUserThreadStart+0x1b
0045fa8c   012e1299 M2+0x1299
0045fa90   7efde000
0045fa94   00000000
0045fa98   00000000
0045fa9c   00000000
[...]
```

We see cal3du module residue and check if it is not coincidental such as a contsant that falls into some module
address range:

```
0:000> ub 6064504a
calc3du!fncalc3d+0x3fd2:
60645032 ff7524            push      dword ptr [ebp+24h]
60645035 ff156c806460      call      dword ptr [calc3du!fncalc3d+0x700c (6064806c)]
6064503b 8bf8              mov       edi,eax
6064503d 56                push      esi
6064503e e860000000        call      calc3du!fncalc3d+0x4043 (606450a3)
60645043 59                pop       ecx
60645044 53                push      ebx
60645045 e859000000        call      calc3du!fncalc3d+0x4043 (606450a3)

0:000> ub  6064503b
calc3du!fncalc3d+0x3fc7:
60645027 eb06              jmp       calc3du!fncalc3d+0x3fcf (6064502f)
60645029 ff7520            push      dword ptr [ebp+20h]
6064502c ff751c            push      dword ptr [ebp+1Ch]
6064502f 57                push      edi
60645030 56                push      esi
60645031 50                push      eax
60645032 ff7524            push      dword ptr [ebp+24h]
60645035 ff156c806460      call      dword ptr [calc3du!fncalc3d+0x700c (6064806c)]
```

Because the preceding instruction is *call* there is much higher probability that this return address was saved during
past execution. We can also check for strings in that region **s-sa** and **s-su** commands or interpret every value as a
pointer to a string by using using **dpa** and **dpu** commands. **dpp** command would treat every value as a memory
address and show a value it points to togteher with possible symbols (double redirection).

11.   We now check the whole modules calc3d and calc3du address ranges for any malicious **String Hints** such as
website, password and HTTP forms:

```
0:000> lm
start    end         module name
012e0000 012ec000    M2        C (no symbols)
5ea70000 5eb46000    msvcr110    (deferred)
60640000 60654000    calc3du   C (export symbols)        calc3du.dll
71610000 71627000    calc3d      (deferred)
751e0000 752f0000    kernel32    (pdb symbols)
75390000 753d7000    KERNELBASE  (pdb symbols)
76fe0000 77160000    ntdll       (pdb symbols)

0:000> s-su 60640000 60654000
[...]
60648178   https://www.dumpanalysis.com
[...]
```

```
0:000> s-su 71610000 71627000
[...]
71618178  https://www.dumpanalysis.com
[...]
```

12.   Let's now check if there are any **Hidden Modules** not shown in loaded module list by using **.imgscan** command that searches for MZ/PE signatures:

```
0:000> .imgscan
MZ at 012e0000, prot 00000002, type 01000000 - size c000
  Name: M2.exe
MZ at 5ea70000, prot 00000002, type 01000000 - size d6000
  Name: MSVCR110.dll
MZ at 60640000, prot 00000002, type 01000000 - size 14000
  Name: calc3d.dll
MZ at 71610000, prot 00000002, type 01000000 - size 17000
  Name: calc3d.dll
MZ at 72e00000, prot 00000002, type 01000000 - size 8000
  Name: wow64cpu.dll
MZ at 72e10000, prot 00000002, type 01000000 - size 5c000
  Name: wow64win.dll
MZ at 72e70000, prot 00000002, type 01000000 - size 3f000
  Name: wow64.dll
MZ at 751e0000, prot 00000002, type 01000000 - size 110000
  Name: KERNEL32.dll
MZ at 75390000, prot 00000002, type 01000000 - size 47000
  Name: KERNELBASE.dll
MZ at 76e00000, prot 00000002, type 01000000 - size 1a9000
  Name: ntdll.dll
MZ at 76fe0000, prot 00000002, type 01000000 - size 180000
  Name: ntdll.dll
```

wow64 modules and two ndll modules can be explained by the fact that this 32-bit dump came from x64 Windows.

Let's double check these findings by searching for MZ strings. By default **s-sa** command ignores 2 byte ASCII sequences so we need to specify *l2* parameter. For example, seaching in M2 module address range reveals a second MZ/PE header and closest strings point to it being packed by UPX packer:

```
0:000> s -[l2]sa 012e0000 012ec000
012e0000  "MZ"
012e004d  "!This program cannot be run in D"
012e006d  "OS mode."
012e00c0  "S;"
012e00c8  "S;"
012e00d8  "S;"
012e00e0  "Rich"
012e00f0  "PE"
012e0170  "D"""
012e017c  "0d"
012e01b8  "8!"
012e01e8  ".text"
012e020f  "`.rdata"
012e0237  "@.data"
012e0260  ".rsrc"
012e0268  "0d"
012e0287  "@.reloc"
012e1002  "!."
```

```
012e1008   " ."
012e100d   "!."
012e1013   " ."
[...]
012e40b0   "MZ"
012e40fd   "!This program cannot be run in D"
012e411d   "OS mode."
012e4188   "Rich"
012e4198   "PE"
012e4210   "tb"
012e4238   " c"
012e4290   "UPX0"
012e42b8   "UPX1"
012e42e0   ".rsrc"
012e448b   "3.08"
012e4490   "UPX!"
[...]
```

Dumping M2 module header shows this hidden module is located inside a resource section:

```
0:000> !dh 012e0000

[...]

SECTION HEADER #4
    .rsrc name
    6430 virtual size
    4000 virtual address
    6600 size of raw data
    1600 file pointer to raw data
       0 file pointer to relocation table
       0 file pointer to line numbers
       0 number of relocations
       0 number of line numbers
40000040 flags
         Initialized Data
         (no align specified)
         Read Only

[...]
```

If we dump ASCII strings we don't find many because the module was packed and not yet loaded for execution. However, we see some **Pre-Obfuscation Residue**, fragments of strings:

```
0:000> s-sa 012e4000 L6600
012e40fd   "!This program cannot be run in D"
012e411d   "OS mode."
012e4188   "Rich"
012e4290   "UPX0"
012e42b8   "UPX1"
012e42e0   ".rsrc"
012e448b   "3.08"
012e4490   "UPX!"
012e449c   "9T5"
012e44d1   "vqx"
[...]
012e84b8   "%BoxW"
012e84c2   "ActiveWindowas"
```

```
[...]
012e9197   "o:\Work\AWMA\M2\ReleaseN"
[...]
012e94da   "ommand"
012e94f1   "IsDe"
012e94f9   "buggerP"
[...]
```

13.   We can even write this embedded binary to some folder and try to unpack (012e40b0 is an address of "MZ" signature) and then later load an unpacked version as a crash dump for further analysis:

```
0:000> .writemem c:\AWMA\module.bin 012e40b0 L6600
Writing 6600 bytes.............
```

14.   Close the log file:

```
0:000> .logclose
Closing open log file C:\AWMA-Dumps\M2.log
```

15.   To avoid possible confusion and glitches we recommend exiting WinDbg after each exercise.

If you are presented with this dialog choose No:

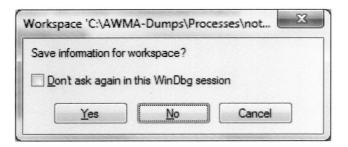

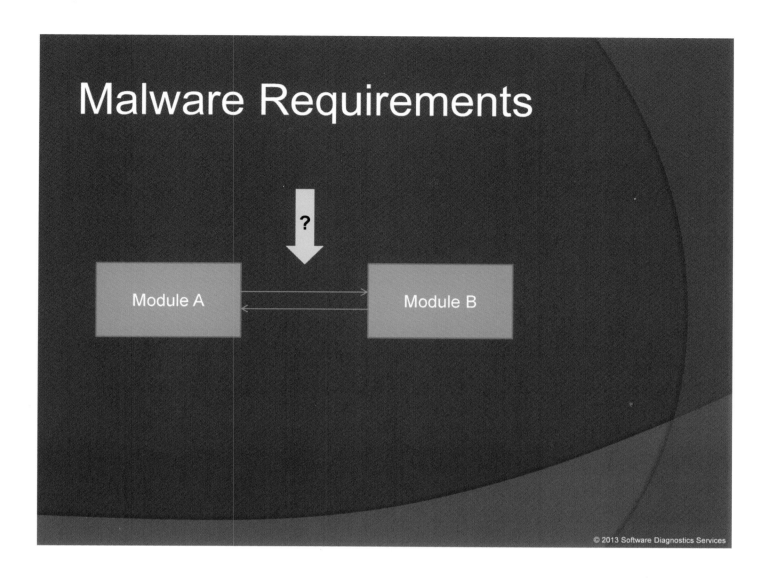

In order for malware to do something malicious its need to be executed. So its basic requirement is to be loaded into memory and get attention of a CPU.

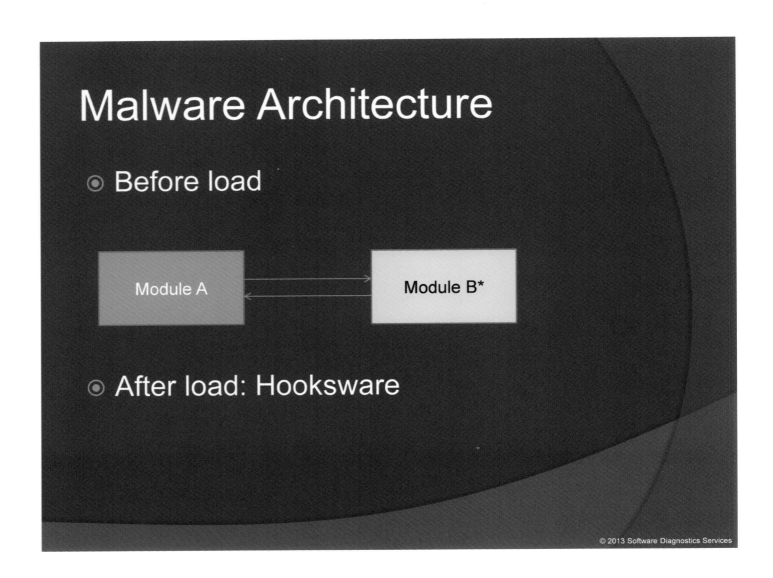

Such requirements can be implemented by replacing modules with fake ones or somehow modifying existing modules before they are loaded into memory. Another way is when genuine malware modules are loaded and they modify existing modules and structures in memory resulting in execution being redirected to them, the so called hooksware method that combines various approaches such as windows hooks, patching, and DLL injection by remote thread execution.

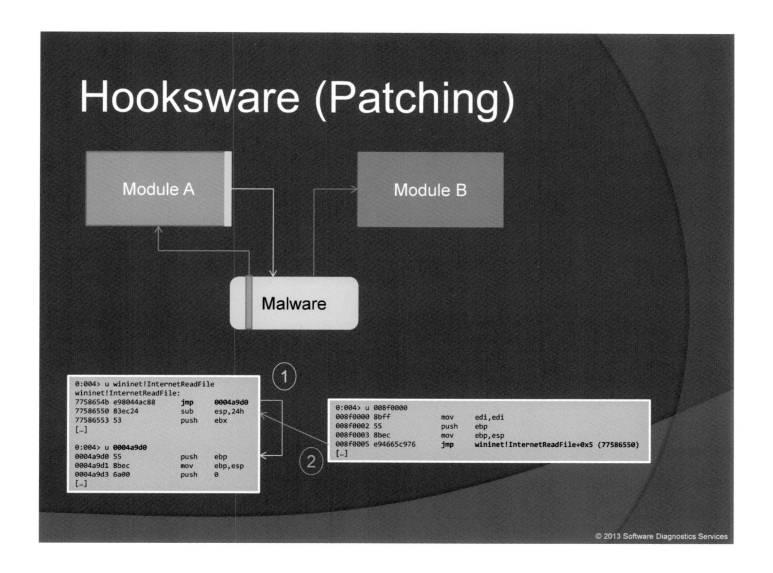

Here we cover only code patching and delegate to free Debugging TV session for DLL Injection case study. In the forthcoming exercise you would see this patching effects in action. Basically initial code in a function is saved and replaced by a jump to another code region and after malicious activity execution is returned back to the previous code after executing its saved portion.

Exercise M3

- **Goal:** Diagnose malware in victimware process memory dumps

- **Patterns:** Stack Trace Collection, RIP Stack Trace, Hooksware, Patched Code, Hidden Module, Deviant Module, String Hint, Fake Module, No Component Symbols, Namespace

- \AWMA-Dumps\Exercise-M3.pdf

Now we analyze a real malware crash dump with many malware analysis patterns.

Goal: Diagnose malware in victimware process memory dumps.

Patterns: Stack Trace Collection, RIP Stack Trace, Hooksware, Patched Code, Hidden Module, Deviant Module, String Hint, FakeModule, No Component Symbols, Namespace

1.   Launch WinDbg from Windows Kits \ Debugging Tools for Windows (X64) or Debugging Tools for Windows (X86)

2.   Open \AWMA-Dumps\Processes\iexplore.exe.5564.dmp

3.   If you are presented with this dialog say No:

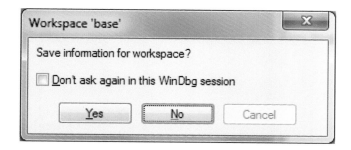

4.   You get the dump file loaded:

```
Microsoft (R) Windows Debugger Version 6.2.9200.20512 X86
Copyright (c) Microsoft Corporation. All rights reserved.


Loading Dump File [C:\AWMA-Dumps\Processes\iexplore.exe.5564.dmp]
User Mini Dump File with Full Memory: Only application data is available


Symbol search path is: *** Invalid ***
****************************************************************
* Symbol loading may be unreliable without a symbol search path.   *
* Use .symfix to have the debugger choose a symbol path.           *
* After setting your symbol path, use .reload to refresh symbol locations. *
****************************************************************
Executable search path is:
Windows Server 2008/Windows Vista Version 6002 (Service Pack 2) MP (2 procs) Free x86
compatible
Product: WinNt, suite: SingleUserTS Personal
Machine Name:
Debug session time: Sun Sep 26 08:19:07.000 2010 (UTC + 0:00)
System Uptime: 0 days 18:41:40.127
Process Uptime: 0 days 0:00:48.000
Loading unloaded module list
...
This dump file has an exception of interest stored in it.
The stored exception information can be accessed via .ecxr.
(15bc.650): Unknown exception - code c0000374 (first/second chance not available)
*** ERROR: Symbol file could not be found.  Defaulted to export symbols for ntdll.dll -
eax=00000000 ebx=00000000 ecx=00000400 edx=00000000 esi=026e0000 edi=000015bc
eip=77815e74 esp=02c9cb1c ebp=02c9cba0 iopl=0         nv up ei pl nz na po nc
cs=001b  ss=0023  ds=0023  es=0023  fs=003b  gs=0000           efl=00040202
```

```
ntdll!KiFastSystemCallRet:
77815e74 c3                    ret
```

Note the message about a stored exception.

5.   Open a log file:

```
0:004> .logopen C:\AWMA-Dumps\M3.log
Opened log file 'C:\AWMA-Dumps\M3.log'
```

6.   Set up a link to Microsoft symbol server and reload symbols:

```
0:004> .symfix c:\mss

0:004> .reload
.........................................................
......................................................
Loading unloaded module list
..
```

7.   We first try to use **!analyzed -v** command:

```
0:004> !analyze -v
*******************************************************************************
*                                                                             *
*                        Exception Analysis                                   *
*                                                                             *
*******************************************************************************

*** ERROR: Symbol file could not be found.  Defaulted to export symbols for msidcrl40.dll -

FAULTING_IP:
ntdll!RtlReportCriticalFailure+5b
7785faf8 eb1c            jmp     ntdll!RtlReportCriticalFailure+0x6f (7785fb16)

EXCEPTION_RECORD:  ffffffff -- (.exr 0xffffffffffffffff)
ExceptionAddress: 7785faf8 (ntdll!RtlReportCriticalFailure+0x0000005b)
   ExceptionCode: c0000374
  ExceptionFlags: 00000001
NumberParameters: 1
   Parameter[0]: 7787c040

PROCESS_NAME:  iexplore.exe

ERROR_CODE: (NTSTATUS) 0xc0000374 - A heap has been corrupted.

EXCEPTION_CODE: (NTSTATUS) 0xc0000374 - A heap has been corrupted.

EXCEPTION_PARAMETER1:  7787c040

NTGLOBALFLAG:  400

APPLICATION_VERIFIER_FLAGS:  0

APP:  iexplore.exe

LAST_CONTROL_TRANSFER:  from 77860704 to 7785faf8

FAULTING_THREAD:  ffffffff

BUGCHECK_STR:  APPLICATION_FAULT_ACTIONABLE_HEAP_CORRUPTION_heap_failure_entry_corruption_AFTER_CALL

PRIMARY_PROBLEM_CLASS:  ACTIONABLE_HEAP_CORRUPTION_heap_failure_entry_corruption_AFTER_CALL

DEFAULT_BUCKET_ID:  ACTIONABLE_HEAP_CORRUPTION_heap_failure_entry_corruption_AFTER_CALL
```

```
STACK_TEXT:
7787c078 7782b1a5 ntdll!RtlpCoalesceFreeBlocks+0x4b9
7787c07c 7781730a ntdll!RtlpFreeHeap+0x1e2
7787c080 77817545 ntdll!RtlFreeHeap+0x14e
7787c084 76277e4b kernel32!GlobalFree+0x47
7787c088 760f7277 ole32!ReleaseStgMedium+0x124
7787c08c 76594a1f urlmon!ReleaseBindInfo+0x4c
7787c090 765f7feb urlmon!CINet::ReleaseCNetObjects+0x3d
7787c094 765b9a87 urlmon!CINetHttp::OnWininetRequestHandleClosing+0x60
7787c098 765b93f0 urlmon!CINet::CINetCallback+0x2de
7787c09c 77582078 wininet!InternetIndicateStatus+0xfc
7787c0a0 77588f5d wininet!HANDLE_OBJECT::~HANDLE_OBJECT+0xc9
7787c0a4 7758937a wininet!INTERNET_CONNECT_HANDLE_OBJECT::~INTERNET_CONNECT_HANDLE_OBJECT+0x209
7787c0a8 7758916b wininet!HTTP_REQUEST_HANDLE_OBJECT::`scalar deleting destructor'+0xd
7787c0ac 77588d5e wininet!HANDLE_OBJECT::Dereference+0x22
7787c0b0 77589419 wininet!_InternetCloseHandle+0x9d
7787c0b4 77589114 wininet!InternetCloseHandle+0x11e


STACK_COMMAND:  .ecxr ; kb ; dps 7787c078 ; kb

FOLLOWUP_IP:
urlmon!ReleaseBindInfo+4c
76594a1f 57              push    edi

SYMBOL_STACK_INDEX:  5

SYMBOL_NAME:  urlmon!ReleaseBindInfo+4c

FOLLOWUP_NAME:  MachineOwner

MODULE_NAME: urlmon

IMAGE_NAME:  urlmon.dll

DEBUG_FLR_IMAGE_TIMESTAMP:  4c2598b9

FAILURE_BUCKET_ID:
ACTIONABLE_HEAP_CORRUPTION_heap_failure_entry_corruption_AFTER_CALL_c0000374_urlmon.dll!ReleaseBindInfo

BUCKET_ID:
APPLICATION_FAULT_ACTIONABLE_HEAP_CORRUPTION_heap_failure_entry_corruption_AFTER_CALL_urlmon!ReleaseBindInfo+4c

WATSON_STAGEONE_URL:
http://watson.microsoft.com/StageOne/iexplore_exe/8_0_6001_18943/4c25813d/ntdll_dll/6_0_6002_18005/49e03821/c0000374/0
00afaf8.htm?Retriage=1

WATSON_IBUCKET:  1989379217

WATSON_IBUCKETTABLE:  1

Followup: MachineOwner
---------
```

We see heap corruption diagnostics. The usual impulse here is to enable full page heap and collect a new dump. We also do it but now analyze the dump a bit further.

8.   Let's check stack traces from all process threads:

```
0:004> ~*k

    0  Id: 15bc.12c4 Suspend: 1 Teb: 7ffdf000 Unfrozen
ChildEBP RetAddr
001df4d8 77815610 ntdll!KiFastSystemCallRet
001df4dc 7627a5d7 ntdll!ZwWaitForMultipleObjects+0xc
001df578 77420f8d kernel32!WaitForMultipleObjectsEx+0x11d
001df5cc 7647334a user32!RealMsgWaitForMultipleObjectsEx+0x13c
001df61c 76474942 iertutil!IsoDispatchMessageToArtifacts+0x22c
001df63c 708c416a iertutil!IsoManagerThreadZero_WindowsPump+0x52
001df68c 00ff12e3 ieframe!LCIEStartAsTabProcess+0x25f
001df7d8 00ff147a iexplore!wWinMain+0x368
001df86c 7627d0e9 iexplore!_initterm_e+0x1b1
001df878 777f19bb kernel32!BaseThreadInitThunk+0xe
001df8b8 777f198e ntdll!__RtlUserThreadStart+0x23
001df8d0 00000000 ntdll!_RtlUserThreadStart+0x1b

    1  Id: 15bc.17a8 Suspend: 1 Teb: 7ffde000 Unfrozen
ChildEBP RetAddr
0258f6d8 77815610 ntdll!KiFastSystemCallRet
0258f6dc 777f2934 ntdll!ZwWaitForMultipleObjects+0xc
0258f870 7627d0e9 ntdll!TppWaiterpThread+0x328
0258f87c 777f19bb kernel32!BaseThreadInitThunk+0xe
0258f8bc 777f198e ntdll!__RtlUserThreadStart+0x23
0258f8d4 00000000 ntdll!_RtlUserThreadStart+0x1b

    2  Id: 15bc.1148 Suspend: 1 Teb: 7ffdc000 Unfrozen
ChildEBP RetAddr
02a2ed3c 77815610 ntdll!KiFastSystemCallRet
02a2ed40 7627a5d7 ntdll!ZwWaitForMultipleObjects+0xc
02a2eddc 7627a6f0 kernel32!WaitForMultipleObjectsEx+0x11d
02a2edf8 7646f08c kernel32!WaitForMultipleObjects+0x18
02a2fe24 76474819 iertutil!CForeignProcessToCurrentProcessMessaging::_vThreadProc+0xa1
02a2fe2c 7627d0e9 iertutil!CForeignProcessToCurrentProcessMessaging::_sThreadProc+0xd
02a2fe38 777f19bb kernel32!BaseThreadInitThunk+0xe
02a2fe78 777f198e ntdll!__RtlUserThreadStart+0x23
02a2fe90 00000000 ntdll!_RtlUserThreadStart+0x1b

    3  Id: 15bc.9e8 Suspend: 1 Teb: 7ffdb000 Unfrozen
ChildEBP RetAddr
028ef9a8 77815610 ntdll!KiFastSystemCallRet
028ef9ac 7627a5d7 ntdll!ZwWaitForMultipleObjects+0xc
028efa48 77420f8d kernel32!WaitForMultipleObjectsEx+0x11d
028efa9c 7647334a user32!RealMsgWaitForMultipleObjectsEx+0x13c
028efaec 764748b6 iertutil!IsoDispatchMessageToArtifacts+0x22c
028efb0c 7627d0e9 iertutil!IsoManagerThreadNonzero_WindowsPump+0x59
028efb18 777f19bb kernel32!BaseThreadInitThunk+0xe
028efb58 777f198e ntdll!__RtlUserThreadStart+0x23
028efb70 00000000 ntdll!_RtlUserThreadStart+0x1b
```

```
#  4  Id: 15bc.650 Suspend: 0 Teb: 7ffda000 Unfrozen
ChildEBP RetAddr
02c9cb18 77815620 ntdll!KiFastSystemCallRet
02c9cb1c 77843c62 ntdll!ZwWaitForSingleObject+0xc
02c9cba0 77843d4b ntdll!RtlReportExceptionEx+0x14b
02c9cbe0 7785fa87 ntdll!RtlReportException+0x3c
02c9cbf4 7785fb0d ntdll!RtlpTerminateFailureFilter+0x14
02c9cc00 777b9bdc ntdll!RtlReportCriticalFailure+0x6b
02c9cc14 777b4067 ntdll!_EH4_CallFilterFunc+0x12
02c9cc3c 77815f79 ntdll!_except_handler4+0x8e
02c9cc60 77815f4b ntdll!ExecuteHandler2+0x26
02c9cd10 77815dd7 ntdll!ExecuteHandler+0x24
02c9cd10 7785faf8 ntdll!KiUserExceptionDispatcher+0xf
02c9d084 77860704 ntdll!RtlReportCriticalFailure+0x5b
02c9d094 778607f2 ntdll!RtlpReportHeapFailure+0x21
02c9d0c8 7782b1a5 ntdll!RtlpLogHeapFailure+0xa1
02c9d110 7781730a ntdll!RtlpCoalesceFreeBlocks+0x4b9
02c9d208 77817545 ntdll!RtlpFreeHeap+0x1e2
02c9d224 76277e4b ntdll!RtlFreeHeap+0x14e
02c9d26c 760f7277 kernel32!GlobalFree+0x47
02c9d280 76594a1f ole32!ReleaseStgMedium+0x124 [d:\longhorn\com\ole32\ole232\base\api.cpp @
964]
02c9d294 765f7feb urlmon!ReleaseBindInfo+0x4c
02c9d2a4 765b9a87 urlmon!CINet::ReleaseCNetObjects+0x3d
02c9d2bc 765b93f0 urlmon!CINetHttp::OnWininetRequestHandleClosing+0x60
02c9d2d0 77582078 urlmon!CINet::CINetCallback+0x2de
02c9d418 77588f5d wininet!InternetIndicateStatus+0xfc
02c9d448 7758937a wininet!HANDLE_OBJECT::~HANDLE_OBJECT+0xc9
02c9d464 7758916b wininet!INTERNET_CONNECT_HANDLE_OBJECT::~INTERNET_CONNECT_HANDLE_OBJECT+0x209
02c9d470 77588d5e wininet!HTTP_REQUEST_HANDLE_OBJECT::`scalar deleting destructor'+0xd
02c9d480 77584e72 wininet!HANDLE_OBJECT::Dereference+0x22
02c9d48c 77589419 wininet!DereferenceObject+0x21
02c9d4b4 77589114 wininet!_InternetCloseHandle+0x9d
02c9d4d4 0004aaaf wininet!InternetCloseHandle+0x11e
WARNING: Frame IP not in any known module. Following frames may be wrong.
02c9d4e0 765a5d25 0x4aaaf
02c9d4fc 765a5c1b urlmon!CINet::TerminateRequest+0x82
02c9d50c 765a5a3c urlmon!CINet::MyTerminate+0x7b
02c9d51c 765a5998 urlmon!CINetProtImpl::Terminate+0x13
02c9d538 765a5b92 urlmon!CINetEmbdFilter::Terminate+0x17
02c9d548 765b9bc1 urlmon!CINet::Terminate+0x23
02c9d55c 765979f2 urlmon!CINetHttp::Terminate+0x48
02c9d574 7659766b urlmon!COInetProt::Terminate+0x1d
02c9d598 765979c0 urlmon!CTransaction::Terminate+0x12d
02c9d5b8 76597a2d urlmon!CBinding::ReportResult+0x92
02c9d5d0 76596609 urlmon!COInetProt::ReportResult+0x1a
02c9d5f8 76596322 urlmon!CTransaction::DispatchReport+0x1d9
02c9d624 7659653e urlmon!CTransaction::DispatchPacket+0x31
02c9d644 765a504b urlmon!CTransaction::OnINetCallback+0x92
02c9d65c 7741fd72 urlmon!TransactionWndProc+0x28
02c9d688 7741fe4a user32!InternalCallWinProc+0x23
02c9d700 7742018d user32!UserCallWinProcCheckWow+0x14b
02c9d764 7742022b user32!DispatchMessageWorker+0x322
02c9d774 7094c1d5 user32!DispatchMessageW+0xf
02c9f87c 708f337e ieframe!CTabWindow::_TabWindowThreadProc+0x54c
02c9f934 7647426d ieframe!LCIETab_ThreadProc+0x2c1
02c9f944 7627d0e9 iertutil!CIsoScope::RegisterThread+0xab
02c9f950 777f19bb kernel32!BaseThreadInitThunk+0xe
02c9f990 777f198e ntdll!__RtlUserThreadStart+0x23
02c9f9a8 00000000 ntdll!_RtlUserThreadStart+0x1b
```

```
   5  Id: 15bc.efc Suspend: 1 Teb: 7ffd9000 Unfrozen
ChildEBP RetAddr
02e8fa48 77815610 ntdll!KiFastSystemCallRet
02e8fa4c 7627a5d7 ntdll!ZwWaitForMultipleObjects+0xc
02e8fae8 7627a6f0 kernel32!WaitForMultipleObjectsEx+0x11d
02e8fb04 275c55c0 kernel32!WaitForMultipleObjects+0x18
WARNING: Stack unwind information not available. Following frames may be wrong.
02e8fc4c 777f4123 msidcrl40!CreatePassportAuthUIContext+0x2ab30
02e8fc88 777f3e23 ntdll!RtlpTpTimerCallback+0x62
02e8fcac 777f2fcf ntdll!TppTimerpExecuteCallback+0x14d
02e8fddc 7627d0e9 ntdll!TppWorkerThread+0x545
02e8fde8 777f19bb kernel32!BaseThreadInitThunk+0xe
02e8fe28 777f198e ntdll!__RtlUserThreadStart+0x23
02e8fe40 00000000 ntdll!_RtlUserThreadStart+0x1b

   6  Id: 15bc.10ec Suspend: 1 Teb: 7ffd8000 Unfrozen
ChildEBP RetAddr
0409fd70 77814780 ntdll!KiFastSystemCallRet
0409fd74 76279990 ntdll!NtDelayExecution+0xc
0409fddc 76231c6c kernel32!SleepEx+0x62
0409fdec 76123f1d kernel32!Sleep+0xf
0409fdf8 7613eb46 ole32!CROIDTable::WorkerThreadLoop+0x14
[d:\longhorn\com\ole32\com\dcomrem\refcache.cxx @ 1345]
0409fe14 761257ab ole32!CRpcThread::WorkerLoop+0x26
[d:\longhorn\com\ole32\com\dcomrem\threads.cxx @ 257]
0409fe24 7627d0e9 ole32!CRpcThreadCache::RpcWorkerThreadEntry+0x16
[d:\longhorn\com\ole32\com\dcomrem\threads.cxx @ 63]
0409fe30 777f19bb kernel32!BaseThreadInitThunk+0xe
0409fe70 777f198e ntdll!__RtlUserThreadStart+0x23
0409fe88 00000000 ntdll!_RtlUserThreadStart+0x1b

   7  Id: 15bc.1500 Suspend: 1 Teb: 7ffd6000 Unfrozen
ChildEBP RetAddr
03f0fb68 778150b0 ntdll!KiFastSystemCallRet
03f0fb6c 7627d11e ntdll!NtRemoveIoCompletion+0xc
03f0fb98 75ec03c8 kernel32!GetQueuedCompletionStatus+0x29
03f0fbd4 75ec04fd rpcrt4!COMMON_ProcessCalls+0xb5
03f0fc44 75ec011c rpcrt4!LOADABLE_TRANSPORT::ProcessIOEvents+0x138
03f0fc4c 75ec00e3 rpcrt4!ProcessIOEventsWrapper+0xd
03f0fc70 75ec0166 rpcrt4!BaseCachedThreadRoutine+0x5c
03f0fc7c 7627d0e9 rpcrt4!ThreadStartRoutine+0x1e
03f0fc88 777f19bb kernel32!BaseThreadInitThunk+0xe
03f0fcc8 777f198e ntdll!__RtlUserThreadStart+0x23
03f0fce0 00000000 ntdll!_RtlUserThreadStart+0x1b

   8  Id: 15bc.1364 Suspend: 1 Teb: 7ffd5000 Unfrozen
ChildEBP RetAddr
0474f5f8 77815620 ntdll!KiFastSystemCallRet
0474f5fc 75471aa6 ntdll!ZwWaitForSingleObject+0xc
0474f63c 7547179d mswsock!SockWaitForSingleObject+0x19f
0474f728 77381693 mswsock!WSPSelect+0x38c
0474f7a8 7757e9a9 ws2_32!select+0x494
0474fb00 7759deab wininet!ICAsyncThread::SelectThread+0x242
0474fb08 7627d0e9 wininet!ICAsyncThread::SelectThreadWrapper+0xd
0474fb14 777f19bb kernel32!BaseThreadInitThunk+0xe
0474fb54 777f198e ntdll!__RtlUserThreadStart+0x23
0474fb6c 00000000 ntdll!_RtlUserThreadStart+0x1b
```

```
   9   Id: 15bc.1224 Suspend: 1 Teb: 7ffaf000 Unfrozen
ChildEBP RetAddr
051ff8a8 778157b0 ntdll!KiFastSystemCallRet
051ff8ac 777f2eb0 ntdll!NtWaitForWorkViaWorkerFactory+0xc
051ff9dc 7627d0e9 ntdll!TppWorkerThread+0x1f6
051ff9e8 777f19bb kernel32!BaseThreadInitThunk+0xe
051ffa28 777f198e ntdll!__RtlUserThreadStart+0x23
051ffa40 00000000 ntdll!_RtlUserThreadStart+0x1b

  10   Id: 15bc.990 Suspend: 1 Teb: 7ffad000 Unfrozen
ChildEBP RetAddr
04dbf860 778150b0 ntdll!KiFastSystemCallRet
04dbf864 754764f1 ntdll!NtRemoveIoCompletion+0xc
04dbf89c 7627d0e9 mswsock!SockAsyncThread+0x69
04dbf8a8 777f19bb kernel32!BaseThreadInitThunk+0xe
04dbf8e8 777f198e ntdll!__RtlUserThreadStart+0x23
04dbf900 00000000 ntdll!_RtlUserThreadStart+0x1b

  11   Id: 15bc.fa4 Suspend: 1 Teb: 7ffac000 Unfrozen
ChildEBP RetAddr
0568fe78 77815620 ntdll!KiFastSystemCallRet
0568fe7c 76279884 ntdll!ZwWaitForSingleObject+0xc
0568feec 762797f2 kernel32!WaitForSingleObjectEx+0xbe
0568ff00 6ca4a731 kernel32!WaitForSingleObject+0x12
0568ff24 6c9b0778 mshtml!CDwnTaskExec::ThreadExec+0x23c
0568ff2c 6c9b083b mshtml!CExecFT::ThreadProc+0x39
0568ff38 7627d0e9 mshtml!CExecFT::StaticThreadProc+0xe
0568ff44 777f19bb kernel32!BaseThreadInitThunk+0xe
0568ff84 777f198e ntdll!__RtlUserThreadStart+0x23
0568ff9c 00000000 ntdll!_RtlUserThreadStart+0x1b

  12   Id: 15bc.d10 Suspend: 1 Teb: 7ffaa000 Unfrozen
ChildEBP RetAddr
06e1fca0 77815620 ntdll!KiFastSystemCallRet
06e1fca4 76279884 ntdll!ZwWaitForSingleObject+0xc
06e1fd14 762797f2 kernel32!WaitForSingleObjectEx+0xbe
06e1fd28 6ca4a731 kernel32!WaitForSingleObject+0x12
06e1fd4c 6c9b0778 mshtml!CDwnTaskExec::ThreadExec+0x23c
06e1fd54 6c9b083b mshtml!CExecFT::ThreadProc+0x39
06e1fd60 7627d0e9 mshtml!CExecFT::StaticThreadProc+0xe
06e1fd6c 777f19bb kernel32!BaseThreadInitThunk+0xe
06e1fdac 777f198e ntdll!__RtlUserThreadStart+0x23
06e1fdc4 00000000 ntdll!_RtlUserThreadStart+0x1b

  13   Id: 15bc.294 Suspend: 1 Teb: 7ffa9000 Unfrozen
ChildEBP RetAddr
06f1f6dc 77815610 ntdll!KiFastSystemCallRet
06f1f6e0 7627a5d7 ntdll!ZwWaitForMultipleObjects+0xc
06f1f77c 7627a6f0 kernel32!WaitForMultipleObjectsEx+0x11d
06f1f798 275b4879 kernel32!WaitForMultipleObjects+0x18
WARNING: Stack unwind information not available. Following frames may be wrong.
06f1fabc 275b4a58 msidcrl40!CreatePassportAuthUIContext+0x19de9
06f1fae4 275c9655 msidcrl40!CreatePassportAuthUIContext+0x19fc8
06f1fb1c 275c96fa msidcrl40!CreatePassportAuthUIContext+0x2ebc5
06f1fb30 777f19bb msidcrl40!CreatePassportAuthUIContext+0x2ec6a
06f1fb70 777f198e ntdll!__RtlUserThreadStart+0x23
06f1fb88 00000000 ntdll!_RtlUserThreadStart+0x1b
```

```
  14   Id: 15bc.ebc Suspend: 1 Teb: 7ffa8000 Unfrozen
ChildEBP RetAddr
0775f5fc 77815610 ntdll!KiFastSystemCallRet
0775f600 7627a5d7 ntdll!ZwWaitForMultipleObjects+0xc
0775f69c 7627a6f0 kernel32!WaitForMultipleObjectsEx+0x11d
0775f6b8 275b4879 kernel32!WaitForMultipleObjects+0x18
WARNING: Stack unwind information not available. Following frames may be wrong.
0775f9dc 275b4a58 msidcrl40!CreatePassportAuthUIContext+0x19de9
0775fa04 275c9655 msidcrl40!CreatePassportAuthUIContext+0x19fc8
0775fa3c 275c96fa msidcrl40!CreatePassportAuthUIContext+0x2ebc5
0775fa50 777f19bb msidcrl40!CreatePassportAuthUIContext+0x2ec6a
0775fa90 777f198e ntdll!__RtlUserThreadStart+0x23
0775faa8 00000000 ntdll!_RtlUserThreadStart+0x1b

  15   Id: 15bc.99c Suspend: 1 Teb: 7ffa6000 Unfrozen
ChildEBP RetAddr
0501faf4 778157b0 ntdll!KiFastSystemCallRet
0501faf8 777f2eb0 ntdll!NtWaitForWorkViaWorkerFactory+0xc
0501fc28 7627d0e9 ntdll!TppWorkerThread+0x1f6
0501fc34 777f19bb kernel32!BaseThreadInitThunk+0xe
0501fc74 777f198e ntdll!__RtlUserThreadStart+0x23
0501fc8c 00000000 ntdll!_RtlUserThreadStart+0x1b

  16   Id: 15bc.1128 Suspend: 1 Teb: 7ffa5000 Unfrozen
ChildEBP RetAddr
0785f748 77815620 ntdll!KiFastSystemCallRet
0785f74c 76279884 ntdll!ZwWaitForSingleObject+0xc
0785f7bc 762797f2 kernel32!WaitForSingleObjectEx+0xbe
0785f7d0 6ca4a731 kernel32!WaitForSingleObject+0x12
0785f7f0 6c9b0778 mshtml!CDwnTaskExec::ThreadExec+0x23c
0785f7f8 6c9b083b mshtml!CExecFT::ThreadProc+0x39
0785f804 7627d0e9 mshtml!CExecFT::StaticThreadProc+0xe
0785f810 777f19bb kernel32!BaseThreadInitThunk+0xe
0785f850 777f198e ntdll!__RtlUserThreadStart+0x23
0785f868 00000000 ntdll!_RtlUserThreadStart+0x1b

  17   Id: 15bc.b44 Suspend: 1 Teb: 7ffa1000 Unfrozen
ChildEBP RetAddr
0868fc78 77815620 ntdll!KiFastSystemCallRet
0868fc7c 76279884 ntdll!ZwWaitForSingleObject+0xc
0868fcec 762797f2 kernel32!WaitForSingleObjectEx+0xbe
0868fd00 6cbe8fed kernel32!WaitForSingleObject+0x12
0868fd24 6c9b0778 mshtml!CTimerMan::ThreadExec+0x90
0868fd2c 6c9b083b mshtml!CExecFT::ThreadProc+0x39
0868fd38 7627d0e9 mshtml!CExecFT::StaticThreadProc+0xe
0868fd44 777f19bb kernel32!BaseThreadInitThunk+0xe
0868fd84 777f198e ntdll!__RtlUserThreadStart+0x23
0868fd9c 00000000 ntdll!_RtlUserThreadStart+0x1b

  18   Id: 15bc.4d0 Suspend: 1 Teb: 7ffa0000 Unfrozen
ChildEBP RetAddr
0b99fbbc 7741feef ntdll!KiFastSystemCallRet
0b99fbc0 77418af3 user32!NtUserGetMessage+0xc
0b99fbe4 7450145c user32!GetMessageA+0x8a
0b99fc1c 7627d0e9 winmm!mciwindow+0x102
0b99fc28 777f19bb kernel32!BaseThreadInitThunk+0xe
0b99fc68 777f198e ntdll!__RtlUserThreadStart+0x23
0b99fc80 00000000 ntdll!_RtlUserThreadStart+0x1b
```

```
  19  Id: 15bc.e10 Suspend: 1 Teb: 7ff9f000 Unfrozen
ChildEBP RetAddr
0bc7fa20 77815610 ntdll!KiFastSystemCallRet
0bc7fa24 7627a5d7 ntdll!ZwWaitForMultipleObjects+0xc
0bc7fac0 742d4f1d kernel32!WaitForMultipleObjectsEx+0x11d
0bc7faf8 742d7e96 wdmaud!CWorker::_ThreadProc+0x5e
0bc7fb04 7627d0e9 wdmaud!CWorker::_StaticThreadProc+0x18
0bc7fb10 777f19bb kernel32!BaseThreadInitThunk+0xe
0bc7fb50 777f198e ntdll!__RtlUserThreadStart+0x23
0bc7fb68 00000000 ntdll!_RtlUserThreadStart+0x1b

  20  Id: 15bc.15b0 Suspend: 1 Teb: 7ffa4000 Unfrozen
ChildEBP RetAddr
0b04fc00 77815610 ntdll!KiFastSystemCallRet
0b04fc04 7627a5d7 ntdll!ZwWaitForMultipleObjects+0xc
0b04fca0 77420f8d kernel32!WaitForMultipleObjectsEx+0x11d
0b04fcf4 77417f5a user32!RealMsgWaitForMultipleObjectsEx+0x13c
0b04fd10 745974b2 user32!MsgWaitForMultipleObjects+0x1f
0b04fd5c 7627d0e9 GdiPlus!BackgroundThreadProc+0x59
0b04fd68 777f19bb kernel32!BaseThreadInitThunk+0xe
0b04fda8 777f198e ntdll!__RtlUserThreadStart+0x23
0b04fdc0 00000000 ntdll!_RtlUserThreadStart+0x1b

  21  Id: 15bc.15a8 Suspend: 1 Teb: 7ffdd000 Unfrozen
ChildEBP RetAddr
0bb7fb08 778150b0 ntdll!KiFastSystemCallRet
0bb7fb0c 7627d11e ntdll!NtRemoveIoCompletion+0xc
0bb7fb38 75ec03c8 kernel32!GetQueuedCompletionStatus+0x29
0bb7fb74 75ec04fd rpcrt4!COMMON_ProcessCalls+0xb5
0bb7fbe4 75ec011c rpcrt4!LOADABLE_TRANSPORT::ProcessIOEvents+0x138
0bb7fbec 75ec00e3 rpcrt4!ProcessIOEventsWrapper+0xd
0bb7fc14 75ec0166 rpcrt4!BaseCachedThreadRoutine+0x5c
0bb7fc20 7627d0e9 rpcrt4!ThreadStartRoutine+0x1e
0bb7fc2c 777f19bb kernel32!BaseThreadInitThunk+0xe
0bb7fc6c 777f198e ntdll!__RtlUserThreadStart+0x23
0bb7fc84 00000000 ntdll!_RtlUserThreadStart+0x1b
```

The only problem thread we see is #4 with exception processing code after detected heap corruption. What we also see is a raw instruction pointer on the stack trace. This can often be seen in managed .NET execution environment with its JIT compiled .NET code. However there is no presence of .NET CLR modules such as mscorwks.dll or clr.dll on the stack trace.

9.   Let's look at this RIP address closely by doing backwards disassembly:

```
0:004> ub 0x4aaaf
0004aa97 740c            je          0004aaa5
0004aa99 8b4508          mov         eax,dword ptr [ebp+8]
0004aa9c 50              push        eax
0004aa9d e82eedffff      call        000497d0
0004aaa2 83c404          add         esp,4
0004aaa5 8b4d08          mov         ecx,dword ptr [ebp+8]
0004aaa8 51              push        ecx
0004aaa9 ff1580aa0500    call        dword ptr ds:[5AA80h]
```

Note that there is an indirect call through another address 5AA80:

```
0:004> db 5AA80
0005aa80  00 00 93 00 00 00 8f 00-00 00 27 00 00 00 90 00  ..........'.....
0005aa90  00 00 25 00 00 00 dc 01-4d 6f 7a 69 6c 6c 61 2f  ..%.....Mozilla/
0005aaa0  34 2e 30 20 28 63 6f 6d-70 61 74 69 62 6c 65 3b  4.0 (compatible;
0005aab0  20 4d 53 49 45 20 38 2e-30 3b 20 57 69 6e 64 6f   MSIE 8.0; Windo
0005aac0  77 73 20 4e 54 20 36 2e-30 3b 20 54 72 69 64 65  ws NT 6.0; Tride
0005aad0  6e 74 2f 34 2e 30 3b 20-4d 61 74 68 50 6c 61 79  nt/4.0; MathPlay
0005aae0  65 72 20 32 2e 31 30 64-3b 20 53 4c 43 43 31 3b  er 2.10d; SLCC1;
0005aaf0  20 2e 4e 45 54 20 43 4c-52 20 32 2e 30 2e 35 30   .NET CLR 2.0.50

0:004> dps 5AA80
0005aa80  00930000
0005aa84  008f0000
0005aa88  00270000
0005aa8c  00900000
0005aa90  00250000
0005aa94  01dc0000
0005aa98  697a6f4d
0005aa9c  2f616c6c
0005aaa0  20302e34
0005aaa4  6d6f6328
0005aaa8  69746170
0005aaac  3b656c62
0005aab0  49534d20
0005aab4  2e382045
0005aab8  57203b30
0005aabc  6f646e69
0005aac0  4e207377
0005aac4  2e362054
0005aac8  54203b30
0005aacc  65646972
0005aad0  342f746e
0005aad4  203b302e
0005aad8  6874614d
0005aadc  79616c50
0005aae0  32207265
0005aae4  6430312e
0005aae8  4c53203b
0005aaec  3b314343
0005aaf0  454e2e20
0005aaf4  4c432054
0005aaf8  2e322052
0005aafc  30352e30

0:004> u 00930000
00930000 8bff           mov     edi,edi
00930002 55             push    ebp
00930003 8bec           mov     ebp,esp
00930005 e98390c576     jmp     wininet!InternetCloseHandle+0x5 (7758908d)
0093000a 0000           add     byte ptr [eax],al
0093000c 0000           add     byte ptr [eax],al
0093000e 0000           add     byte ptr [eax],al
00930010 0000           add     byte ptr [eax],al
```

Let's check all other addresses from **dps** command output before ASCII data:

```
0:004> u 008f0000
008f0000 8bff               mov      edi,edi
008f0002 55                 push     ebp
008f0003 8bec               mov      ebp,esp
008f0005 e94665c976         jmp      wininet!InternetReadFile+0x5 (77586550)
008f000a 0000               add      byte ptr [eax],al
008f000c 0000               add      byte ptr [eax],al
008f000e 0000               add      byte ptr [eax],al
008f0010 0000               add      byte ptr [eax],al

0:004> u 00270000
00270000 8bff               mov      edi,edi
00270002 55                 push     ebp
00270003 8bec               mov      ebp,esp
00270005 e905a73877         jmp      wininet!HttpSendRequestExA+0x5 (775fa70f)
0027000a 0000               add      byte ptr [eax],al
0027000c 0000               add      byte ptr [eax],al
0027000e 0000               add      byte ptr [eax],al
00270010 0000               add      byte ptr [eax],al

0:004> u 00900000
00900000 8bff               mov      edi,edi
00900002 55                 push     ebp
00900003 8bec               mov      ebp,esp
00900005 e97c33ca76         jmp      wininet!InternetReadFileExA+0x5 (775a3386)
0090000a 0000               add      byte ptr [eax],al
0090000c 0000               add      byte ptr [eax],al
0090000e 0000               add      byte ptr [eax],al
00900010 0000               add      byte ptr [eax],al

0:004> u 00250000
00250000 8bff               mov      edi,edi
00250002 55                 push     ebp
00250003 8bec               mov      ebp,esp
00250005 e984ee3477         jmp      wininet!HttpSendRequestA+0x5 (7759ee8e)
0025000a 0000               add      byte ptr [eax],al
0025000c 0000               add      byte ptr [eax],al
0025000e 0000               add      byte ptr [eax],al
00250010 0000               add      byte ptr [eax],al
```

All these code jumps look like return to original hooked function code. Let's check the first instructions in all these functions:

```
0:004> u wininet!InternetCloseHandle
wininet!InternetCloseHandle:
77589088 e9031aac88         jmp      0004aa90
7758908d 51                 push     ecx
7758908e 51                 push     ecx
7758908f 53                 push     ebx
77589090 56                 push     esi
77589091 57                 push     edi
77589092 33db               xor      ebx,ebx
77589094 33ff               xor      edi,edi
```

83

```
0:004> u wininet!InternetReadFile
wininet!InternetReadFile:
7758654b e98044ac88      jmp       0004a9d0
77586550 83ec24          sub       esp,24h
77586553 53              push      ebx
77586554 56              push      esi
77586555 57              push      edi
77586556 33ff            xor       edi,edi
77586558 393db8116277    cmp       dword ptr [wininet!GlobalDataInitialized (776211b8)],edi
7758655e 897df4          mov       dword ptr [ebp-0Ch],edi

0:004> u wininet!HttpSendRequestExA
wininet!HttpSendRequestExA:
775fa70a e9f1faa488      jmp       0004a200
775fa70f 53              push      ebx
775fa710 56              push      esi
775fa711 57              push      edi
775fa712 33db            xor       ebx,ebx
775fa714 33c9            xor       ecx,ecx
775fa716 33d2            xor       edx,edx
775fa718 33f6            xor       esi,esi

0:004> u wininet!InternetReadFileExA
wininet!InternetReadFileExA:
775a3381 e97a76aa88      jmp       0004aa00
775a3386 83ec20          sub       esp,20h
775a3389 53              push      ebx
775a338a 33db            xor       ebx,ebx
775a338c 391db8116277    cmp       dword ptr [wininet!GlobalDataInitialized (776211b8)],ebx
775a3392 56              push      esi
775a3393 57              push      edi
775a3394 895dfc          mov       dword ptr [ebp-4],ebx

0:004> u wininet!HttpSendRequestA
wininet!HttpSendRequestA:
7759ee89 e952b2aa88      jmp       0004a0e0
7759ee8e 6a10            push      10h
7759ee90 6a00            push      0
7759ee92 ff7518          push      dword ptr [ebp+18h]
7759ee95 ff7514          push      dword ptr [ebp+14h]
7759ee98 ff7510          push      dword ptr [ebp+10h]
7759ee9b ff750c          push      dword ptr [ebp+0Ch]
7759ee9e ff7508          push      dword ptr [ebp+8]
```

Let's check the address attribute:

```
0:004> !address 0x4aaaf


Mapping file section regions...
Mapping module regions...
Mapping PEB regions...
Mapping TEB and stack regions...
*** Failure in mapping Heap (80004005: ExtRemoteTyped::Field: unable to retrieve field
'BaseAddress' at ffffffff99654a5f)
Mapping page heap regions...
Mapping other regions...
Mapping stack trace database regions...
Mapping activation context regions...
```

```
Usage:                    <unknown>
Base Address:             00040000
End Address:              0005d000
Region Size:              0001d000
State:                    00001000 MEM_COMMIT
Protect:                  00000040 PAGE_EXECUTE_READWRITE
Type:                     00020000 MEM_PRIVATE
Allocation Base:          00040000
Allocation Protect:       00000040 PAGE_EXECUTE_READWRITE
```

We see that the region is also writable compared to normal code:

```
0:004> !address 775fa70a
```

```
Usage:                    Image
Base Address:             77571000
End Address:              77621000
Region Size:              000b0000
State:                    00001000 MEM_COMMIT
Protect:                  00000020 PAGE_EXECUTE_READ
Type:                     01000000 MEM_IMAGE
Allocation Base:          77570000
Allocation Protect:       00000080 PAGE_EXECUTE_WRITECOPY
Image Path:               C:\Windows\System32\wininet.dll
Module Name:              wininet
Loaded Image Name:        wininet.dll
Mapped Image Name:
More info:                lmv m wininet
More info:                !lmi wininet
More info:                ln 0x775fa70a
More info:                !dh 0x77570000
```

10.   Now we check if the base address contains any module information:

```
0:004> dc 00040000
00040000   00905a4d 00000003 00000004 0000ffff   MZ..............
00040010   000000b8 00000000 00000040 00000000   ........@.......
00040020   00000000 00000000 00000000 00000000   ................
00040030   00000000 00000000 00000000 000000d8   ................
00040040   0eba1f0e cd09b400 4c01b821 685421cd   ........!..L.!Th
00040050   70207369 72676f72 63206d61 6f6e6e61   is program canno
00040060   65622074 6e757220 206e6920 20534f44   t be run in DOS
00040070   65646f6d 0a0d0d2e 00000024 00000000   mode....$.......

0:004> !dh 00040000

File Type: EXECUTABLE IMAGE
FILE HEADER VALUES
     14C machine (i386)
       4 number of sections
4C9E36D3 time date stamp Sat Sep 25 18:52:19 2010

       0 file pointer to symbol table
       0 number of symbols
      E0 size of optional header
     102 characteristics
            Executable
            32 bit word machine
```

```
OPTIONAL HEADER VALUES
      10B magic #
     9.00 linker version
    12200 size of code
     7000 size of initialized data
        0 size of uninitialized data
     D5F0 address of entry point
     1000 base of code
          ----- new -----
 00400000 image base
     1000 section alignment
      200 file alignment
        2 subsystem (Windows GUI)
     5.00 operating system version
     0.00 image version
     5.00 subsystem version
    1D000 size of image
      400 size of headers
        0 checksum
 00100000 size of stack reserve
 00001000 size of stack commit
 00100000 size of heap reserve
 00001000 size of heap commit
     8540 DLL characteristics
              Dynamic base
              NX compatible
              No structured exception handler
              Terminal server aware
        0 [        0] address [size] of Export Directory
        0 [        0] address [size] of Import Directory
        0 [        0] address [size] of Resource Directory
        0 [        0] address [size] of Exception Directory
        0 [        0] address [size] of Security Directory
    1C000 [      3F0] address [size] of Base Relocation Directory
        0 [        0] address [size] of Debug Directory
        0 [        0] address [size] of Description Directory
        0 [        0] address [size] of Special Directory
        0 [        0] address [size] of Thread Storage Directory
        0 [        0] address [size] of Load Configuration Directory
        0 [        0] address [size] of Bound Import Directory
        0 [        0] address [size] of Import Address Table Directory
        0 [        0] address [size] of Delay Import Directory
        0 [        0] address [size] of COR20 Header Directory
        0 [        0] address [size] of Reserved Directory


SECTION HEADER #1
    .text name
    1203B virtual size
     1000 virtual address
    12200 size of raw data
      400 file pointer to raw data
        0 file pointer to relocation table
        0 file pointer to line numbers
        0 number of relocations
        0 number of line numbers
 60000020 flags
          Code
          (no align specified)
```

```
          Execute Read

SECTION HEADER #2
  .rdata name
     7D0 virtual size
   14000 virtual address
     800 size of raw data
   12600 file pointer to raw data
       0 file pointer to relocation table
       0 file pointer to line numbers
       0 number of relocations
       0 number of line numbers
40000040 flags
         Initialized Data
         (no align specified)
         Read Only

SECTION HEADER #3
  .data name
    6008 virtual size
   15000 virtual address
    4000 size of raw data
   12E00 file pointer to raw data
       0 file pointer to relocation table
       0 file pointer to line numbers
       0 number of relocations
       0 number of line numbers
C0000040 flags
         Initialized Data
         (no align specified)
         Read Write

SECTION HEADER #4
  .reloc name
     5F0 virtual size
   1C000 virtual address
     600 size of raw data
   16E00 file pointer to raw data
       0 file pointer to relocation table
       0 file pointer to line numbers
       0 number of relocations
       0 number of line numbers
42000040 flags
         Initialized Data
         Discardable
         (no align specified)
         Read Only
```

We see the module doesn't have any import tables.

11.   We now check the module range for any string hints:

```
0:004> s-sa 00040000 0005d000
0004004d  "!This program cannot be run in D"
0004006d  "OS mode."
00040081  "3y@"
000400b8  "Rich"
000401d0  ".text"
000401f7  "`.rdata"
```

```
0004021f    "@.data"
00040248    ".reloc"
[...]
00054000    "HELLO"
00054008    "%s:%s"
00054010    "READY"
00054018    "GET /stat?uptime=%d&downlink=%d&"
00054038    "uplink=%d&id=%s&statpass=%s&comm"
00054058    "ent=%s HTTP/1.0"
000540ac    "%s%s%s"
000540d8    "ftp://%s:%s@%s:%d"
000540fc    "Accept-Encoding:"
00054118    "Accept-Encoding:"
00054130    "0123456789ABCDEF"
00054144    "://"
00054160    "POST %s HTTP/1.0"
00054172    "Host: %s"
0005417c    "User-Agent: %s"
0005418c    "Accept: text/html"
0005419f    "Connection: Close"
000541b2    "Content-Type: application/x-www-"
000541d2    "form-urlencoded"
000541e3    "Content-Length: %d"
000541fc    "id="
00054208    "POST %s HTTP/1.1"
0005421a    "Host: %s"
00054224    "User-Agent: %s"
00054234    "Accept: text/html"
00054247    "Connection: Close"
0005425a    "Content-Type: application/x-www-"
0005427a    "form-urlencoded"
0005428b    "Content-Length: %d"
000542a4    "id=%s&base="
000542b8    "id=%s&brw=%d&type=%d&data="
000542d8    "POST %s HTTP/1.1"
000542ea    "Host: %s"
000542f4    "User-Agent: %s"
00054304    "Accept: text/html"
00054317    "Connection: Close"
0005432a    "Content-Type: application/x-www-"
0005434a    "form-urlencoded"
0005435b    "Content-Length: %d"
00054378    "id=%s&os=%s&plist="
00054390    "POST %s HTTP/1.1"
000543a2    "Host: %s"
000543ac    "User-Agent: %s"
000543bc    "Accept: text/html"
000543cf    "Connection: Close"
000543e2    "Content-Type: application/x-www-"
00054402    "form-urlencoded"
00054413    "Content-Length: %d"
00054430    "id=%s&data=%s"
00054440    "POST %s HTTP/1.1"
00054452    "Host: %s"
0005445c    "User-Agent: %s"
0005446c    "Accept: text/html"
0005447f    "Connection: Close"
00054492    "Content-Type: application/x-www-"
000544b2    "form-urlencoded"
000544c3    "Content-Length: %d"
```

```
000544e0    "GET %s HTTP/1.0"
000544f1    "Host: %s"
000544fb    "User-Agent: %s"
0005450b    "Connection: close"
00054528    "POST /get/scr.html HTTP/1.0"
00054545    "Host: %s"
0005454f    "User-Agent: %s"
0005455f    "Connection: close"
00054572    "Content-Length: %d"
00054586    "Content-Type: multipart/form-dat"
000545a6    "a; boundary=--------------------"
000545c6    "-------%d"
000545d4    "---------------------------%d"
000545f8    "%sContent-Disposition: form-data"
00054618    "; name="id""
00054630    "%sContent-Disposition: form-data"
00054650    "; name="screen"; filename="%d""
00054670    "Content-Type: application/octet-"
00054690    "stream"
000546a0    "%s(%d) : %s"
000546ac    "%s failed with error %d: %s"
000546c8    "%02X"
000546d8    "BlackwoodPRO"
000546e8    "FinamDirect"
000546f4    "GrayBox"
000546fc    "MbtPRO"
00054704    "Laser"
0005470c    "LightSpeed"
00054718    "LTGroup"
00054720    "Mbt"
00054724    "ScotTrader"
00054730    "SaxoTrader"
00054740    "Program:    %s"
0005474f    "Username:   %s"
0005475e    "Password:   %s"
0005476d    "AccountNO: %s"
0005477c    "Server:     %s"
00054790    "%s %s"
0005479c    "PROCESSOR_IDENTIFIER"
[...]
0005a8e0    "glebk"
0005aa98    "Mozilla/4.0 (compatible; MSIE 8."
0005aab8    "0; Windows NT 6.0; Trident/4.0; "
0005aad8    "MathPlayer 2.10d; SLCC1; .NET CL"
0005aaf8    "R 2.0.50727; Media Center PC 5.0"
0005ab18    "; .NET CLR 3.5.30729; .NET CLR 3"
0005ab38    ".0.30729)"
[...]

0:004> s-su 00040000 0005d000
[...]
00055004    "\chkntfs.exe"
00055020    "\chkntfs.dat"
[...]
00058e20    "kernel32.dll"
00058e3c    "user32.dll"
00058e54    "ws2_32.dll"
00058e6c    "ntdll.dll"
00058e80    "wininet.dll"
00058e98    "nspr4.dll"
```

```
00058eac  "ssl3.dll"
0005a4e0  "C:\Users\dima\AppData\Roaming\ch"
0005a520  "kntfs.dat"
[...]
```

We find some references to the fake chkntfs.exe here and the list of modules needed for this malware. Also "gleb" is a Russian name but it could be just a coincidence.

12.   Let's now check if there are any Hidden Modules not shown in loaded module list by using **.imgscan** command that searches for MZ/PE signatures:

```
0:004> .imgscan
MZ at 00040000, prot 00000040, type 00020000 - size 1d000
MZ at 00fa0000, prot 00000002, type 00040000 - size 2000
MZ at 00ff0000, prot 00000002, type 01000000 - size 9c000
  Name: iexplore.exe
MZ at 044b0000, prot 00000002, type 00040000 - size 2000
MZ at 08f50000, prot 00000002, type 01000000 - size 335000
  Name: igdumd32.dll
MZ at 0a390000, prot 00000002, type 00040000 - size 191000
MZ at 10000000, prot 00000004, type 00020000 - size 5000
  Name: screens_dll.dll
MZ at 16080000, prot 00000002, type 01000000 - size 25000
  Name: mdnsNSP.dll
MZ at 27500000, prot 00000002, type 01000000 - size 11a000
  Name: msidcrl40.dll
MZ at 29500000, prot 00000002, type 01000000 - size 67000
  Name: IDBHO.DLL
MZ at 633d0000, prot 00000002, type 01000000 - size 4f000
  Name: rpbrowserrecordplugin.dll
MZ at 634b0000, prot 00000002, type 01000000 - size 1d000
  Name: rpchromebrowserrecordhelper.dll
MZ at 68f80000, prot 00000002, type 01000000 - size 5e3000
  Name: Flash.ocx
MZ at 6a2b0000, prot 00000002, type 01000000 - size 45b000
  Name: agcore.dll
MZ at 6bfb0000, prot 00000002, type 01000000 - size d8000
  Name: NPCTRL.dll
MZ at 6c8c0000, prot 00000002, type 01000000 - size 6a000
  Name: VBSCRIPT.dll
MZ at 6c9a0000, prot 00000002, type 01000000 - size 5b0000
  Name: MSHTML.dll
MZ at 6d150000, prot 00000002, type 01000000 - size 39000
  Name: dxtrans.dll
MZ at 6d1d0000, prot 00000002, type 01000000 - size b4000
  Name: JSCRIPT.dll
MZ at 6d2c0000, prot 00000002, type 01000000 - size a000
  Name: DDRAWEX.DLL
MZ at 6d3e0000, prot 00000002, type 01000000 - size e000
  Name: PNGFILTER.DLL
MZ at 6d440000, prot 00000002, type 01000000 - size c000
  Name: jp2ssv.dll
MZ at 6dbf0000, prot 00000002, type 01000000 - size 33000
  Name: IEShims.dll
MZ at 6e080000, prot 00000002, type 01000000 - size 29000
  Name: msls31.dll
MZ at 6e100000, prot 00000002, type 01000000 - size 40000
  Name: SWEEPRX.dll
MZ at 6e150000, prot 00000002, type 01000000 - size 2f000
```

90

```
   Name: iepeers.DLL
MZ at 6e520000, prot 00000002, type 01000000 - size b000
   Name: msimtf.dll
MZ at 6e550000, prot 00000002, type 01000000 - size c000
   Name: ImgUtil.dll
MZ at 6e8a0000, prot 00000002, type 01000000 - size 1b000
   Name: CRYPTNET.dll
MZ at 6e960000, prot 00000002, type 01000000 - size 26000
   Name: DSSENH.dll
MZ at 6ea00000, prot 00000002, type 01000000 - size 30000
   Name: MLANG.dll
MZ at 6f320000, prot 00000002, type 01000000 - size 6000
   Name: SensApi.dll
MZ at 6f340000, prot 00000002, type 01000000 - size 31000
   Name: TAPI32.dll
MZ at 6f3c0000, prot 00000002, type 01000000 - size 14000
   Name: rasman.dll
MZ at 6f3e0000, prot 00000002, type 01000000 - size 4a000
   Name: RASAPI32.dll
MZ at 6f840000, prot 00000002, type 01000000 - size 70000
   Name: DSOUND.dll
MZ at 6f8d0000, prot 00000002, type 01000000 - size 136000
   Name: MSXML3.dll
MZ at 6fa40000, prot 00000002, type 01000000 - size c000
   Name: rtutils.dll
MZ at 70320000, prot 00000002, type 01000000 - size 3e000
   Name: pdh.dll
MZ at 70620000, prot 00000002, type 01000000 - size e5000
   Name: DDRAW.dll
MZ at 70820000, prot 00000002, type 01000000 - size a94000
   Name: IEFRAME.dll
MZ at 71a70000, prot 00000002, type 01000000 - size 62000
   Name: mscms.dll
MZ at 71bb0000, prot 00000002, type 01000000 - size 12000
   Name: PNRPNSP.dll
MZ at 723c0000, prot 00000002, type 01000000 - size 53000
   Name: SWEEPRX.dll
MZ at 72430000, prot 00000002, type 01000000 - size 42000
   Name: WINSPOOL.DRV
MZ at 72ff0000, prot 00000002, type 01000000 - size 6000
   Name: rasadhlp.dll
MZ at 73320000, prot 00000002, type 01000000 - size c000
   Name: dwmapi.dll
MZ at 74120000, prot 00000002, type 01000000 - size 14000
   Name: MSACM32.dll
MZ at 74140000, prot 00000002, type 01000000 - size 66000
   Name: audioeng.dll
MZ at 74240000, prot 00000002, type 01000000 - size 7000
   Name: MIDIMAP.dll
MZ at 74260000, prot 00000002, type 01000000 - size 9000
   Name: MSACM32.DRV
MZ at 742a0000, prot 00000002, type 01000000 - size 21000
   Name: AudioSes.DLL
MZ at 742d0000, prot 00000002, type 01000000 - size 2f000
   Name: WINMMDRV.dll
MZ at 74300000, prot 00000002, type 01000000 - size bb000
   Name: PROPSYS.dll
MZ at 743e0000, prot 00000002, type 01000000 - size 8000
   Name: WINRNR.dll
MZ at 743f0000, prot 00000002, type 01000000 - size c000
```

```
  Name: wshbth.dll
MZ at 74400000, prot 00000002, type 01000000 - size 3d000
  Name: OLEACC.dll
MZ at 744e0000, prot 00000002, type 01000000 - size 14000
  Name: ATL.DLL
MZ at 74500000, prot 00000002, type 01000000 - size 32000
  Name: WINMM.dll
MZ at 74570000, prot 00000002, type 01000000 - size 6000
  Name: DCIMAN32.dll
MZ at 74580000, prot 00000002, type 01000000 - size 1ab000
  Name: gdiplus.dll
MZ at 748a0000, prot 00000002, type 01000000 - size f000
  Name: NAPINSP.dll
MZ at 74bd0000, prot 00000002, type 01000000 - size 19e000
  Name: COMCTL32.dll
MZ at 74d70000, prot 00000002, type 01000000 - size f000
  Name: nlaapi.dll
MZ at 74db0000, prot 00000002, type 01000000 - size 28000
  Name: MMDevAPI.DLL
MZ at 74e40000, prot 00000002, type 01000000 - size 15000
  Name: Cabinet.dll
MZ at 74e80000, prot 00000002, type 01000000 - size 4000
  Name: ksuser.dll
MZ at 74e90000, prot 00000002, type 01000000 - size 7000
  Name: AVRT.dll
MZ at 74ed0000, prot 00000002, type 01000000 - size 3f000
  Name: UxTheme.dll
MZ at 74f60000, prot 00000002, type 01000000 - size 2d000
  Name: WINTRUST.dll
MZ at 75140000, prot 00000002, type 01000000 - size 5000
  Name: WSHTCPIP.dll
MZ at 75150000, prot 00000002, type 01000000 - size 5000
  Name: MSIMG32.dll
MZ at 75160000, prot 00000002, type 01000000 - size 1a000
  Name: POWRPROF.dll
MZ at 75180000, prot 00000002, type 01000000 - size 21000
  Name: NTMARTA.dll
MZ at 751e0000, prot 00000002, type 01000000 - size 15000
  Name: GPAPI.dll
MZ at 75220000, prot 00000002, type 01000000 - size 3b000
  Name: RSAENH.dll
MZ at 75260000, prot 00000002, type 01000000 - size 46000
  Name: SCHANNEL.dll
MZ at 75470000, prot 00000002, type 01000000 - size 3b000
  Name: MSWSOCK.dll
MZ at 754e0000, prot 00000002, type 01000000 - size 5000
  Name: WSHIP6.dll
MZ at 75570000, prot 00000002, type 01000000 - size 45000
  Name: bcrypt.dll
MZ at 755c0000, prot 00000002, type 01000000 - size 35000
  Name: ncrypt.dll
MZ at 75610000, prot 00000002, type 01000000 - size 8000
  Name: VERSION.dll
MZ at 75630000, prot 00000002, type 01000000 - size 7000
  Name: CREDSSP.dll
MZ at 75670000, prot 00000002, type 01000000 - size 22000
  Name: dhcpcsvc6.DLL
MZ at 756a0000, prot 00000002, type 01000000 - size 7000
  Name: WINNSI.DLL
MZ at 756b0000, prot 00000002, type 01000000 - size 35000
```

```
        Name: dhcpcsvc.DLL
MZ at 756f0000, prot 00000002, type 01000000 - size 19000
        Name: IPHLPAPI.DLL
MZ at 75750000, prot 00000002, type 01000000 - size 3a000
        Name: slc.dll
MZ at 75790000, prot 00000002, type 01000000 - size f2000
        Name: CRYPT32.dll
MZ at 758f0000, prot 00000002, type 01000000 - size 12000
        Name: MSASN1.dll
MZ at 75930000, prot 00000002, type 01000000 - size 11000
        Name: SAMLIB.dll
MZ at 759a0000, prot 00000002, type 01000000 - size 76000
        Name: NETAPI32.dll
MZ at 75a20000, prot 00000002, type 01000000 - size 2c000
        Name: DNSAPI.dll
MZ at 75c30000, prot 00000002, type 01000000 - size 5f000
        Name: sxs.dll
MZ at 75c90000, prot 00000002, type 01000000 - size 2c000
        Name: apphelp.dll
MZ at 75cf0000, prot 00000002, type 01000000 - size 14000
        Name: Secur32.dll
MZ at 75d10000, prot 00000002, type 01000000 - size 1e000
        Name: USERENV.dll
MZ at 75e50000, prot 00000002, type 01000000 - size 7000
        Name: PSAPI.DLL
MZ at 75e60000, prot 00000002, type 01000000 - size 6000
        Name: NSI.dll
MZ at 75e70000, prot 00000002, type 01000000 - size c3000
        Name: RPCRT4.dll
MZ at 75f40000, prot 00000002, type 01000000 - size 18a000
        Name: SETUPAPI.dll
MZ at 760d0000, prot 00000002, type 01000000 - size 9000
        Name: LPK.dll
MZ at 760e0000, prot 00000002, type 01000000 - size 145000
        Name: ole32.dll
MZ at 76230000, prot 00000002, type 01000000 - size dc000
        Name: KERNEL32.dll
MZ at 76310000, prot 00000002, type 01000000 - size 1e8000
        Name: iertutil.dll
MZ at 76500000, prot 00000002, type 01000000 - size 8d000
        Name: OLEAUT32.dll
MZ at 76590000, prot 00000002, type 01000000 - size 133000
        Name: urlmon.dll
MZ at 766d0000, prot 00000002, type 01000000 - size b10000
        Name: SHELL32.dll
MZ at 771e0000, prot 00000002, type 01000000 - size 84000
        Name: CLBCatQ.DLL
MZ at 77270000, prot 00000002, type 01000000 - size aa000
        Name: msvcrt.dll
MZ at 77320000, prot 00000002, type 01000000 - size 59000
        Name: SHLWAPI.dll
MZ at 77380000, prot 00000002, type 01000000 - size 2d000
        Name: WS2_32.dll
MZ at 773b0000, prot 00000002, type 01000000 - size 4b000
        Name: GDI32.dll
MZ at 77400000, prot 00000002, type 01000000 - size 9d000
        Name: USER32.dll
MZ at 774a0000, prot 00000002, type 01000000 - size 73000
        Name: COMDLG32.dll
MZ at 77520000, prot 00000002, type 01000000 - size 49000
```

```
      Name: WLDAP32.dll
MZ at 77570000, prot 00000002, type 01000000 - size e6000
      Name: WININET.dll
MZ at 77660000, prot 00000002, type 01000000 - size 7d000
      Name: USP10.dll
MZ at 776e0000, prot 00000002, type 01000000 - size c6000
      Name: ADVAPI32.dll
MZ at 777b0000, prot 00000002, type 01000000 - size 127000
      Name: ntdll.dll
MZ at 778e0000, prot 00000002, type 01000000 - size 3000
      Name: Normaliz.dll
MZ at 778f0000, prot 00000002, type 01000000 - size 1e000
      Name: IMM32.dll
MZ at 77910000, prot 00000002, type 01000000 - size 29000
      Name: imagehlp.dll
MZ at 77940000, prot 00000002, type 01000000 - size c8000
      Name: MSCTF.dll
MZ at 7c340000, prot 00000002, type 01000000 - size 56000
      Name: MSVCR71.dll
MZ at 7c3a0000, prot 00000002, type 01000000 - size 7b000
      Name: MSVCP71.dll
```

We see screens_dll.dll module with read/write protection attribute different from all other found modules:

```
0:004> !address 10000000

Usage:                    <unknown>
Base Address:             10000000
End Address:              10001000
Region Size:              00001000
State:                    00001000 MEM_COMMIT
Protect:                  00000004 PAGE_READWRITE
Type:                     00020000 MEM_PRIVATE
Allocation Base:          10000000
Allocation Protect:       00000004 PAGE_READWRITE
```

13.   We now check module headers for this dll:

```
0:004> !dh 10000000

File Type: DLL
FILE HEADER VALUES
     14C machine (i386)
       4 number of sections
4C8FEE9E time date stamp Tue Sep 14 22:52:30 2010

       0 file pointer to symbol table
       0 number of symbols
      E0 size of optional header
    2102 characteristics
            Executable
            32 bit word machine
            DLL

OPTIONAL HEADER VALUES
     10B magic #
    9.00 linker version
     400 size of code
     800 size of initialized data
```

94

```
       0 size of uninitialized data
    12F3 address of entry point
    1000 base of code
         ----- new -----
10000000 image base
    1000 section alignment
     200 file alignment
       2 subsystem (Windows GUI)
    5.00 operating system version
    0.00 image version
    5.00 subsystem version
    5000 size of image
     400 size of headers
       0 checksum
00100000 size of stack reserve
00001000 size of stack commit
00100000 size of heap reserve
00001000 size of heap commit
     140  DLL characteristics
             Dynamic base
             NX compatible
    2330 [        50] address [size] of Export Directory
    20E0 [        78] address [size] of Import Directory
       0 [         0] address [size] of Resource Directory
       0 [         0] address [size] of Exception Directory
       0 [         0] address [size] of Security Directory
    4000 [        34] address [size] of Base Relocation Directory
    2060 [        1C] address [size] of Debug Directory
       0 [         0] address [size] of Description Directory
       0 [         0] address [size] of Special Directory
       0 [         0] address [size] of Thread Storage Directory
       0 [         0] address [size] of Load Configuration Directory
       0 [         0] address [size] of Bound Import Directory
    2000 [        58] address [size] of Import Address Table Directory
       0 [         0] address [size] of Delay Import Directory
       0 [         0] address [size] of COR20 Header Directory
       0 [         0] address [size] of Reserved Directory


SECTION HEADER #1
   .text name
10001000 virtual size
    1000 virtual address
     400 size of raw data
     400 file pointer to raw data
       0 file pointer to relocation table
       0 file pointer to line numbers
       0 number of relocations
       0 number of line numbers
60000020 flags
         Code
         (no align specified)
         Execute Read

SECTION HEADER #2
  .rdata name
10002000 virtual size
    2000 virtual address
     400 size of raw data
     800 file pointer to raw data
```

```
        0 file pointer to relocation table
        0 file pointer to line numbers
        0 number of relocations
        0 number of line numbers
40000040 flags
         Initialized Data
         (no align specified)
         Read Only


Debug Directories(1)
      Type      Size    Address  Pointer
       cv        46       2094      894   Format: RSDS, guid, 1,
C:\MyWork\screens_dll\Release\screens_dll.pdb

SECTION HEADER #3
   .data name
10003000 virtual size
    3000 virtual address
       0 size of raw data
       0 file pointer to raw data
       0 file pointer to relocation table
       0 file pointer to line numbers
       0 number of relocations
       0 number of line numbers
C0000040 flags
         Initialized Data
         (no align specified)
         Read Write

SECTION HEADER #4
   .reloc name
10004000 virtual size
    4000 virtual address
     200 size of raw data
     C00 file pointer to raw data
       0 file pointer to relocation table
       0 file pointer to line numbers
       0 number of relocations
       0 number of line numbers
42000040 flags
         Initialized Data
         Discardable
         (no align specified)
         Read Only
```

It looks like a normal DLL but its import address table reveals its purpose - screen capture:

```
0:004> dps 10000000+2000 L58/4
10002000   773b6101 gdi32!CreateCompatibleDC
10002004   773b93d6 gdi32!StretchBlt
10002008   773b7461 gdi32!CreateDIBSection
1000200c   773b62a0 gdi32!SelectObject
10002010   00000000
10002014   7627a411 kernel32!lstrcmpW
10002018   762740aa kernel32!VirtualFree
1000201c   7627ad55 kernel32!VirtualAlloc
10002020   00000000
10002024   77419ced user32!ReleaseDC
```

```
10002028   77413ba7  user32!NtUserGetWindowDC
1000202c   77420e21  user32!GetWindowRect
10002030   00000000
10002034   745975e9  GdiPlus!GdiplusStartup
10002038   745876dd  GdiPlus!GdipSaveImageToStream
1000203c   745bdd38  GdiPlus!GdipGetImageEncodersSize
10002040   745871cf  GdiPlus!GdipDisposeImage
10002044   74598591  GdiPlus!GdipCreateBitmapFromHBITMAP
10002048   745bdbae  GdiPlus!GdipGetImageEncoders
1000204c   00000000
10002050   7613d51b  ole32!CreateStreamOnHGlobal
10002054   00000000
```

14.   And finally heap analysis of a corrupt entry reveals the captured password:

```
0:004> !heap -s -v
***********************************************************
*                                                         *
*                  HEAP  ERROR  DETECTED                  *
*                                                         *
***********************************************************

Details:

Heap address:    00290000
Error address:   04f1ffe0
Error type:      HEAP_FAILURE_ENTRY_CORRUPTION
Details:         The heap manager detected a corrupt heap entry.
Follow-up:       Enable pageheap.

Stack trace:
               7782b1a5: ntdll!RtlpCoalesceFreeBlocks+0x000004b9
               7781730a: ntdll!RtlpFreeHeap+0x000001e2
               77817545: ntdll!RtlFreeHeap+0x0000014e
               76277e4b: kernel32!GlobalFree+0x00000047
               760f7277: ole32!ReleaseStgMedium+0x00000124
               76594a1f: urlmon!ReleaseBindInfo+0x0000004c
               765f7feb: urlmon!CINet::ReleaseCNetObjects+0x0000003d
               765b9a87: urlmon!CINetHttp::OnWininetRequestHandleClosing+0x00000060
               765b93f0: urlmon!CINet::CINetCallback+0x000002de
               77582078: wininet!InternetIndicateStatus+0x000000fc
               77588f5d: wininet!HANDLE_OBJECT::~HANDLE_OBJECT+0x000000c9
               7758937a:
wininet!INTERNET_CONNECT_HANDLE_OBJECT::~INTERNET_CONNECT_HANDLE_OBJECT+0x00000209
               7758916b: wininet!HTTP_REQUEST_HANDLE_OBJECT::`scalar deleting
destructor'+0x0000000d
               77588d5e: wininet!HANDLE_OBJECT::Dereference+0x00000022
               77589419: wininet!_InternetCloseHandle+0x0000009d
               77589114: wininet!InternetCloseHandle+0x0000011e

0:004> dc 04f1ffe0-20
04f1ffc0  6161613d 61616161 26616161 50747874   =aaaaaaaaaa&txtP
04f1ffd0  77737361 3d64726f 61616161 61616161   assword=aaaaaaaa
04f1ffe0  74933b00 0310f0ba 00000000 00000000   .;.t............
04f1fff0  04e20038 04e20038 04f20000 00000000   8...8...........
04f20000  ???????? ???????? ???????? ????????   ????????????????
04f20010  ???????? ???????? ???????? ????????   ????????????????
04f20020  ???????? ???????? ???????? ????????   ????????????????
04f20030  ???????? ???????? ???????? ????????   ????????????????
```

15.   We should also check for any patched module code in all modules to which we have matching file binary access:

```
0:004> !for_each_module "!chkimg -v -d @#ModuleName"

[...]

Scanning section:    .text
Size: 1307933
Range to scan: 74bd1000-74d1051d
    74ca8814-74ca8818  5 bytes - comctl32!PropertySheetW
        [ 8b ff 55 8b ec:e9 e8 d8 d9 fb ]
    74ca882c-74ca8830  5 bytes - comctl32!PropertySheetA (+0x18)
        [ 8b ff 55 8b ec:e9 70 d9 d9 fb ]
Total bytes compared: 1307933(100%)
Number of errors: 10
10 errors : comctl32 (74ca8814-74ca8830)
Searching for module with expression: nlaapi
Will apply relocation fixups to file used for comparison
Will ignore NOP/LOCK errors
Will ignore patched instructions
Image specific ignores will be applied
Comparison image path: C:\WSDK8\Debuggers\x86\sym\nlaapi.dll\4791A746f000\nlaapi.dll
No range specified

Scanning section:    .text
Size: 1204234
Range to scan: 760e1000-7620700a
    76101e12-76101e16  5 bytes - ole32!OleLoadFromStream
        [ 8b ff 55 8b ec:e9 b9 30 94 fa ]
    76139ea6-76139eaa  5 bytes - ole32!CoCreateInstance (+0x38094)
        [ 8b ff 55 8b ec:e9 d5 3c 81 fa ]
Total bytes compared: 1204234(100%)
Number of errors: 10

[...]

Scanning section:    .text
Size: 528293
Range to scan: 76501000-76581fa5
    76503df0-76503df4  5 bytes - oleaut32!VariantClear
        [ 8b ff 55 8b ec:e9 1f 1d 54 fa ]
    76503e40-76503e44  5 bytes - oleaut32!SysFreeString (+0x50)
        [ 8b ff 55 8b ec:e9 f3 10 54 fa ]
    7650462b-7650462f  5 bytes - oleaut32!SysAllocStringByteLen (+0x7eb)
        [ 8b ff 55 8b ec:e9 4a 14 54 fa ]
    765074bc-765074c0  5 bytes - oleaut32!VariantChangeType (+0x2e91)
        [ 8b ff 55 8b ec:e9 04 e6 53 fa ]
    765670ae-765670b2  5 bytes - oleaut32!OleCreatePropertyFrameIndirect (+0x5fbf2)
        [ 8b ff 55 8b ec:e9 96 e6 4d fa ]
Total bytes compared: 528293(100%)
Number of errors: 25

[...]

Scanning section:    .text
Size: 3612636
Range to scan: 766d1000-76a42fdc
    767589a8-767589ab  4 bytes - shell32!CRegFolder::`vftable'
        [ 88 20 76 76:4d 30 c1 6d ]
```

```
    767589b0-767589b7  8 bytes - shell32!CRegFolder::`vftable'+8 (+0x08)
       [ 2f 92 75 76 df e4 75 76:57 2f c1 6d 9c 5b c0 6d ]
Total bytes compared: 3612636(100%)
Number of errors: 12
12 errors : shell32 (767589a8-767589b7)
Searching for module with expression: clbcatq
Will apply relocation fixups to file used for comparison
Will ignore NOP/LOCK errors
Will ignore patched instructions
Image specific ignores will be applied
Comparison image path: C:\WSDK8\Debuggers\x86\sym\clbcatq.dll\4791A66F84000\clbcatq.dll
No range specified

[...]

Scanning section:      .text
Size: 422527
Range to scan: 77401000-7746827f
    774072a2-774072a6  5 bytes - user32!CreateDialogParamW
       [ 8b ff 55 8b ec:e9 09 6c 54 f9 ]
    7740863c-77408640  5 bytes - user32!GetAsyncKeyState (+0x139a)
       [ 8b ff 55 8b ec:e9 f6 08 46 f9 ]
    774087ad-774087b1  5 bytes - user32!SetWindowsHookExW (+0x171)
       [ 8b ff 55 8b ec:e9 23 13 54 f9 ]
    77408e3b-77408e3f  5 bytes - user32!CallNextHookEx (+0x68e)
       [ 8b ff 55 8b ec:e9 f5 42 53 f9 ]
    774098db-774098df  5 bytes - user32!NtUserUnhookWindowsHookEx (+0xaa0)
       [ b8 52 12 00 00:e9 86 ad 4a f9 ]
    7740cd8b-7740cd8f  5 bytes - user32!EnableWindow (+0x34b0)
       [ 8b ff 55 8b ec:e9 ad 0f 54 f9 ]
    77411305-77411309  5 bytes - user32!CreateWindowExW (+0x457a)
       [ 8b ff 55 8b ec:e9 1a c8 53 f9 ]
    77418cb1-77418cb5  5 bytes - user32!GetKeyState (+0x79ac)
       [ 8b ff 55 8b ec:e9 35 46 53 f9 ]
    77420745-77420749  5 bytes - user32!IsDialogMessageW (+0x7a94)
       [ 8b ff 55 8b ec:e9 c9 52 45 f9 ]
    774217aa-774217ae  5 bytes - user32!CreateDialogParamA (+0x1065)
       [ 8b ff 55 8b ec:e9 27 40 62 f9 ]
    77421847-7742184b  5 bytes - user32!IsDialogMessageA (+0x9d)
       [ 8b ff 55 8b ec:e9 26 38 62 f9 ]
    774226f1-774226f5  5 bytes - user32!CreateDialogIndirectParamA (+0xeaa)
       [ 8b ff 55 8b ec:e9 17 31 62 f9 ]
    77429a62-77429a66  5 bytes - user32!CreateDialogIndirectParamW (+0x7371)
       [ 8b ff 55 8b ec:e9 dd bd 61 f9 ]
    77430987-7743098b  5 bytes - user32!NtUserSetKeyboardState (+0x6f25)
       [ b8 20 12 00 00:e9 55 4a 61 f9 ]
    774310b0-774310b4  5 bytes - user32!DialogBoxParamW (+0x729)
       [ 8b ff 55 8b ec:e9 4c 44 44 f9 ]
    77432ef5-77432ef9  5 bytes - user32!DialogBoxIndirectParamW (+0x1e45)
       [ 8b ff 55 8b ec:e9 55 1c 61 f9 ]
    77432f75-77432f79  5 bytes - user32!NtUserSendInput (+0x80)
       [ b8 0d 12 00 00:e9 25 30 61 f9 ]
    7743326e-77433272  5 bytes - user32!EndDialog (+0x2f9)
       [ 8b ff 55 8b ec:e9 47 4c 44 f9 ]
    77446fb2-77446fb6  5 bytes - user32!SetCursorPos (+0x13d44)
       [ 8b ff 55 8b ec:e9 3c f0 5f f9 ]
    77448152-77448156  5 bytes - user32!DialogBoxParamA (+0x11a0)
       [ 8b ff 55 8b ec:e9 95 c9 5f f9 ]
    7744847d-77448481  5 bytes - user32!DialogBoxIndirectParamA (+0x32b)
       [ 8b ff 55 8b ec:e9 30 c7 5f f9 ]
```

```
    7745d4d9-7745d4dd  5 bytes - user32!MessageBoxIndirectA (+0x1505c)
      [ 8b ff 55 8b ec:e9 a3 75 5e f9 ]
    7745d5d3-7745d5d7  5 bytes - user32!MessageBoxIndirectW (+0xfa)
      [ 8b ff 55 8b ec:e9 3e 74 5e f9 ]
    7745d639-7745d63d  5 bytes - user32!MessageBoxExA (+0x66)
      [ 8b ff 55 8b ec:e9 76 73 5e f9 ]
    7745d65d-7745d661  5 bytes - user32!MessageBoxExW (+0x24)
      [ 8b ff 55 8b ec:e9 f0 72 5e f9 ]
    7745d972-7745d976  5 bytes - user32!keybd_event (+0x315)
      [ 8b ff 55 8b ec:e9 ac 89 5e f9 ]
Total bytes compared: 422527(100%)
Number of errors: 130
130 errors : user32 (774072a2-7745d976)
Searching for module with expression: comdlg32
Will apply relocation fixups to file used for comparison
Will ignore NOP/LOCK errors
Will ignore patched instructions
Image specific ignores will be applied
Comparison image path: C:\WSDK8\Debuggers\x86\sym\comdlg32.dll\49E0380973000\comdlg32.dll
No range specified

[...]


Scanning section:     .text
Size: 320529
Range to scan: 774a1000-774ef411
    774a30cf-774a30d3  5 bytes - comdlg32!PrintDlgW
      [ 8b ff 55 8b ec:e9 41 28 5a f9 ]
    774ced29-774ced2d  5 bytes - comdlg32!PageSetupDlgW (+0x2bc5a)
      [ 8b ff 55 8b ec:e9 4d 6b 57 f9 ]
Total bytes compared: 320529(100%)
Number of errors: 10
10 errors : comdlg32 (774a30cf-774ced2d)

[...]


Scanning section:     .text
Size: 794010
Range to scan: 777b1000-77872d9a
    77814dba-77814dbd  4 bytes - ntdll!ZwQueryDirectoryFile+6
      [ 00 03 fe 7f:e8 af 05 00 ]
    778151ba-778151bd  4 bytes - ntdll!ZwResumeThread+6 (+0x400)
      [ 00 03 fe 7f:d8 af 05 00 ]
Total bytes compared: 794010(100%)
Number of errors: 8

[...]
```

When we look at reported patched address we find out that most of them belong to IE:

```
0:004> u 774a30cf
comdlg32!PrintDlgW:
774a30cf e941285af9      jmp      ieframe!Detour_PrintDlgW (70a45915)
774a30d4 81eca0040000    sub      esp,4A0h
774a30da a1ac034f77      mov      eax,dword ptr [comdlg32!__security_cookie (774f03ac)]
774a30df 33c5            xor      eax,ebp
774a30e1 8945fc          mov      dword ptr [ebp-4],eax
774a30e4 56              push     esi
774a30e5 8b7508          mov      esi,dword ptr [ebp+8]
774a30e8 689c040000      push     49Ch
```

However, the last two addresses are suspicious as they do not belong to IE and show "garbage":

```
0:004> u 77814dba
ntdll!ZwQueryDirectoryFile+0x6:
77814dba e8af0500ff      call    shell32!MetadataLayout::UpdateDesiredSize+0x218 (7681536e)
77814dbf 12c2            adc     al,dl
77814dc1 2c00            sub     al,0
77814dc3 90              nop
ntdll!NtQueryDirectoryObject:
77814dc4 b8db000000      mov     eax,0DBh
77814dc9 ba0003fe7f      mov     edx,offset SharedUserData!SystemCallStub (7ffe0300)
77814dce ff12            call    dword ptr [edx]
77814dd0 c21c00          ret     1Ch

0:004> u 7681536e
shell32!MetadataLayout::UpdateDesiredSize+0x218:
7681536e 46              inc     esi
7681536f 18894df80f82    sbb     byte ptr [ecx-7DF007B3h],cl
76815375 51              push    ecx
76815376 ff              ???
76815377 ff              ???
76815378 ff8b46288b55    dec     dword ptr [ebx+558B2846h]
7681537e 108d04988b08    adc     byte ptr [ebp+88B9804h],cl
76815384 014df0          add     dword ptr [ebp-10h],ecx

0:004> ub 77814dba
             ^ Unable to find valid previous instruction for 'ub 77814dba'
```

Here we needed to check the beginning of the function because the patching may be be done for the part of an instruction such as changing an address or an offset:

```
0:004> u ntdll!ZwQueryDirectoryFile
ntdll!ZwQueryDirectoryFile:
77814db4 b8da000000      mov     eax,0DAh
77814db9 bae8af0500      mov     edx,5AFE8h
77814dbe ff12            call    dword ptr [edx]
77814dc0 c22c00          ret     2Ch
77814dc3 90              nop
ntdll!NtQueryDirectoryObject:
77814dc4 b8db000000      mov     eax,0DBh
77814dc9 ba0003fe7f      mov     edx,offset SharedUserData!SystemCallStub (7ffe0300)
77814dce ff12            call    dword ptr [edx]
```

Note that a pointer to an indirect call has changed: in the normal case we see this:

```
0:004> dps 7ffe0300 L1
7ffe0300  77815e70 ntdll!KiFastSystemCall
```

In the abnormal case we have execution diversion to already discovered malware module:

```
0:004> dps 5AFE8h L1
0005afe8  0004efe0
```

```
0:004> u 0004efe0
0004efe0 58              pop     eax
0004efe1 8d0510ec0400    lea     eax,ds:[4EC10h]
0004efe7 ffe0            jmp     eax
0004efe9 c3              ret
0004efea cc              int     3
0004efeb cc              int     3
0004efec cc              int     3
0004efed cc              int     3

0:004> u 4EC10h
0004ec10 55              push    ebp
0004ec11 8bec            mov     ebp,esp
0004ec13 83ec38          sub     esp,38h
0004ec16 0fb64530        movzx   eax,byte ptr [ebp+30h]
0004ec1a 50              push    eax
0004ec1b 8b4d2c          mov     ecx,dword ptr [ebp+2Ch]
0004ec1e 51              push    ecx
0004ec1f 0fb65528        movzx   edx,byte ptr [ebp+28h]

0:004> !address 4EC10h

Usage:              <unknown>
Base Address:       00040000
End Address:        0005d000
Region Size:        0001d000
State:              00001000 MEM_COMMIT
Protect:            00000040 PAGE_EXECUTE_READWRITE
Type:               00020000 MEM_PRIVATE
Allocation Base:    00040000
Allocation Protect: 00000040 PAGE_EXECUTE_READWRITE
```

Note that here we have execution redirection based on system call dispatch. This is a different pathway as Import Address Table. Here ntdll!Zw* functions are meant to transition to kernel space to execute corresponding system services there. This transitions is commonly done through pseudo module SharedUserData:

```
0:004> !address SharedUserData

Usage:              Other
Base Address:       7ffe0000
End Address:        7ffe1000
Region Size:        00001000
State:              00001000 MEM_COMMIT
Protect:            00000002 PAGE_READONLY
Type:               00020000 MEM_PRIVATE
Allocation Base:    7ffe0000
Allocation Protect: 00000002 PAGE_READONLY
Additional info:    User Shared Data

0:004> dps SharedUserData!SystemCallStub L1
7ffe0300  77815e70 ntdll!KiFastSystemCall

0:004> uf ntdll!KiFastSystemCall
ntdll!KiFastSystemCall:
77815e70 8bd4            mov     edx,esp
77815e72 0f34            sysenter
77815e74 c3              ret
```

16.   Another check is for exception handlers. We can check the current problem thread or for all threads via **~*e** command. Note that an exception can happen on each threads each having different handlers.

```
0:004> !exchain
02c9cb90: ntdll!_except_handler4+0 (777b99fa)
  CRT scope  0, func:    ntdll!RtlReportExceptionEx+187 (77843ca3)
02c9cbd0: ntdll!_except_handler4+0 (777b99fa)
  CRT scope  0, filter: ntdll!RtlReportException+53 (77843d67)
                func:    ntdll!RtlReportException+57 (77843d70)
02c9cc54: ntdll!ExecuteHandler2+3a (77815f8d)
02c9d074: ntdll!_except_handler4+0 (777b99fa)
  CRT scope  0, filter: ntdll!RtlReportCriticalFailure+5d (7785faff)
                func:    ntdll!RtlReportCriticalFailure+6c (7785fb13)
02c9d0b8: ntdll!_except_handler4+0 (777b99fa)
  CRT scope  0, filter: ntdll!RtlpLogHeapFailure+83 (778607cf)
                func:    ntdll!RtlpLogHeapFailure+90 (778607e1)
02c9d1f8: ntdll!_except_handler4+0 (777b99fa)
  CRT scope  0, func:    ntdll!RtlpFreeHeap+b0c (7782b9f7)
02c9d25c: kernel32!_except_handler4+0 (7626fd89)
  CRT scope  0, filter: kernel32!GlobalFree+11c (7628e1e7)
                func:    kernel32!GlobalFree+133 (7628e203)
02c9d6f0: user32!_except_handler4+0 (7746522d)
  CRT scope  0, func:    user32!UserCallWinProcCheckWow+150 (77436e2c)
02c9d754: user32!_except_handler4+0 (7746522d)
  CRT scope  0, filter: user32!DispatchMessageWorker+144 (77437cbc)
                func:    user32!DispatchMessageWorker+157 (77437cd4)
02c9f980: ntdll!_except_handler4+0 (777b99fa)
  CRT scope  0, filter: ntdll!__RtlUserThreadStart+3b (77827f8d)
                func:    ntdll!__RtlUserThreadStart+70 (77827fc7)

0:004> ~*e !exchain
001df568: kernel32!_except_handler4+0 (7626fd89)
  CRT scope  1, func:    kernel32!WaitForMultipleObjectsEx+18a (7627a628)
  CRT scope  0, func:    kernel32!WaitForMultipleObjectsEx+186 (7627a630)
001df85c: iexplore!_except_handler4+0 (00ff6944)
  CRT scope  1, filter: iexplore!_initterm_e+1da (00ff3153)
                func:    iexplore!_initterm_e+1ee (00ff316c)
001df8a8: ntdll!_except_handler4+0 (777b99fa)
  CRT scope  0, filter: ntdll!__RtlUserThreadStart+3b (77827f8d)
                func:    ntdll!__RtlUserThreadStart+70 (77827fc7)
0258f860: ntdll!_except_handler4+0 (777b99fa)
  CRT scope  2, func:    ntdll!TppWaiterpThread+63c (7783a9bb)
  CRT scope  1, func:    ntdll!TppWaiterpThread+6e9 (777c098e)
  CRT scope  0, filter: ntdll!TppWaiterpThread+6f2 (7783aa39)
                func:    ntdll!TppWaiterpThread+703 (7783aa4f)
0258f8ac: ntdll!_except_handler4+0 (777b99fa)
  CRT scope  0, filter: ntdll!__RtlUserThreadStart+3b (77827f8d)
                func:    ntdll!__RtlUserThreadStart+70 (77827fc7)
02a2edcc: kernel32!_except_handler4+0 (7626fd89)
  CRT scope  1, func:    kernel32!WaitForMultipleObjectsEx+18a (7627a628)
  CRT scope  0, func:    kernel32!WaitForMultipleObjectsEx+186 (7627a630)
02a2fe68: ntdll!_except_handler4+0 (777b99fa)
  CRT scope  0, filter: ntdll!__RtlUserThreadStart+3b (77827f8d)
                func:    ntdll!__RtlUserThreadStart+70 (77827fc7)
028efa38: kernel32!_except_handler4+0 (7626fd89)
  CRT scope  1, func:    kernel32!WaitForMultipleObjectsEx+18a (7627a628)
  CRT scope  0, func:    kernel32!WaitForMultipleObjectsEx+186 (7627a630)
028efb48: ntdll!_except_handler4+0 (777b99fa)
  CRT scope  0, filter: ntdll!__RtlUserThreadStart+3b (77827f8d)
                func:    ntdll!__RtlUserThreadStart+70 (77827fc7)
```

```
02c9cb90: ntdll!_except_handler4+0 (777b99fa)
  CRT scope  0, func:    ntdll!RtlReportExceptionEx+187 (77843ca3)
02c9cbd0: ntdll!_except_handler4+0 (777b99fa)
  CRT scope  0, filter: ntdll!RtlReportException+53 (77843d67)
                func:    ntdll!RtlReportException+57 (77843d70)
02c9cc54: ntdll!ExecuteHandler2+3a (77815f8d)
02c9d074: ntdll!_except_handler4+0 (777b99fa)
  CRT scope  0, filter: ntdll!RtlReportCriticalFailure+5d (7785faff)
                func:    ntdll!RtlReportCriticalFailure+6c (7785fb13)
02c9d0b8: ntdll!_except_handler4+0 (777b99fa)
  CRT scope  0, filter: ntdll!RtlpLogHeapFailure+83 (778607cf)
                func:    ntdll!RtlpLogHeapFailure+90 (778607e1)
02c9d1f8: ntdll!_except_handler4+0 (777b99fa)
  CRT scope  0, func:    ntdll!RtlpFreeHeap+b0c (7782b9f7)
02c9d25c: kernel32!_except_handler4+0 (7626fd89)
  CRT scope  0, filter: kernel32!GlobalFree+11c (7628e1e7)
                func:    kernel32!GlobalFree+133 (7628e203)
02c9d6f0: user32!_except_handler4+0 (7746522d)
  CRT scope  0, func:    user32!UserCallWinProcCheckWow+150 (77436e2c)
02c9d754: user32!_except_handler4+0 (7746522d)
  CRT scope  0, filter: user32!DispatchMessageWorker+144 (77437cbc)
                func:    user32!DispatchMessageWorker+157 (77437cd4)
02c9f980: ntdll!_except_handler4+0 (777b99fa)
  CRT scope  0, filter: ntdll!__RtlUserThreadStart+3b (77827f8d)
                func:    ntdll!__RtlUserThreadStart+70 (77827fc7)
02e8fad8: kernel32!_except_handler4+0 (7626fd89)
  CRT scope  1, func:    kernel32!WaitForMultipleObjectsEx+18a (7627a628)
  CRT scope  0, func:    kernel32!WaitForMultipleObjectsEx+186 (7627a630)
02e8fc40: *** ERROR: Symbol file could not be found.  Defaulted to export symbols for
msidcrl40.dll -
msidcrl40!CreatePassportAuthUIContext+5e13b (275f8bcb)
02e8fc78: ntdll!_except_handler4+0 (777b99fa)
  CRT scope  0, func:    ntdll!RtlpTpTimerCallback+8e (7783b037)
02e8fdcc: ntdll!_except_handler4+0 (777b99fa)
  CRT scope  8, filter: ntdll!TppWorkerThread+515 (77839f8d)
                func:    ntdll!TppWorkerThread+531 (77839fae)
  CRT scope  2, func:    ntdll!TppWorkerThread+6c2 (777e6fdb)
  CRT scope  1, func:    ntdll!TppWorkerThread+78e (777e70cf)
  CRT scope  0, filter: ntdll!TppWorkerThread+79f (7783a09f)
                func:    ntdll!TppWorkerThread+7b4 (7783a0b9)
02e8fe18: ntdll!_except_handler4+0 (777b99fa)
  CRT scope  0, filter: ntdll!__RtlUserThreadStart+3b (77827f8d)
                func:    ntdll!__RtlUserThreadStart+70 (77827fc7)
0409fdcc: kernel32!_except_handler4+0 (7626fd89)
  CRT scope  0, func:    kernel32!SleepEx+91 (76293fa6)
0409fe60: ntdll!_except_handler4+0 (777b99fa)
  CRT scope  0, filter: ntdll!__RtlUserThreadStart+3b (77827f8d)
                func:    ntdll!__RtlUserThreadStart+70 (77827fc7)
03f0fcb8: ntdll!_except_handler4+0 (777b99fa)
  CRT scope  0, filter: ntdll!__RtlUserThreadStart+3b (77827f8d)
                func:    ntdll!__RtlUserThreadStart+70 (77827fc7)
0474f718: mswsock!_except_handler4+0 (7549148b)
  CRT scope  0, filter: mswsock!WSPSelect+52d (7547e749)
                func:    mswsock!WSPSelect+531 (7547e752)
0474f798: ws2_32!_except_handler4+0 (773a24ba)
  CRT scope  0, filter: ws2_32!select+3ba (7738fe6e)
                func:    ws2_32!select+3be (7738fe77)
0474fb44: ntdll!_except_handler4+0 (777b99fa)
  CRT scope  0, filter: ntdll!__RtlUserThreadStart+3b (77827f8d)
                func:    ntdll!__RtlUserThreadStart+70 (77827fc7)
```

```
051ff9cc: ntdll!_except_handler4+0 (777b99fa)
   CRT scope  5, filter: ntdll!TppWorkerThread+219 (77839e5c)
                  func:   ntdll!TppWorkerThread+230 (77839e78)
   CRT scope  2, func:    ntdll!TppWorkerThread+6c2 (777e6fdb)
   CRT scope  1, func:    ntdll!TppWorkerThread+78e (777e70cf)
   CRT scope  0, filter: ntdll!TppWorkerThread+79f (7783a09f)
                  func:   ntdll!TppWorkerThread+7b4 (7783a0b9)
051ffa18: ntdll!_except_handler4+0 (777b99fa)
   CRT scope  0, filter: ntdll!__RtlUserThreadStart+3b (77827f8d)
                  func:   ntdll!__RtlUserThreadStart+70 (77827fc7)
04dbf8d8: ntdll!_except_handler4+0 (777b99fa)
   CRT scope  0, filter: ntdll!__RtlUserThreadStart+3b (77827f8d)
                  func:   ntdll!__RtlUserThreadStart+70 (77827fc7)
0568fedc: kernel32!_except_handler4+0 (7626fd89)
   CRT scope  1, func:    kernel32!WaitForSingleObjectEx+fc (762937c7)
   CRT scope  0, func:    kernel32!WaitForSingleObjectEx+110 (762937e2)
0568ff74: ntdll!_except_handler4+0 (777b99fa)
   CRT scope  0, filter: ntdll!__RtlUserThreadStart+3b (77827f8d)
                  func:   ntdll!__RtlUserThreadStart+70 (77827fc7)
06e1fd04: kernel32!_except_handler4+0 (7626fd89)
   CRT scope  1, func:    kernel32!WaitForSingleObjectEx+fc (762937c7)
   CRT scope  0, func:    kernel32!WaitForSingleObjectEx+110 (762937e2)
06e1fd9c: ntdll!_except_handler4+0 (777b99fa)
   CRT scope  0, filter: ntdll!__RtlUserThreadStart+3b (77827f8d)
                  func:   ntdll!__RtlUserThreadStart+70 (77827fc7)
06f1f76c: kernel32!_except_handler4+0 (7626fd89)
   CRT scope  1, func:    kernel32!WaitForMultipleObjectsEx+18a (7627a628)
   CRT scope  0, func:    kernel32!WaitForMultipleObjectsEx+186 (7627a630)
06f1fad8: msidcrl40!CreatePassportAuthUIContext+5c340 (275f6dd0)
06f1fb0c: msidcrl40!CreatePassportAuthUIContext+2dc00 (275c8690)
06f1fb60: ntdll!_except_handler4+0 (777b99fa)
   CRT scope  0, filter: ntdll!__RtlUserThreadStart+3b (77827f8d)
                  func:   ntdll!__RtlUserThreadStart+70 (77827fc7)
0775f68c: kernel32!_except_handler4+0 (7626fd89)
   CRT scope  1, func:    kernel32!WaitForMultipleObjectsEx+18a (7627a628)
   CRT scope  0, func:    kernel32!WaitForMultipleObjectsEx+186 (7627a630)
0775f9f8: msidcrl40!CreatePassportAuthUIContext+5c340 (275f6dd0)
0775fa2c: msidcrl40!CreatePassportAuthUIContext+2dc00 (275c8690)
0775fa80: ntdll!_except_handler4+0 (777b99fa)
   CRT scope  0, filter: ntdll!__RtlUserThreadStart+3b (77827f8d)
                  func:   ntdll!__RtlUserThreadStart+70 (77827fc7)
0501fc18: ntdll!_except_handler4+0 (777b99fa)
   CRT scope  5, filter: ntdll!TppWorkerThread+219 (77839e5c)
                  func:   ntdll!TppWorkerThread+230 (77839e78)
   CRT scope  2, func:    ntdll!TppWorkerThread+6c2 (777e6fdb)
   CRT scope  1, func:    ntdll!TppWorkerThread+78e (777e70cf)
   CRT scope  0, filter: ntdll!TppWorkerThread+79f (7783a09f)
                  func:   ntdll!TppWorkerThread+7b4 (7783a0b9)
0501fc64: ntdll!_except_handler4+0 (777b99fa)
   CRT scope  0, filter: ntdll!__RtlUserThreadStart+3b (77827f8d)
                  func:   ntdll!__RtlUserThreadStart+70 (77827fc7)
0785f7ac: kernel32!_except_handler4+0 (7626fd89)
   CRT scope  1, func:    kernel32!WaitForSingleObjectEx+fc (762937c7)
   CRT scope  0, func:    kernel32!WaitForSingleObjectEx+110 (762937e2)
0785f840: ntdll!_except_handler4+0 (777b99fa)
   CRT scope  0, filter: ntdll!__RtlUserThreadStart+3b (77827f8d)
                  func:   ntdll!__RtlUserThreadStart+70 (77827fc7)
0868fcdc: kernel32!_except_handler4+0 (7626fd89)
   CRT scope  1, func:    kernel32!WaitForSingleObjectEx+fc (762937c7)
   CRT scope  0, func:    kernel32!WaitForSingleObjectEx+110 (762937e2)
```

```
0868fd74: ntdll!_except_handler4+0 (777b99fa)
   CRT scope  0, filter: ntdll!__RtlUserThreadStart+3b (77827f8d)
                   func:  ntdll!__RtlUserThreadStart+70 (77827fc7)
0b99fc58: ntdll!_except_handler4+0 (777b99fa)
   CRT scope  0, filter: ntdll!__RtlUserThreadStart+3b (77827f8d)
                   func:  ntdll!__RtlUserThreadStart+70 (77827fc7)
0bc7fab0: kernel32!_except_handler4+0 (7626fd89)
   CRT scope  1, func:    kernel32!WaitForMultipleObjectsEx+18a (7627a628)
   CRT scope  0, func:    kernel32!WaitForMultipleObjectsEx+186 (7627a630)
0bc7fb40: ntdll!_except_handler4+0 (777b99fa)
   CRT scope  0, filter: ntdll!__RtlUserThreadStart+3b (77827f8d)
                   func:  ntdll!__RtlUserThreadStart+70 (77827fc7)
0b04fc90: kernel32!_except_handler4+0 (7626fd89)
   CRT scope  1, func:    kernel32!WaitForMultipleObjectsEx+18a (7627a628)
   CRT scope  0, func:    kernel32!WaitForMultipleObjectsEx+186 (7627a630)
0b04fd98: ntdll!_except_handler4+0 (777b99fa)
   CRT scope  0, filter: ntdll!__RtlUserThreadStart+3b (77827f8d)
                   func:  ntdll!__RtlUserThreadStart+70 (77827fc7)
0bb7fc5c: ntdll!_except_handler4+0 (777b99fa)
   CRT scope  0, filter: ntdll!__RtlUserThreadStart+3b (77827f8d)
                   func:  ntdll!__RtlUserThreadStart+70 (77827fc7)
```

Note that here we look at anythong abnormal such as raw moduless pointers. None found.

17.   Close the log file:

```
0:004> .logclose
Closing open log file C:\AWMA-Dumps\M3.log
```

18.   To avoid possible confusion and glitches we recommend exiting WinDbg after each exercise.

If you are presented with this dialog choose No:

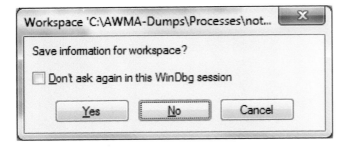

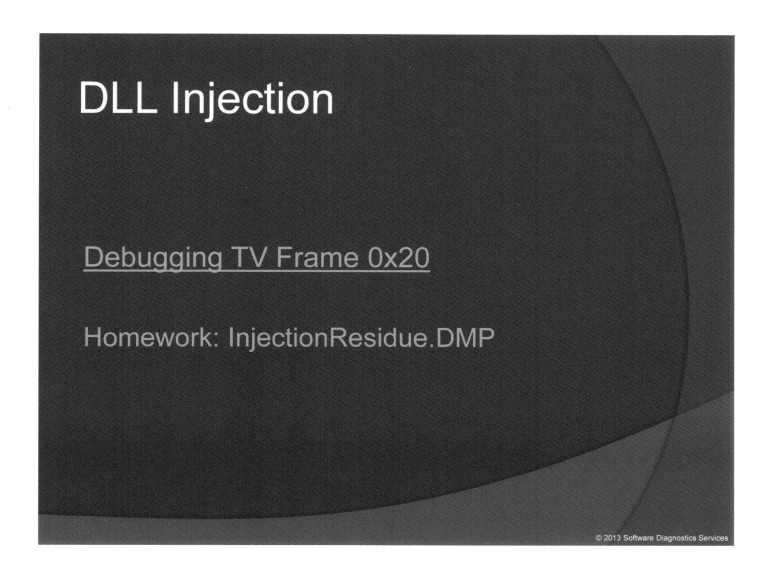

We don't cover DLL injection via remote threads and its possible execution residue in this training because there is a free case study available. However, we provide you a crash dump for homework so you can follow the presentation.

Debugging TV: http://www.debugging.tv/

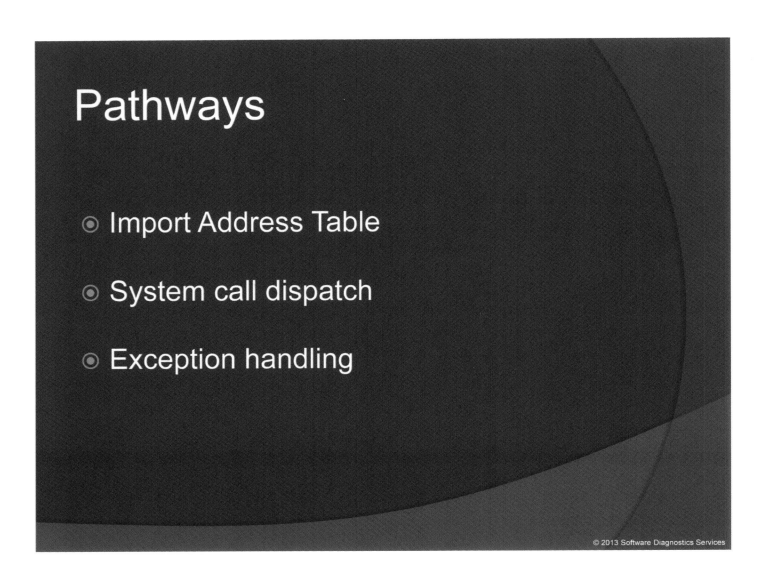

To summarize, in exercise M3 we have seen 3 basic ways to drive malware execution: by hooking Import Address Table, by patching system call dispatch mechanism and by modifying exception handling chains and tables that deal with exception propagation.

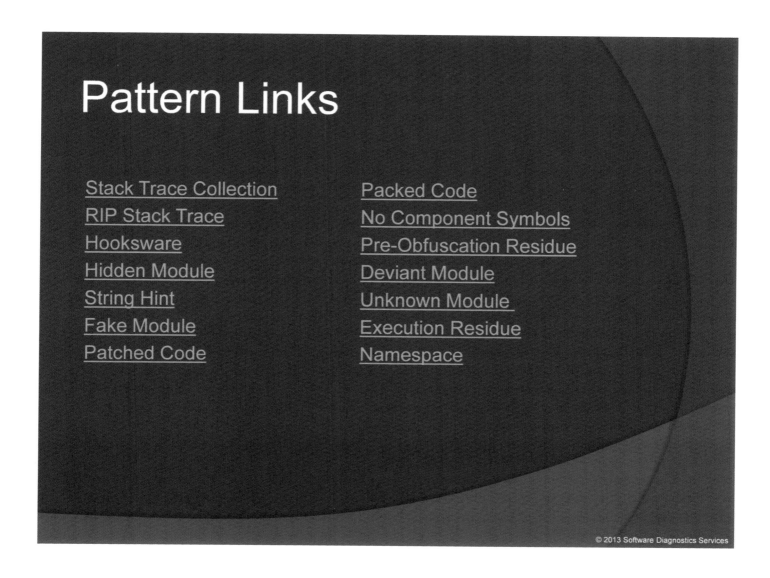

Here are links to descriptions of patterns we found in our examples:

Stack Trace Collection
http://www.dumpanalysis.org/blog/index.php/2007/09/14/crash-dump-analysis-patterns-part-27/

Packed Code
http://www.dumpanalysis.org/blog/index.php/2013/01/19/malware-analysis-patterns-part-3/

RIP Stack Trace
http://www.dumpanalysis.org/blog/index.php/2013/01/20/malware-analysis-patterns-part-11/

No Component Symbols
http://www.dumpanalysis.org/blog/index.php/2007/04/20/crash-dump-analysis-patterns-part-12/

Hooksware
http://www.dumpanalysis.org/blog/index.php/2008/08/10/hooksware/

Pre-Obfuscation Residue
http://www.dumpanalysis.org/blog/index.php/2013/01/19/malware-analysis-patterns-part-4/

Hidden Module
http://www.dumpanalysis.org/blog/index.php/2008/08/07/crash-dump-analysis-patterns-part-75/

Deviant Module
http://www.dumpanalysis.org/blog/index.php/2012/07/15/crash-dump-analysis-patterns-part-179/

String Hint
http://www.dumpanalysis.org/blog/index.php/2013/02/01/malware-analysis-patterns-part-18/

Unknown Module
http://www.dumpanalysis.org/blog/index.php/2007/08/16/crash-dump-analysis-patterns-part-22/

Fake Module
http://www.dumpanalysis.org/blog/index.php/2012/12/29/malware-analysis-patterns-part-2/

Execution Residue
http://www.dumpanalysis.org/blog/index.php/2008/04/29/crash-dump-analysis-patterns-part-60/

Patched Code
http://www.dumpanalysis.org/blog/index.php/2013/02/09/malware-analysis-patterns-part-21/

Namespace
http://www.dumpanalysis.org/blog/index.php/2013/02/05/malware-analysis-patterns-part-20/

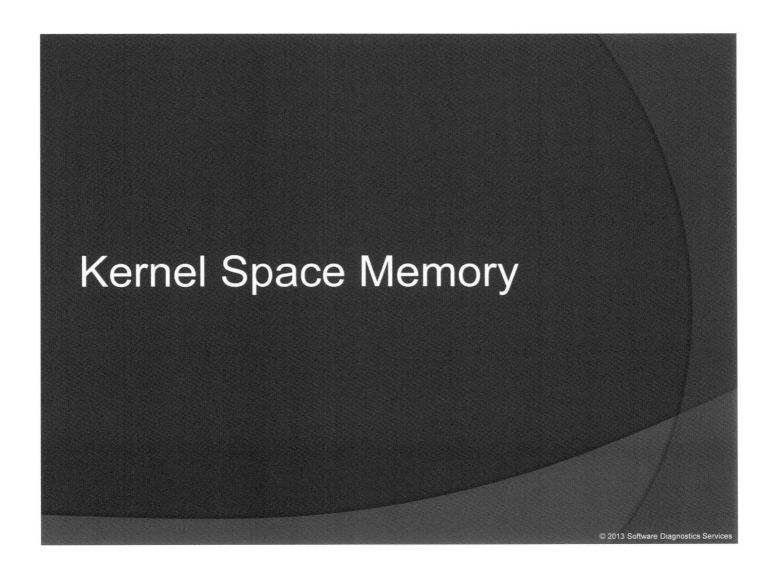

Kernel Space Memory

Now we come to kernel space. Our goal is to show important commands and how their output helps in recognizing patterns of malware in case of detected abnormal software behaviour.

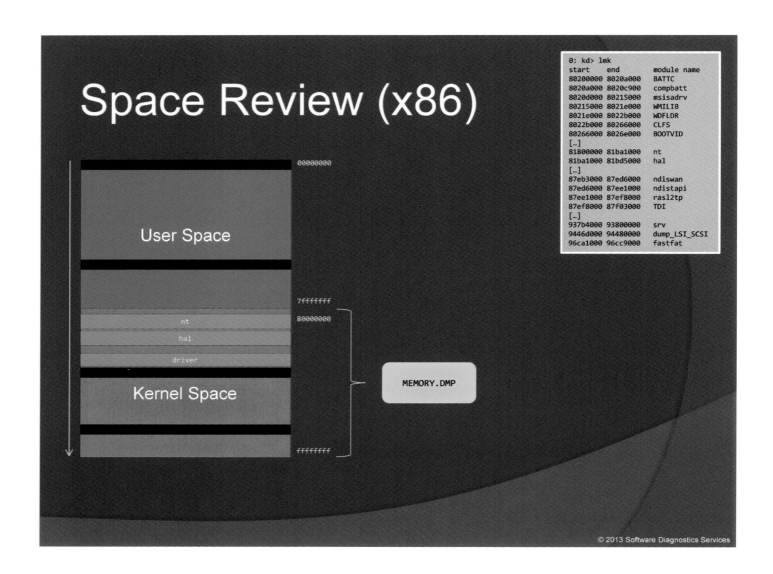

Similar to a user space slide I just briefly repeat that when operating system is booted its executable file is loaded into memory together with additional modules such as **hal.** This OS executable file can be found as **nt** module. During the driver loading stage they are loaded dynamically like DLLs and if they reference other DLLs they are loaded too. Everything we learnt about PE header format is applicable here. In fact .SYS file can be viewed as a system DLL so there is no mystery there. There may be gaps between modules and other space regions like black regions on this picture. Some memory is also allocated for additional working regions needed for system execution. Kernel space usually has 2 GB range and we see addresses where modules are loaded by using **lm** or **lmk** command. When we save a dump all accessible memory including loaded drivers are saved. The dump is usually much smaller than 2 GB unless we have a kernel memory leak or some drivers are memory demanding.

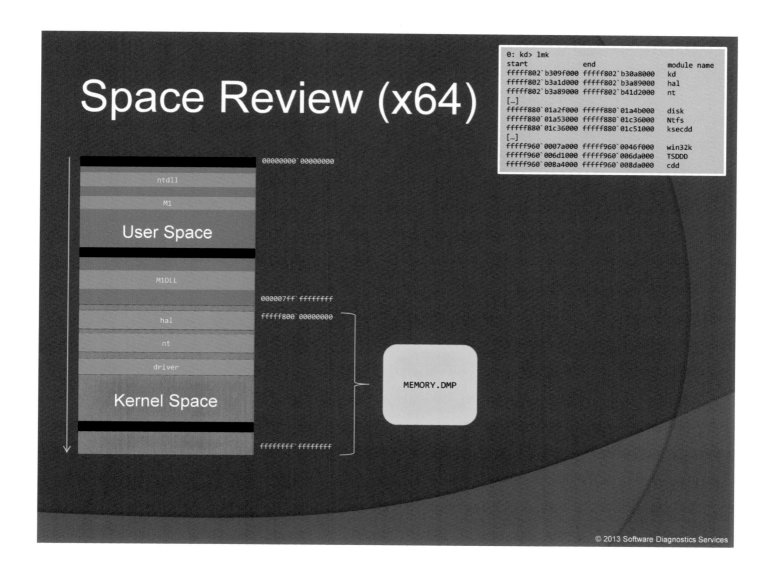

Here we provide a picture for process space in 64-bit Windows. You see that kernel space is no longer restricted to 2 or 1 GB. We see that space distribution when we do an exercise. We now look at a typical driver PE header to see a few differences compared to user space modules.

Driver PE Format

- Non-Paged code

- Page code

- Non-Paged data

- Paged data

- Discardable code and data

In user space executable files and dynamic link libraries we saw one section for code and one for data. In kernel space some code and data need to be always present in physical memory and their sections are declared non-pageable. We also have sections for pageable code and data and also for discardable driver initialization code. All the rest is the same including Import Address Tables.

Suspicious Behaviour

- BSOD

- CPU consumption

- Network communication

- Slow system

There are several cases of suspicious and abnormal system behaviour that could have been potentially caused by malware or defective malware. For example, similar to heap corruption a kernel level rootkit could corrupt a kernel pool causing blue screen with a corresponding bugcheck.

BSOD

```
CRITICAL_STRUCTURE_CORRUPTION (109)
This bugcheck is generated when the kernel detects that critical kernel code or
data have been corrupted. There are generally three causes for a corruption:
1) A driver has inadvertently or deliberately modified critical kernel code
 or data. See http://www.microsoft.com/whdc/driver/kernel/64bitPatching.mspx
2) A developer attempted to set a normal kernel breakpoint using a kernel
 debugger that was not attached when the system was booted. Normal breakpoints,
 "bp", can only be set if the debugger is attached at boot time. Hardware
 breakpoints, "ba", can be set at any time.
3) A hardware corruption occurred, e.g. failing RAM holding kernel code or data.
Arguments:
Arg1: a4a039d897c2787e, Reserved
Arg2: b4b7465eea408b28, Reserved
Arg3: fffff88000f2ef1c, Failure type dependent information
Arg4: 0000000000000002, Type of corrupted region, can be
        0 : A generic data region
        1 : Modification of a function or .pdata
        2 : A processor IDT
        3 : A processor GDT
        4 : Type 1 process list corruption
        5 : Type 2 process list corruption
        6 : Debug routine modification
        7 : Critical MSR modification
```

Latest Windows OS detect kernel structure modifications such as patching and when detected trigger a bugcheck. An example you see on this slide (the output from **!analyze -v** command). Here a modification of IDT (Interrupt Descriptor Table) was detected. We cover IDT later in the next exercise.

The First Steps

- Check the current thread: `!thread -1 3f`

- Check the current process: `!process -1 3f`

- Check the current CPU IDT

- Check the current thread raw stack

- Check running and ready threads

- List all processes and threads

- List all CPUs IDT

What are the first steps? In case of BSOD we might want to check the current thread and then the current process and CPU. The *3f* flag will be needed for physical memory dump analysis and it is good to learn it from the beginning as it has the same output for kernel space even for just kernel memory dumps. Depending on the problem we might also want to check running and ready for execution threads, and also all processes and their threads. When looking at thread output we might want to check kernel and user times spent, modules on stack traces, the presence of any raw addresses. For CPUs we might want to check their interrupt descriptor tables.

IDT

- Interrupt processing

- One for each CPU

- !idt

- !idt -a

IDT or Interrupt Descriptor Table is used to transfer an execution to kernel functions upon an interrupt. Each entry in that table corresponds to an interrupt number (0 to 255) and has an associated pointer to some kernel procedure. Typical interrupts include page fault, divide-by-zero, and also hardware interrupts. We see this command in our next exercise. Just to mention that we might also want to check all interrupt table entries for the presence of any suspicious pointers because normally unused interrupt entries may potentially be used for communication. Also note that each CPU has its own IDT.

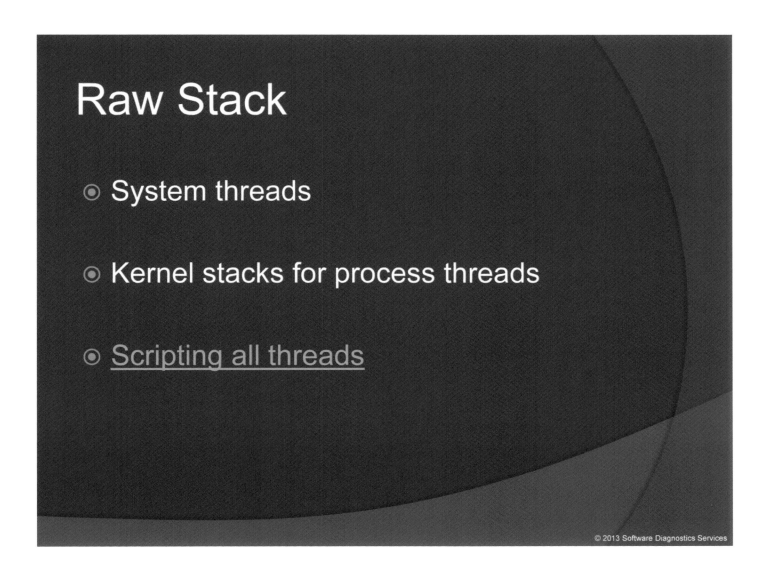

Please recall that we mentioned user space stack region in the previous exercises. The same region exists in kernel for each thread be it a system thread originated from kernel or a thread originated from some process. In the latter case we have 2 separate stack regions in different spaces.

Scripting all threads
http://www.dumpanalysis.org/blog/index.php/2012/01/22/raw-stack-dump-of-all-threads-part-5/

Processes and Threads

- `!process 0 0`

- `!process 0 3f`

- `!sprocess <session> 3f`

- `!for_each_thread "command"`

- `!vm`

Obviously the next thing we would like to check are processes and their thread stacks. There are different ways to do. The first 2 commands are similar to the individual thread and process commands except that instead of -1 we put 0 to indicate all. Also, if we have terminal sessions environment or just interested in the one session we can use the 3rd command. And we can customize thread stack output with the 4th command. An example is given in the previous slide scripting link. Process output is also available with the 5th command where terminated but still referenced processes (the so called "zombie processes") are nicely grouped at the end of the output.

Attached Threads

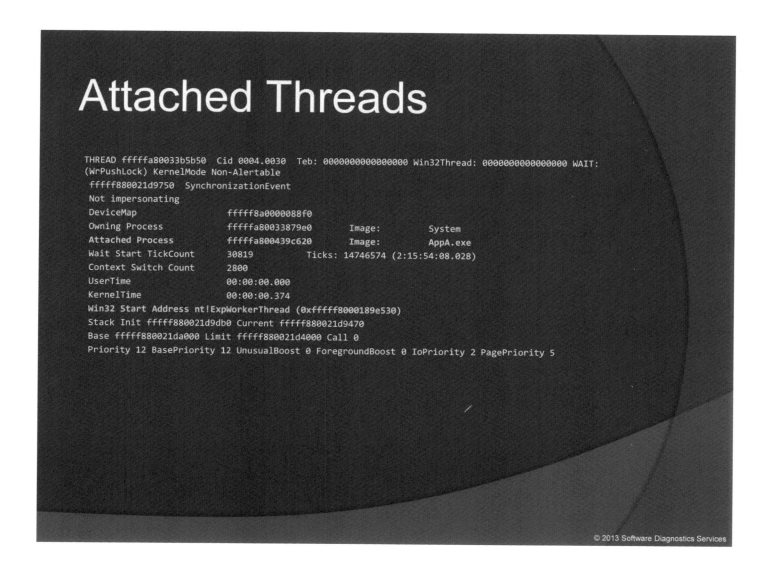

```
THREAD fffffa80033b5b50  Cid 0004.0030  Teb: 0000000000000000 Win32Thread: 0000000000000000 WAIT:
(WrPushLock) KernelMode Non-Alertable
    fffff880021d9750  SynchronizationEvent
Not impersonating
DeviceMap                fffff8a0000088f0
Owning Process           fffffa80033879e0      Image:          System
Attached Process         fffffa800439c620      Image:          AppA.exe
Wait Start TickCount     30819         Ticks: 14746574 (2:15:54:08.028)
Context Switch Count     2800
UserTime                 00:00:00.000
KernelTime               00:00:00.374
Win32 Start Address nt!ExpWorkerThread (0xfffff8000189e530)
Stack Init fffff880021d9db0 Current fffff880021d9470
Base fffff880021da000 Limit fffff880021d4000 Call 0
Priority 12 BasePriority 12 UnusualBoost 0 ForegroundBoost 0 IoPriority 2 PagePriority 5
```

Some system threads can be attached to a particular process if they need its resources. On this fragment we see the thread originated in kernel space but was attached to AppA process so it can access that process address space if needed.

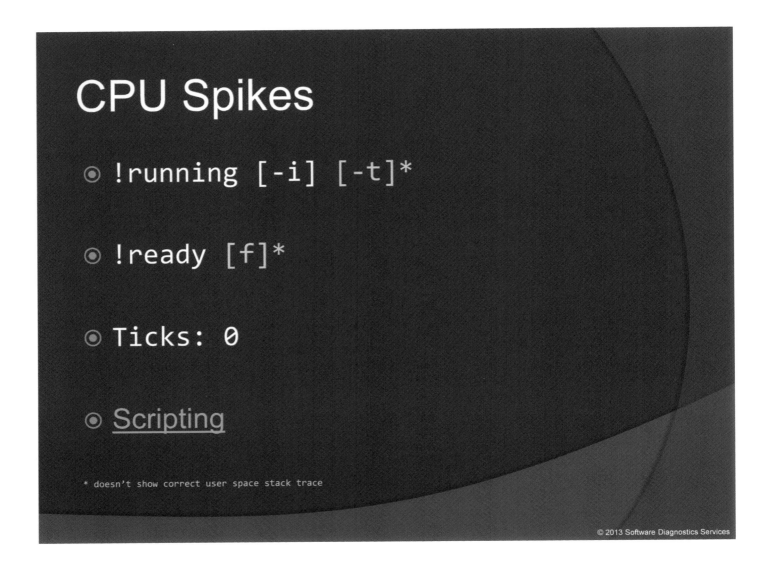

To check for CPU spiking activity and associated threads we can use different commands. I also provided a link to WinDbg scripts that allow you to find out the most time consuming thread in kernel and user modes in case it was consuming CPU some time in the past and this is not visible from the output of the first 2 commands or Ticks output.

Scripting CPU consumption
http://www.dumpanalysis.org/blog/index.php/2011/12/03/2-windbg-scripts-that-changed-the-world/

Exercise M4

- **Goal:** Navigate through kernel space memory regions, list and analyze CPUs, processes and threads

- **Patterns:** Stack Trace Collection, Execution Residue, Self-Diagnosis

- \AWMA-Dumps\Exercise-M4.pdf

Now we analyze a complete memory dump but mainly focus on kernel part for now.

Goal: Navigate through kernel space memory regions, list and analyze CPUs, processes and threads.

Patterns: Stack Trace Collection, Execution Residue, Self-Diagnosis

1.   Launch WinDbg from Windows Kits \ Debugging Tools for Windows (X64) or Debugging Tools for Windows (X86)

2.   Open \AWMA-Dumps\Complete\MEMORY.DMP

3.   If you are presented with this dialog say No:

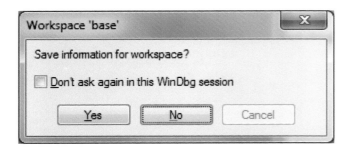

4.   You get the dump file loaded:

```
Microsoft (R) Windows Debugger Version 6.2.9200.20512 X86
Copyright (c) Microsoft Corporation. All rights reserved.


Loading Dump File [C:\AWMA-Dumps\Complete\MEMORY.DMP]
Kernel Bitmap Dump File: Full address space is available

Symbol search path is: *** Invalid ***
************************************************************************
* Symbol loading may be unreliable without a symbol search path.       *
* Use .symfix to have the debugger choose a symbol path.               *
* After setting your symbol path, use .reload to refresh symbol locations. *
************************************************************************
Executable search path is:
************************************************************************
* Symbols can not be loaded because symbol path is not initialized. *
*                                                                   *
* The Symbol Path can be set by:                                    *
*    using the _NT_SYMBOL_PATH environment variable.                *
*    using the -y <symbol_path> argument when starting the debugger. *
*    using .sympath and .sympath+                                   *
************************************************************************
*** ERROR: Symbol file could not be found.  Defaulted to export symbols for ntkrnlmp.exe -
Windows 8 Kernel Version 9200 MP (2 procs) Free x64
Product: WinNt, suite: TerminalServer SingleUserTS
Built by: 9200.16424.amd64fre.win8_gdr.120926-1855
Machine Name:
Kernel base = 0xfffff802`b3a89000 PsLoadedModuleList = 0xfffff802`b3d53a60
Debug session time: Tue Oct 30 20:22:24.413 2012 (UTC + 0:00)
System Uptime: 2 days 20:12:43.173
************************************************************************
```

```
* Symbols can not be loaded because symbol path is not initialized. *
*                                                                   *
* The Symbol Path can be set by:                                    *
*    using the _NT_SYMBOL_PATH environment variable.                *
*    using the -y <symbol_path> argument when starting the debugger.*
*    using .sympath and .sympath+                                   *
*********************************************************************
*** ERROR: Symbol file could not be found.  Defaulted to export symbols for ntkrnlmp.exe -
Loading Kernel Symbols
.........................................................
.........................................................
.......................
Loading User Symbols
.........................................................
............
Loading unloaded module list
..................***  ERROR: Symbol file could not be found.  Defaulted to export symbols for
ntdll.dll -

*********************************************************************
*                                                                   *
*                      Bugcheck Analysis                            *
*                                                                   *
*********************************************************************

Use !analyze -v to get detailed debugging information.

BugCheck EF, {fffffa8002e6b1c0, 0, 0, 0}

*** ERROR: Symbol file could not be found.  Defaulted to export symbols for KERNELBASE.dll -
***** Kernel symbols are WRONG. Please fix symbols to do analysis.


-------------------------------------------------
|                                               |
|          NT symbols are not available         |
|          reduced functionality                |
|                                               |
-------------------------------------------------
unable to get nt!KiCurrentEtwBufferOffset
unable to get nt!KiCurrentEtwBufferBase
*********************************************************************
***                                                             ***
***                                                             ***
***     Either you specified an unqualified symbol, or your debugger ***
***     doesn't have full symbol information.  Unqualified symbol ***
***     resolution is turned off by default. Please either specify a ***
***     fully qualified symbol module!symbolname, or enable resolution ***
***     of unqualified symbols by typing ".symopt- 100". Note that  ***
***     enabling unqualified symbol resolution with network symbol ***
***     server shares in the symbol path may cause the debugger to ***
***     appear to hang for long periods of time when an incorrect ***
***     symbol name is typed or the network symbol server is down. ***
***                                                             ***
***     For some commands to work properly, your symbol path     ***
***     must point to .pdb files that have full type information. ***
***                                                             ***
***     Certain .pdb files (such as the public OS symbols) do not ***
***     contain the required information.  Contact the group that ***
***     provided you with these symbols if you need this command to ***
***     work.                                                    ***
```

```
***                                                                    ***
***     Type referenced: nt!_KPRCB                                     ***
***                                                                    ***
************************************************************************
************************************************************************
***                                                                    ***
***                                                                    ***
***     Either you specified an unqualified symbol, or your debugger   ***
***     doesn't have full symbol information.  Unqualified symbol      ***
***     resolution is turned off by default. Please either specify a   ***
***     fully qualified symbol module!symbolname, or enable resolution ***
***     of unqualified symbols by typing ".symopt- 100". Note that     ***
***     enabling unqualified symbol resolution with network symbol     ***
***     server shares in the symbol path may cause the debugger to     ***
***     appear to hang for long periods of time when an incorrect      ***
***     symbol name is typed or the network symbol server is down.     ***
***                                                                    ***
***     For some commands to work properly, your symbol path           ***
***     must point to .pdb files that have full type information.      ***
***                                                                    ***
***     Certain .pdb files (such as the public OS symbols) do not      ***
***     contain the required information.  Contact the group that      ***
***     provided you with these symbols if you need this command to    ***
***     work.                                                          ***
***                                                                    ***
***     Type referenced: nt!KPRCB                                      ***
***                                                                    ***
************************************************************************
************************************************************************
***                                                                    ***
***                                                                    ***
***     Either you specified an unqualified symbol, or your debugger   ***
***     doesn't have full symbol information.  Unqualified symbol      ***
***     resolution is turned off by default. Please either specify a   ***
***     fully qualified symbol module!symbolname, or enable resolution ***
***     of unqualified symbols by typing ".symopt- 100". Note that     ***
***     enabling unqualified symbol resolution with network symbol     ***
***     server shares in the symbol path may cause the debugger to     ***
***     appear to hang for long periods of time when an incorrect      ***
***     symbol name is typed or the network symbol server is down.     ***
***                                                                    ***
***     For some commands to work properly, your symbol path           ***
***     must point to .pdb files that have full type information.      ***
***                                                                    ***
***     Certain .pdb files (such as the public OS symbols) do not      ***
***     contain the required information.  Contact the group that      ***
***     provided you with these symbols if you need this command to    ***
***     work.                                                          ***
***                                                                    ***
***     Type referenced: nt!_KPRCB                                     ***
***                                                                    ***
************************************************************************
************************************************************************
***                                                                    ***
***                                                                    ***
***     Either you specified an unqualified symbol, or your debugger   ***
***     doesn't have full symbol information.  Unqualified symbol      ***
***     resolution is turned off by default. Please either specify a   ***
***     fully qualified symbol module!symbolname, or enable resolution ***
***     of unqualified symbols by typing ".symopt- 100". Note that     ***
```

```
***     enabling unqualified symbol resolution with network symbol       ***
***     server shares in the symbol path may cause the debugger to        ***
***     appear to hang for long periods of time when an incorrect         ***
***     symbol name is typed or the network symbol server is down.        ***
***                                                                       ***
***     For some commands to work properly, your symbol path              ***
***     must point to .pdb files that have full type information.         ***
***                                                                       ***
***     Certain .pdb files (such as the public OS symbols) do not         ***
***     contain the required information.  Contact the group that         ***
***     provided you with these symbols if you need this command to       ***
***     work.                                                             ***
***                                                                       ***
***     Type referenced: nt!KPRCB                                         ***
***                                                                       ***
*************************************************************************
*************************************************************************
***                                                                       ***
***                                                                       ***
***     Either you specified an unqualified symbol, or your debugger      ***
***     doesn't have full symbol information.  Unqualified symbol         ***
***     resolution is turned off by default. Please either specify a      ***
***     fully qualified symbol module!symbolname, or enable resolution ***
***     of unqualified symbols by typing ".symopt- 100". Note that     ***
***     enabling unqualified symbol resolution with network symbol       ***
***     server shares in the symbol path may cause the debugger to        ***
***     appear to hang for long periods of time when an incorrect         ***
***     symbol name is typed or the network symbol server is down.        ***
***                                                                       ***
***     For some commands to work properly, your symbol path              ***
***     must point to .pdb files that have full type information.         ***
***                                                                       ***
***     Certain .pdb files (such as the public OS symbols) do not         ***
***     contain the required information.  Contact the group that         ***
***     provided you with these symbols if you need this command to       ***
***     work.                                                             ***
***                                                                       ***
***     Type referenced: nt!_KPRCB                                        ***
***                                                                       ***
*************************************************************************
*************************************************************************
***                                                                       ***
***                                                                       ***
***     Either you specified an unqualified symbol, or your debugger      ***
***     doesn't have full symbol information.  Unqualified symbol         ***
***     resolution is turned off by default. Please either specify a      ***
***     fully qualified symbol module!symbolname, or enable resolution ***
***     of unqualified symbols by typing ".symopt- 100". Note that     ***
***     enabling unqualified symbol resolution with network symbol       ***
***     server shares in the symbol path may cause the debugger to        ***
***     appear to hang for long periods of time when an incorrect         ***
***     symbol name is typed or the network symbol server is down.        ***
***                                                                       ***
***     For some commands to work properly, your symbol path              ***
***     must point to .pdb files that have full type information.         ***
***                                                                       ***
***     Certain .pdb files (such as the public OS symbols) do not         ***
***     contain the required information.  Contact the group that         ***
***     provided you with these symbols if you need this command to       ***
***     work.                                                             ***
```

127

```
***                                                         ***
***     Type referenced: nt!_KPRCB                          ***
***                                                         ***
****************************************************************
****************************************************************
***                                                         ***
***                                                         ***
***     Either you specified an unqualified symbol, or your debugger  ***
***     doesn't have full symbol information.  Unqualified symbol     ***
***     resolution is turned off by default. Please either specify a  ***
***     fully qualified symbol module!symbolname, or enable resolution ***
***     of unqualified symbols by typing ".symopt- 100". Note that     ***
***     enabling unqualified symbol resolution with network symbol    ***
***     server shares in the symbol path may cause the debugger to    ***
***     appear to hang for long periods of time when an incorrect     ***
***     symbol name is typed or the network symbol server is down.    ***
***                                                         ***
***     For some commands to work properly, your symbol path     ***
***     must point to .pdb files that have full type information.  ***
***                                                         ***
***     Certain .pdb files (such as the public OS symbols) do not  ***
***     contain the required information.  Contact the group that  ***
***     provided you with these symbols if you need this command to  ***
***     work.                                               ***
***                                                         ***
***     Type referenced: nt!_KPRCB                          ***
***                                                         ***
****************************************************************
****************************************************************
***                                                         ***
***                                                         ***
***     Either you specified an unqualified symbol, or your debugger  ***
***     doesn't have full symbol information.  Unqualified symbol     ***
***     resolution is turned off by default. Please either specify a  ***
***     fully qualified symbol module!symbolname, or enable resolution ***
***     of unqualified symbols by typing ".symopt- 100". Note that     ***
***     enabling unqualified symbol resolution with network symbol    ***
***     server shares in the symbol path may cause the debugger to    ***
***     appear to hang for long periods of time when an incorrect     ***
***     symbol name is typed or the network symbol server is down.    ***
***                                                         ***
***     For some commands to work properly, your symbol path     ***
***     must point to .pdb files that have full type information.  ***
***                                                         ***
***     Certain .pdb files (such as the public OS symbols) do not  ***
***     contain the required information.  Contact the group that  ***
***     provided you with these symbols if you need this command to  ***
***     work.                                               ***
***                                                         ***
***     Type referenced: nt!_KPRCB                          ***
***                                                         ***
****************************************************************
****************************************************************
* Symbols can not be loaded because symbol path is not initialized. *
*                                                                   *
* The Symbol Path can be set by:                                    *
*    using the _NT_SYMBOL_PATH environment variable.                *
*    using the -y <symbol_path> argument when starting the debugger. *
*    using .sympath and .sympath+                                   *
*********************************************************************
```

128

Probably caused by : ntkrnlmp.exe

Followup: MachineOwner

Note: we see more diagnostics related to missing symbols coming out than with the previous version of WinDbg.

5.   Open a log file:

```
0: kd> .logopen C:\AWMA-Dumps\M4.log
Opened log file 'C:\AWMA-Dumps\M4.log'
```

6.   Set up a link to Microsoft symbol server and reload symbols:

```
0: kd> .symfix c:\mss

0: kd> .reload
Loading Kernel Symbols
...............................................................
...............................................................
.....................
Loading User Symbols
...............................................................
............
Loading unloaded module list
..............................................................
```

7.   How this dump was created is of no interest to us here so we skip **!analyze -v** step and look at kernel modules:

```
0: kd> lmk
start             end               module name
fffff802`b309f000 fffff802`b30a8000   kd          (deferred)
fffff802`b3a1d000 fffff802`b3a89000   hal         (deferred)
fffff802`b3a89000 fffff802`b41d2000   nt          (pdb symbols)
c:\mss\ntkrnlmp.pdb\9C419ACB04574E6D91857E85E46682032\ntkrnlmp.pdb
fffff880`00c00000 fffff880`00c7f000   CI          (deferred)
fffff880`00c7f000 fffff880`00ce2000   msrpc       (deferred)
fffff880`00cfd000 fffff880`00d5c000   mcupdate_GenuineIntel   (deferred)
fffff880`00d5c000 fffff880`00db8000   CLFS        (deferred)
fffff880`00db8000 fffff880`00ddb000   tm          (deferred)
fffff880`00ddb000 fffff880`00df0000   PSHED       (deferred)
fffff880`00df0000 fffff880`00dfa000   BOOTVID     (deferred)
fffff880`01000000 fffff880`0106d000   ACPI        (deferred)
fffff880`0106d000 fffff880`01077000   WMILIB      (deferred)
fffff880`01077000 fffff880`01081000   msisadrv    (deferred)
fffff880`010a8000 fffff880`0116a000   Wdf01000    (deferred)
fffff880`0116a000 fffff880`0117a000   WDFLDR      (deferred)
fffff880`0117a000 fffff880`01191000   acpiex      (deferred)
fffff880`01191000 fffff880`0119c000   WppRecorder (deferred)
fffff880`0119c000 fffff880`011d9000   pci         (deferred)
fffff880`01200000 fffff880`01260000   volmgrx     (deferred)
fffff880`01264000 fffff880`012f0000   cng         (deferred)
fffff880`012f0000 fffff880`01318000   tpm         (deferred)
fffff880`01323000 fffff880`01330000   vdrvroot    (deferred)
fffff880`01330000 fffff880`01347000   pdc         (deferred)
fffff880`01347000 fffff880`01361000   partmgr     (deferred)
fffff880`01361000 fffff880`013aa000   spaceport   (deferred)
fffff880`013aa000 fffff880`013c2000   volmgr      (deferred)
fffff880`013c2000 fffff880`013cb000   intelide    (deferred)
fffff880`013cb000 fffff880`013da000   PCIIDEX     (deferred)
fffff880`01400000 fffff880`01456000   CLASSPNP    (deferred)
fffff880`01456000 fffff880`01465000   mouclass    (deferred)
fffff880`01465000 fffff880`0147c000   BTHUSB      (deferred)
```

```
fffff880`0148d000 fffff880`01516000   bxvbda       (deferred)
fffff880`01516000 fffff880`01576000   fltmgr       (deferred)
fffff880`01576000 fffff880`015b8000   WdFilter     (deferred)
fffff880`015b8000 fffff880`015c6000   TDI          (deferred)
fffff880`015c6000 fffff880`015f9580   usbvideo     (deferred)
fffff880`01600000 fffff880`01622000   tdx          (deferred)
fffff880`01622000 fffff880`0162e000   mouhid       (deferred)
fffff880`0162f000 fffff880`01969000   evbda        (deferred)
fffff880`01969000 fffff880`01983000   mountmgr     (deferred)
fffff880`01983000 fffff880`0198d000   atapi        (deferred)
fffff880`0198d000 fffff880`019c1000   ataport      (deferred)
fffff880`019c1000 fffff880`019db000   EhStorClass    (deferred)
fffff880`019db000 fffff880`019ef000   fileinfo     (deferred)
fffff880`019ef000 fffff880`019fc000   BasicRender    (deferred)
fffff880`01a00000 fffff880`01a2f000   ksecpkg      (deferred)
fffff880`01a2f000 fffff880`01a4b000   disk         (deferred)
fffff880`01a53000 fffff880`01c36000   Ntfs         (deferred)
fffff880`01c36000 fffff880`01c51000   ksecdd       (deferred)
fffff880`01c51000 fffff880`01c62000   pcw          (deferred)
fffff880`01c62000 fffff880`01c6c000   Fs_Rec       (deferred)
fffff880`01c6c000 fffff880`01d67000   ndis         (deferred)
fffff880`01d67000 fffff880`01dd7000   NETIO        (deferred)
fffff880`01df5000 fffff880`01dfd000   Beep         (deferred)
fffff880`01e00000 fffff880`01e3b000   rdyboost     (deferred)
fffff880`01e48000 fffff880`0207e000   tcpip        (deferred)
fffff880`0207e000 fffff880`020e6000   fwpkclnt     (deferred)
fffff880`020e6000 fffff880`02101000   wfplwfs      (deferred)
fffff880`02101000 fffff880`02177000   fvevol       (deferred)
fffff880`02177000 fffff880`021cc000   volsnap      (deferred)
fffff880`021cc000 fffff880`021e3000   mup          (deferred)
fffff880`021e3000 fffff880`021f7000   crashdmp     (deferred)
fffff880`021f7000 fffff880`02200000   Null         (deferred)
fffff880`03406000 fffff880`0356d000   dxgkrnl      (deferred)
fffff880`0356d000 fffff880`0357e000   watchdog     (deferred)
fffff880`0357e000 fffff880`035cc000   dxgmms1      (deferred)
fffff880`035cc000 fffff880`035dd000   BasicDisplay   (deferred)
fffff880`035dd000 fffff880`035ef000   Npfs         (deferred)
fffff880`035ef000 fffff880`035fb000   Msfs         (deferred)
fffff880`03600000 fffff880`0362a000   pacer        (deferred)
fffff880`0362a000 fffff880`03640000   vwififlt     (deferred)
fffff880`03640000 fffff880`03650000   netbios      (deferred)
fffff880`03650000 fffff880`036c2000   rdbss        (deferred)
fffff880`036c2000 fffff880`036ce000   BATTC        (deferred)
fffff880`036ce000 fffff880`036f1000   usbccgp      (deferred)
fffff880`036f1000 fffff880`03749000   netbt        (deferred)
fffff880`03749000 fffff880`037db000   afd          (deferred)
fffff880`037db000 fffff880`037e8000   kbdhid       (deferred)
fffff880`037e8000 fffff880`037f7000   kbdclass     (deferred)
fffff880`03800000 fffff880`0384b000   portcls      (deferred)
fffff880`0384d000 fffff880`038c8000   USBPORT      (deferred)
fffff880`038c8000 fffff880`038de000   usbehci      (deferred)
fffff880`038de000 fffff880`038f4000   HDAudBus     (deferred)
fffff880`038f4000 fffff880`03972000   usbhub       (deferred)
fffff880`03972000 fffff880`039ca000   HdAudio      (deferred)
fffff880`039ca000 fffff880`039d7000   hidusb       (deferred)
fffff880`039d7000 fffff880`039f2000   HIDCLASS     (deferred)
fffff880`039f2000 fffff880`039fa000   HIDPARSE     (deferred)
fffff880`03a00000 fffff880`03a0f000   CompositeBus   (deferred)
fffff880`03a0f000 fffff880`03a1a000   kdnic        (deferred)
fffff880`03a1a000 fffff880`03a2c000   umbus        (deferred)
fffff880`03a2c000 fffff880`03a48000   intelppm     (deferred)
fffff880`03a4c000 fffff880`03add000   csc          (deferred)
fffff880`03add000 fffff880`03af7000   wanarp       (deferred)
fffff880`03af7000 fffff880`03b05000   nsiproxy     (deferred)
fffff880`03b05000 fffff880`03b11000   npsvctrig    (deferred)
fffff880`03b11000 fffff880`03b1d000   mssmbios     (deferred)
fffff880`03b1d000 fffff880`03b2e000   discache     (deferred)
fffff880`03b2e000 fffff880`03b4f000   dfsc         (deferred)
fffff880`03b4f000 fffff880`03b55400   CmBatt       (deferred)
fffff880`03b5f000 fffff880`03b6b000   ndistapi     (deferred)
fffff880`03b6b000 fffff880`03b9a000   ndiswan      (deferred)
fffff880`03b9a000 fffff880`03bb8000   rassstp      (deferred)
fffff880`03bb8000 fffff880`03bd0000   AgileVpn     (deferred)
fffff880`03bd0000 fffff880`03bfc000   tunnel       (deferred)
fffff880`03e00000 fffff880`03e0e000   usbuhci      (deferred)
fffff880`03e17000 fffff880`043fee00   igdkmd64     (deferred)
```

```
fffff880`04400000 fffff880`04422000   bthpan       (deferred)
fffff880`04422000 fffff880`0443f000   hidbth       (deferred)
fffff880`0443f000 fffff880`0444c000   dump_dumpata    (deferred)
fffff880`0444c000 fffff880`04456000   dump_atapi    (deferred)
fffff880`04456000 fffff880`0446a000   dump_dumpfve    (deferred)
fffff880`0449c000 fffff880`045c0000   bthport      (deferred)
fffff880`045c0000 fffff880`045eb000   rfcomm       (deferred)
fffff880`045eb000 fffff880`045fd000   BthEnum      (deferred)
fffff880`04800000 fffff880`0480b000   rdpbus       (deferred)
fffff880`0480b000 fffff880`0481f000   NDProxy      (deferred)
fffff880`0481f000 fffff880`0482a000   USBD        (deferred)
fffff880`0482a000 fffff880`0484c000   drmk        (deferred)
fffff880`0484c000 fffff880`04851380   ksthunk      (deferred)
fffff880`04852000 fffff880`04d3f000   bcmwl63a     (deferred)
fffff880`04d3f000 fffff880`04d4c000   vwifibus     (deferred)
fffff880`04d4c000 fffff880`04d6d000   raspptp      (deferred)
fffff880`04d6d000 fffff880`04d92000   rasl2tp      (deferred)
fffff880`04d92000 fffff880`04dac000   raspppoe     (deferred)
fffff880`04dac000 fffff880`04dad480   swenum       (deferred)
fffff880`04dae000 fffff880`04dfd000   ks          (deferred)
fffff880`15262000 fffff880`1528a000   luafv        (deferred)
fffff880`1528a000 fffff880`1529e000   lltdio       (deferred)
fffff880`1529e000 fffff880`1530c000   nwifi        (deferred)
fffff880`1530c000 fffff880`15320000   ndisuio      (deferred)
fffff880`15320000 fffff880`15338000   rspndr       (deferred)
fffff880`15338000 fffff880`15342000   vwifimp      (deferred)
fffff880`15342000 fffff880`1535e000   Ndu         (deferred)
fffff880`1535e000 fffff880`153eb000   srv         (deferred)
fffff880`15a00000 fffff880`15a62000   mrxsmb       (deferred)
fffff880`15a62000 fffff880`15aad000   mrxsmb10     (deferred)
fffff880`15ab3000 fffff880`15b8f000   HTTP        (deferred)
fffff880`15b8f000 fffff880`15baf000   bowser       (deferred)
fffff880`15baf000 fffff880`15bc6000   mpsdrv       (deferred)
fffff880`15bc6000 fffff880`15c00000   mrxsmb20     (deferred)
fffff880`15c00000 fffff880`15ca0000   srv2        (deferred)
fffff880`15ca0000 fffff880`15cab000   rdpvideominiport    (deferred)
fffff880`15cae000 fffff880`15cbc000   monitor      (deferred)
fffff880`15cbc000 fffff880`15cc9000   condrv       (deferred)
fffff880`15ccd000 fffff880`15d98000   peauth       (deferred)
fffff880`15d98000 fffff880`15da3000   secdrv       (deferred)
fffff880`15da3000 fffff880`15de7000   srvnet       (deferred)
fffff880`15de7000 fffff880`15df9000   tcpipreg     (deferred)
fffff960`0007a000 fffff960`0046f000   win32k       (deferred)
fffff960`006d1000 fffff960`006da000   TSDDD        (deferred)
fffff960`008a4000 fffff960`008da000   cdd         (deferred)

Unloaded modules:
fffff880`153eb000 fffff880`153f8000   hiber_ataport.sys
fffff880`15200000 fffff880`1520a000   hiber_atapi.sys
fffff880`1520a000 fffff880`1521e000   hiber_dumpfve.sys
fffff880`15ca0000 fffff880`15ca8000   drmkaud.sys
fffff880`15dfc000 fffff880`15dfe000   MSTEE.sys
fffff880`15df9000 fffff880`15dfc000   MSKSSRV.sys
fffff880`15ccb000 fffff880`15ccd000   MSPQM.sys
fffff880`15cc9000 fffff880`15ccb000   MSPCLOCK.sys
fffff880`15ca0000 fffff880`15cae000   monitor.sys
fffff880`0446a000 fffff880`04478000   monitor.sys
fffff880`01e3b000 fffff880`01e48000   dump_ataport.sys
fffff880`01dd7000 fffff880`01de1000   dump_atapi.sys
fffff880`01de1000 fffff880`01df5000   dump_dumpfve.sys
fffff880`03b4f000 fffff880`03b5f000   dam.sys
fffff880`01456000 fffff880`01487000   cdrom.sys
fffff880`01318000 fffff880`01323000   WdBoot.sys
fffff880`021e3000 fffff880`021ef000   hwpolicy.sys
fffff880`00cf0000 fffff880`00cfd000   ApiSetSchema.dll
000007fe`eb670000 000007fe`eb682000   BROWCLI.DLL
000007fe`f48c0000 000007fe`f48e4000   srvcli.dll
000007fe`e6830000 000007fe`e68c5000   tiptsf.dll
000007fe`e7820000 000007fe`e7897000   verifier.dll
000007fe`f7b20000 000007fe`f7b27000   psapi.dll
000007fe`f0ca0000 000007fe`f0ca9000   version.dll
000007fe`eb1c0000 000007fe`eb237000   verifier.dll
000007fe`f7b20000 000007fe`f7b27000   psapi.dll
000007fe`f0ca0000 000007fe`f0ca9000   version.dll
000007fe`f4110000 000007fe`f4157000   AUTHZ.dll
000007fe`f1b70000 000007fe`f1b88000   slc.dll
```

```
000007fe`efcc0000 000007fe`efcd7000    MPR.dll
000007fe`ea520000 000007fe`ea619000    ACLUI.dll
000007fe`f3840000 000007fe`f3864000    NTDSAPI.dll
000007fe`f3790000 000007fe`f3799000    DSROLE.dll
000007fe`ec300000 000007fe`ec32e000    srmshell.dll
000007fe`f3800000 000007fe`f381d000    ATL.DLL
000007fe`ec2e0000 000007fe`ec2fb000    SrmTrace.DLL
000007fe`ec330000 000007fe`ec345000    cryptext.dll
000007fe`eb1a0000 000007fe`eb233000    CRYPTUI.dll
000007fe`ecb90000 000007fe`ecbc0000    syncui.dll
000007fe`ec350000 000007fe`ec36b000    SYNCENG.dll
000007fe`efc50000 000007fe`efc5b000    LINKINFO.dll
000007fe`f0f00000 000007fe`f0f0f000    acppage.dll
000007fe`ebf20000 000007fe`ebf23000    sfc.dll
000007fe`e8e20000 000007fe`e90dd000    msi.dll
000007fe`eef30000 000007fe`eef40000    sfc_os.DLL
000007fe`f4ec0000 000007fe`f4f15000    WINTRUST.DLL
000007fe`f7ce0000 000007fe`f7cf4000    imagehlp.dll
000007fe`f5100000 000007fe`f52d7000    CRYPT32.dll
000007fe`f4ea0000 000007fe`f4eb6000    MSASN1.dll
000007fe`f4870000 000007fe`f4897000    ncrypt.dll
000007fe`f4830000 000007fe`f4865000    NTASN1.dll
000007fe`e8620000 000007fe`e8773000    wdc.dll
000007fe`ea680000 000007fe`ea693000    pdhui.dll
000007fe`f7a20000 000007fe`f7ac1000    COMDLG32.dll
000007fe`e8560000 000007fe`e861e000    ODBC32.dll
000007fe`edf30000 000007fe`edf3b000    Secur32.dll
000007fe`f0ca0000 000007fe`f0ca9000    VERSION.dll
000007fe`e7740000 000007fe`e7893000    PLA.dll
000007fe`e8b30000 000007fe`e8b7c000    pdh.dll
000007fe`f3690000 000007fe`f3774000    tdh.dll
000007fe`ec170000 000007fe`ec195000    Cabinet.dll
000007fe`f3a50000 000007fe`f3abc000    wevtapi.dll
000007fe`ea440000 000007fe`ea457000    UTILDLL.dll
000007fe`f3820000 000007fe`f3835000    NETAPI32.dll
000007fe`f4440000 000007fe`f4474000    LOGONCLI.DLL
000007fe`eb670000 000007fe`eb682000    BROWCLI.DLL
000007fe`f48c0000 000007fe`f48e4000    srvcli.dll
000007fe`f4ba0000 000007fe`f4bcc000    SSPICLI.DLL
000007fe`e8620000 000007fe`e8773000    wdc.dll
000007fe`ea680000 000007fe`ea693000    pdhui.dll
000007fe`f7a20000 000007fe`f7ac1000    COMDLG32.dll
000007fe`e8560000 000007fe`e861e000    ODBC32.dll
000007fe`edf30000 000007fe`edf3b000    Secur32.dll
000007fe`f0ca0000 000007fe`f0ca9000    VERSION.dll
000007fe`e7740000 000007fe`e7893000    PLA.dll
000007fe`e8b30000 000007fe`e8b7c000    pdh.dll
000007fe`f3690000 000007fe`f3774000    tdh.dll
000007fe`ec170000 000007fe`ec195000    Cabinet.dll
000007fe`f3a50000 000007fe`f3abc000    wevtapi.dll
000007fe`ea440000 000007fe`ea457000    UTILDLL.dll
000007fe`f3820000 000007fe`f3835000    NETAPI32.dll
000007fe`f4440000 000007fe`f4474000    LOGONCLI.DLL
```

Notice the unload modules list. These names can also be considered a part of execution residue.

8.   Let's check a typical driver module header and IAT:

```
0: kd> !dh disk

File Type: EXECUTABLE IMAGE
FILE HEADER VALUES
    8664 machine (X64)
       9 number of sections
5010AB85 time date stamp Thu Jul 26 03:29:25 2012

       0 file pointer to symbol table
       0 number of symbols
      F0 size of optional header
```

```
     22 characteristics
            Executable
            App can handle >2gb addresses

OPTIONAL HEADER VALUES
        20B magic #
      10.10 linker version
       EA00 size of code
       8200 size of initialized data
          0 size of uninitialized data
       215C address of entry point
       1000 base of code
            ----- new -----
fffff802b5567000 image base
       1000 section alignment
        200 file alignment
          1 subsystem (Native)
       6.02 operating system version
       6.02 image version
       6.02 subsystem version
      1C000 size of image
        400 size of headers
      24F95 checksum
0000000000040000 size of stack reserve
0000000000001000 size of stack commit
0000000000100000 size of heap reserve
0000000000001000 size of heap commit
          0   DLL characteristics
          0 [        0] address [size] of Export Directory
      15118 [       3C] address [size] of Import Directory
      16000 [     4258] address [size] of Resource Directory
       A000 [      EAC] address [size] of Exception Directory
      17000 [     20F0] address [size] of Security Directory
      1B000 [       A0] address [size] of Base Relocation Directory
       5A54 [       38] address [size] of Debug Directory
          0 [        0] address [size] of Description Directory
          0 [        0] address [size] of Special Directory
          0 [        0] address [size] of Thread Storage Directory
       6810 [       70] address [size] of Load Configuration Directory
          0 [        0] address [size] of Bound Import Directory
       6000 [      2D8] address [size] of Import Address Table Directory
          0 [        0] address [size] of Delay Import Directory
          0 [        0] address [size] of COR20 Header Directory
          0 [        0] address [size] of Reserved Directory


SECTION HEADER #1
   .text name
   4AB5 virtual size
   1000 virtual address
   4C00 size of raw data
    400 file pointer to raw data
      0 file pointer to relocation table
      0 file pointer to line numbers
      0 number of relocations
      0 number of line numbers
68000020 flags
        Code
        Not Paged
        (no align specified)
```

```
        Execute Read

Debug Directories(2)
      Type        Size    Address   Pointer
      cv          21        5a94      4e94    Format: RSDS, guid, 2, disk.pdb
      (    10)     8         5a8c      4e8c


SECTION HEADER #2
   .rdata name
    2270 virtual size
    6000 virtual address
    2400 size of raw data
    5000 file pointer to raw data
       0 file pointer to relocation table
       0 file pointer to line numbers
       0 number of relocations
       0 number of line numbers
48000040 flags
         Initialized Data
         Not Paged
         (no align specified)
         Read Only


SECTION HEADER #3
   .data name
     2C5 virtual size
    9000 virtual address
     400 size of raw data
    7400 file pointer to raw data
       0 file pointer to relocation table
       0 file pointer to line numbers
       0 number of relocations
       0 number of line numbers
C8000040 flags
         Initialized Data
         Not Paged
         (no align specified)
         Read Write


SECTION HEADER #4
   .pdata name
     EAC virtual size
    A000 virtual address
    1000 size of raw data
    7800 file pointer to raw data
       0 file pointer to relocation table
       0 file pointer to line numbers
       0 number of relocations
       0 number of line numbers
48000040 flags
         Initialized Data
         Not Paged
         (no align specified)
         Read Only
```

```
SECTION HEADER #5
    PAGE name
    7E59 virtual size
    B000 virtual address
    8000 size of raw data
    8800 file pointer to raw data
 1A3A000 file pointer to relocation table
FFFFF880 file pointer to line numbers
       0 number of relocations
       0 number of line numbers
60000020 flags
         Code
         (no align specified)
         Execute Read

SECTION HEADER #6
    PAGE name
     2A0 virtual size
   13000 virtual address
     400 size of raw data
   10800 file pointer to raw data
 1A42000 file pointer to relocation table
FFFFF880 file pointer to line numbers
       0 number of relocations
       0 number of line numbers
C0000040 flags
         Initialized Data
         (no align specified)
         Read Write

SECTION HEADER #7
    INIT name
    1C9C virtual size
   14000 virtual address
    1E00 size of raw data
   10C00 file pointer to raw data
       0 file pointer to relocation table
       0 file pointer to line numbers
       0 number of relocations
       0 number of line numbers
E2000020 flags
         Code
         Discardable
         (no align specified)
         Execute Read Write

SECTION HEADER #8
   .rsrc name
    4258 virtual size
   16000 virtual address
    4400 size of raw data
   12A00 file pointer to raw data
       0 file pointer to relocation table
       0 file pointer to line numbers
       0 number of relocations
       0 number of line numbers
42000040 flags
         Initialized Data
         Discardable
         (no align specified)
```

```
          Read Only

SECTION HEADER #9
   .reloc name
      A0 virtual size
   1B000 virtual address
     200 size of raw data
   16E00 file pointer to raw data
       0 file pointer to relocation table
       0 file pointer to line numbers
       0 number of relocations
       0 number of line numbers
42000040 flags
         Initialized Data
         Discardable
         (no align specified)
         Read Only
```

Note different code and data sections for non-pageable, pageable and discardable code and data. For image base address we need to take the value from the output of **lm m** command:

```
0: kd> lm m disk
start             end               module name
fffff880`01a2f000 fffff880`01a4b000  disk       (deferred)

0: kd> dps fffff880`01a2f000+6000 L2D8/8
fffff880`01a35000  fffff802`b3aeb4d0 nt!IoGetAttachedDeviceReference
fffff880`01a35008  fffff802`b3b8cc10 nt!IoAttachDeviceToDeviceStack
fffff880`01a35010  fffff802`b3b63b10 nt!IoAllocateIrp
fffff880`01a35018  fffff802`b3b2b120 nt!RtlCompareMemory
fffff880`01a35020  fffff802`b3af99a0 nt!ObfDereferenceObject
fffff880`01a35028  fffff802`b3aeb1f0 nt!IoQueueWorkItem
fffff880`01a35030  fffff802`b3b3c3b0 nt!IofCallDriver
fffff880`01a35038  fffff802`b3b3d1f0 nt!IoGetIoPriorityHint
fffff880`01a35040  fffff802`b3c48d7c nt!ExInterlockedPopEntryList
fffff880`01a35048  fffff802`b3b72a70 nt!MmBuildMdlForNonPagedPool
fffff880`01a35050  fffff802`b3b4d960 nt!IoFreeMdl
fffff880`01a35058  fffff802`b3b471e0 nt!IoFreeIrp
fffff880`01a35060  fffff802`b3c48e14 nt!ExInterlockedPushEntryList
fffff880`01a35068  fffff802`b3aef97c nt!ExInitializePushLock
fffff880`01a35070  fffff802`b3b29a50 nt!KeWaitForSingleObject
fffff880`01a35078  fffff802`b3f69f30 nt!IoReadDiskSignature
fffff880`01a35080  fffff802`b3b04be0 nt!ZwQueryValueKey
fffff880`01a35088  fffff802`b3ec3bac nt!RtlUnicodeStringToInteger
fffff880`01a35090  fffff802`b3b04b40 nt!ZwOpenKey
fffff880`01a35098  fffff802`b3f87600 nt!IoGetConfigurationInformation
fffff880`01a350a0  fffff802`b3f94cf0 nt!IoDeleteSymbolicLink
fffff880`01a350a8  fffff802`b3ac6f60 nt!KeInitializeMutex
fffff880`01a350b0  fffff802`b3a8c0a0 nt!HalExamineMBR
fffff880`01a350b8  fffff802`b3f5a0cc nt!RtlQueryRegistryValues
fffff880`01a350c0  fffff802`b3d70104 nt!InitSafeBootMode
fffff880`01a350c8  fffff802`b3b8148c nt!vsnprintf
fffff880`01a350d0  fffff802`b3f94c70 nt!IoCreateSymbolicLink
fffff880`01a350d8  fffff802`b3e1d280 nt!IoOpenDeviceRegistryKey
fffff880`01a350e0  fffff802`b3bac250 nt!IoSetActivityIdIrp
fffff880`01a350e8  fffff802`b3b04ae0 nt!ZwClose
fffff880`01a350f0  fffff802`b3af33cc nt!vsnwprintf
fffff880`01a350f8  fffff802`b3ab17dc nt!IoAllocateWorkItem
fffff880`01a35100  fffff802`b3ad7d70 nt!EtwWrite
```

```
fffff880`01a35108  fffff802`b3f6a9e0  nt!IoRegisterBootDriverReinitialization
fffff880`01a35110  fffff802`b3b06820  nt!ZwMakeTemporaryObject
fffff880`01a35118  fffff802`b3b41fd0  nt!KeReleaseMutex
fffff880`01a35120  fffff802`b3ba2140  nt!IoAllocateErrorLogEntry
fffff880`01a35128  fffff802`b3b466b0  nt!IoGetActivityIdIrp
fffff880`01a35130  fffff802`b3b8fe54  nt!IoInvalidateDeviceRelations
fffff880`01a35138  fffff802`b3e0e500  nt!EtwRegister
fffff880`01a35140  fffff802`b3b05c40  nt!ZwCreateDirectoryObject
fffff880`01a35148  fffff802`b3b3d0e0  nt!KeInitializeEvent
fffff880`01a35150  fffff802`b3f059d4  nt!MmGetSystemRoutineAddress
fffff880`01a35158  fffff802`b3ab17c0  nt!IoFreeWorkItem
fffff880`01a35160  fffff802`b3afa000  nt!KeSetEvent
fffff880`01a35168  fffff802`b3a8ddd0  nt!IoDeleteDevice
fffff880`01a35170  fffff802`b3b47190  nt!RtlInitUnicodeString
fffff880`01a35178  fffff802`b3ba8080  nt!IoSetHardErrorOrVerifyDevice
fffff880`01a35180  fffff802`b3a8d890  nt!IoReportTargetDeviceChangeAsynchronous
fffff880`01a35188  fffff802`b3e08240  nt!IoBuildSynchronousFsdRequest
fffff880`01a35190  fffff802`b3f86de0  nt!IoRegisterDriverReinitialization
fffff880`01a35198  fffff802`b3afae90  nt!strncmp
fffff880`01a351a0  fffff802`b3cf7010  nt!ExFreePoolWithTag
fffff880`01a351a8  fffff802`b3ae84e0  nt!IoBuildDeviceIoControlRequest
fffff880`01a351b0  fffff802`b3e0d890  nt!EtwUnregister
fffff880`01a351b8  fffff802`b3ba2030  nt!IoWriteErrorLogEntry
fffff880`01a351c0  fffff802`b3f994ac  nt!IoWMIRegistrationControl
fffff880`01a351c8  fffff802`b3b4d300  nt!IoAllocateMdl
fffff880`01a351d0  fffff802`b3cf8040  nt!ExAllocatePoolWithTag
fffff880`01a351d8  00000000`00000000
fffff880`01a351e0  fffff880`0143e6d0  CLASSPNP!ClassInitializeSrbLookasideList
fffff880`01a351e8  fffff880`014438a4  CLASSPNP!ClassDeleteSrbLookasideList
fffff880`01a351f0  fffff880`0143f7a0  CLASSPNP!ClassInitializeMediaChangeDetection
fffff880`01a351f8  fffff880`0143eff0  CLASSPNP!ClassUpdateInformationInRegistry
fffff880`01a35200  fffff880`0143ee10  CLASSPNP!ClassGetDeviceParameter
fffff880`01a35208  fffff880`014402d0  CLASSPNP!ClassQueryTimeOutRegistryValue
fffff880`01a35210  fffff880`01401660  CLASSPNP!ClassSignalCompletion
fffff880`01a35218  fffff880`014056e0  CLASSPNP!ClassReadDriveCapacity
fffff880`01a35220  fffff880`01403540  CLASSPNP!ClassInterpretSenseInfo
fffff880`01a35228  fffff880`01408990  CLASSPNP!ClassWmiCompleteRequest
fffff880`01a35230  fffff880`0140ee70  CLASSPNP!ClassNotifyFailurePredicted
fffff880`01a35238  fffff880`014135f8  CLASSPNP!ClassReleaseQueue
fffff880`01a35240  fffff880`0143fdf0  CLASSPNP!ClassSetFailurePredictionPoll
fffff880`01a35248  fffff880`01407e10  CLASSPNP!ClassAcquireRemoveLockEx
fffff880`01a35250  fffff880`0143d440  CLASSPNP!ClassModeSense
fffff880`01a35258  fffff880`0143e5a0  CLASSPNP!ClassClaimDevice
fffff880`01a35260  fffff880`014015e0  CLASSPNP!ClassReleaseRemoveLock
fffff880`01a35268  fffff880`014091c0  CLASSPNP!ClassSpinDownPowerHandler
fffff880`01a35270  fffff880`01440180  CLASSPNP!ClassInitializeEx
fffff880`01a35278  fffff880`014049d0  CLASSPNP!ClassDeviceControl
fffff880`01a35280  fffff880`01405640  CLASSPNP!ClassCompleteRequest
fffff880`01a35288  fffff880`014042f0  CLASSPNP!ClassSendSrbSynchronous
fffff880`01a35290  fffff880`014138a0  CLASSPNP!ClassAsynchronousCompletion
fffff880`01a35298  fffff880`0144377c  CLASSPNP!ClassSetDeviceParameter
fffff880`01a352a0  fffff880`0143ccc0  CLASSPNP!ClassSendDeviceIoControlSynchronous
fffff880`01a352a8  fffff880`01408b00  CLASSPNP!ClassFindModePage
fffff880`01a352b0  fffff880`01440470  CLASSPNP!ClassInitialize
fffff880`01a352b8  fffff880`01402e80  CLASSPNP!ClassIoComplete
fffff880`01a352c0  fffff880`0143e160  CLASSPNP!ClassCreateDeviceObject
fffff880`01a352c8  fffff880`0143da10  CLASSPNP!ClassScanForSpecial
fffff880`01a352d0  00000000`00000000
```

9.	We can check if there was any patching by using **!for_each_module** command like we did for user space in the previous exercise:

```
0: kd> !for_each_module "!chkimg -v -d @#ModuleName"
[…]
```

There are only errors for win32k.sys but they do not point to any code and are possibly related to some internal modification done by Windows itself.

10.	Let's check the current thread:

```
0: kd> !thread -1 3f
THREAD fffffa8003db4740  Cid 0ca0.03e0  Teb: 000007f770b7d000 Win32Thread: fffff90104094830
RUNNING on processor 0
Not impersonating
DeviceMap                 fffff8a007e2e6a0
Owning Process            fffffa8002d74180       Image:         Taskmgr.exe
Attached Process          N/A           Image:         N/A
Wait Start TickCount      15741128      Ticks: 0
Context Switch Count      31359         IdealProcessor: 0
UserTime                  00:00:09.859
KernelTime                00:00:07.394
Win32 Start Address taskmgr!wWinMainCRTStartup (0x000007f770e68688)
Stack Init fffff88015925dd0 Current fffff88015925800
Base fffff88015926000 Limit fffff88015920000 Call 0
Priority 13 BasePriority 9 UnusualBoost 0 ForegroundBoost 2 IoPriority 2 PagePriority 5
Child-SP          RetAddr           Call Site
fffff880`15925ae8 fffff802`b400f0dd nt!KeBugCheckEx
fffff880`15925af0 fffff802`b3ea8f6d nt!PspCatchCriticalBreak+0xad
fffff880`15925b30 fffff802`b3ea8019 nt! ?? ::NNGAKEGL::`string'+0x46f60
fffff880`15925b90 fffff802`b3ea7e52 nt!PspTerminateProcess+0x6d
fffff880`15925bd0 fffff802`b3b02d53 nt!NtTerminateProcess+0x9e
fffff880`15925c40 000007fe`f7ec2eaa nt!KiSystemServiceCopyEnd+0x13 (TrapFrame @
fffff880`15925c40)
000000f0`6e86f3e8 000007fe`f4ff1295 ntdll!NtTerminateProcess+0xa
000000f0`6e86f3f0 000007f7`70e012ba KERNELBASE!TerminateProcess+0x25
000000f0`6e86f420 000007f7`70df3698 taskmgr!WdcProcessMonitor::OnProcessCommand+0x1b6
000000f0`6e86f4b0 000007f7`70df55bb taskmgr!WdcListView::OnProcessCommand+0x1e0
000000f0`6e86f5a0 000007f7`70df5b47 taskmgr!WdcListView::OnCommand+0x123
000000f0`6e86f5f0 000007fe`f2227239 taskmgr!WdcListView::OnMessage+0x287
000000f0`6e86f710 000007fe`f2a82d23 DUI70!DirectUI::HWNDHost::_CtrlWndProc+0xa1
000000f0`6e86f770 000007fe`f56c171e DUser!WndBridge::RawWndProc+0x73
000000f0`6e86f7e0 000007fe`f56c14d7 USER32!UserCallWinProcCheckWow+0x13a
000000f0`6e86f8a0 000007f7`70e1b0e1 USER32!DispatchMessageWorker+0x1a7
000000f0`6e86f920 000007f7`70e685e6 taskmgr!wWinMain+0x44d
000000f0`6e86fde0 000007fe`f601167e taskmgr!CBaseRPCTimeout::Disarm+0x31a
000000f0`6e86fea0 000007fe`f7ee3501 KERNEL32!BaseThreadInitThunk+0x1a
000000f0`6e86fed0 00000000`00000000 ntdll!RtlUserThreadStart+0x1d
```

Note that the small number of Ticks value may be also helpful in finding threads that execute frequently or just recently spent some time executing. Also in kernel memory dumps we won't see user space portion of thread stack. Here we see it because we use a complete memory dump.

11.   Then we check the current process:

```
0: kd> !process -1 3f
PROCESS fffffa8002d74180
    SessionId: 2  Cid: 0ca0    Peb: 7f770b7f000  ParentCid: 0d68
    DirBase: 08818000  ObjectTable: fffff8a001f18d80  HandleCount: <Data Not Accessible>
    Image: Taskmgr.exe
    VadRoot fffffa8003e9d1e0 Vads 239 Clone 0 Private 2297. Modified 243564. Locked 0.
    DeviceMap fffff8a007e2e6a0
    Token                            fffff8a007e3b8c0
    ElapsedTime                      00:10:57.072
    UserTime                         00:00:11.325
    KernelTime                       00:00:26.878
    QuotaPoolUsage[PagedPool]        482336
    QuotaPoolUsage[NonPagedPool]     31280
    Working Set Sizes (now,min,max)  (7136, 50, 345) (28544KB, 200KB, 1380KB)
    PeakWorkingSetSize               7337
    VirtualSize                      216 Mb
    PeakVirtualSize                  343 Mb
    PageFaultCount                   51873
    MemoryPriority                   BACKGROUND
    BasePriority                     8
    CommitCharge                     2905

    PEB at 000007f770b7f000
        InheritedAddressSpace:    No
        ReadImageFileExecOptions: No
        BeingDebugged:            No
        ImageBaseAddress:         000007f770dd0000
        Ldr                       000007fef7ff88a0
        Ldr.Initialized:          Yes
        Ldr.InInitializationOrderModuleList: 000000f06e9b1a10 . 000000f070e6d150
        Ldr.InLoadOrderModuleList:           000000f06e9b1b70 . 000000f070e6d130
        Ldr.InMemoryOrderModuleList:         000000f06e9b1b80 . 000000f070e6d140
                    Base TimeStamp                   Module
              7f770dd0000 50107c26 Jul 26 00:07:18 2012 C:\WINDOWS\system32\taskmgr.exe
              7fef7ec0000 505ab405 Sep 20 07:13:25 2012 C:\WINDOWS\SYSTEM32\ntdll.dll
              7fef6010000 5010a83a Jul 26 03:15:22 2012 C:\WINDOWS\system32\KERNEL32.DLL
              7fef4fd0000 5010ab2d Jul 26 03:27:57 2012 C:\WINDOWS\system32\KERNELBASE.dll
              7fef5810000 50108b7f Jul 26 01:12:47 2012 C:\WINDOWS\system32\GDI32.dll
              7fef56c0000 505a9a92 Sep 20 05:24:50 2012 C:\WINDOWS\system32\USER32.dll
              7fef7820000 5010ac20 Jul 26 03:32:00 2012 C:\WINDOWS\system32\msvcrt.dll
              7fef5500000 50108a1d Jul 26 01:06:53 2012 C:\WINDOWS\system32\OLEAUT32.dll
              7fef52e0000 50108a89 Jul 26 01:08:41 2012 C:\WINDOWS\SYSTEM32\cfgmgr32.dll
              7fef4d90000 501089e8 Jul 26 01:06:00 2012 C:\WINDOWS\SYSTEM32\powrprof.dll
              7fef4080000 5010ac3a Jul 26 03:32:26 2012 C:\WINDOWS\system32\pcwum.dll
              7fef2760000 501084f0 Jul 26 00:44:48 2012 C:\WINDOWS\WinSxS\amd64_microsoft.windows.common-
controls_6595b64144ccf1df_6.0.9200.16384_none_418c2a697189c07f\COMCTL32.dll
              7fef3c80000 505a9614 Sep 20 05:05:40 2012 C:\WINDOWS\system32\UxTheme.dll
              7fef7ad0000 501080dd Jul 26 00:27:25 2012 C:\WINDOWS\system32\SHLWAPI.dll
              7fef6520000 507635b5 Oct 11 03:57:57 2012 C:\WINDOWS\system32\SHELL32.dll
              7fef1750000 5010969b Jul 26 02:00:11 2012 C:\WINDOWS\system32\credui.dll
              7fef2a80000 5010846e Jul 26 00:42:38 2012 C:\WINDOWS\system32\DUser.dll
              7fef21c0000 50108e6a Jul 26 01:25:14 2012 C:\WINDOWS\system32\DUI70.dll
              7feeef40000 505ab1f8 Sep 20 07:04:40 2012 C:\WINDOWS\system32\apphelp.dll
              7fef7b30000 505a9af2 Sep 20 05:26:26 2012 C:\WINDOWS\system32\combase.dll
              7fef5be0000 50108bb9 Jul 26 01:13:45 2012 C:\WINDOWS\system32\RPCRT4.dll
              7fef2ed0000 505a97e0 Sep 20 05:13:20 2012 C:\WINDOWS\system32\SHCORE.DLL
              7fef54c0000 501088ce Jul 26 01:01:18 2012 C:\WINDOWS\system32\IMM32.DLL
              7fef5d20000 50108881 Jul 26 01:00:01 2012 C:\WINDOWS\system32\MSCTF.dll
              7fef4c30000 5010ab50 Jul 26 03:28:32 2012 C:\WINDOWS\system32\CRYPTBASE.dll
              7fef4bd0000 50108a4c Jul 26 01:07:40 2012 C:\WINDOWS\system32\bcryptPrimitives.dll
              7fef2a10000 5010894e Jul 26 01:03:26 2012 C:\WINDOWS\system32\dwmapi.dll
              7fef5340000 50108270 Jul 26 00:34:08 2012 C:\WINDOWS\system32\ole32.dll
              7fef55d0000 50108a41 Jul 26 01:07:29 2012 C:\WINDOWS\SYSTEM32\sechost.dll
              7fef4d00000 5010a79e Jul 26 03:12:46 2012 C:\WINDOWS\system32\WTSAPI32.dll
              7fef4d20000 5010876c Jul 26 00:55:24 2012 C:\WINDOWS\system32\WINSTA.dll
              7feebbe0000 501089d1 Jul 26 01:05:37 2012 C:\WINDOWS\system32\srumapi.dll
              7fef5620000 501081c1 Jul 26 00:31:13 2012 C:\WINDOWS\SYSTEM32\clbcatq.dll
              7fef0b80000 505a9be8 Sep 20 05:30:32 2012 C:\WINDOWS\system32\IPHLPAPI.DLL
              7fef5330000 5010ac24 Jul 26 03:32:04 2012 C:\WINDOWS\system32\NSI.dll
              7fef0b20000 50108ad1 Jul 26 01:09:53 2012 C:\WINDOWS\system32\WINNSI.DLL
              7fef2420000 505a924c Sep 20 04:49:32 2012 C:\Windows\System32\Windows.UI.Immersive.dll
              7fef4d70000 50108a11 Jul 26 01:06:41 2012 C:\WINDOWS\system32\samcli.dll
```

```
       7fef0f50000 50108a13 Jul 26 01:06:43 2012 C:\WINDOWS\system32\SAMLIB.dll
       7fef4100000 50108a19 Jul 26 01:06:49 2012 C:\WINDOWS\system32\netutils.dll
       7fef1980000 505a9949 Sep 20 05:19:21 2012 C:\WINDOWS\system32\WindowsCodecs.dll
       7fef46a0000 50108ad9 Jul 26 01:10:01 2012 C:\WINDOWS\system32\CRYPTSP.dll
       7fef4320000 50108ac4 Jul 26 01:09:40 2012 C:\WINDOWS\system32\rsaenh.dll
       7fef26f0000 5010877b Jul 26 00:55:39 2012 C:\WINDOWS\system32\OLEACC.dll
       7fef06b0000 505a9bdc Sep 20 05:30:20 2012 C:\WINDOWS\system32\dhcpcsvc6.DLL
       7fef5b80000 50108abf Jul 26 01:09:35 2012 C:\WINDOWS\system32\WS2_32.dll
       7fef06e0000 505a9b9c Sep 20 05:29:16 2012 C:\WINDOWS\system32\dhcpcsvc.DLL
       7fef1740000 5010ac6c Jul 26 03:33:16 2012 C:\WINDOWS\system32\wlanutil.dll
       7fef03b0000 5063dc6b Sep 27 05:56:11 2012 C:\WINDOWS\system32\wlanapi.dll
       7fef37e0000 501089ec Jul 26 01:06:04 2012 C:\WINDOWS\system32\wkscli.dll
       7fef2e90000 50108843 Jul 26 00:58:59 2012 C:\WINDOWS\system32\XmlLite.dll
       7fef4df0000 50108ab9 Jul 26 01:09:29 2012 C:\WINDOWS\system32\profapi.dll
       7feed830000 501080ee Jul 26 00:27:42 2012 C:\Windows\System32\thumbcache.dll
       7fef78d0000 5010a732 Jul 26 03:10:58 2012 C:\WINDOWS\SYSTEM32\advapi32.dll
       7fef0cb0000 505a95dd Sep 20 05:04:45 2012 C:\Windows\System32\PROPSYS.dll
       7feeb9d0000 505aafdf Sep 20 06:55:43 2012 C:\Windows\System32\actxprxy.dll
       7fef2580000 501089b7 Jul 26 01:05:11 2012 C:\WINDOWS\system32\Bcp47Langs.dll
       7fef48f0000 50108aca Jul 26 01:09:46 2012 C:\WINDOWS\SYSTEM32\bcrypt.dll
       7feeeb70000 50107f98 Jul 26 00:22:00 2012 C:\Windows\System32\MrmCoreR.dll
       7fef7d60000 505a9257 Sep 20 04:49:43 2012 C:\WINDOWS\system32\urlmon.dll
       7fef6160000 505aa96c Sep 20 06:28:12 2012 C:\WINDOWS\system32\iertutil.dll
       7fef5950000 505a9365 Sep 20 04:54:13 2012 C:\WINDOWS\system32\WININET.dll
       7fef5e40000 501080fc Jul 26 00:27:56 2012 C:\WINDOWS\system32\SETUPAPI.dll
       7fef50d0000 5010898b Jul 26 01:04:27 2012 C:\WINDOWS\system32\DEVOBJ.dll
       7fee8a40000 505a9555 Sep 20 05:02:29 2012 C:\Windows\System32\twinapi.dll
       7fef31b0000 50108834 Jul 26 00:58:44 2012 C:\WINDOWS\system32\dbghelp.dll
       7feeb770000 50109564 Jul 26 01:55:00 2012 C:\WINDOWS\System32\cscui.dll
       7fef30c0000 5010a9be Jul 26 03:21:50 2012 C:\WINDOWS\System32\CSCDLL.dll
       7fef30d0000 5010a183 Jul 26 02:46:43 2012 C:\WINDOWS\System32\cscobj.dll
       7fef4420000 50108843 Jul 26 00:58:59 2012 C:\WINDOWS\System32\USERENV.dll
       7feec150000 501089ad Jul 26 01:05:01 2012 C:\WINDOWS\system32\CSCAPI.dll
       7fee72f0000 50109745 Jul 26 02:03:01 2012 C:\Windows\System32\EhStorShell.dll
       7feef920000 501089fe Jul 26 01:06:22 2012 C:\WINDOWS\SYSTEM32\ntmarta.dll
       7feeb240000 501081d7 Jul 26 00:31:35 2012 C:\WINDOWS\SYSTEM32\profext.dll
       7fef4ba0000 505a9be9 Sep 20 05:30:33 2012 C:\WINDOWS\system32\SSPICLI.DLL
       7fef3320000 50108655 Jul 26 00:50:45 2012 C:\Windows\System32\taskschd.dll
SubSystemData:     0000000000000000
ProcessHeap:       000000f06e9b0000
ProcessParameters: 000000f06e9b11e0
CurrentDirectory:  'C:\WINDOWS\system32\'
WindowTitle: 'C:\WINDOWS\system32\taskmgr.exe'
ImageFile:   'C:\WINDOWS\system32\taskmgr.exe'
CommandLine: '"C:\WINDOWS\system32\taskmgr.exe" /4'
DllPath:     '< Name not readable >'
Environment: 000000f06e9b0860
    ALLUSERSPROFILE=C:\ProgramData
    APPDATA=C:\Users\Dmitry\AppData\Roaming
    CommonProgramFiles=C:\Program Files\Common Files
    CommonProgramFiles(x86)=C:\Program Files (x86)\Common Files
    CommonProgramW6432=C:\Program Files\Common Files
    COMPUTERNAME=MACAIR1
    ComSpec=C:\WINDOWS\system32\cmd.exe
    FP_NO_HOST_CHECK=NO
    HOMEDRIVE=C:
    HOMEPATH=\Users\Dmitry
    LOCALAPPDATA=C:\Users\Dmitry\AppData\Local
    LOGONSERVER=\\MicrosoftAccount
    NUMBER_OF_PROCESSORS=2
    OS=Windows_NT
    Path=C:\WINDOWS\system32;C:\WINDOWS;C:\WINDOWS\System32\Wbem;C:\WINDOWS\System32\WindowsPowerShell\v1.0\
    PATHEXT=.COM;.EXE;.BAT;.CMD;.VBS;.VBE;.JS;.JSE;.WSF;.WSH;.MSC
    PROCESSOR_ARCHITECTURE=AMD64
    PROCESSOR_IDENTIFIER=Intel64 Family 6 Model 15 Stepping 11, GenuineIntel
    PROCESSOR_LEVEL=6
    PROCESSOR_REVISION=0f0b
    ProgramData=C:\ProgramData
    ProgramFiles=C:\Program Files
    ProgramFiles(x86)=C:\Program Files (x86)
    ProgramW6432=C:\Program Files
    PSModulePath=C:\WINDOWS\system32\WindowsPowerShell\v1.0\Modules\
    PUBLIC=C:\Users\Public
    SystemDrive=C:
    SystemRoot=C:\WINDOWS
    TEMP=C:\Users\Dmitry\AppData\Local\Temp
```

```
TMP=C:\Users\Dmitry\AppData\Local\Temp
USERDOMAIN=MACAIR1
USERDOMAIN_ROAMINGPROFILE=MACAIR1
USERNAME=Dmitry
USERPROFILE=C:\Users\Dmitry
windir=C:\WINDOWS


    THREAD fffffa8003db4740  Cid 0ca0.03e0  Teb: 000007f770b7d000 Win32Thread: fffff90104094830 RUNNING on
processor 0
    Not impersonating
    DeviceMap                    fffff8a007e2e6a0
    Owning Process               fffffa8002d74180       Image:         Taskmgr.exe
    Attached Process             N/A         Image:         N/A
    Wait Start TickCount         15741128    Ticks: 0
    Context Switch Count         31359       IdealProcessor: 0
    UserTime                     00:00:09.859
    KernelTime                   00:00:07.394
    Win32 Start Address taskmgr!wWinMainCRTStartup (0x000007f770e68688)
    Stack Init fffff88015925dd0 Current fffff88015925800
    Base fffff88015926000 Limit fffff88015920000 Call 0
    Priority 13 BasePriority 9 UnusualBoost 0 ForegroundBoost 2 IoPriority 2 PagePriority 5
    Child-SP          RetAddr           Call Site
    fffff880`15925ae8 fffff802`b400f0dd nt!KeBugCheckEx
    fffff880`15925af0 fffff802`b3ea8f6d nt!PspCatchCriticalBreak+0xad
    fffff880`15925b30 fffff802`b3ea8019 nt! ?? ::NNGAKEGL::`string'+0x46f60
    fffff880`15925b90 fffff802`b3ea7e52 nt!PspTerminateProcess+0x6d
    fffff880`15925bd0 fffff802`b3b02d53 nt!NtTerminateProcess+0x9e
    fffff880`15925c40 000007fe`f7ec2eaa nt!KiSystemServiceCopyEnd+0x13 (TrapFrame @ fffff880`15925c40)
    000000f0`6e86f3e8 000007fe`f4ff1295 ntdll!NtTerminateProcess+0xa
    000000f0`6e86f3f0 000007f7`70e012ba KERNELBASE!TerminateProcess+0x25
    000000f0`6e86f420 000007f7`70df3698 taskmgr!WdcProcessMonitor::OnProcessCommand+0x1b6
    000000f0`6e86f4b0 000007f7`70df55bb taskmgr!WdcListView::OnProcessCommand+0x1e0
    000000f0`6e86f5a0 000007f7`70df5b47 taskmgr!WdcListView::OnCommand+0x123
    000000f0`6e86f5f0 000007fe`f2227239 taskmgr!WdcListView::OnMessage+0x287
    000000f0`6e86f710 000007fe`f2a82d23 DUI70!DirectUI::HWNDHost::_CtrlWndProc+0xa1
    000000f0`6e86f770 000007fe`f56c171e DUser!WndBridge::RawWndProc+0x73
    000000f0`6e86f7e0 000007fe`f56c14d7 USER32!UserCallWinProcCheckWow+0x13a
    000000f0`6e86f8a0 000007f7`70e1b0e1 USER32!DispatchMessageWorker+0x1a7
    000000f0`6e86f920 000007f7`70e685e6 taskmgr!wWinMain+0x44d
    000000f0`6e86fde0 000007fe`f601167e taskmgr!CBaseRPCTimeout::Disarm+0x31a
    000000f0`6e86fea0 000007fe`f7ee3501 KERNEL32!BaseThreadInitThunk+0x1a
    000000f0`6e86fed0 00000000`00000000 ntdll!RtlUserThreadStart+0x1d


    THREAD fffffa80039dfb00  Cid 0ca0.0564  Teb: 000007f770b7b000 Win32Thread: fffff90103f44710 WAIT:
(UserRequest) UserMode Non-Alertable
        fffffa8003665fe0  SynchronizationEvent
        fffffa8002cc1d30  SynchronizationEvent
    Not impersonating
    DeviceMap                    fffff8a007e2e6a0
    Owning Process               fffffa8002d74180       Image:         Taskmgr.exe
    Attached Process             N/A         Image:         N/A
    Wait Start TickCount         15699020    Ticks: 42108 (0:00:10:56.889)
    Context Switch Count         4           IdealProcessor: 0
    UserTime                     00:00:00.000
    KernelTime                   00:00:00.000
    Win32 Start Address msvcrt!endthreadex (0x000007fef7845e10)
    Stack Init fffff880155d5dd0 Current fffff880155d5180
    Base fffff880155d6000 Limit fffff880155d0000 Call 0
    Priority 9 BasePriority 8 UnusualBoost 0 ForegroundBoost 0 IoPriority 2 PagePriority 5
    Kernel stack not resident.
    Child-SP          RetAddr           Call Site
    fffff880`155d51c0 fffff802`b3b2d99c nt!KiSwapContext+0x76
    fffff880`155d5300 fffff802`b3b293cd nt!KiCommitThreadWait+0x23c
    fffff880`155d53c0 fffff802`b3eca2ac nt!KeWaitForMultipleObjects+0x25d
    fffff880`155d5470 fffff802`b3eca723 nt!ObWaitForMultipleObjects+0x29c
    fffff880`155d5980 fffff802`b3b02d53 nt!NtWaitForMultipleObjects+0xe3
    fffff880`155d5bd0 000007fe`f7ec319b nt!KiSystemServiceCopyEnd+0x13 (TrapFrame @ fffff880`155d5c40)
    000000f0`7025f938 000007fe`f4fd12c6 ntdll!NtWaitForMultipleObjects+0xa
    000000f0`7025f940 000007fe`f56c2c83 KERNELBASE!WaitForMultipleObjectsEx+0xe5
    000000f0`7025fc20 000007fe`f2aa160b USER32!MsgWaitForMultipleObjectsEx+0x144
    000000f0`7025fcd0 000007fe`f2aa15db DUser!CoreSC::xwProcessNL+0x5bb
    000000f0`7025fda0 000007fe`f2aa14fe DUser!GetMessageExA+0x6b
    000000f0`7025fdf0 000007fe`f782707b DUser!ResourceManager::SharedThreadProc+0xfe
    000000f0`7025fe80 000007fe`f7845e6d msvcrt!endthreadex+0xcb
    000000f0`7025feb0 000007fe`f601167e msvcrt!endthreadex+0xac
```

141

```
      000000f0`7025fee0 000007fe`f7ee3501 KERNEL32!BaseThreadInitThunk+0x1a
      000000f0`7025ff10 00000000`00000000 ntdll!RtlUserThreadStart+0x1d
      THREAD fffffa8003253b00  Cid 0ca0.0d64  Teb: 000007f770b79000 Win32Thread: 0000000000000000 WAIT:
(UserRequest) UserMode Non-Alertable
          fffffa800307aca0  NotificationEvent
          fffffa80036357a0  SynchronizationEvent
      Not impersonating
      DeviceMap                fffff8a007e2e6a0
      Owning Process           fffffa8002d74180     Image:        Taskmgr.exe
      Attached Process         N/A          Image:        N/A
      Wait Start TickCount     15741108     Ticks: 20 (0:00:00.312)
      Context Switch Count     653          IdealProcessor: 0
      UserTime                 00:00:00.000
      KernelTime               00:00:00.000
      Win32 Start Address taskmgr!WdcDataMonitor::UpdateThread (0x000007f770dfdf1c)
      Stack Init fffff880159dadd0 Current fffff880159da180
      Base fffff880159db000 Limit fffff880159d5000 Call 0
      Priority 11 BasePriority 8 UnusualBoost 0 ForegroundBoost 2 IoPriority 2 PagePriority 5
      Child-SP          RetAddr           Call Site
      fffff880`159da1c0 fffff802`b3b2d99c nt!KiSwapContext+0x76
      fffff880`159da300 fffff802`b3b293cd nt!KiCommitThreadWait+0x23c
      fffff880`159da3c0 fffff802`b3eca2ac nt!KeWaitForMultipleObjects+0x25d
      fffff880`159da470 fffff802`b3eca723 nt!ObWaitForMultipleObjects+0x29c
      fffff880`159da980 fffff802`b3b02d53 nt!NtWaitForMultipleObjects+0xe3
      fffff880`159dabd0 000007fe`f7ec319b nt!KiSystemServiceCopyEnd+0x13 (TrapFrame @ fffff880`159dac40)
      000000f0`7238f4f8 000007fe`f4fd12c6 ntdll!NtWaitForMultipleObjects+0xa
      000000f0`7238f500 000007fe`f6011292 KERNELBASE!WaitForMultipleObjectsEx+0xe5
      000000f0`7238f7e0 000007f7`70dfdc81 KERNEL32!WaitForMultipleObjects+0x12
      000000f0`7238f820 000007f7`70dfdf54 taskmgr!WdcDataMonitor::DoUpdates+0x3d
      000000f0`7238f860 000007fe`f601167e taskmgr!WdcDataMonitor::UpdateThread+0x38
      000000f0`7238f8a0 000007fe`f7ee3501 KERNEL32!BaseThreadInitThunk+0x1a
      000000f0`7238f8d0 00000000`00000000 ntdll!RtlUserThreadStart+0x1d

      THREAD fffffa8003b45b00  Cid 0ca0.0824  Teb: 000007f770b77000 Win32Thread: fffff90103f5cb90 WAIT:
(UserRequest) UserMode Non-Alertable
          fffffa8003612250  NotificationEvent
          fffffa8002cb6890  SynchronizationEvent
      Not impersonating
      DeviceMap                fffff8a007e2e6a0
      Owning Process           fffffa8002d74180     Image:        Taskmgr.exe
      Attached Process         N/A          Image:        N/A
      Wait Start TickCount     15741108     Ticks: 20 (0:00:00.312)
      Context Switch Count     2818         IdealProcessor: 0
      UserTime                 00:00:00.031
      KernelTime               00:00:00.124
      Win32 Start Address taskmgr!WdcDataMonitor::UpdateThread (0x000007f770dfdf1c)
      Stack Init fffff8801595ddd0 Current fffff8801595d180
      Base fffff8801595e000 Limit fffff88015958000 Call 0
      Priority 13 BasePriority 10 UnusualBoost 0 ForegroundBoost 2 IoPriority 2 PagePriority 5
      Child-SP          RetAddr           Call Site
      fffff880`1595d1c0 fffff802`b3b2d99c nt!KiSwapContext+0x76
      fffff880`1595d300 fffff802`b3b293cd nt!KiCommitThreadWait+0x23c
      fffff880`1595d3c0 fffff802`b3eca2ac nt!KeWaitForMultipleObjects+0x25d
      fffff880`1595d470 fffff802`b3eca723 nt!ObWaitForMultipleObjects+0x29c
      fffff880`1595d980 fffff802`b3b02d53 nt!NtWaitForMultipleObjects+0xe3
      fffff880`1595dbd0 000007fe`f7ec319b nt!KiSystemServiceCopyEnd+0x13 (TrapFrame @ fffff880`1595dc40)
      000000f0`7240f9f8 000007fe`f4fd12c6 ntdll!NtWaitForMultipleObjects+0xa
      000000f0`7240fa00 000007fe`f6011292 KERNELBASE!WaitForMultipleObjectsEx+0xe5
      000000f0`7240fce0 000007f7`70dfdc81 KERNEL32!WaitForMultipleObjects+0x12
      000000f0`7240fd20 000007f7`70dfdf54 taskmgr!WdcDataMonitor::DoUpdates+0x3d
      000000f0`7240fd60 000007fe`f601167e taskmgr!WdcDataMonitor::UpdateThread+0x38
      000000f0`7240fda0 000007fe`f7ee3501 KERNEL32!BaseThreadInitThunk+0x1a
      000000f0`7240fdd0 00000000`00000000 ntdll!RtlUserThreadStart+0x1d

      THREAD fffffa80018eab00  Cid 0ca0.0888  Teb: 000007f770b75000 Win32Thread: fffff90103ff8b90 WAIT:
(UserRequest) UserMode Non-Alertable
          fffffa8001c81ca0  NotificationEvent
          fffffa80036767a0  SynchronizationEvent
      Not impersonating
      DeviceMap                fffff8a007e2e6a0
      Owning Process           fffffa8002d74180     Image:        Taskmgr.exe
      Attached Process         N/A          Image:        N/A
      Wait Start TickCount     15741108     Ticks: 20 (0:00:00.312)
      Context Switch Count     4747         IdealProcessor: 0
      UserTime                 00:00:00.000
      KernelTime               00:00:00.078
```

```
Win32 Start Address taskmgr!WdcDataMonitor::UpdateThread (0x000007f770dfdf1c)
Stack Init fffff8801594fdd0 Current fffff8801594f180
Base fffff88015950000 Limit fffff8801594a000 Call 0
Priority 11 BasePriority 8 UnusualBoost 0 ForegroundBoost 2 IoPriority 2 PagePriority 5
Child-SP          RetAddr           Call Site
fffff880`1594f1c0 fffff802`b3b2d99c nt!KiSwapContext+0x76
fffff880`1594f300 fffff802`b3b293cd nt!KiCommitThreadWait+0x23c
fffff880`1594f3c0 fffff802`b3eca2ac nt!KeWaitForMultipleObjects+0x25d
fffff880`1594f470 fffff802`b3eca723 nt!ObWaitForMultipleObjects+0x29c
fffff880`1594f980 fffff802`b3b02d53 nt!NtWaitForMultipleObjects+0xe3
fffff880`1594fbd0 000007fe`f7ec319b nt!KiSystemServiceCopyEnd+0x13 (TrapFrame @ fffff880`1594fc40)
000000f0`7248f548 000007fe`f4fd12c6 ntdll!NtWaitForMultipleObjects+0xa
000000f0`7248f550 000007fe`f6011292 KERNELBASE!WaitForMultipleObjectsEx+0xe5
000000f0`7248f830 000007f7`70dfdc81 KERNEL32!WaitForMultipleObjects+0x12
000000f0`7248f870 000007f7`70dfdf54 taskmgr!WdcDataMonitor::DoUpdates+0x3d
000000f0`7248f8b0 000007fe`f601167e taskmgr!WdcDataMonitor::UpdateThread+0x38
000000f0`7248f8f0 000007fe`f7ee3501 KERNEL32!BaseThreadInitThunk+0x1a
000000f0`7248f920 00000000`00000000 ntdll!RtlUserThreadStart+0x1d

   THREAD fffffa80033f63c0 Cid 0ca0.0e28 Teb: 000007f770b73000 Win32Thread: fffff901006bb710 WAIT:
(UserRequest) UserMode Non-Alertable
       fffffa80040844b0 NotificationEvent
       fffffa8002e58710 SynchronizationEvent
   Not impersonating
   DeviceMap                fffff8a007e2e6a0
   Owning Process           fffffa8002d74180     Image:         Taskmgr.exe
   Attached Process         N/A          Image:        N/A
   Wait Start TickCount     15699023     Ticks: 42105 (0:00:10:56.842)
   Context Switch Count     6            IdealProcessor: 0
   UserTime                 00:00:00.000
   KernelTime               00:00:00.000
   Win32 Start Address taskmgr!WdcDataMonitor::UpdateThread (0x000007f770dfdf1c)
   Stack Init fffff880159ccdd0 Current fffff880159cc180
   Base fffff880159cd000 Limit fffff880159c7000 Call 0
   Priority 11 BasePriority 8 UnusualBoost 0 ForegroundBoost 2 IoPriority 2 PagePriority 5
   Kernel stack not resident.
   Child-SP          RetAddr           Call Site
   fffff880`159cc1c0 fffff802`b3b2d99c nt!KiSwapContext+0x76
   fffff880`159cc300 fffff802`b3b293cd nt!KiCommitThreadWait+0x23c
   fffff880`159cc3c0 fffff802`b3eca2ac nt!KeWaitForMultipleObjects+0x25d
   fffff880`159cc470 fffff802`b3eca723 nt!ObWaitForMultipleObjects+0x29c
   fffff880`159cc980 fffff802`b3b02d53 nt!NtWaitForMultipleObjects+0xe3
   fffff880`159ccbd0 000007fe`f7ec319b nt!KiSystemServiceCopyEnd+0x13 (TrapFrame @ fffff880`159ccc40)
   000000f0`7250f448 000007fe`f4fd12c6 ntdll!NtWaitForMultipleObjects+0xa
   000000f0`7250f450 000007fe`f56c2c83 KERNELBASE!WaitForMultipleObjectsEx+0xe5
   000000f0`7250f730 000007f7`70e43c03 USER32!MsgWaitForMultipleObjectsEx+0x144
   000000f0`7250f7e0 000007f7`70dfdf54 taskmgr!WdcAppHistoryMonitor::DoUpdates+0x3f
   000000f0`7250f850 000007fe`f601167e taskmgr!WdcDataMonitor::UpdateThread+0x38
   000000f0`7250f890 000007fe`f7ee3501 KERNEL32!BaseThreadInitThunk+0x1a
   000000f0`7250f8c0 00000000`00000000 ntdll!RtlUserThreadStart+0x1d

   THREAD fffffa8001f075c0 Cid 0ca0.06d4 Teb: 000007f770a4c000 Win32Thread: fffff901040b5b90 WAIT:
(UserRequest) UserMode Non-Alertable
       fffffa8002d94de0 NotificationEvent
       fffffa800371fc70 SynchronizationEvent
       fffffa8002d704f0 SynchronizationEvent
   Not impersonating
   DeviceMap                fffff8a007e2e6a0
   Owning Process           fffffa8002d74180     Image:         Taskmgr.exe
   Attached Process         N/A          Image:        N/A
   Wait Start TickCount     15741108     Ticks: 20 (0:00:00:00.312)
   Context Switch Count     19727        IdealProcessor: 0
   UserTime                 00:00:00.000
   KernelTime               00:00:00.078
   Win32 Start Address taskmgr!TmTraceControl::IncrementThread (0x000007f770df1fc4)
   Stack Init fffff880159efdd0 Current fffff880159ef180
   Base fffff880159f0000 Limit fffff880159ea000 Call 0
   Priority 11 BasePriority 8 UnusualBoost 0 ForegroundBoost 2 IoPriority 2 PagePriority 5
   Child-SP          RetAddr           Call Site
   fffff880`159ef1c0 fffff802`b3b2d99c nt!KiSwapContext+0x76
   fffff880`159ef300 fffff802`b3b293cd nt!KiCommitThreadWait+0x23c
   fffff880`159ef3c0 fffff802`b3eca2ac nt!KeWaitForMultipleObjects+0x25d
   fffff880`159ef470 fffff802`b3eca723 nt!ObWaitForMultipleObjects+0x29c
   fffff880`159ef980 fffff802`b3b02d53 nt!NtWaitForMultipleObjects+0xe3
   fffff880`159efbd0 000007fe`f7ec319b nt!KiSystemServiceCopyEnd+0x13 (TrapFrame @ fffff880`159efc40)
   000000f0`7260fb58 000007fe`f4fd12c6 ntdll!NtWaitForMultipleObjects+0xa
```

```
000000f0`7260fb60 000007fe`f6011292 KERNELBASE!WaitForMultipleObjectsEx+0xe5
000000f0`7260fe40 000007f7`70df2118 KERNEL32!WaitForMultipleObjects+0x12
000000f0`7260fe80 000007fe`f601167e taskmgr!TmTraceControl::IncrementThreadInternal+0x148
000000f0`7260ff30 000007fe`f7ee3501 KERNEL32!BaseThreadInitThunk+0x1a
000000f0`7260ff60 00000000`00000000 ntdll!RtlUserThreadStart+0x1d

        THREAD fffffa8003f23b00  Cid 0ca0.0db8  Teb: 000007f770a4a000 Win32Thread: fffff90103fa5610 WAIT:
(UserRequest) UserMode Non-Alertable
            fffffa80036d1420  NotificationEvent
            fffffa80036c8cb0  SynchronizationEvent
        Not impersonating
        DeviceMap                 fffff8a007e2e6a0
        Owning Process            fffffa8002d74180      Image:         Taskmgr.exe
        Attached Process          N/A            Image:         N/A
        Wait Start TickCount      15741106       Ticks: 22 (0:00:00.343)
        Context Switch Count      811            IdealProcessor: 0
        UserTime                  00:00:00.000
        KernelTime                00:00:00.000
        Win32 Start Address taskmgr!CRUMAPIHelper::SrumThread (0x000007f770e0db10)
        Stack Init fffff88015e0ddd0 Current fffff88015e0d180
        Base fffff88015e0e000 Limit fffff88015e08000 Call 0
        Priority 11 BasePriority 8 UnusualBoost 0 ForegroundBoost 2 IoPriority 2 PagePriority 5
        Child-SP          RetAddr           Call Site
        fffff880`15e0d1c0 fffff802`b3b2d99c nt!KiSwapContext+0x76
        fffff880`15e0d300 fffff802`b3b293cd nt!KiCommitThreadWait+0x23c
        fffff880`15e0d3c0 fffff802`b3eca2ac nt!KeWaitForMultipleObjects+0x25d
        fffff880`15e0d470 fffff802`b3eca723 nt!ObWaitForMultipleObjects+0x29c
        fffff880`15e0d980 fffff802`b3b02d53 nt!NtWaitForMultipleObjects+0xe3
        fffff880`15e0dbd0 000007fe`f7ec319b nt!KiSystemServiceCopyEnd+0x13 (TrapFrame @ fffff880`15e0dc40)
        000000f0`7268f4b8 000007fe`f4fd12c6 ntdll!NtWaitForMultipleObjects+0xa
        000000f0`7268f4c0 000007fe`f56c2c83 KERNELBASE!WaitForMultipleObjectsEx+0xe5
        000000f0`7268f7a0 000007f7`70e0dd3a USER32!MsgWaitForMultipleObjectsEx+0x144
        000000f0`7268f850 000007fe`f601167e taskmgr!CRUMAPIHelper::SrumThread+0x22a
        000000f0`7268f940 000007fe`f7ee3501 KERNEL32!BaseThreadInitThunk+0x1a
        000000f0`7268f970 00000000`00000000 ntdll!RtlUserThreadStart+0x1d

        THREAD fffffa800404a080  Cid 0ca0.0c88  Teb: 000007f770a48000 Win32Thread: fffff901006b9710 WAIT:
(UserRequest) UserMode Non-Alertable
            fffffa8001c95500  NotificationEvent
            fffffa8003f37990  SynchronizationEvent
            fffffa800409e6c0  SynchronizationEvent
        Not impersonating
        DeviceMap                 fffff8a007e2e6a0
        Owning Process            fffffa8002d74180      Image:         Taskmgr.exe
        Attached Process          N/A            Image:         N/A
        Wait Start TickCount      15699025       Ticks: 42103 (0:00:10:56.811)
        Context Switch Count      7              IdealProcessor: 0
        UserTime                  00:00:00.000
        KernelTime                00:00:00.000
        Win32 Start Address taskmgr!WdcDataMonitor::UpdateThread (0x000007f770dfdf1c)
        Stack Init fffff88015e22dd0 Current fffff88015e22180
        Base fffff88015e23000 Limit fffff88015e1d000 Call 0
        Priority 11 BasePriority 8 UnusualBoost 0 ForegroundBoost 2 IoPriority 2 PagePriority 5
        Kernel stack not resident.
        Child-SP          RetAddr           Call Site
        fffff880`15e221c0 fffff802`b3b2d99c nt!KiSwapContext+0x76
        fffff880`15e22300 fffff802`b3b293cd nt!KiCommitThreadWait+0x23c
        fffff880`15e223c0 fffff802`b3eca2ac nt!KeWaitForMultipleObjects+0x25d
        fffff880`15e22470 fffff802`b3eca723 nt!ObWaitForMultipleObjects+0x29c
        fffff880`15e22980 fffff802`b3b02d53 nt!NtWaitForMultipleObjects+0xe3
        fffff880`15e22bd0 000007fe`f7ec319b nt!KiSystemServiceCopyEnd+0x13 (TrapFrame @ fffff880`15e22c40)
        000000f0`7270f448 000007fe`f4fd12c6 ntdll!NtWaitForMultipleObjects+0xa
        000000f0`7270f450 000007fe`f56c2c83 KERNELBASE!WaitForMultipleObjectsEx+0xe5
        000000f0`7270f730 000007f7`70e475fd USER32!MsgWaitForMultipleObjectsEx+0x144
        000000f0`7270f7e0 000007f7`70dfdf54 taskmgr!WdcUserMonitor::DoUpdates+0x65
        000000f0`7270f870 000007fe`f601167e taskmgr!WdcDataMonitor::UpdateThread+0x38
        000000f0`7270f8b0 000007fe`f7ee3501 KERNEL32!BaseThreadInitThunk+0x1a
        000000f0`7270f8e0 00000000`00000000 ntdll!RtlUserThreadStart+0x1d

        THREAD fffffa8001de0b00  Cid 0ca0.0c84  Teb: 000007f770a46000 Win32Thread: fffff9010065f010 WAIT:
(UserRequest) UserMode Non-Alertable
            fffffa800372dc50  NotificationEvent
            fffffa80041961c0  SynchronizationEvent
        Not impersonating
        DeviceMap                 fffff8a007e2e6a0
        Owning Process            fffffa8002d74180      Image:         Taskmgr.exe
```

```
    Attached Process        N/A             Image:          N/A
    Wait Start TickCount    15741108        Ticks: 20 (0:00:00:00.312)
    Context Switch Count    2887            IdealProcessor: 0
    UserTime                00:00:00.015
    KernelTime              00:00:00.000
    Win32 Start Address taskmgr!WdcDataMonitor::UpdateThread (0x000007f770dfdf1c)
    Stack Init fffff88015e29dd0 Current fffff88015e29180
    Base fffff88015e2a000 Limit fffff88015e24000 Call 0
    Priority 11 BasePriority 8 UnusualBoost 0 ForegroundBoost 2 IoPriority 2 PagePriority 5
    Child-SP          RetAddr           Call Site
    fffff880`15e291c0 fffff802`b3b2d99c nt!KiSwapContext+0x76
    fffff880`15e29300 fffff802`b3b293cd nt!KiCommitThreadWait+0x23c
    fffff880`15e293c0 fffff802`b3eca2ac nt!KeWaitForMultipleObjects+0x25d
    fffff880`15e29470 fffff802`b3eca723 nt!ObWaitForMultipleObjects+0x29c
    fffff880`15e29980 fffff802`b3b02d53 nt!NtWaitForMultipleObjects+0xe3
    fffff880`15e29bd0 000007fe`f7ec319b nt!KiSystemServiceCopyEnd+0x13 (TrapFrame @ fffff880`15e29c40)
    000000f0`7278f348 000007fe`f4fd12c6 ntdll!NtWaitForMultipleObjects+0xa
    000000f0`7278f350 000007fe`f56c2c83 KERNELBASE!WaitForMultipleObjectsEx+0xe5
    000000f0`7278f630 000007f7`70e43c03 USER32!MsgWaitForMultipleObjectsEx+0x144
    000000f0`7278f6e0 000007f7`70dfdf54 taskmgr!WdcAppHistoryMonitor::DoUpdates+0x3f
    000000f0`7278f750 000007fe`f601167e taskmgr!WdcDataMonitor::UpdateThread+0x38
    000000f0`7278f790 000007fe`f7ee3501 KERNEL32!BaseThreadInitThunk+0x1a
    000000f0`7278f7c0 00000000`00000000 ntdll!RtlUserThreadStart+0x1d


    THREAD fffffa80039d3b00  Cid 0ca0.07e4  Teb: 000007f770a44000 Win32Thread: fffff901040e2530 WAIT:
(UserRequest) UserMode Non-Alertable
        fffffa8002067370  SynchronizationEvent
        fffffa8003f46e10  NotificationEvent
        fffffa800205cce0  SynchronizationEvent
        fffffa8003826490  SynchronizationEvent
        fffffa8003ee0dc0  SynchronizationEvent
        fffffa80030959b8  NotificationEvent
        fffffa800362fd18  NotificationEvent
    IRP List:
        fffffa800211ac10: (0006,03e8) Flags: 00060000  Mdl: 00000000
        fffffa800198a360: (0006,03e8) Flags: 00060000  Mdl: 00000000
    Not impersonating
    DeviceMap               fffff8a007e2e6a0
    Owning Process          fffffa8002d74180        Image:          Taskmgr.exe
    Attached Process        N/A             Image:          N/A
    Wait Start TickCount    15699048        Ticks: 42080 (0:00:10:56.452)
    Context Switch Count    40              IdealProcessor: 0
    UserTime                00:00:00.000
    KernelTime              00:00:00.000
    Win32 Start Address taskmgr!WdcDataMonitor::UpdateThread (0x000007f770dfdf1c)
    Stack Init fffff88015e3edd0 Current fffff88015e3e180
    Base fffff88015e3f000 Limit fffff88015e39000 Call 0
    Priority 11 BasePriority 8 UnusualBoost 0 ForegroundBoost 2 IoPriority 2 PagePriority 5
    Kernel stack not resident.
    Child-SP          RetAddr           Call Site
    fffff880`15e3e1c0 fffff802`b3b2d99c nt!KiSwapContext+0x76
    fffff880`15e3e300 fffff802`b3b293cd nt!KiCommitThreadWait+0x23c
    fffff880`15e3e3c0 fffff802`b3eca2ac nt!KeWaitForMultipleObjects+0x25d
    fffff880`15e3e470 fffff802`b3eca723 nt!ObWaitForMultipleObjects+0x29c
    fffff880`15e3e980 fffff802`b3b02d53 nt!NtWaitForMultipleObjects+0xe3
    fffff880`15e3ebd0 000007fe`f7ec319b nt!KiSystemServiceCopyEnd+0x13 (TrapFrame @ fffff880`15e3ec40)
    000000f0`7280f588 000007fe`f4fd12c6 ntdll!NtWaitForMultipleObjects+0xa
    000000f0`7280f590 000007fe`f6011292 KERNELBASE!WaitForMultipleObjectsEx+0xe5
    000000f0`7280f870 000007f7`70e57ed5 KERNEL32!WaitForMultipleObjects+0x12
    000000f0`7280f8b0 000007f7`70dfdf54 taskmgr!WdcStartupMonitor::DoUpdates+0x2ad
    000000f0`7280fdc0 000007fe`f601167e taskmgr!WdcDataMonitor::UpdateThread+0x38
    000000f0`7280fe00 000007fe`f7ee3501 KERNEL32!BaseThreadInitThunk+0x1a
    000000f0`7280fe30 00000000`00000000 ntdll!RtlUserThreadStart+0x1d


    THREAD fffffa8002d01200  Cid 0ca0.0a9c  Teb: 000007f770a42000 Win32Thread: fffff901040f7b90 WAIT: (WrQueue)
UserMode Alertable
        fffffa8001e75ec0  QueueObject
    Not impersonating
    DeviceMap               fffff8a007e2e6a0
    Owning Process          fffffa8002d74180        Image:          Taskmgr.exe
    Attached Process        N/A             Image:          N/A
    Wait Start TickCount    15740913        Ticks: 215 (0:00:00:03.354)
    Context Switch Count    565             IdealProcessor: 0
    UserTime                00:00:00.000
    KernelTime              00:00:00.000
    Win32 Start Address ntdll!TppWorkerThread (0x000007fef7ee38c0)
```

145

```
Stack Init fffff88015e4cdd0 Current fffff88015e4c760
Base fffff88015e4d000 Limit fffff88015e47000 Call 0
Priority 10 BasePriority 8 UnusualBoost 0 ForegroundBoost 2 IoPriority 2 PagePriority 5
Child-SP          RetAddr           Call Site
fffff880`15e4c7a0 fffff802`b3b2d99c nt!KiSwapContext+0x76
fffff880`15e4c8e0 fffff802`b3b38ddb nt!KiCommitThreadWait+0x23c
fffff880`15e4c9a0 fffff802`b3ed0b6c nt!KeRemoveQueueEx+0x26b
fffff880`15e4ca50 fffff802`b3b434d5 nt!IoRemoveIoCompletion+0x4c
fffff880`15e4cae0 fffff802`b3b02d53 nt!NtWaitForWorkViaWorkerFactory+0x295
fffff880`15e4cc40 000007fe`f7ec46ab nt!KiSystemServiceCopyEnd+0x13 (TrapFrame @ fffff880`15e4cc40)
000000f0`7288f808 000007fe`f7ec84b3 ntdll!NtWaitForWorkViaWorkerFactory+0xa
000000f0`7288f810 000007fe`f601167e ntdll!TppWorkerThread+0x275
000000f0`7288fab0 000007fe`f7ee3501 KERNEL32!BaseThreadInitThunk+0x1a
000000f0`7288fae0 00000000`00000000 ntdll!RtlUserThreadStart+0x1d

        THREAD fffffa80040036c0  Cid 0ca0.0244  Teb: 000007f770a3c000 Win32Thread: 0000000000000000 WAIT:
(UserRequest) UserMode Non-Alertable
        fffffa80021566a0  SynchronizationEvent
        fffffa8002cd3ce0  SynchronizationEvent
    Not impersonating
    DeviceMap                    fffff8a007e2e6a0
    Owning Process               fffffa8002d74180       Image:         Taskmgr.exe
    Attached Process             N/A            Image:         N/A
    Wait Start TickCount         15739266       Ticks: 1862 (0:00:00:29.047)
    Context Switch Count         1896           IdealProcessor: 0
    UserTime                     00:00:00.015
    KernelTime                   00:00:00.000
    Win32 Start Address taskmgr!WdcServiceCache::s_InformClientsThread (0x000007f770e07be4)
    Stack Init fffff88015f10dd0 Current fffff88015f10180
    Base fffff88015f11000 Limit fffff88015f0b000 Call 0
    Priority 11 BasePriority 8 UnusualBoost 0 ForegroundBoost 2 IoPriority 2 PagePriority 5
    Child-SP          RetAddr           Call Site
    fffff880`15f101c0 fffff802`b3b2d99c nt!KiSwapContext+0x76
    fffff880`15f10300 fffff802`b3b293cd nt!KiCommitThreadWait+0x23c
    fffff880`15f103c0 fffff802`b3eca2ac nt!KeWaitForMultipleObjects+0x25d
    fffff880`15f10470 fffff802`b3eca723 nt!ObWaitForMultipleObjects+0x29c
    fffff880`15f10980 fffff802`b3b02d53 nt!NtWaitForMultipleObjects+0xe3
    fffff880`15f10bd0 000007fe`f7ec319b nt!KiSystemServiceCopyEnd+0x13 (TrapFrame @ fffff880`15f10c40)
    000000f0`72a2f428 000007fe`f4fd12c6 ntdll!NtWaitForMultipleObjects+0xa
    000000f0`72a2f430 000007fe`f6011292 KERNELBASE!WaitForMultipleObjectsEx+0xe5
    000000f0`72a2f710 000007f7`70e07c1b KERNEL32!WaitForMultipleObjects+0x12
    000000f0`72a2f750 000007fe`f601167e taskmgr!WdcServiceCache::s_InformClientsThread+0x37
    000000f0`72a2f790 000007fe`f7ee3501 KERNEL32!BaseThreadInitThunk+0x1a
    000000f0`72a2f7c0 00000000`00000000 ntdll!RtlUserThreadStart+0x1d

        THREAD fffffa8002198b00  Cid 0ca0.0aa4  Teb: 000007f770a36000 Win32Thread: 0000000000000000 WAIT: (WrQueue)
UserMode Alertable
        fffffa8003798d80  QueueObject
    Not impersonating
    DeviceMap                    fffff8a007e2e6a0
    Owning Process               fffffa8002d74180       Image:         Taskmgr.exe
    Attached Process             N/A            Image:         N/A
    Wait Start TickCount         15715946       Ticks: 25182 (0:00:06:32.841)
    Context Switch Count         3              IdealProcessor: 0
    UserTime                     00:00:00.000
    KernelTime                   00:00:00.000
    Win32 Start Address ntdll!TppWorkerThread (0x000007fef7ee38c0)
    Stack Init fffff880160eddd0 Current fffff880160ed760
    Base fffff880160ee000 Limit fffff880160e8000 Call 0
    Priority 8 BasePriority 8 UnusualBoost 0 ForegroundBoost 0 IoPriority 2 PagePriority 5
    Kernel stack not resident.
    Child-SP          RetAddr           Call Site
    fffff880`160ed7a0 fffff802`b3b2d99c nt!KiSwapContext+0x76
    fffff880`160ed8e0 fffff802`b3b38ddb nt!KiCommitThreadWait+0x23c
    fffff880`160ed9a0 fffff802`b3ed0b6c nt!KeRemoveQueueEx+0x26b
    fffff880`160eda50 fffff802`b3b434d5 nt!IoRemoveIoCompletion+0x4c
    fffff880`160edae0 fffff802`b3b02d53 nt!NtWaitForWorkViaWorkerFactory+0x295
    fffff880`160edc40 000007fe`f7ec46ab nt!KiSystemServiceCopyEnd+0x13 (TrapFrame @ fffff880`160edc40)
    000000f0`77f5f608 000007fe`f7ec84b3 ntdll!NtWaitForWorkViaWorkerFactory+0xa
    000000f0`77f5f610 000007fe`f601167e ntdll!TppWorkerThread+0x275
    000000f0`77f5f8b0 000007fe`f7ee3501 KERNEL32!BaseThreadInitThunk+0x1a
    000000f0`77f5f8e0 00000000`00000000 ntdll!RtlUserThreadStart+0x1d
```

```
     THREAD fffffa8001f3b080  Cid 0ca0.0d2c  Teb: 000007f770a4e000 Win32Thread: fffff90103f2ab90 WAIT:
(UserRequest) UserMode Non-Alertable
          fffffa80040e0220  SynchronizationEvent
          fffffa8003da2630  SynchronizationEvent
     Not impersonating
     DeviceMap                fffff8a007e2e6a0
     Owning Process           fffffa8002d74180      Image:         Taskmgr.exe
     Attached Process         N/A            Image:         N/A
     Wait Start TickCount     15741108       Ticks: 20 (0:00:00.312)
     Context Switch Count     2113           IdealProcessor: 0
     UserTime                 00:00:00.000
     KernelTime               00:00:00.000
     Win32 Start Address taskmgr!WdcProcessMonitor::HangDetectionThread (0x000007f770e01354)
     Stack Init fffff88016222dd0 Current fffff88016222180
     Base fffff88016223000 Limit fffff8801621d000 Call 0
     Priority 11 BasePriority 8 UnusualBoost 0 ForegroundBoost 2 IoPriority 2 PagePriority 5
     Child-SP          RetAddr           Call Site
     fffff880`162221c0 fffff802`b3b2d99c nt!KiSwapContext+0x76
     fffff880`16222300 fffff802`b3b293cd nt!KiCommitThreadWait+0x23c
     fffff880`162223c0 fffff802`b3eca2ac nt!KeWaitForMultipleObjects+0x25d
     fffff880`16222470 fffff802`b3eca723 nt!ObWaitForMultipleObjects+0x29c
     fffff880`16222980 fffff802`b3b02d53 nt!NtWaitForMultipleObjects+0xe3
     fffff880`16222bd0 000007fe`f7ec319b nt!KiSystemServiceCopyEnd+0x13 (TrapFrame @ fffff880`16222c40)
     000000f0`72ddf648 000007fe`f4fd12c6 ntdll!NtWaitForMultipleObjects+0xa
     000000f0`72ddf650 000007fe`f6011292 KERNELBASE!WaitForMultipleObjectsEx+0xe5
     000000f0`72ddf930 000007f7`70e01398 KERNEL32!WaitForMultipleObjects+0x12
     000000f0`72ddf970 000007fe`f601167e taskmgr!WdcProcessMonitor::HangDetectionThread+0x44
     000000f0`72ddf9b0 000007fe`f7ee3501 KERNEL32!BaseThreadInitThunk+0x1a
     000000f0`72ddf9e0 00000000`00000000 ntdll!RtlUserThreadStart+0x1d

     THREAD fffffa8003bbdb00  Cid 0ca0.0ae8  Teb: 000007f770a3a000 Win32Thread: fffff90103f6e530 WAIT: (WrQueue)
UserMode Alertable
          fffffa8001e75ec0   QueueObject
     Not impersonating
     DeviceMap                fffff8a007e2e6a0
     Owning Process           fffffa8002d74180      Image:         Taskmgr.exe
     Attached Process         N/A            Image:         N/A
     Wait Start TickCount     15741108       Ticks: 20 (0:00:00.312)
     Context Switch Count     7261           IdealProcessor: 0
     UserTime                 00:00:00.031
     KernelTime               00:00:00.015
     Win32 Start Address ntdll!TppWorkerThread (0x000007fef7ee38c0)
     Stack Init fffff880150c3dd0 Current fffff880150c3760
     Base fffff880150c4000 Limit fffff880150be000 Call 0
     Priority 8 BasePriority 8 UnusualBoost 0 ForegroundBoost 0 IoPriority 2 PagePriority 5
     Child-SP          RetAddr           Call Site
     fffff880`150c37a0 fffff802`b3b2d99c nt!KiSwapContext+0x76
     fffff880`150c38e0 fffff802`b3b38ddb nt!KiCommitThreadWait+0x23c
     fffff880`150c39a0 fffff802`b3ed0b6c nt!KeRemoveQueueEx+0x26b
     fffff880`150c3a50 fffff802`b3b434d5 nt!IoRemoveIoCompletion+0x4c
     fffff880`150c3ae0 fffff802`b3b02d53 nt!NtWaitForWorkViaWorkerFactory+0x295
     fffff880`150c3c40 000007fe`f7ec46ab nt!KiSystemServiceCopyEnd+0x13 (TrapFrame @ fffff880`150c3c40)
     000000f0`0010fbd8 000007fe`f7ec84b3 ntdll!NtWaitForWorkViaWorkerFactory+0xa
     000000f0`0010fbe0 000007fe`f601167e ntdll!TppWorkerThread+0x275
     000000f0`0010fe80 000007fe`f7ee3501 KERNEL32!BaseThreadInitThunk+0x1a
     000000f0`0010feb0 00000000`00000000 ntdll!RtlUserThreadStart+0x1d

     THREAD fffffa8001e74b00  Cid 0ca0.0c34  Teb: 000007f770a34000 Win32Thread: 0000000000000000 WAIT:
(UserRequest) UserMode Non-Alertable
          fffffa8003e58460  SynchronizationTimer
     Not impersonating
     DeviceMap                fffff8a007e2e6a0
     Owning Process           fffffa8002d74180      Image:         Taskmgr.exe
     Attached Process         N/A            Image:         N/A
     Wait Start TickCount     15740965       Ticks: 163 (0:00:02.542)
     Context Switch Count     10             IdealProcessor: 0
     UserTime                 00:00:00.000
     KernelTime               00:00:00.000
     Win32 Start Address combase!CRpcThreadCache::RpcWorkerThreadEntry (0x000007fef7b323a8)
     Stack Init fffff880173bedd0 Current fffff880173be0f0
     Base fffff880173bf000 Limit fffff880173b9000 Call 0
     Priority 10 BasePriority 8 UnusualBoost 0 ForegroundBoost 2 IoPriority 2 PagePriority 5
     Child-SP          RetAddr           Call Site
     fffff880`173be130 fffff802`b3b2d99c nt!KiSwapContext+0x76
     fffff880`173be270 fffff802`b3b29c1f nt!KiCommitThreadWait+0x23c
     fffff880`173be330 fffff802`b3b2943e nt!KeWaitForSingleObject+0x1cf
```

```
ffffff880`173be3c0 fffff802`b3eca2ac nt!KeWaitForMultipleObjects+0x2ce
ffffff880`173be470 fffff802`b3eca723 nt!ObWaitForMultipleObjects+0x29c
ffffff880`173be980 fffff802`b3b02d53 nt!NtWaitForMultipleObjects+0xe3
ffffff880`173bebd0 000007fe`f7ec319b nt!KiSystemServiceCopyEnd+0x13 (TrapFrame @ fffff880`173bec40)
000000f0`0028f418 000007fe`f4fd12c6 ntdll!NtWaitForMultipleObjects+0xa
000000f0`0028f420 000007fe`f7b3196a KERNELBASE!WaitForMultipleObjectsEx+0xe5
000000f0`0028f700 000007fe`f7b31a03 combase!WaitCoalesced+0x96
000000f0`0028f950 000007fe`f7b32218 combase!CROIDTable::WorkerThreadLoop+0x63
000000f0`0028f9a0 000007fe`f7b3241f combase!CRpcThread::WorkerLoop+0x48
000000f0`0028fc10 000007fe`f601167e combase!CRpcThreadCache::RpcWorkerThreadEntry+0x73
000000f0`0028fc40 000007fe`f7ee3501 KERNEL32!BaseThreadInitThunk+0x1a
000000f0`0028fc70 00000000`00000000 ntdll!RtlUserThreadStart+0x1d

    THREAD fffffa80020b5900  Cid 0ca0.0154  Teb: 000007f770a40000 Win32Thread: 0000000000000000 WAIT: (WrQueue)
UserMode Alertable
        fffffa8001e75ec0  QueueObject
    Not impersonating
    DeviceMap               fffff8a007e2e6a0
    Owning Process          fffffa8002d74180      Image:          Taskmgr.exe
    Attached Process        N/A            Image:        N/A
    Wait Start TickCount    15740913       Ticks: 215 (0:00:00:03.354)
    Context Switch Count    6              IdealProcessor: 0
    UserTime                00:00:00.000
    KernelTime              00:00:00.000
    Win32 Start Address ntdll!TppWorkerThread (0x000007fef7ee38c0)
    Stack Init fffff88014e29dd0 Current fffff88014e29760
    Base fffff88014e2a000 Limit fffff88014e24000 Call 0
    Priority 8 BasePriority 8 UnusualBoost 0 ForegroundBoost 0 IoPriority 2 PagePriority 5
    Child-SP          RetAddr           Call Site
    fffff880`14e297a0 fffff802`b3b2d99c nt!KiSwapContext+0x76
    fffff880`14e298e0 fffff802`b3b38ddb nt!KiCommitThreadWait+0x23c
    fffff880`14e299a0 fffff802`b3ed0b6c nt!KeRemoveQueueEx+0x26b
    fffff880`14e29a50 fffff802`b3b434d5 nt!IoRemoveIoCompletion+0x4c
    fffff880`14e29ae0 fffff802`b3b02d53 nt!NtWaitForWorkViaWorkerFactory+0x295
    fffff880`14e29c40 000007fe`f7ec46ab nt!KiSystemServiceCopyEnd+0x13 (TrapFrame @ fffff880`14e29c40)
    000000f0`0018fc78 000007fe`f7ec84b3 ntdll!NtWaitForWorkViaWorkerFactory+0xa
    000000f0`0018fc80 000007fe`f601167e ntdll!TppWorkerThread+0x275
    000000f0`0018ff20 000007fe`f7ee3501 KERNEL32!BaseThreadInitThunk+0x1a
    000000f0`0018ff50 00000000`00000000 ntdll!RtlUserThreadStart+0x1d
```

12.   Let's now check the current CPU IDT:

```
0: kd> !pcr
KPCR for Processor 0 at fffff802b3d7f000:
    Major 1 Minor 1
        NtTib.ExceptionList: fffff802b30b8000
          NtTib.StackBase: fffff802b30b9080
         NtTib.StackLimit: 000000f06e86f3e8
        NtTib.SubSystemTib: fffff802b3d7f000
            NtTib.Version: 00000000b3d7f180
         NtTib.UserPointer: fffff802b3d7f7f0
            NtTib.SelfTib: 000007f770b7d000

                  SelfPcr: 0000000000000000
                     Prcb: fffff802b3d7f180
                     Irql: 0000000000000000
                      IRR: 0000000000000000
                      IDR: 0000000000000000
            InterruptMode: 0000000000000000
                      IDT: 0000000000000000
                      GDT: 0000000000000000
                      TSS: 0000000000000000

            CurrentThread: fffffa8003db4740
               NextThread: 0000000000000000
               IdleThread: fffff802b3dd9880

                 DpcQueue:
```

If you like structure format you can use **dt** command:

```
0: kd> dt nt!_KPCR fffff802b3d7f000
   +0x000 NtTib            : _NT_TIB
   +0x000 GdtBase          : 0xfffff802`b30b8000 _KGDTENTRY64
   +0x008 TssBase          : 0xfffff802`b30b9080 _KTSS64
   +0x010 UserRsp          : 0x000000f0`6e86f3e8
   +0x018 Self             : 0xfffff802`b3d7f000 _KPCR
   +0x020 CurrentPrcb      : 0xfffff802`b3d7f180 _KPRCB
   +0x028 LockArray        : 0xfffff802`b3d7f7f0 _KSPIN_LOCK_QUEUE
   +0x030 Used_Self        : 0x000007f7`70b7d000 Void
   +0x038 IdtBase          : 0xfffff802`b30b8080 _KIDTENTRY64
   +0x040 Unused           : [2] 0
   +0x050 Irql             : 0 ''
   +0x051 SecondLevelCacheAssociativity : 0x10 ''
   +0x052 ObsoleteNumber   : 0 ''
   +0x053 Fill0            : 0 ''
   +0x054 Unused0          : [3] 0
   +0x060 MajorVersion     : 1
   +0x062 MinorVersion     : 1
   +0x064 StallScaleFactor : 0x63c
   +0x068 Unused1          : [3] (null)
   +0x080 KernelReserved   : [15] 0
   +0x0bc SecondLevelCacheSize : 0x400000
   +0x0c0 HalReserved      : [16] 0x5f217c30
   +0x100 Unused2          : 0
   +0x108 KdVersionBlock   : (null)
   +0x110 Unused3          : (null)
   +0x118 PcrAlign1        : [24] 0
   +0x180 Prcb             : _KPRCB

0: kd> !prcb
PRCB for Processor 0 at fffff802b3d7f180:
Current IRQL -- 0
Threads--  Current ffffffa8003db4740 Next 0000000000000000 Idle fffff802b3dd9880
Processor Index 0 Number (0, 0) GroupSetMember 1
Interrupt Count -- 00146891
Times -- Dpc      0000026d Interrupt 00000159
         Kernel 0001cc95 User       00002a1d

0: kd> dt nt!_KPRCB  fffff802b3d7f180
   +0x000 MxCsr            : 0x1f80
   +0x004 LegacyNumber     : 0 ''
   +0x005 ReservedMustBeZero : 0 ''
   +0x006 InterruptRequest : 0 ''
   +0x007 IdleHalt         : 0 ''
   +0x008 CurrentThread    : 0xffffffa80`03db4740 _KTHREAD
   +0x010 NextThread       : (null)
   +0x018 IdleThread       : 0xfffff802`b3dd9880 _KTHREAD
   +0x020 NestingLevel     : 0 ''
   +0x021 ClockOwner       : 0x1 ''
   +0x022 PendingTick      : 0 ''
   +0x023 PrcbPad00        : [1]  ""
   +0x024 Number           : 0
   +0x028 RspBase          : 0xfffff880`15925dd0
   +0x030 PrcbLock         : 0
   +0x038 PrcbPad01        : 0
   +0x040 ProcessorState   : _KPROCESSOR_STATE
   +0x5f0 CpuType          : 6 ''
   +0x5f1 CpuID            : 1 ''
```

```
+0x5f2 CpuStep             : 0xf0b
+0x5f2 CpuStepping         : 0xb ''
+0x5f3 CpuModel            : 0xf ''
+0x5f4 MHz                 : 0x63c
+0x5f8 HalReserved         : [8] 0
+0x638 MinorVersion        : 1
+0x63a MajorVersion        : 1
+0x63c BuildType           : 0 ''
+0x63d CpuVendor           : 0x2 ''
+0x63e CoresPerPhysicalProcessor : 0x2 ''
+0x63f LogicalProcessorsPerCore : 0x1 ''
+0x640 ApicMask            : 0xfffffffe
+0x644 CFlushSize          : 0x40
+0x648 AcpiReserved        : (null)
+0x650 InitialApicId       : 0
+0x654 Stride              : 2
+0x658 Group               : 0
+0x660 GroupSetMember      : 1
+0x668 GroupIndex          : 0 ''
+0x670 LockQueue           : [17] _KSPIN_LOCK_QUEUE
+0x780 PPLookasideList     : [16] _PP_LOOKASIDE_LIST
+0x880 PPNxPagedLookasideList : [32] _GENERAL_LOOKASIDE_POOL
+0x1480 PPNPagedLookasideList : [32] _GENERAL_LOOKASIDE_POOL
+0x2080 PPPagedLookasideList : [32] _GENERAL_LOOKASIDE_POOL
+0x2c80 PrcbPad20          : 0
+0x2c88 DeferredReadyListHead : _SINGLE_LIST_ENTRY
+0x2c90 MmPageFaultCount    : 0n1729599
+0x2c94 MmCopyOnWriteCount  : 0n27918
+0x2c98 MmTransitionCount   : 0n593150
+0x2c9c MmDemandZeroCount   : 0n882660
+0x2ca0 MmPageReadCount     : 0n382444
+0x2ca4 MmPageReadIoCount   : 0n57376
+0x2ca8 MmDirtyPagesWriteCount : 0n35128
+0x2cac MmDirtyWriteIoCount : 0n582
+0x2cb0 MmMappedPagesWriteCount : 0n178
+0x2cb4 MmMappedWriteIoCount : 0n15
+0x2cb8 KeSystemCalls       : 0x20f77d0
+0x2cbc KeContextSwitches   : 0x1aecf6
+0x2cc0 CcFastReadNoWait    : 0
+0x2cc4 CcFastReadWait      : 0x6850
+0x2cc8 CcFastReadNotPossible : 0x32
+0x2ccc CcCopyReadNoWait    : 0
+0x2cd0 CcCopyReadWait      : 0x7793
+0x2cd4 CcCopyReadNoWaitMiss : 0
+0x2cd8 LookasideIrpFloat   : 0n2147483647
+0x2cdc IoReadOperationCount : 0n50462
+0x2ce0 IoWriteOperationCount : 0n56714
+0x2ce4 IoOtherOperationCount : 0n323985
+0x2ce8 IoReadTransferCount : _LARGE_INTEGER 0x1e1e96d6
+0x2cf0 IoWriteTransferCount : _LARGE_INTEGER 0x2168e9a3
+0x2cf8 IoOtherTransferCount : _LARGE_INTEGER 0x1335cfe
+0x2d00 PacketBarrier       : 0n0
+0x2d04 TargetCount         : 0n0
+0x2d08 IpiFrozen           : 0
+0x2d0c PrcbPad40           : [29] 0
+0x2d80 DpcData             : [2] _KDPC_DATA
+0x2dc0 DpcStack            : 0xfffff802`b30c5fb0 Void
+0x2dc8 MaximumDpcQueueDepth : 0n4
+0x2dcc DpcRequestRate      : 8
+0x2dd0 MinimumDpcRate      : 3
```

```
+0x2dd4 DpcLastCount        : 0x5c62b
+0x2dd8 ThreadDpcEnable     : 0x1 ''
+0x2dd9 QuantumEnd          : 0 ''
+0x2dda DpcRoutineActive    : 0 ''
+0x2ddb IdleSchedule        : 0 ''
+0x2ddc DpcRequestSummary   : 0n0
+0x2ddc DpcRequestSlot      : [2] 0n0
+0x2ddc NormalDpcState      : 0n0
+0x2dde ThreadDpcState      : 0n0
+0x2ddc DpcNormalProcessingActive : 0y0
+0x2ddc DpcNormalProcessingRequested : 0y0
+0x2ddc DpcNormalThreadSignal : 0y0
+0x2ddc DpcNormalTimerExpiration : 0y0
+0x2ddc DpcNormalDpcPresent : 0y0
+0x2ddc DpcNormalLocalInterrupt : 0y0
+0x2ddc DpcNormalSpare      : 0y0000000000 (0)
+0x2ddc DpcThreadActive     : 0y0
+0x2ddc DpcThreadRequested  : 0y0
+0x2ddc DpcThreadSpare      : 0y00000000000000 (0)
+0x2de0 LastTimerHand       : 0x8eefc3
+0x2de4 LastTick            : 0xf030c8
+0x2de8 ClockInterrupts     : 0x1e7f4
+0x2dec ReadyScanTick       : 0xf03113
+0x2df0 BalanceState        : 0 ''
+0x2df1 PrcbPad50           : [7]  ""
+0x2df8 InterruptLastCount  : 0x146853
+0x2dfc InterruptRate       : 3
+0x2e00 TimerTable          : _KTIMER_TABLE
+0x5000 DpcGate             : _KGATE
+0x5018 PrcbPad52           : (null)
+0x5020 CallDpc             : _KDPC
+0x5060 ClockKeepAlive      : 0n1
+0x5064 PrcbPad60           : [2]  ""
+0x5066 NmiActive           : 0
+0x5068 DpcWatchdogPeriod   : 0n1924
+0x506c DpcWatchdogCount    : 0n1918
+0x5070 KeSpinLockOrdering  : 0n0
+0x5074 PrcbPad70           : [1] 0
+0x5078 CachedPtes          : (null)
+0x5080 WaitListHead        : _LIST_ENTRY [ 0xfffffa80`01e03158 - 0xfffffa80`0419abd8 ]
+0x5090 WaitLock            : 0
+0x5098 ReadySummary        : 0x1000
+0x509c QueueIndex          : 1
+0x50a0 ReadyQueueWeight    : 0xc
+0x50a4 PrcbPad75           : 0
+0x50a8 TimerExpirationDpc  : _KDPC
+0x50e8 BuddyPrcb           : (null)
+0x50f0 ScbQueue            : _RTL_RB_TREE
+0x5100 DispatcherReadyListHead : [32] _LIST_ENTRY [ 0xfffff802`b3d84280 -
0xfffff802`b3d84280 ]
+0x5300 InterruptCount      : 0x146891
+0x5304 KernelTime          : 0x1cc95
+0x5308 UserTime            : 0x2a1d
+0x530c DpcTime             : 0x26d
+0x5310 InterruptTime       : 0x159
+0x5314 AdjustDpcThreshold  : 2
+0x5318 DebuggerSavedIRQL   : 0 ''
+0x5319 GroupSchedulingOverQuota : 0 ''
+0x531a DeepSleep           : 0 ''
+0x531b PrcbPad80           : [1]  ""
```

```
+0x531c  ScbOffset          : 0x40
+0x5320  DpcTimeCount       : 0
+0x5324  DpcTimeLimit       : 0x282
+0x5328  PeriodicCount      : 0
+0x532c  PeriodicBias       : 0
+0x5330  AvailableTime      : 0xc07
+0x5334  KeExceptionDispatchCount : 0x324
+0x5338  ParentNode         : 0xfffff802`b3d0d000 _KNODE
+0x5340  StartCycles        : 0x0000020d`2f5acf08
+0x5348  GenerationTarget : 0x2431db
+0x5350  AffinitizedCycles : 0x00000004`0f38cfd0
+0x5358  PrcbPad81          : 0
+0x5360  MmSpinLockOrdering : 0n0
+0x5364  PageColor          : 0x498b
+0x5368  NodeColor          : 0
+0x536c  NodeShiftedColor   : 0
+0x5370  SecondaryColorMask : 0x3f
+0x5374  PrcbPad83          : 0
+0x5378  CycleTime          : 0x00000007`8a855d30
+0x5380  CcFastMdlReadNoWait : 0
+0x5384  CcFastMdlReadWait : 0
+0x5388  CcFastMdlReadNotPossible : 0
+0x538c  CcMapDataNoWait    : 0
+0x5390  CcMapDataWait      : 0x468c4
+0x5394  CcPinMappedDataCount : 0xa006
+0x5398  CcPinReadNoWait    : 2
+0x539c  CcPinReadWait      : 0x3cd4
+0x53a0  CcMdlReadNoWait    : 0
+0x53a4  CcMdlReadWait      : 0x32
+0x53a8  CcLazyWriteHotSpots : 0x76
+0x53ac  CcLazyWriteIos     : 0xb75
+0x53b0  CcLazyWritePages   : 0x2692c
+0x53b4  CcDataFlushes      : 0x1c52
+0x53b8  CcDataPages        : 0x309c2
+0x53bc  CcLostDelayedWrites : 0
+0x53c0  CcFastReadResourceMiss : 0
+0x53c4  CcCopyReadWaitMiss : 0xd84c
+0x53c8  CcFastMdlReadResourceMiss : 0
+0x53cc  CcMapDataNoWaitMiss : 0
+0x53d0  CcMapDataWaitMiss : 0xead
+0x53d4  CcPinReadNoWaitMiss : 0
+0x53d8  CcPinReadWaitMiss : 0x148
+0x53dc  CcMdlReadNoWaitMiss : 0
+0x53e0  CcMdlReadWaitMiss : 0
+0x53e4  CcReadAheadIos     : 0x111d
+0x53e8  MmCacheTransitionCount : 0n0
+0x53ec  MmCacheReadCount   : 0n0
+0x53f0  MmCacheIoCount     : 0n0
+0x53f4  PrcbPad91          : [3] 0
+0x5400  PowerState         : _PROCESSOR_POWER_STATE
+0x55c8  ScbList            : _LIST_ENTRY [ 0xfffffa80`030575f0 - 0xfffffa80`036ab930 ]
+0x55d8  PrcbPad92          : [22] 0
+0x5630  KeAlignmentFixupCount : 0
+0x5638  DpcWatchdogDpc     : _KDPC
+0x5678  DpcWatchdogTimer   : _KTIMER
+0x56b8  Cache              : [5] _CACHE_DESCRIPTOR
+0x56f4  CacheCount         : 3
+0x56f8  CachedCommit       : 0xfe
+0x56fc  CachedResidentAvailable : 0x91
+0x5700  HyperPte           : 0xfffff880`00800005 Void
```

```
+0x5708 WheaInfo            : 0xfffffa80`0182d7c0 Void
+0x5710 EtwSupport          : 0xfffffa80`01815010 Void
+0x5720 InterruptObjectPool : _SLIST_HEADER
+0x5730 HypercallPageList   : _SLIST_HEADER
+0x5740 HypercallPageVirtual : (null)
+0x5748 VirtualApicAssist   : (null)
+0x5750 StatisticsPage      : (null)
+0x5758 PackageProcessorSet : _KAFFINITY_EX
+0x5800 CacheProcessorMask  : [5] 1
+0x5828 ScanSiblingMask     : 3
+0x5830 ScanSiblingIndex    : 0
+0x5834 LLCLevel            : 2
+0x5838 CoreProcessorSet    : 1
+0x5840 ProcessorProfileControlArea : (null)
+0x5848 ProfileEventIndexAddress : 0xfffff802`b3d849c8 Void
+0x5850 PrcbPad94           : [6] 0
+0x5880 SynchCounters       : _SYNCH_COUNTERS
+0x5938 FsCounters          : _FILESYSTEM_DISK_COUNTERS
+0x5948 VendorString        : [13]  "GenuineIntel"
+0x5955 PrcbPad10           : [3]  ""
+0x5958 FeatureBits         : 0x291b3ffe
+0x5960 UpdateSignature     : _LARGE_INTEGER 0x000000ba`00000000
+0x5968 Context             : 0xfffff802`b3d7f2a0 _CONTEXT
+0x5970 ContextFlagsInit    : 0x10000b
+0x5978 ExtendedState       : (null)
+0x5980 EntropyTimingState  : _KENTROPY_TIMING_STATE
+0x5b00 Mailbox             : (null)
+0x5b40 RequestMailbox      : [1] _REQUEST_MAILBOX

0: kd> !idt

Dumping IDT: fffff802b30b8080

22c4d9ca00000000:    fffff802b3b00440 nt!KiDivideErrorFault
22c4d9ca00000001:    fffff802b3b00540 nt!KiDebugTrapOrFault
22c4d9ca00000002:    fffff802b3b00700 nt!KiNmiInterrupt        Stack = 0xFFFFF802B30CA000

22c4d9ca00000003:    fffff802b3b00a80 nt!KiBreakpointTrap
22c4d9ca00000004:    fffff802b3b00b80 nt!KiOverflowTrap
22c4d9ca00000005:    fffff802b3b00c80 nt!KiBoundFault
22c4d9ca00000006:    fffff802b3b00d80 nt!KiInvalidOpcodeFault
22c4d9ca00000007:    fffff802b3b00fc0 nt!KiNpxNotAvailableFault
22c4d9ca00000008:    fffff802b3b01080 nt!KiDoubleFaultAbort Stack = 0xFFFFF802B30C8000

22c4d9ca00000009:    fffff802b3b01140 nt!KiNpxSegmentOverrunAbort
22c4d9ca0000000a:    fffff802b3b01200 nt!KiInvalidTssFault
22c4d9ca0000000b:    fffff802b3b012c0 nt!KiSegmentNotPresentFault
22c4d9ca0000000c:    fffff802b3b01400 nt!KiStackFault
22c4d9ca0000000d:    fffff802b3b01540 nt!KiGeneralProtectionFault
22c4d9ca0000000e:    fffff802b3b01680 nt!KiPageFault
22c4d9ca00000010:    fffff802b3b01a40 nt!KiFloatingErrorFault
22c4d9ca00000011:    fffff802b3b01bc0 nt!KiAlignmentFault
22c4d9ca00000012:    fffff802b3b01cc0 nt!KiMcheckAbort         Stack = 0xFFFFF802B30CC000

22c4d9ca00000013:    fffff802b3b02340 nt!KiXmmException
22c4d9ca0000001f:    fffff802b3b65ad0 nt!KiApcInterrupt
22c4d9ca00000029:    fffff802b3b02500 nt!KiRaiseSecurityCheckFailure
22c4d9ca0000002c:    fffff802b3b02600 nt!KiRaiseAssertion
22c4d9ca0000002d:    fffff802b3b02700 nt!KiDebugServiceTrap
22c4d9ca0000002f:    fffff802b3bc5190 nt!KiDpcInterrupt
```

```
22c4d9ca00000030:    fffff802b3afb6d0 nt!KiHvInterrupt
22c4d9ca00000031:    fffff802b3afba20 nt!KiVmbusInterrupt0
22c4d9ca00000032:    fffff802b3afbd60 nt!KiVmbusInterrupt1
22c4d9ca00000033:    fffff802b3afc0a0 nt!KiVmbusInterrupt2
22c4d9ca00000034:    fffff802b3afc3e0 nt!KiVmbusInterrupt3
22c4d9ca00000037:    fffff802b3a69560 hal!HalpInterruptSpuriousService (KINTERRUPT
fffff802b3a694d0)
22c4d9ca0000003f:    fffff802b3a691f0 hal!HalpInterruptSpuriousService (KINTERRUPT
fffff802b3a69160)
22c4d9ca00000050:    fffff802b3a69090 hal!HalpInterruptCmciService (KINTERRUPT fffff802b3a69000)
22c4d9ca00000060:    fffff88000993ed0 pci!ExpressRootPortMessageRoutine (KINTERRUPT
fffff88000993e40)
22c4d9ca00000071:    fffff88000993990 USBPORT!USBPORT_InterruptService (KINTERRUPT
fffff88000993900)

                     USBPORT!USBPORT_InterruptService (KINTERRUPT fffff88000993780)
                     ndis!ndisMiniportIsr (KINTERRUPT fffff880009936c0)
                     dxgkrnl!DpiFdoLineInterruptRoutine (KINTERRUPT fffff88000993300)
22c4d9ca00000081:    fffff88000993b10 USBPORT!USBPORT_InterruptService (KINTERRUPT
fffff88000993a80)

                     USBPORT!USBPORT_InterruptService (KINTERRUPT fffff880009933c0)
                     HDAudBus!HdaController::Isr (KINTERRUPT fffff88000993600)
22c4d9ca00000091:    fffff88000993c90 ataport+0xd770 (KINTERRUPT fffff88000993c00)
                     ataport+0xd770 (KINTERRUPT fffff88000993b40)
                     USBPORT!USBPORT_InterruptService (KINTERRUPT fffff88000993540)
22c4d9ca000000a1:    fffff88000993a50 ataport+0xd770 (KINTERRUPT fffff880009939c0)
                     ataport+0xd770 (KINTERRUPT fffff88000993cc0)
                     USBPORT!USBPORT_InterruptService (KINTERRUPT fffff88000993840)
                     USBPORT!USBPORT_InterruptService (KINTERRUPT fffff88000993480)
22c4d9ca000000b0:    fffff88000993f90 ACPI!ACPIInterruptServiceRoutine (KINTERRUPT
fffff88000993f00)
22c4d9ca000000b1:    fffff88000993e10 pci!ExpressRootPortMessageRoutine (KINTERRUPT
fffff88000993d80)
22c4d9ca000000c0:    fffff802b3a692a0 hal!HalpInterruptStubService (KINTERRUPT fffff802b3a69210)
22c4d9ca000000c2:    fffff802b3a696c0 hal!HalpDmaControllerInterruptRoutine (KINTERRUPT
fffff802b3a69630)
22c4d9ca000000d1:    fffff802b3a69610 hal!HalpTimerClockInterrupt (KINTERRUPT fffff802b3a69580)
22c4d9ca000000df:    fffff802b3a69400 hal!HalpInterruptRebootService (KINTERRUPT
fffff802b3a69370)
22c4d9ca000000e1:    fffff802b3b30f10 nt!KiIpiInterrupt
22c4d9ca000000e2:    fffff802b3a69350 hal!HalpInterruptLocalErrorService (KINTERRUPT
fffff802b3a692c0)
22c4d9ca000000e3:    fffff802b3a69140 hal!HalpInterruptDeferredRecoveryService (KINTERRUPT
fffff802b3a690b0)
22c4d9ca000000fe:    fffff802b3a694b0 hal!HalpPerfInterrupt (KINTERRUPT fffff802b3a69420)

0: kd> !idt -a

Dumping IDT: fffff802b30b8080

22c4d9ca00000000:    fffff802b3b00440 nt!KiDivideErrorFault
22c4d9ca00000001:    fffff802b3b00540 nt!KiDebugTrapOrFault
22c4d9ca00000002:    fffff802b3b00700 nt!KiNmiInterrupt       Stack = 0xFFFFF802B30CA000

22c4d9ca00000003:    fffff802b3b00a80 nt!KiBreakpointTrap
22c4d9ca00000004:    fffff802b3b00b80 nt!KiOverflowTrap
22c4d9ca00000005:    fffff802b3b00c80 nt!KiBoundFault
22c4d9ca00000006:    fffff802b3b00d80 nt!KiInvalidOpcodeFault
22c4d9ca00000007:    fffff802b3b00fc0 nt!KiNpxNotAvailableFault
22c4d9ca00000008:    fffff802b3b01080 nt!KiDoubleFaultAbort Stack = 0xFFFFF802B30C8000
```

```
22c4d9ca00000009:    fffff802b3b01140 nt!KiNpxSegmentOverrunAbort
22c4d9ca0000000a:    fffff802b3b01200 nt!KiInvalidTssFault
22c4d9ca0000000b:    fffff802b3b012c0 nt!KiSegmentNotPresentFault
22c4d9ca0000000c:    fffff802b3b01400 nt!KiStackFault
22c4d9ca0000000d:    fffff802b3b01540 nt!KiGeneralProtectionFault
22c4d9ca0000000e:    fffff802b3b01680 nt!KiPageFault
22c4d9ca0000000f:    fffff802b3cfa0f0 nt!KxUnexpectedInterrupt0+0xF0
22c4d9ca00000010:    fffff802b3b01a40 nt!KiFloatingErrorFault
22c4d9ca00000011:    fffff802b3b01bc0 nt!KiAlignmentFault
22c4d9ca00000012:    fffff802b3b01cc0 nt!KiMcheckAbort        Stack = 0xFFFFF802B30CC000

22c4d9ca00000013:    fffff802b3b02340 nt!KiXmmException
22c4d9ca00000014:    fffff802b3cfa140 nt!KxUnexpectedInterrupt0+0x140
22c4d9ca00000015:    fffff802b3cfa150 nt!KxUnexpectedInterrupt0+0x150
22c4d9ca00000016:    fffff802b3cfa160 nt!KxUnexpectedInterrupt0+0x160
22c4d9ca00000017:    fffff802b3cfa170 nt!KxUnexpectedInterrupt0+0x170
22c4d9ca00000018:    fffff802b3cfa180 nt!KxUnexpectedInterrupt0+0x180
22c4d9ca00000019:    fffff802b3cfa190 nt!KxUnexpectedInterrupt0+0x190
22c4d9ca0000001a:    fffff802b3cfa1a0 nt!KxUnexpectedInterrupt0+0x1A0
22c4d9ca0000001b:    fffff802b3cfa1b0 nt!KxUnexpectedInterrupt0+0x1B0
22c4d9ca0000001c:    fffff802b3cfa1c0 nt!KxUnexpectedInterrupt0+0x1C0
22c4d9ca0000001d:    fffff802b3cfa1d0 nt!KxUnexpectedInterrupt0+0x1D0
[…]
```

Note that some interrupts have their own stack.

13.   Let's now check the raw stack data for the current thread:

```
0: kd> !thread -1 3f
THREAD fffffa8003db4740  Cid 0ca0.03e0   Teb: 000007f770b7d000 Win32Thread: fffff90104094830
RUNNING on processor 0
Not impersonating
DeviceMap                  fffff8a007e2e6a0
Owning Process             fffffa8002d74180      Image:        Taskmgr.exe
Attached Process           N/A              Image:        N/A
Wait Start TickCount       15741128         Ticks: 0
Context Switch Count       31359            IdealProcessor: 0
UserTime                   00:00:09.859
KernelTime                 00:00:07.394
Win32 Start Address taskmgr!wWinMainCRTStartup (0x000007f770e68688)
Stack Init fffff88015925dd0 Current fffff88015925800
Base fffff88015926000 Limit fffff88015920000 Call 0
Priority 13 BasePriority 9 UnusualBoost 0 ForegroundBoost 2 IoPriority 2 PagePriority 5
Child-SP          RetAddr            Call Site
fffff880`15925ae8 fffff802`b400f0dd nt!KeBugCheckEx
fffff880`15925af0 fffff802`b3ea8f6d nt!PspCatchCriticalBreak+0xad
fffff880`15925b30 fffff802`b3ea8019 nt! ?? ::NNGAKEGL::`string'+0x46f60
fffff880`15925b90 fffff802`b3ea7e52 nt!PspTerminateProcess+0x6d
fffff880`15925bd0 fffff802`b3b02d53 nt!NtTerminateProcess+0x9e
fffff880`15925c40 000007fe`f7ec2eaa nt!KiSystemServiceCopyEnd+0x13 (TrapFrame @
fffff880`15925c40)
000000f0`6e86f3e8 000007fe`f4ff1295 ntdll!NtTerminateProcess+0xa
000000f0`6e86f3f0 000007f7`70e012ba KERNELBASE!TerminateProcess+0x25
000000f0`6e86f420 000007f7`70df3698 taskmgr!WdcProcessMonitor::OnProcessCommand+0x1b6
000000f0`6e86f4b0 000007f7`70df55bb taskmgr!WdcListView::OnProcessCommand+0x1e0
000000f0`6e86f5a0 000007f7`70df5b47 taskmgr!WdcListView::OnCommand+0x123
000000f0`6e86f5f0 000007fe`f2227239 taskmgr!WdcListView::OnMessage+0x287
000000f0`6e86f710 000007fe`f2a82d23 DUI70!DirectUI::HWNDHost::_CtrlWndProc+0xa1
000000f0`6e86f770 000007fe`f56c171e DUser!WndBridge::RawWndProc+0x73
```

```
000000f0`6e86f7e0 000007fe`f56c14d7 USER32!UserCallWinProcCheckWow+0x13a
000000f0`6e86f8a0 000007f7`70e1b0e1 USER32!DispatchMessageWorker+0x1a7
000000f0`6e86f920 000007f7`70e685e6 taskmgr!wWinMain+0x44d
000000f0`6e86fde0 000007fe`f601167e taskmgr!CBaseRPCTimeout::Disarm+0x31a
000000f0`6e86fea0 000007fe`f7ee3501 KERNEL32!BaseThreadInitThunk+0x1a
000000f0`6e86fed0 00000000`00000000 ntdll!RtlUserThreadStart+0x1d


0: kd> dps fffff88015920000 fffff88015926000
[…]
fffff880`15924098 00000000`00000000
fffff880`159240a0 00000000`00000000
fffff880`159240a8 00000000`00000000
fffff880`159240b0 00000000`00000000
fffff880`159240b8 00000000`00000000
fffff880`159240c0 fffff880`00000000
fffff880`159240c8 fffff880`040067e4 igdkmd64!PORTCONTROLLER_EnumEnabledPortsOnPipe+0x64
fffff880`159240d0 fffff880`03cec200
fffff880`159240d8 04524320`00000048
fffff880`159240e0 00000500`000005a0
fffff880`159240e8 fffff880`03f8b652 igdkmd64!ExtInterface_ReadULONG+0x52
fffff880`159240f0 fffffa80`01a2e000
fffff880`159240f8 fffff880`03cec200
fffff880`15924100 00000320`abcd0003
fffff880`15924108 00000323`00000336
fffff880`15924110 fffff880`03cec204
fffff880`15924118 fffffa80`01a2eefc
fffff880`15924120 04524320`00000048
fffff880`15924128 fffff880`03f8b5ec igdkmd64!ExtInterface_WriteULONG+0x5c
fffff880`15924130 fffffa80`01a2e000
fffff880`15924138 fffff880`03cec204
fffff880`15924140 00000337`00000003
fffff880`15924148 00000320`00000320
fffff880`15924150 fffffa80`01a2e000
fffff880`15924158 fffffa80`01a2eefc
fffff880`15924160 00000000`0800000c
fffff880`15924168 fffff880`04033015 igdkmd64!MMIOREG_WriteValue+0x55
fffff880`15924170 fffffa80`01a6d010
fffff880`15924178 fffff880`00061204
fffff880`15924180 fffff880`00000003
fffff880`15924188 fffff880`00000000
fffff880`15924190 fffffa80`01a6d010
fffff880`15924198 00000005`00000000
fffff880`159241a0 fffff801`00000001
fffff880`159241a8 fffff880`0406efd8 igdkmd64!PORTBASE_SetEncoderRegisterValue+0x1c8
fffff880`159241b0 fffff880`159241f0
fffff880`159241b8 fffff880`00000003
fffff880`159241c0 fffff880`00000000
fffff880`159241c8 fffff880`00000000
fffff880`159241d0 fffff880`0000fffc
fffff880`159241d8 fffff880`04033270 igdkmd64!MMIOREG_WriteMaskedByteValue
fffff880`159241e0 fffff801`00000002
fffff880`159241e8 fffff880`04033320 igdkmd64!MMIOREG_Commit
fffff880`159241f0 fffff880`040330e0 igdkmd64!MMIOREG_ReadValue
fffff880`159241f8 fffff880`04033160 igdkmd64!MMIOREG_ReadByteValue
fffff880`15924200 fffff880`04032fc0 igdkmd64!MMIOREG_WriteValue
fffff880`15924208 fffff880`04033040 igdkmd64!MMIOREG_WriteByteValue
fffff880`15924210 fffff880`04033200 igdkmd64!MMIOREG_WriteMaskedValue
fffff880`15924218 fffff880`04033270 igdkmd64!MMIOREG_WriteMaskedByteValue
fffff880`15924220 fffff880`04033300 igdkmd64!MMIOREG_EnableCaching
```

```
fffff880`15924228    fffff880`04033320  igdkmd64!MMIOREG_Commit
fffff880`15924230    fffff880`04033390  igdkmd64!MMIOREG_ReadWrite
fffff880`15924238    fffff880`040333d0  igdkmd64!MMIOREG_SaveValue
fffff880`15924240    fffff880`04033410  igdkmd64!MMIOREG_RestoreValue
fffff880`15924248    fffff880`04033460  igdkmd64!MMIOREG_RestoreMaskedValue
fffff880`15924250    fffff880`04033550  igdkmd64!MMIOREG_ReadMultiValue
fffff880`15924258    fffff880`040334e0  igdkmd64!MMIOREG_WriteMultiValue
fffff880`15924260    00000000`00061204
fffff880`15924268    0000fffc`00000000
fffff880`15924270    00000000`01a6cd00
fffff880`15924278    fffff800`00061200
fffff880`15924280    fffff880`04032fb0  igdkmd64!MMIOREG_Destroy
fffff880`15924288    fffff880`03fbc52c  igdkmd64!GMCHBASE_GetPortObject+0x2c
fffff880`15924290    00000000`00000028
fffff880`15924298    abcd0003`abcd0003
fffff880`159242a0    00000000`00000000
fffff880`159242a8    fffff880`03fbc404  igdkmd64!GMCHBASE_SetInternalEncoderRegister+0xb4
fffff880`159242b0    fffffa80`01a6cde0
fffff880`159242b8    fffff880`00061204
fffff880`159242c0    fffff880`00000003
fffff880`159242c8    fffff880`00000001
fffff880`159242d0    fffffa01`00000005
fffff880`159242d8    fffffa80`01a6cde0
fffff880`159242e0    00000001`00000001
fffff880`159242e8    fffffa80`01a6cde0
fffff880`159242f0    fffff880`15924388
fffff880`159242f8    fffff880`03fd1d32  igdkmd64!INTLVDSENCODER_SetTiming+0x552
fffff880`15924300    fffffa80`01a97000
fffff880`15924308    fffff880`00000001
fffff880`15924310    fffff880`00061204
fffff880`15924318    fffff880`00000003
fffff880`15924320    fffff880`159244b0
fffff880`15924328    00000000`00000000
fffff880`15924330    00000000`00000000
fffff880`15924338    00000000`00000000
fffff880`15924340    04524320`00000048
fffff880`15924348    00000500`000005a0
fffff880`15924350    0000059f`00000500
fffff880`15924358    0000054f`00000530
fffff880`15924360    00000337`0000c4ab
fffff880`15924368    00000320`00000320
fffff880`15924370    00000323`00000336
fffff880`15924378    0000003d`00000328
fffff880`15924380    00000000`0800000c
fffff880`15924388    00000000`00000000
fffff880`15924390    00000002`00000000
fffff880`15924398    00000000`00000000
fffff880`159243a0    00000000`00000000
fffff880`159243a8    00000000`00000000
fffff880`159243b0    00001000`00000000
fffff880`159243b8    00000000`00000001
fffff880`159243c0    fffffa80`01a97000
fffff880`159243c8    00000000`00000003
fffff880`159243d0    04524320`00000048
fffff880`159243d8    00000500`000005a0
fffff880`159243e0    0000059f`00000500
fffff880`159243e8    0000054f`00000530
fffff880`159243f0    00000337`0000c4ab
fffff880`159243f8    00000320`00000320
fffff880`15924400    00000323`00000336
```

```
fffff880`15924408    0000003d`00000328
fffff880`15924410    00000000`0000000c
fffff880`15924418    00000000`00000407
fffff880`15924420    04524320`00000048
fffff880`15924428    00000500`000005a0
fffff880`15924430    0000059f`00000500
fffff880`15924438    0000054f`00000530
fffff880`15924440    00000337`0000c4ab
fffff880`15924448    00000320`00000320
fffff880`15924450    00000323`00000336
fffff880`15924458    0000003d`00000328
fffff880`15924460    00000000`0800000c
fffff880`15924468    00000000`00000000
fffff880`15924470    000001e0`00000280
fffff880`15924478    00000000`00000004
fffff880`15924480    00000000`0000003c
fffff880`15924488    00000280`00000000
fffff880`15924490    0000003c`000001e0
fffff880`15924498    00000000`00000000
fffff880`159244a0    00000000`00000000
fffff880`159244a8    00000000`00000001
fffff880`159244b0    0000007f`00000000
fffff880`159244b8    0000007f`0000007f
fffff880`159244c0    00000001`00000001
fffff880`159244c8    00000000`00000005
fffff880`159244d0    00000000`00000000
fffff880`159244d8    fffff880`03f8ce7a igdkmd64!GetCSLSBIOSProtocolObject+0x3a
fffff880`159244e0    fffffa80`01a08830
fffff880`159244e8    00000000`00000000
fffff880`159244f0    00000000`00000000
fffff880`159244f8    00000000`00000000
fffff880`15924500    fffffa80`01a145f0
fffff880`15924508    fffffa80`01a06010
fffff880`15924510    000001e0`00000280
fffff880`15924518    fffff880`03fa4b0e igdkmd64!MODESMANAGER_PostSetMode+0x1e
fffff880`15924520    00000000`0000003c
fffff880`15924528    00000280`00000000
fffff880`15924530    0000003c`000001e0
fffff880`15924538    00000000`00000000
fffff880`15924540    00000000`00000000
fffff880`15924548    fffffa80`01a06010
fffff880`15924550    fffffa80`01a12e00
fffff880`15924558    fffff880`15924a4c
fffff880`15924560    fffffa80`01a151b6
fffff880`15924568    fffff880`03f975f9 igdkmd64!MODESMANAGER_SetMode+0x6b9
fffff880`15924570    fffffa80`01a15010
fffff880`15924578    fffff880`15924da0
fffff880`15924580    fffff880`15924da0
fffff880`15924588    fffff880`15924a10
fffff880`15924590    fffff880`15924a50
fffff880`15924598    fffffa80`017e0700
fffff880`159245a0    fffffa80`01a2d010
fffff880`159245a8    fffff8a0`01be49a0
fffff880`159245b0    00000000`00000000
fffff880`159245b8    0000007f`0000007f
fffff880`159245c0    00000001`0000007f
fffff880`159245c8    00000005`00000001
fffff880`159245d0    00000000`00000000
fffff880`159245d8    00000000`00000000
fffff880`159245e0    00000000`00000000
```

```
fffff880`159245e8    00000000`00000000
fffff880`159245f0    00000000`00000000
fffff880`159245f8    00000000`00000000
fffff880`15924600    00000000`00000000
fffff880`15924608    0000007f`00000000
fffff880`15924610    0000007f`0000007f
fffff880`15924618    00000001`0000007f
fffff880`15924620    00000000`00000000
fffff880`15924628    00000000`00000000
fffff880`15924630    00000000`00000000
fffff880`15924638    00000000`00000000
fffff880`15924640    00000000`00000000
fffff880`15924648    00000000`00000000
fffff880`15924650    00000000`00000000
fffff880`15924658    00000000`00000000
fffff880`15924660    fffff901`00000000
fffff880`15924668    fffff901`000d2e20
fffff880`15924670    fffff880`00000000
fffff880`15924678    ffff fa80`01a10010
fffff880`15924680    00000000`00000000
fffff880`15924688    00000000`00000000
fffff880`15924690    00000000`00000000
fffff880`15924698    00000000`00000000
fffff880`159246a0    00000000`00000000
fffff880`159246a8    00000000`00000000
fffff880`159246b0    00000000`00000000
fffff880`159246b8    00000000`00000000
fffff880`159246c0    00000000`00000000
fffff880`159246c8    00000000`00000000
fffff880`159246d0    00000000`00000000
fffff880`159246d8    fffff802`b3ec289b  nt!RtlAnsiCharToUnicodeChar+0x4b
fffff880`159246e0    04070400`00000201
fffff880`159246e8    ffff fa80`01a97000
fffff880`159246f0    00000000`00000000
fffff880`159246f8    00000000`000007ff
fffff880`15924700    04070400`00000001
fffff880`15924708    00000000`00000000
fffff880`15924710    00000000`00000000
fffff880`15924718    00000000`00000000
fffff880`15924720    00000000`00000000
fffff880`15924728    00000000`00000000
fffff880`15924730    00000000`00000000
fffff880`15924738    00000000`00000000
fffff880`15924740    00000000`00000000
fffff880`15924748    00000000`00000000
fffff880`15924750    00000000`00000000
fffff880`15924758    00000000`00000000
fffff880`15924760    00000000`00000000
fffff880`15924768    00000000`00000000
fffff880`15924770    00000000`00000000
fffff880`15924778    00000000`00000000
fffff880`15924780    00000000`00000000
fffff880`15924788    fffff880`ffffff00
fffff880`15924790    000001e0`00000280
fffff880`15924798    00000000`00000004
fffff880`159247a0    00000000`0000003c
fffff880`159247a8    00000280`00000000
fffff880`159247b0    0000003c`000001e0
fffff880`159247b8    00000000`00000000
fffff880`159247c0    00000000`00000000
```

```
fffff880`159247c8    fffff880`00000001
fffff880`159247d0    ffffffff`00000001
fffff880`159247d8    00000000`00000000
fffff880`159247e0    04000000`00010001
fffff880`159247e8    00000000`00000407
fffff880`159247f0    00000000`00000000
fffff880`159247f8    00000000`00000000
fffff880`15924800    00000000`00000000
fffff880`15924808    00000000`00000000
fffff880`15924810    00000000`00000000
fffff880`15924818    00000000`00000000
fffff880`15924820    00000000`00000000
fffff880`15924828    00000000`00000000
fffff880`15924830    00000000`00000000
fffff880`15924838    00000000`00000000
fffff880`15924840    00000000`00000000
fffff880`15924848    00000000`00000000
fffff880`15924850    00000000`00000000
fffff880`15924858    00000000`00000000
fffff880`15924860    00000000`00000000
fffff880`15924868    00000000`00000000
fffff880`15924870    00000000`00ffff00
fffff880`15924878    00000000`00000000
fffff880`15924880    00000000`00000000
fffff880`15924888    fffff880`035cd8e0 BasicDisplay!CopyBitsTo_4+0x3d0
fffff880`15924890    00000000`00000000
fffff880`15924898    00000000`00000000
fffff880`159248a0    00000000`00000000
fffff880`159248a8    00000000`00000000
fffff880`159248b0    00000004`00008007
fffff880`159248b8    00000001`00000018
fffff880`159248c0    00000018`00000001
fffff880`159248c8    fffff880`159249f0
fffff880`159248d0    fffff880`15924a18
fffff880`159248d8    fffff880`00bdc0a8
fffff880`159248e0    00000000`00000001
fffff880`159248e8    00000000`00000031
fffff880`159248f0    00000000`00000000
fffff880`159248f8    00000000`00000000
fffff880`15924900    00000000`00000000
fffff880`15924908    00000000`00000000
fffff880`15924910    fffff880`00000000
fffff880`15924918    00000000`00000000
fffff880`15924920    00000000`00000000
fffff880`15924928    fffff880`035cd8e0 BasicDisplay!CopyBitsTo_4+0x3d0
fffff880`15924930    00000280`00000000
fffff880`15924938    0000003c`000001e0
fffff880`15924940    00000000`00000000
fffff880`15924948    00000000`00000000
fffff880`15924950    ffff3753`3e069d3e
fffff880`15924958    00000001`0000000d
fffff880`15924960    00000000`00000018
fffff880`15924968    00000000`00000004
fffff880`15924970    00000000`00000000
fffff880`15924978    fffff880`00bdc078
fffff880`15924980    00000000`ffffff23
fffff880`15924988    fffff880`035cdd4e BasicDisplay!BltBits+0x42
fffff880`15924990    00000000`fffffe73
fffff880`15924998    fffff880`15924a51
fffff880`159249a0    fffffa80`02c55d20
```

```
ffffff880`159249a8    00000000`0000000d
ffffff880`159249b0    00000004`0000e001
ffffff880`159249b8    00000001`00000018
ffffff880`159249c0    00000000`0000018d
ffffff880`159249c8    ffffff880`035cd416  BasicDisplay!BddDdiSystemDisplayWrite+0x11e
ffffff880`159249d0    ffffff880`15924a18
ffffff880`159249d8    ffffff880`159249f0
ffffff880`159249e0    00000000`00000001
ffffff880`159249e8    00000000`00000030
ffffff880`159249f0    ffffff880`00bdc078
ffffff880`159249f8    00000004`00000002
ffffff880`15924a00    ffffff23`fffffe73
ffffff880`15924a08    00000004`00000001
ffffff880`15924a10    00000000`00000018
ffffff880`15924a18    ffffff880`03c6b000
ffffff880`15924a20    00000004`00000050
ffffff880`15924a28    00000000`00000000
ffffff880`15924a30    00000280`00000001
ffffff880`15924a38    ffffff880`000001e0
ffffff880`15924a40    000000dd`0000018d
ffffff880`15924a48    000000f5`00000191
ffffff880`15924a50    ffff3753`3e069c7e
ffffff880`15924a58    00000000`00000000
ffffff880`15924a60    00000000`00000004
ffffff880`15924a68    00000000`00000001
ffffff880`15924a70    00000000`00000018
ffffff880`15924a78    00000000`00000018
ffffff880`15924a80    00000000`00000004
ffffff880`15924a88    00000000`00000004
ffffff880`15924a90    ffffff880`15924b00
ffffff880`15924a98    ffffff880`03418c9e  dxgkrnl!DpiSystemDisplayWrite+0xee
ffffff880`15924aa0    ffffff880`00bdc0a7
ffffff880`15924aa8    00000000`00000000
ffffff880`15924ab0    00000000`00000001
ffffff880`15924ab8    ffffff802`b3bc7f84  nt!RaspAntiAlias+0x104
ffffff880`15924ac0    ffffff880`00000002
ffffff880`15924ac8    ffffff880`0000018d
ffffff880`15924ad0    00000000`000000dd
ffffff880`15924ad8    00000000`00000001
ffffff880`15924ae0    00000000`00000000
ffffff880`15924ae8    00000000`00000018
ffffff880`15924af0    ffffff880`15924ce8
ffffff880`15924af8    ffffff880`15924b99
ffffff880`15924b00    ffffff880`15924b99
ffffff880`15924b08    ffffff802`b3bd77f6  nt!GxpWriteFrameBufferPixels+0x13e
ffffff880`15924b10    ffffff880`00bdc030
ffffff880`15924b18    ffffff880`15924ce8
ffffff880`15924b20    ffffff880`15924b60
ffffff880`15924b28    ffffff802`b3bc7e02  nt!BgpRasPrintGlyph+0x28a
ffffff880`15924b30    ffffff880`15924b60
ffffff880`15924b38    00000004`00000018
ffffff880`15924b40    00014af4`00000001
ffffff880`15924b48    ffffff880`00bdc078
ffffff880`15924b50    ffffffa80`00000004
ffffff880`15924b58    ffffff880`00000000
ffffff880`15924b60    00000004`00000018
ffffff880`15924b68    00014af4`00000004
ffffff880`15924b70    ffffffa80`00000000
ffffff880`15924b78    ffffff880`00bdc078
ffffff880`15924b80    00000000`00000001
```

161

```
fffff880`15924b88  fffff880`04440f79  dump_dumpata!IdeDumpNotification+0x1e1
fffff880`15924b90  00000000`00000000
fffff880`15924b98  00000000`00000002
fffff880`15924ba0  fffff880`15924c20
fffff880`15924ba8  fffff880`15924ce0
fffff880`15924bb0  fffffa80`03337000
fffff880`15924bb8  fffff880`04440f39  dump_dumpata!IdeDumpNotification+0x1a1
fffff880`15924bc0  00000000`00000200
fffff880`15924bc8  fffff802`b3d17fe0  nt!BcpCharacterCache
fffff880`15924bd0  00000000`00000000
fffff880`15924bd8  fffffa80`018289a0
fffff880`15924be0  fffff880`15924ce8
fffff880`15924be8  fffff880`00bdc030
fffff880`15924bf0  00000000`00000001
fffff880`15924bf8  fffff880`04442614  dump_dumpata!AtaPortGetPhysicalAddress+0x2c
fffff880`15924c00  00000000`000050e0
fffff880`15924c08  fffffa80`03337260
fffff880`15924c10  00000000`00000000
fffff880`15924c18  fffff880`00baebc9
fffff880`15924c20  fffffa80`0000000c
fffff880`15924c28  fffffa80`03337798
fffff880`15924c30  00000000`7afe7000
fffff880`15924c38  fffffa80`027e7000
fffff880`15924c40  00000000`00000000
fffff880`15924c48  fffff802`b3b15490  nt!RtlDecompressFragmentProcs
fffff880`15924c50  fffff880`00000000
fffff880`15924c58  fffffa80`03337798
fffff880`15924c60  fffffa80`033375a8
fffff880`15924c68  fffff880`0444e8ce*** ERROR: Module load completed but symbols could not be
loaded for dump_atapi.sys
 dump_atapi+0x28ce
fffff880`15924c70  00000000`00000000
fffff880`15924c78  fffff880`00bdc030
fffff880`15924c80  ffff7cad`450c35aa
fffff880`15924c88  fffff880`0444e7bc  dump_atapi+0x27bc
fffff880`15924c90  00000000`00000103
fffff880`15924c98  fffffa80`033377a0
fffff880`15924ca0  00000000`00000000
fffff880`15924ca8  00000000`00000001
fffff880`15924cb0  fffffa80`03337798
fffff880`15924cb8  fffff880`0444e297  dump_atapi+0x2297
fffff880`15924cc0  fffffa80`033375a8
fffff880`15924cc8  fffffa80`033375f0
fffff880`15924cd0  fffffa80`033375f0
fffff880`15924cd8  fffffa80`03337798
fffff880`15924ce0  00000000`00000000
fffff880`15924ce8  fffff880`0444e0f4  dump_atapi+0x20f4
fffff880`15924cf0  fffffa80`033375f0
fffff880`15924cf8  fffff802`b3a24d07  hal!IoMapTransfer+0x1b
fffff880`15924d00  00000000`00000103
fffff880`15924d08  fffff802`b3a3b110  hal!HalpTimerStallExecutionProcessor+0x161
fffff880`15924d10  00000000`00000000
fffff880`15924d18  fffff880`15924ec8
fffff880`15924d20  fffffa80`03337798
fffff880`15924d28  fffff880`0444deb1  dump_atapi+0x1eb1
fffff880`15924d30  fffffa80`03337650
fffff880`15924d38  fffff880`0444d6c8  dump_atapi+0x16c8
fffff880`15924d40  fffff880`15924f00
fffff880`15924d48  00000000`00000000
fffff880`15924d50  fffff157`9399fa4b
```

```
fffff880`15924d58   fffff880`0444d678   dump_atapi+0x1678
fffff880`15924d60   00000000`00000103
fffff880`15924d68   ffffa80`033371c0
fffff880`15924d70   00000000`000003e8
fffff880`15924d78   fffff880`15924ec8
fffff880`15924d80   00000000`00000103
fffff880`15924d88   ffffa80`033371c0
fffff880`15924d90   00000000`000000e6
fffff880`15924d98   fffff880`04440cab   dump_dumpata!IdeDumpPollInterrupt+0x37
fffff880`15924da0   00000000`00000000
fffff880`15924da8   00000000`00000000
fffff880`15924db0   00000000`ffffffff
fffff880`15924db8   00000000`ffffff44
fffff880`15924dc0   ffffa80`033371c0
fffff880`15924dc8   fffff880`04441982   dump_dumpata!IdeDumpWaitOnRequest+0xce
fffff880`15924dd0   ffffa80`03337001
fffff880`15924dd8   00000000`ffffffff
fffff880`15924de0   00000000`ffffffff
fffff880`15924de8   00000000`ffffffff
fffff880`15924df0   00000000`00000000
fffff880`15924df8   00000000`00000000
fffff880`15924e00   00000000`ffffffff
fffff880`15924e08   fffff880`04440794   dump_dumpata!IdeDumpIoIssue+0x110
fffff880`15924e10   ffffa80`03337000
fffff880`15924e18   ffffa80`03337000
fffff880`15924e20   fffff880`15924f00
fffff880`15924e28   00000000`00000000
fffff880`15924e30   ffffa80`033371c0
fffff880`15924e38   ffffa80`027b0103
fffff880`15924e40   00000000`00000020
fffff880`15924e48   00000000`00000002
fffff880`15924e50   00000000`00010000
fffff880`15924e58   fffff880`021e8097   crashdmp!CrashdmpWriteRoutine+0x4f
fffff880`15924e60   00000000`066e2000
fffff880`15924e68   fffff880`15924ec8
fffff880`15924e70   fffff880`15924f00
fffff880`15924e78   ffffa80`027b5950
fffff880`15924e80   00000000`13746000
fffff880`15924e88   fffff880`021ed3e0   crashdmp!Context+0x30
fffff880`15924e90   00000000`13746000
fffff880`15924e98   fffff880`021e62dc   crashdmp!WritePageSpanToDisk+0x200
fffff880`15924ea0   00000000`066e2000
fffff880`15924ea8   fffff880`15924fa0
fffff880`15924eb0   fffff880`021ed3e0   crashdmp!Context+0x30
fffff880`15924eb8   fffff880`00000002
fffff880`15924ec0   fffff880`00000000
fffff880`15924ec8   0000000d`09886000
fffff880`15924ed0   fffff880`021e8048   crashdmp!CrashdmpWriteRoutine
fffff880`15924ed8   fffff880`021e812c   crashdmp!CrashdmpWritePendingRoutine
fffff880`15924ee0   00000000`00010000
fffff880`15924ee8   00000000`0002dc63
fffff880`15924ef0   fffff880`021ed3e0   crashdmp!Context+0x30
fffff880`15924ef8   ffff802`b3b8149d   nt!vsnprintf+0x11
fffff880`15924f00   00000000`00000000
fffff880`15924f08   00000000`20030000
fffff880`15924f10   00000000`00000000
fffff880`15924f18   fffff880`00841000
fffff880`15924f20   fffff880`00841000
fffff880`15924f28   00000000`00010000
fffff880`15924f30   00000000`0002dc63
```

```
fffff880`15924f38    00000000`0002dc64
fffff880`15924f40    00000000`0002dc65
fffff880`15924f48    00000000`0002dc66
fffff880`15924f50    00000000`0002dc67
fffff880`15924f58    00000000`0002dc68
fffff880`15924f60    00000000`0002dc69
fffff880`15924f68    00000000`0002dc6a
fffff880`15924f70    00000000`0002dc6b
fffff880`15924f78    00000000`0002dc6c
fffff880`15924f80    00000000`0002dc6d
fffff880`15924f88    00000000`0002dc6e
fffff880`15924f90    00000000`0002dc6f
fffff880`15924f98    00000000`0002dc70
fffff880`15924fa0    00000000`0002dc71
fffff880`15924fa8    00000000`0002dc72
fffff880`15924fb0    00000000`00000000
fffff880`15924fb8    00000000`0017c85d
fffff880`15924fc0    ffffcbba`a93076e8
fffff880`15924fc8    fffff802`b3d17590    nt!NtVhdBootFile+0x15d8
fffff880`15924fd0    fffff880`15925510
fffff880`15924fd8    00000000`0004fae9
fffff880`15924fe0    00000000`00000000
fffff880`15924fe8    00000000`0002dc63
fffff880`15924ff0    00000000`00000000
fffff880`15924ff8    00000000`00000010
fffff880`15925000    fffff880`15925400
fffff880`15925008    fffff880`021e5e2a    crashdmp!WriteBitmapDump+0x25e
fffff880`15925010    fffff880`159250d0
fffff880`15925018    fffff880`021ed3e0    crashdmp!Context+0x30
fffff880`15925020    00000000`00000050
fffff880`15925028    00000000`00000000
fffff880`15925030    fffff880`00000050
fffff880`15925038    fffff880`00000001
fffff880`15925040    00000000`00066bec
fffff880`15925048    fffff880`00016ae9
fffff880`15925050    00000000`00000000
fffff880`15925058    00000000`00000000
fffff880`15925060    00000000`00000000
fffff880`15925068    00000000`00066c63
fffff880`15925070    00000000`0007d74c
fffff880`15925078    fffffa80`02c02038
fffff880`15925080    00000000`00000010
fffff880`15925088    fffff802`b3bfe96c    nt!KiBugCheckProgress
fffff880`15925090    00000000`0007d6d5
fffff880`15925098    00000000`00066bec
fffff880`159250a0    fffff880`021ed3e0    crashdmp!Context+0x30
fffff880`159250a8    fffff802`b3bfe96c    nt!KiBugCheckProgress
fffff880`159250b0    00000000`00000000
fffff880`159250b8    fffffa80`02c02030
fffff880`159250c0    00000000`0007d6d5
fffff880`159250c8    00000000`00000000
fffff880`159250d0    20676e69`706d7544
fffff880`159250d8    6c616369`73796870
fffff880`159250e0    2079726f`6d656d20
fffff880`159250e8    3a6b7369`64206f74
fffff880`159250f0    000d2025`30382020
fffff880`159250f8    00000000`00000000
fffff880`15925100    00000000`00000000
fffff880`15925108    00000000`00000000
fffff880`15925110    00000000`00000000
```

```
fffff880`15925118    00000000`00000000
fffff880`15925120    00000000`00000000
fffff880`15925128    00000000`00000000
fffff880`15925130    ffffcbba`00000000
fffff880`15925138    00000000`0badf00d
fffff880`15925140    ffffcbba`a9306858
fffff880`15925148    fffff802`b3bfe96c    nt!KiBugCheckProgress
fffff880`15925150    fffff802`b3bfe96c    nt!KiBugCheckProgress
fffff880`15925158    fffff802`b3bfe96c    nt!KiBugCheckProgress
fffff880`15925160    00000000`00000001
fffff880`15925168    00000000`00000000
fffff880`15925170    00000000`0000f08b
fffff880`15925178    fffff880`021e5985    crashdmp!DumpWrite+0x1c5
fffff880`15925180    fffff880`021ed3e0    crashdmp!Context+0x30
fffff880`15925188    fffff880`021ed3e0    crashdmp!Context+0x30
fffff880`15925190    fffff880`021ed3e0    crashdmp!Context+0x30
fffff880`15925198    fffff802`b3d7f100    nt!KiInitialPCR+0x100
fffff880`159251a0    fffff802`b3bfe96c    nt!KiBugCheckProgress
fffff880`159251a8    00000000`00000001
fffff880`159251b0    fffff802`b3d7f100    nt!KiInitialPCR+0x100
fffff880`159251b8    fffff880`021e4a4e    crashdmp!CrashdmpWrite+0x9e
fffff880`159251c0    00000000`00000000
fffff880`159251c8    fffff880`15925490
fffff880`159251d0    fffff802`b3d60200    nt!IopTriageDumpDataBlocks
fffff880`159251d8    fffff802`b3bfe96c    nt!KiBugCheckProgress
fffff880`159251e0    00000000`00000001
fffff880`159251e8    fffff802`b3bf4ea7    nt!IoWriteCrashDump+0x5e3
fffff880`159251f0    00000000`00000000
fffff880`159251f8    fffff880`15925490
fffff880`15925200    fffff802`b3d5ae00    nt!KeBugCheckAddPagesCallbackListHead
fffff880`15925208    00000000`00000001
fffff880`15925210    00300030`00300030
fffff880`15925218    00300030`00300030
fffff880`15925220    00300030`00300030
fffff880`15925228    00300030`00300030
fffff880`15925230    00300078`00300000
fffff880`15925238    00300030`00300030
fffff880`15925240    00300030`00300030
fffff880`15925248    00300030`00300030
fffff880`15925250    000000ef`00300130
fffff880`15925258    00000000`00000000
fffff880`15925260    00000000`00000000
fffff880`15925268    fffff802`b3d5ae00    nt!KeBugCheckAddPagesCallbackListHead
fffff880`15925270    fffffa80`02e6b1c0
fffff880`15925278    fffff802`b3d5ae00    nt!KeBugCheckAddPagesCallbackListHead
fffff880`15925280    fffffa80`02c02000
fffff880`15925288    0000000a`000d0044
fffff880`15925290    00000000`00000000
fffff880`15925298    00000000`000000ef
fffff880`159252a0    00000000`00000000
fffff880`159252a8    00000000`00000000
fffff880`159252b0    fffff880`15925510
fffff880`159252b8    00000000`00000000
fffff880`159252c0    00000000`00000000
fffff880`159252c8    00000000`00000000
fffff880`159252d0    00000000`00000000
fffff880`159252d8    fffff802`b3bfe96c    nt!KiBugCheckProgress
fffff880`159252e0    fffffa80`02c02000
fffff880`159252e8    fffff802`b3bf4710    nt!IoSetDumpRange
fffff880`159252f0    fffff802`b3bf4670    nt!IoFreeDumpRange
```

```
fffff880`159252f8    fffffa80`02e6b1c0
fffff880`15925300    00000000`00000000
fffff880`15925308    00000000`00000000
fffff880`15925310    00000000`0007d74c
fffff880`15925318    fffffa80`02c02038
fffff880`15925320    fffffa80`02e6b1c0
fffff880`15925328    00000000`00000000
fffff880`15925330    00000000`00000000
fffff880`15925338    00000000`00000000
fffff880`15925340    ffff7cad`450c285a
fffff880`15925348    fffff802`b3d7f180   nt!KiInitialPCR+0x180
fffff880`15925350    00000000`00000000
fffff880`15925358    fffff802`b3d7f180   nt!KiInitialPCR+0x180
fffff880`15925360    00000000`00000000
fffff880`15925368    00000000`000000ef
fffff880`15925370    fffffa80`02e6b100
fffff880`15925378    00000000`00000001
fffff880`15925380    00000000`00000000
fffff880`15925388    fffff802`b3bfe5b0   nt!KeBugCheck2+0x9c1
fffff880`15925390    fffff802`b3d1a5a0   nt!EtwpBugCheckCallback
fffff880`15925398    fffff802`b3d5adf0   nt!KeBugCheckReasonCallbackListHead
fffff880`159253a0    fffff802`b3d5adf0   nt!KeBugCheckReasonCallbackListHead
fffff880`159253a8    00000000`00000001
fffff880`159253b0    00000000`00000000
fffff880`159253b8    fffff880`15925510
fffff880`159253c0    fffffa80`03db4740
fffff880`159253c8    fffff802`b3bfe96c   nt!KiBugCheckProgress
fffff880`159253d0    fffff8a0`02c8dc01
fffff880`159253d8    fffff802`b3f5bbf4   nt!CmpCallCallBacks+0x3e4
fffff880`159253e0    01010001`0101dc40
fffff880`159253e8    00000000`00000000
fffff880`159253f0    fffff880`159255d0
fffff880`159253f8    00000000`00000000
fffff880`15925400    00000000`00000000
fffff880`15925408    fffff802`b3b3c95d   nt!ExQueueWorkItem+0x1fd
fffff880`15925410    fffff8a0`00000000
fffff880`15925418    fffff802`b3d7f180   nt!KiInitialPCR+0x180
fffff880`15925420    fffffa80`03db4740
fffff880`15925428    fffff800`00000000
fffff880`15925430    ffffffff`ffffffff
fffff880`15925438    fffff802`b3bfe96c   nt!KiBugCheckProgress
fffff880`15925440    fffff8a0`013d2f0c
fffff880`15925448    fffff802`b3d0d000   nt!ExNode0
fffff880`15925450    fffff880`15925b10
fffff880`15925458    00000000`0fa79f0a
fffff880`15925460    00000000`00140001
fffff880`15925468    00000000`00000002
fffff880`15925470    fffff880`15925500
fffff880`15925478    ffffffff`ffffffff
fffff880`15925480    fffff880`15925b10
fffff880`15925488    00000000`c0000034
fffff880`15925490    00000000`00000000
fffff880`15925498    00000000`00000001
fffff880`159254a0    fffffa80`03de4750
fffff880`159254a8    fffff8a0`00935380
fffff880`159254b0    00000000`00000000
fffff880`159254b8    fffff802`b3ebca64   nt!CmpParseKey+0x865
fffff880`159254c0    fffff880`0000001d
fffff880`159254c8    fffff880`15925698
fffff880`159254d0    fffff8a0`00b49000
```

```
fffff880`159254d8    fffff880`0000001d
fffff880`159254e0    00000000`00000000
fffff880`159254e8    fffff880`15925628
fffff880`159254f0    fffff880`159255d8
fffff880`159254f8    fffff880`15925580
fffff880`15925500    fffff880`15925b10
fffff880`15925508    fffff880`15925620
fffff880`15925510    00000000`00000000
fffff880`15925518    00000000`00000000
fffff880`15925520    00000000`00000000
fffff880`15925528    00000000`00000000
fffff880`15925530    00000000`00000000
fffff880`15925538    00000000`00000000
fffff880`15925540    00001f80`0010000f
fffff880`15925548    0053002b`002b0010
fffff880`15925550    00000246`0018002b
fffff880`15925558    00000000`00000000
fffff880`15925560    00000000`00000000
fffff880`15925568    00000000`00000000
fffff880`15925570    00000000`00000000
fffff880`15925578    00000000`00000000
fffff880`15925580    00000000`00000000
fffff880`15925588    fffff880`15925b03
fffff880`15925590    00000000`000000ef
fffff880`15925598    fffffa80`02e6b1c0
fffff880`159255a0    fffffa80`02e6b100
fffff880`159255a8    fffff880`15925ae8
fffff880`159255b0    00000000`00000001
fffff880`159255b8    00000000`00000000
fffff880`159255c0    fffffa80`02e6b1c0
fffff880`159255c8    00000000`00000000
fffff880`159255d0    00000000`00000000
fffff880`159255d8    00000000`144d2c09
fffff880`159255e0    fffff880`15925c38
fffff880`159255e8    00000000`00000001
fffff880`159255f0    00000000`00000000
fffff880`159255f8    fffffa80`03db4740
fffff880`15925600    fffffa80`03db4740
fffff880`15925608    fffff802`b3b03d40 nt!KeBugCheckEx
fffff880`15925610    00000000`0000027f
fffff880`15925618    00000000`00000000
fffff880`15925620    00000000`00000000
fffff880`15925628    00000000`00001f80
fffff880`15925630    00000000`00000000
fffff880`15925638    00000000`00000000
fffff880`15925640    00000000`00000000
[…]
fffff880`159259d8    00000000`00000000
fffff880`159259e0    fffffa80`02e6b100
fffff880`159259e8    00000000`00000000
fffff880`159259f0    00000000`ffffffff
fffff880`159259f8    00000000`00f800ca
fffff880`15925a00    fffff8a0`005e7560
fffff880`15925a08    fffff802`b3d7f180 nt!KiInitialPCR+0x180
fffff880`15925a10    00000000`00000001
fffff880`15925a18    000000f0`6e86e760
fffff880`15925a20    00000000`00000001
fffff880`15925a28    00000000`00000000
fffff880`15925a30    00000000`00000000
fffff880`15925a38    00000000`00000000
```

```
fffff880`15925a40  fffff880`15925cc0
fffff880`15925a48  fffff802`b3ec1e8d  nt!CmOpenKey+0x31c
fffff880`15925a50  00000000`00000000
fffff880`15925a58  000000f0`6e86e780
fffff880`15925a60  00000000`00000001
fffff880`15925a68  fffffa80`03db4740
fffff880`15925a70  fffffa80`03db4740
fffff880`15925a78  00000000`00000000
fffff880`15925a80  00000000`00000001
fffff880`15925a88  fffffa80`02e6b1c0
fffff880`15925a90  00000000`00000000
fffff880`15925a98  fffffa80`02e6b100
fffff880`15925aa0  00000000`00000001
fffff880`15925aa8  fffff802`b3b03e44  nt!KeBugCheckEx+0x104
fffff880`15925ab0  00000000`00000000
fffff880`15925ab8  00000000`00000000
fffff880`15925ac0  00000000`00000000
fffff880`15925ac8  00000000`00000001
fffff880`15925ad0  00000000`00000000
fffff880`15925ad8  00000000`00000000
fffff880`15925ae0  00000000`00000246
fffff880`15925ae8  fffff802`b400f0dd  nt!PspCatchCriticalBreak+0xad
fffff880`15925af0  00000000`000000ef
fffff880`15925af8  fffffa80`02e6b1c0
fffff880`15925b00  00000000`00000000
fffff880`15925b08  00000000`00000000
fffff880`15925b10  00000000`00000000
fffff880`15925b18  00000000`00000000
fffff880`15925b20  fffffa80`02e6b1c0
fffff880`15925b28  fffff802`b3ea8f6d  nt! ?? ::NNGAKEGL::`string'+0x46f60
fffff880`15925b30  fffffa80`02e6b1c0
fffff880`15925b38  00000000`144d2c01
fffff880`15925b40  00000000`00000000
fffff880`15925b48  ffff7cad`450c235a
fffff880`15925b50  fffffa80`03db4740
fffff880`15925b58  00000000`00000001
fffff880`15925b60  00000000`00000000
fffff880`15925b68  00000000`00000000
fffff880`15925b70  00000000`00000000
fffff880`15925b78  00000000`00000000
fffff880`15925b80  00000000`144d2c01
fffff880`15925b88  fffff802`b3ea8019  nt!PspTerminateProcess+0x6d
fffff880`15925b90  fffffa80`02e6b1c0
fffff880`15925b98  00000000`144d2c01
fffff880`15925ba0  fffffa80`02e6b1c0
fffff880`15925ba8  00000000`00000000
fffff880`15925bb0  00000000`00000001
fffff880`15925bb8  00000000`00000601
fffff880`15925bc0  fffffa80`03db4740
fffff880`15925bc8  fffff802`b3ea7e52  nt!NtTerminateProcess+0x9e
fffff880`15925bd0  ffffffff`ffffffff
fffff880`15925bd8  fffffa80`02d74180
fffff880`15925be0  fffffa80`02e6b1c0
fffff880`15925be8  00000000`00000001
fffff880`15925bf0  fffffa80`65547350
fffff880`15925bf8  fffff880`15925c40
fffff880`15925c00  00000000`00000000
fffff880`15925c08  ffff7cad`450c223a
fffff880`15925c10  000000f0`6edd7480
fffff880`15925c18  00000000`00000648
```

```
fffff880`15925c20    00000000`00000190
fffff880`15925c28    00000000`00000000
fffff880`15925c30    00000000`00000000
fffff880`15925c38    fffff802`b3b02d53 nt!KiSystemServiceCopyEnd+0x13
fffff880`15925c40    ffffffa80`02e6b1c0
fffff880`15925c48    ffffffa80`03db4740
fffff880`15925c50    fffff880`15925cc0
fffff880`15925c58    00000000`00000000
fffff880`15925c60    000000f0`00000000
fffff880`15925c68    00001fa0`02080000
fffff880`15925c70    00000000`00000000
fffff880`15925c78    00000000`000006b4
fffff880`15925c80    000007fe`f2956890 COMCTL32!DirectUI::InvokeHelper::s_uInvokeHelperMsg+0x88
fffff880`15925c88    000000f0`6e86f068
fffff880`15925c90    00000000`00000000
fffff880`15925c98    00000000`00000000
fffff880`15925ca0    00000000`00000246
fffff880`15925ca8    000007f7`70b7d000
fffff880`15925cb0    00000000`00000000
fffff880`15925cb8    00000000`00000000
fffff880`15925cc0    00000000`00000000
fffff880`15925cc8    00000000`00000000
fffff880`15925cd0    00000000`00000000
fffff880`15925cd8    00000000`00000000
fffff880`15925ce0    00000000`00000000
fffff880`15925ce8    00000000`00000000
fffff880`15925cf0    00000000`00000000
fffff880`15925cf8    00000000`00000000
fffff880`15925d00    00000000`00000000
fffff880`15925d08    00000000`00000000
fffff880`15925d10    000007fe`f2901000
COMCTL32!DirectUI::StyleSheetCache::CCacheThread::Initialize+0x54
fffff880`15925d18    00000000`00000000
fffff880`15925d20    00000000`00000000
fffff880`15925d28    00000000`00000000
fffff880`15925d30    00000000`00000000
fffff880`15925d38    00000000`00000000
fffff880`15925d40    00000000`00000000
fffff880`15925d48    00000000`00000000
fffff880`15925d50    00000000`00000000
fffff880`15925d58    00000000`00000000
fffff880`15925d60    00000000`00000000
fffff880`15925d68    00000000`00000000
fffff880`15925d70    00000000`00000000
fffff880`15925d78    00000000`00000000
fffff880`15925d80    00000000`00000648
fffff880`15925d88    00000000`00000001
fffff880`15925d90    00000000`00000000
fffff880`15925d98    000000f0`6e86f470
fffff880`15925da0    00000000`00000014
fffff880`15925da8    000007fe`f7ec2eaa ntdll!NtTerminateProcess+0xa
fffff880`15925db0    00000000`00000033
fffff880`15925db8    00000000`00000202
fffff880`15925dc0    000000f0`6e86f3e8
fffff880`15925dc8    00000000`0000002b
fffff880`15925dd0    fffff880`15926000
[…]
fffff880`15925ff0    00000000`00000000
fffff880`15925ff8    00000000`00000000
fffff880`15926000    ????????`????????
```

We can examine any suspicious module using **lmv** and **!lmi** commands.

```
0: kd> lmv m igdkmd64
start               end                 module name
fffff880`03e17000 fffff880`043fee00    igdkmd64   (pdb symbols)
c:\mss\igdkmd64.pdb\32FCA049C8194A398B9BE29BAF0CA69C1\igdkmd64.pdb
    Loaded symbol image file: igdkmd64.sys
    Image path: \SystemRoot\system32\DRIVERS\igdkmd64.sys
    Image name: igdkmd64.sys
    Timestamp:        Fri Mar 23 04:33:47 2012 (4F6BFD2B)
    CheckSum:         005EBF0F
    ImageSize:        005E7E00
    Translations:     0000.04b0 0000.04e4 0409.04b0 0409.04e4

0: kd> !lmi igdkmd64
Loaded Module Info: [igdkmd64]
         Module: igdkmd64
   Base Address: fffff88003e17000
     Image Name: igdkmd64.sys
   Machine Type: 34404 (X64)
     Time Stamp: 4f6bfd2b Fri Mar 23 04:33:47 2012
           Size: 5e7e00
       CheckSum: 5ebf0f
Characteristics: 2022
Debug Data Dirs: Type  Size      VA  Pointer
         CODEVIEW    89, 4cf978,   4cf978 RSDS - GUID: {32FCA049-C819-4A39-8B9B-
E29BAF0CA69C}
             Age: 1, Pdb: D:\ccViews\autobuild1_BR-1203-
0FZG_15.12.75_Snapshot\gfx_Development\dump64\igfx\lh\release\AIM3Lib\igdkmd64.pdb
     Image Type: MEMORY   - Image read successfully from loaded memory.
    Symbol Type: PDB       - Symbols loaded successfully from symbol server.
             c:\mss\igdkmd64.pdb\32FCA049C8194A398B9BE29BAF0CA69C1\igdkmd64.pdb
    Load Report: public symbols , not source indexed
             c:\mss\igdkmd64.pdb\32FCA049C8194A398B9BE29BAF0CA69C1\igdkmd64.pdb
```

Note that this module has symbols that come from Microsoft symbol server so it should be Microsoft module. Additionally we can also inspect module header using **!dh** command. Now we search for strings using various commands like we did in user space:

```
0: kd> s-sa fffff88015920000 fffff88015926000
fffff880`1592341c  " CR"
fffff880`15923474  " CR"
fffff880`159235bc  " CR"
fffff880`1592388c  " CR"
fffff880`15923aa4  " CR"
fffff880`15923b94  " CR"
fffff880`15923cfc  " CR"
fffff880`15923db4  " CR"
fffff880`15923f84  " CR"
fffff880`159240dc  " CR"
fffff880`15924124  " CR"
fffff880`15924344  " CR"
fffff880`159243d4  " CR"
fffff880`15924424  " CR"
fffff880`15924953  ">S7"
fffff880`15924a53  ">S7"
```

```
fffff880`15924c08    "`r3"
fffff880`15924d30    "Pv3"
fffff880`15924e78    "PY{"
fffff880`159250d0    "Dumping physical memory to disk:"
fffff880`159250f0    "  80% "
fffff880`15925140    "Xh0"
fffff880`15925a00    "`u^"
fffff880`15925bf0    "PsTe"

0: kd> dpa fffff88015920000 fffff88015926000
[…]
fffff880`15925000   fffff880`15925400 ""
fffff880`15925008   fffff880`021e5e2a "D...D$4..$."
fffff880`15925010   fffff880`159250d0 "Dumping physical memory to disk:  80% ."
fffff880`15925018   fffff880`021ed3e0 "PY{......."
fffff880`15925020   00000000`00000050
[…]
```

Note that the stack page was saved to a dump file when the progress bar was at 80%.

14.   Now we can list all processes and their stack traces. The first **!process** command type only lists the sort summary:

```
0: kd> !process 0 0
**** NT ACTIVE PROCESS DUMP ****
PROCESS fffffa800182e480
    SessionId: none  Cid: 0004    Peb: 00000000  ParentCid: 0000
    DirBase: 00187000  ObjectTable: fffff8a000003000  HandleCount: <Data Not Accessible>
    Image: System

PROCESS fffffa8002d78500
    SessionId: none  Cid: 011c    Peb: 7f6a68af000  ParentCid: 0004
    DirBase: 06696000  ObjectTable: fffff8a000b3b840  HandleCount: <Data Not Accessible>
    Image: smss.exe

PROCESS fffffa8002e6b1c0
    SessionId: 0  Cid: 0190    Peb: 7f7688e8000  ParentCid: 0188
    DirBase: 114d5000  ObjectTable: fffff8a001c6c680  HandleCount: <Data Not Accessible>
    Image: csrss.exe

PROCESS fffffa8002e7b940
    SessionId: 0  Cid: 01c4    Peb: 7f6f01fc000  ParentCid: 0188
    DirBase: 2449b000  ObjectTable: fffff8a00156ed80  HandleCount: <Data Not Accessible>
    Image: wininit.exe

PROCESS fffffa80033c3080
    SessionId: 0  Cid: 0220    Peb: 7f75ab5d000  ParentCid: 01c4
    DirBase: 2e23b000  ObjectTable: fffff8a0016a32c0  HandleCount: <Data Not Accessible>
    Image: services.exe
[…]
```

To list all thread stacks in detail you can use the same command with different flags (**3f** will be necessary to get correct user space portion of stack traces for complete memory dumps):

```
0: kd> !process 0 3f
**** NT ACTIVE PROCESS DUMP ****
[…]
```

Note that we skip the output here because it will fill a book. We can also list processes from a specific session:

```
0: kd> !session
Sessions on machine: 3
Valid Sessions: 0 1 2
Current Session 2

0: kd> !sprocess 2 3f
Dumping Session 2
```

[…]

We skip the output here too. Finally the last command show zombie processes at the end:

```
0: kd> !vm

*** Virtual Memory Usage ***
        Physical Memory:      513749 (    2054996 Kb)
        Page File: \??\C:\pagefile.sys
          Current:   2359296 Kb  Free Space:    2272648 Kb
          Minimum:   2359296 Kb  Maximum:       6291456 Kb
        Page File: \??\C:\swapfile.sys
          Current:    262144 Kb  Free Space:     262136 Kb
          Minimum:    262144 Kb  Maximum:       3082492 Kb
        Available Pages:      216378 (     865512 Kb)
        ResAvail Pages:       445904 (    1783616 Kb)
        Locked IO Pages:           0 (          0 Kb)
        Free System PTEs:   33460094 (  133840376 Kb)
        Modified Pages:         5403 (      21612 Kb)
        Modified PF Pages:      5400 (      21600 Kb)
        NonPagedPool Usage:      784 (       3136 Kb)
        NonPagedPoolNx Usage:   7868 (      31472 Kb)
        NonPagedPool Max:     979551 (    3918204 Kb)
        PagedPool 0 Usage:     17859 (      71436 Kb)
        PagedPool 1 Usage:      3094 (      12376 Kb)
        PagedPool 2 Usage:      1385 (       5540 Kb)
        PagedPool 3 Usage:      1362 (       5448 Kb)
        PagedPool 4 Usage:      1430 (       5720 Kb)
        PagedPool Usage:       25130 (     100520 Kb)
        PagedPool Maximum: 100663296 (  402653184 Kb)
        Session Commit:         6322 (      25288 Kb)
        Shared Commit:         57010 (     228040 Kb)
        Special Pool:              0 (          0 Kb)
        Shared Process:         4259 (      17036 Kb)
        PagedPool Commit:      25146 (     100584 Kb)
        Driver Commit:         10957 (      43828 Kb)
        Committed pages:      267388 (    1069552 Kb)
        Commit limit:        1103573 (    4414292 Kb)

        Total Private:        124369 (     497476 Kb)
           0598 MsMpEng.exe     17114 (      68456 Kb)
           06f8 dwm.exe         13202 (      52808 Kb)
           03f0 svchost.exe     12699 (      50796 Kb)
           0d04 iexplore.exe     9242 (      36968 Kb)
           0314 svchost.exe      8943 (      35772 Kb)
           0d68 explorer.exe     8899 (      35596 Kb)
           0478 WWAHost.exe      5574 (      22296 Kb)
           04e4 svchost.exe      4281 (      17124 Kb)
```

```
02f0 svchost.exe        4051 (    16204 Kb)
0270 SearchIndexer.     3928 (    15712 Kb)
0f98 msiexec.exe        3725 (    14900 Kb)
0bdc LiveComm.exe       3185 (    12740 Kb)
0ca0 Taskmgr.exe        2905 (    11620 Kb)
03b8 svchost.exe        2353 (     9412 Kb)
0c80 iexplore.exe       2314 (     9256 Kb)
0a50 mspaint.exe        2145 (     8580 Kb)
0360 svchost.exe        1993 (     7972 Kb)
02a0 taskhostex.exe     1826 (     7304 Kb)
08a8 svchost.exe        1556 (     6224 Kb)
07e8 svchost.exe        1532 (     6128 Kb)
0ba8 wmpnetwk.exe       1441 (     5764 Kb)
0228 lsass.exe          1107 (     4428 Kb)
04c8 spoolsv.exe        1046 (     4184 Kb)
0220 services.exe       1007 (     4028 Kb)
03e4 RuntimeBroker.      985 (     3940 Kb)
02b0 svchost.exe         903 (     3612 Kb)
063c dasHost.exe         881 (     3524 Kb)
0814 BackgroundTran      781 (     3124 Kb)
0288 svchost.exe         702 (     2808 Kb)
0e74 iexplore.exe        610 (     2440 Kb)
0dd0 browserchoice.      495 (     1980 Kb)
0cdc csrss.exe           442 (     1768 Kb)
0e80 WmiPrvSE.exe        436 (     1744 Kb)
02e4 svchost.exe         384 (     1536 Kb)
0bac dllhost.exe         361 (     1444 Kb)
0190 csrss.exe           349 (     1396 Kb)
0d7c notepad.exe         315 (     1260 Kb)
0a28 winlogon.exe        291 (     1164 Kb)
01c4 wininit.exe         255 (     1020 Kb)
011c smss.exe             80 (      320 Kb)
0004 System               31 (      124 Kb)
0dac LogonUI.exe           0 (        0 Kb)
0acc explorer.exe          0 (        0 Kb)
0a3c smss.exe              0 (        0 Kb)
```

15.   Now we check commands related to CPU consumption:

```
0: kd> !running -i

System Processors:  (0000000000000003)
  Idle Processors:  (0000000000000000)

      Prcbs              Current           (pri) Next             (pri) Idle
  0   fffff802b3d7f180   fffffa8003db4740  (13)                        fffff802b3dd9880  ................
  1   fffff880009e6180   fffffa80037b4080  (13)                        fffff880009f1dc0  ................
```

To quickly check kernel space thread stack portion we can use **-t** flag:

```
0: kd> !running -i -t

System Processors:  (0000000000000003)
  Idle Processors:  (0000000000000000)

      Prcbs              Current           (pri) Next             (pri) Idle
  0   fffff802b3d7f180   fffffa8003db4740  (13)                        fffff802b3dd9880  ................

Child-SP          RetAddr           Call Site
fffff880`15925ae8 fffff802`b400f0dd nt!KeBugCheckEx
fffff880`15925af0 fffff802`b3ea8f6d nt!PspCatchCriticalBreak+0xad
fffff880`15925b30 fffff802`b3ea8019 nt! ?? ::NNGAKEGL::`string'+0x46f60
```

```
ffffff880`15925b90 ffffff802`b3ea7e52 nt!PspTerminateProcess+0x6d
ffffff880`15925bd0 ffffff802`b3b02d53 nt!NtTerminateProcess+0x9e
ffffff880`15925c40 000007fe`f7ec2eaa nt!KiSystemServiceCopyEnd+0x13
000000f0`6e86f3e8 00000000`00000000 ntdll!NtTerminateProcess+0xa

  1     ffffff880009e6180   fffffa80037b4080 (13)                    ffffff880009f1dc0 ...............

Child-SP          RetAddr           Call Site
ffffff880`159e39b0 ffffff960`001862d3 win32k!xxxInternalDoPaint+0x19
ffffff880`159e3a00 ffffff960`001862d3 win32k!xxxInternalDoPaint+0x43
ffffff880`159e3a50 ffffff960`001862d3 win32k!xxxInternalDoPaint+0x43
ffffff880`159e3aa0 ffffff960`001862d3 win32k!xxxInternalDoPaint+0x43
ffffff880`159e3af0 ffffff960`001862d3 win32k!xxxInternalDoPaint+0x43
ffffff880`159e3b40 ffffff960`001862d3 win32k!xxxInternalDoPaint+0x43
ffffff880`159e3b90 ffffff960`0018608c win32k!xxxInternalDoPaint+0x43
ffffff880`159e3be0 ffffff960`001532e3 win32k!xxxDoPaint+0x4c
ffffff880`159e3c20 ffffff960`00225974 win32k!xxxRealInternalGetMessage+0xa73
ffffff880`159e3d40 ffffff802`b3b02d53 win32k!NtUserRealInternalGetMessage+0x74
ffffff880`159e3dd0 000007fe`f56c1b4a nt!KiSystemServiceCopyEnd+0x13
00000000`034af598 000007fe`f2a810fb USER32!NtUserRealInternalGetMessage+0xa
00000000`034af5a0 00000000`00000012 0x000007fe`f2a810fb
00000000`034af5a8 000007fe`e5e31f20 0x12
00000000`034af5b0 00000000`000100dc 0x000007fe`e5e31f20
00000000`034af5b8 00000000`00000000 0x100dc
```

Unfortunately, it doesn't show correct user space portion of the full stack trace so we use **!thread** command:

```
0: kd> !thread fffffa80037b4080 3f
THREAD fffffa80037b4080  Cid 0d68.0638  Teb: 000007f68f179000 Win32Thread: ffffff9010063e5b0 RUNNING on
processor 1
Not impersonating
DeviceMap                     ffffff8a000290b20
Owning Process                fffffa8003ed3600      Image:          explorer.exe
Attached Process              N/A           Image:          N/A
Wait Start TickCount          15741128      Ticks: 0
Context Switch Count          18325         IdealProcessor: 0
UserTime                      00:00:00.280
KernelTime                    00:00:00.405
Win32 Start Address SHCORE!COplockFileHandle::v_GetHandlerCLSID (0x000007fef2ef4020)
Stack Init ffffff880159e3fd0 Current ffffff880171fc7f0
Base ffffff880159e4000 Limit ffffff880159de000 Call 0
Priority 13 BasePriority 9 UnusualBoost 0 ForegroundBoost 2 IoPriority 2 PagePriority 5
Child-SP          RetAddr           Call Site
ffffff880`159e39b0 ffffff960`001862d3 win32k!xxxInternalDoPaint+0x19
ffffff880`159e3a00 ffffff960`001862d3 win32k!xxxInternalDoPaint+0x43
ffffff880`159e3a50 ffffff960`001862d3 win32k!xxxInternalDoPaint+0x43
ffffff880`159e3aa0 ffffff960`001862d3 win32k!xxxInternalDoPaint+0x43
ffffff880`159e3af0 ffffff960`001862d3 win32k!xxxInternalDoPaint+0x43
ffffff880`159e3b40 ffffff960`001862d3 win32k!xxxInternalDoPaint+0x43
ffffff880`159e3b90 ffffff960`0018608c win32k!xxxInternalDoPaint+0x43
ffffff880`159e3be0 ffffff960`001532e3 win32k!xxxDoPaint+0x4c
ffffff880`159e3c20 ffffff960`00225974 win32k!xxxRealInternalGetMessage+0xa73
ffffff880`159e3d40 ffffff802`b3b02d53 win32k!NtUserRealInternalGetMessage+0x74
ffffff880`159e3dd0 000007fe`f56c1b4a nt!KiSystemServiceCopyEnd+0x13 (TrapFrame @ ffffff880`159e3e40)
00000000`034af598 000007fe`f2a810fb USER32!NtUserRealInternalGetMessage+0xa
00000000`034af5a0 000007fe`f2a8120b DUser!CoreSC::xwProcessNL+0xe7
00000000`034af670 000007fe`f56c1bad DUser!MphProcessMessage+0xb3
00000000`034af6d0 000007fe`f7ec4b67 USER32!_ClientGetMessageMPH+0x3d
00000000`034af760 000007fe`f56c120a ntdll!KiUserCallbackDispatcherContinue (TrapFrame @
00000000`034af628)
00000000`034af7d8 000007fe`f56c1250 USER32!NtUserPeekMessage+0xa
00000000`034af7e0 000007fe`f56c1145 USER32!PeekMessage+0x2c
00000000`034af820 000007f6`8f66105a USER32!PeekMessageW+0x85
00000000`034af860 000007f6`8f68b41e Explorer!CTray::_MessageLoop+0x4b
00000000`034af8f0 000007fe`f2ef410c Explorer!CTray::MainThreadProc+0x86
00000000`034af920 000007fe`f601167e SHCORE!COplockFileHandle::v_GetHandlerCLSID+0x12c
```

174

```
00000000`034afa10 000007fe`f7ee3501 KERNEL32!BaseThreadInitThunk+0x1a
00000000`034afa40 00000000`00000000 ntdll!RtlUserThreadStart+0x1d
```

And finally for this exercise we try **!ready** command to list thread ready for execution:

```
0: kd> !ready
Processor 0: Ready Threads at priority 12
    THREAD fffffa80040667c0  Cid 0d68.0d3c  Teb: 000007f68f026000 Win32Thread: fffff90103f08b90 READY on processor 0
Processor 1: Ready Threads at priority 12
    THREAD fffffa8001da2380  Cid 0004.0f28  Teb: 0000000000000000 Win32Thread: 0000000000000000 READY on processor 1
Processor 1: Ready Threads at priority 10
    THREAD fffffa8003f0ca00  Cid 0d68.03b4  Teb: 000007f68f048000 Win32Thread: fffff90103ede780 READY on processor 1
    THREAD fffffa8002cdf300  Cid 0d68.0854  Teb: 000007f68f03c000 Win32Thread: fffff90103f544e0 READY on processor 1
```

16.   Close the log file:

```
0: kd> .logclose
Closing open log file C:\AWMA-Dumps\M4.log
```

17.   To avoid possible confusion and glitches we recommend exiting WinDbg after each exercise.

If you are presented with this dialog choose No:

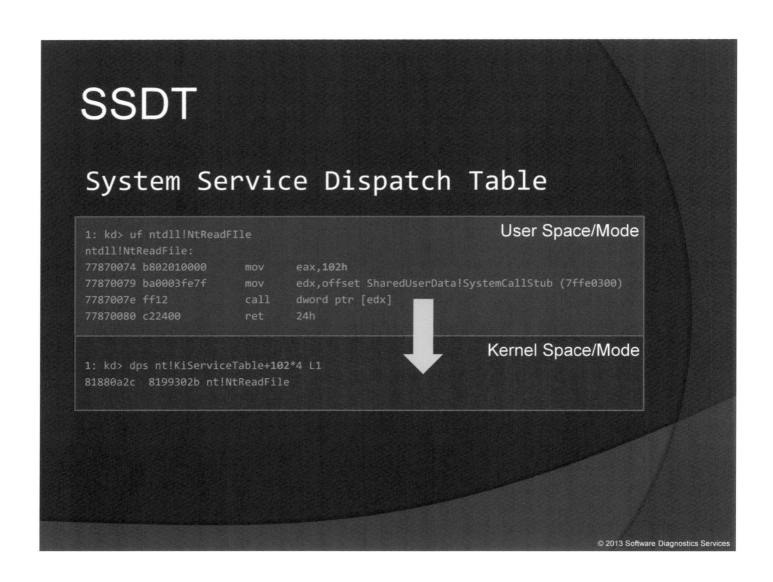

SSDT

System Service Dispatch Table

```
1: kd> uf ntdll!NtReadFIle                                    User Space/Mode
ntdll!NtReadFile:
77870074 b802010000      mov      eax,102h
77870079 ba0003fe7f      mov      edx,offset SharedUserData!SystemCallStub (7ffe0300)
7787007e ff12            call     dword ptr [edx]
77870080 c22400          ret      24h

                                                              Kernel Space/Mode

1: kd> dps nt!KiServiceTable+102*4 L1
81880a2c  8199302b nt!NtReadFile
```

User space calls from DLLs such as user32, gdi32 and kernel32 are forwarded to ntdll module from which they transition to kernel space. The kernel maintains a special table containing pointers to corresponding kernel functions. On this slide, for example, we see ReadFile API call is mapped to 102nd entry in service table. This table can be hooked too and the presence of any raw pointers or pointers to code outside nt module range should trigger a suspicion. The example here is from 32-bit Windows SSDT. On x64 Windows system SSDT is more complicated and I show you that too.

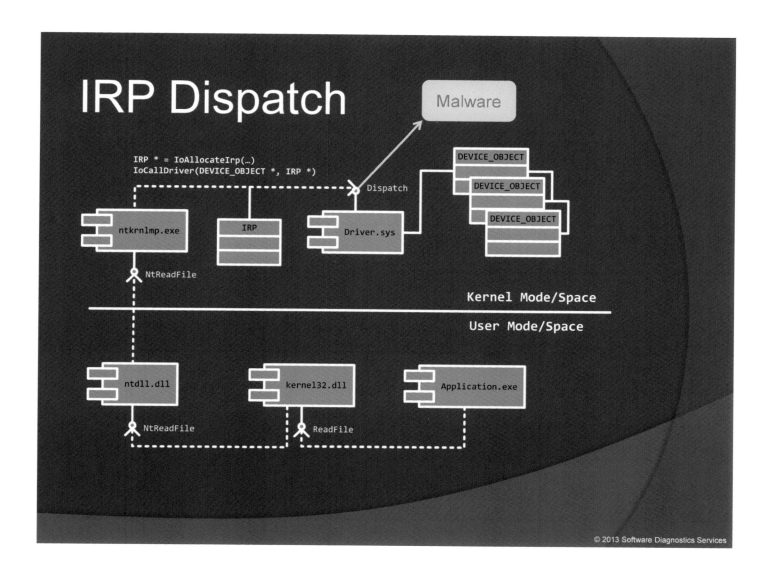

This is a big picture of I/O. Requests such as reading and writing to a device are implemented by a packet-driven architecture. Upon such a request, I/O Manager (a loosely defined component in kernel space) allocates a structure to describe a request including pointers to buffers for device data and then passes it through device driver stack (for example, file system -> volume -> disk array -> disk). Notice that an IRP is created and passed to Driver.sys code. There, according to an IRP dispatch table, an appropriate function is called. This table can be hooked by malware.

Device Driver Example

```
1: kd> !drvobj \Driver\CmBatt 3
Driver object (87668378) is for:
 \Driver\CmBatt
Driver Extension List: (id , addr)

Device Object list:
849e38a0  848c29b8


DriverEntry:    85a399bc   CmBatt!GsDriverEntry
DriverStartIo: 00000000
DriverUnload:   85a38b06   CmBatt!CmBattUnload
AddDevice:      85a38588   CmBatt!CmBattAddDevice

Dispatch routines:
[00] IRP_MJ_CREATE                    85a38b40    CmBatt!CmBattOpenClose
[01] IRP_MJ_CREATE_NAMED_PIPE         8181d171    nt!IopInvalidDeviceRequest
[02] IRP_MJ_CLOSE                     85a38b40    CmBatt!CmBattOpenClose
[03] IRP_MJ_READ                      87fe6226    ModuleA+0x3464
[04] IRP_MJ_WRITE                     8181d171    nt!IopInvalidDeviceRequest
[05] IRP_MJ_QUERY_INFORMATION         8181d171    nt!IopInvalidDeviceRequest
[06] IRP_MJ_SET_INFORMATION           8181d171    nt!IopInvalidDeviceRequest
[07] IRP_MJ_QUERY_EA                  8181d171    nt!IopInvalidDeviceRequest
[08] IRP_MJ_SET_EA                    8181d171    nt!IopInvalidDeviceRequest
[...]
```

Here's a typical device driver example with IRP dispatch table. Notice a hooked entry there.

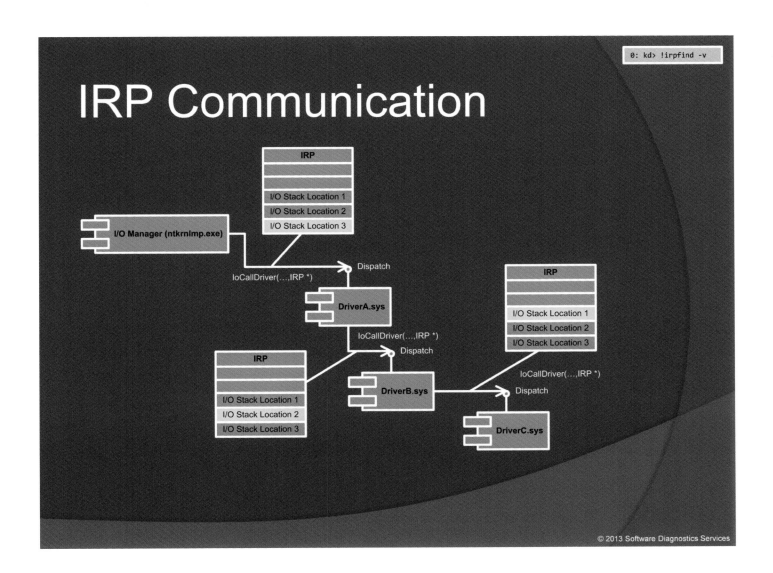

To keep track of the current device driver in device driver stack each I/O Request Packet (IRP) contains a stack at the end of its structure. It is implemented similar to a thread stack: its pointer (slot index) is decremented from bottom to top. We can dump all such I/O stacks and look for any anomalies.

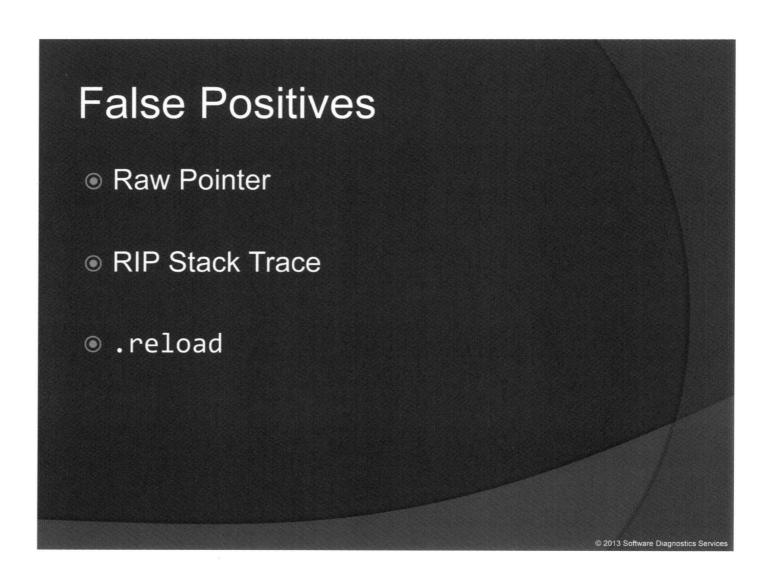

Just before we continue with our next exercise I would like to mention the possible occurrence of raw pointers or strange references outside expected range. These might be false positives due to recent change of context and we should first try to resolve symbols by **.reload** command.

Exercise M5

- **Goal:** Navigate CPUs, check IDT and SSDT, navigate through drivers and check their dispatch tables

- **Patterns:** Driver Device Collection, Raw Pointer, Out-of-Module Pointer

- \AWMA-Dumps\Exercise-M5.pdf

Now we analyze a 32-bit complete memory dump.

Goal: Navigate CPUs, check IDT and SSDT, navigate through drivers and check their dispatch tables.

Patterns: Driver Device Collection, Raw Pointer, Out-of-Module Pointer

1.   Launch WinDbg from Windows Kits \ Debugging Tools for Windows (X64) or Debugging Tools for Windows (X86)

2.   Open \AWMA-Dumps\Complete\MEMORY2.DMP

3.   If you are presented with this dialog say No:

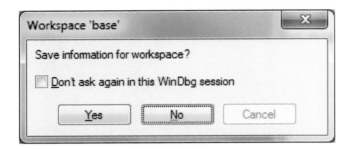

4.   You get the dump file loaded:

```
Microsoft (R) Windows Debugger Version 6.2.9200.20512 X86
Copyright (c) Microsoft Corporation. All rights reserved.


Loading Dump File [C:\AWMA-Dumps\Complete\MEMORY2.DMP]
Kernel Complete Dump File: Full address space is available

Symbol search path is: *** Invalid ***
****************************************************************
* Symbol loading may be unreliable without a symbol search path.   *
* Use .symfix to have the debugger choose a symbol path.           *
* After setting your symbol path, use .reload to refresh symbol locations. *
****************************************************************
Executable search path is:
****************************************************************
* Symbols can not be loaded because symbol path is not initialized. *
*                                                                  *
* The Symbol Path can be set by:                                   *
*    using the _NT_SYMBOL_PATH environment variable.               *
*    using the -y <symbol_path> argument when starting the debugger. *
*    using .sympath and .sympath+                                  *
****************************************************************
*** ERROR: Symbol file could not be found.  Defaulted to export symbols for ntkrpamp.exe -
Windows Vista Kernel Version 6000 MP (2 procs) Free x86 compatible
Product: WinNt, suite: TerminalServer SingleUserTS Personal
Built by: 6000.16386.x86fre.vista_rtm.061101-2205
Machine Name:
Kernel base = 0x81800000 PsLoadedModuleList = 0x81911db0
Debug session time: Wed Jul 20 21:26:14.859 2011 (UTC + 0:00)
System Uptime: 0 days 0:15:30.657
```

```
*********************************************************************
* Symbols can not be loaded because symbol path is not initialized. *
*                                                                   *
* The Symbol Path can be set by:                                    *
*    using the _NT_SYMBOL_PATH environment variable.                *
*    using the -y <symbol_path> argument when starting the debugger.*
*    using .sympath and .sympath+                                   *
*********************************************************************
*** ERROR: Symbol file could not be found.  Defaulted to export symbols for ntkrpamp.exe -
Loading Kernel Symbols
...............................................................
...............................................................
...........
Loading User Symbols
..................................
Loading unloaded module list
.........*** ERROR: Symbol file could not be found.  Defaulted to export symbols for ntdll.dll
-

*********************************************************************************
*                                                                             *
*                          Bugcheck Analysis                                  *
*                                                                             *
*********************************************************************************

Use !analyze -v to get detailed debugging information.

BugCheck F4, {3, 876a72a0, 876a73ec, 81aaa4b0}

***** Kernel symbols are WRONG. Please fix symbols to do analysis.


        -------------------------------------------------
        |                                               |
        |         NT symbols are not available          |
        |                                               |
        -------------------------------------------------
*********************************************************************************
***                                                                         ***
***                                                                         ***
***     Either you specified an unqualified symbol, or your debugger        ***
***     doesn't have full symbol information.  Unqualified symbol           ***
***     resolution is turned off by default. Please either specify a        ***
***     fully qualified symbol module!symbolname, or enable resolution      ***
***     of unqualified symbols by typing ".symopt- 100". Note that          ***
***     enabling unqualified symbol resolution with network symbol          ***
***     server shares in the symbol path may cause the debugger to          ***
***     appear to hang for long periods of time when an incorrect           ***
***     symbol name is typed or the network symbol server is down.          ***
***                                                                         ***
***     For some commands to work properly, your symbol path                ***
***     must point to .pdb files that have full type information.           ***
***                                                                         ***
***     Certain .pdb files (such as the public OS symbols) do not           ***
***     contain the required information.  Contact the group that           ***
***     provided you with these symbols if you need this command to         ***
***     work.                                                               ***
***                                                                         ***
***     Type referenced: nt!_KPRCB                                          ***
***                                                                         ***
*********************************************************************************
```

```
***************************************************************************
***                                                                     ***
***                                                                     ***
***     Either you specified an unqualified symbol, or your debugger    ***
***     doesn't have full symbol information.  Unqualified symbol       ***
***     resolution is turned off by default. Please either specify a    ***
***     fully qualified symbol module!symbolname, or enable resolution  ***
***     of unqualified symbols by typing ".symopt- 100". Note that      ***
***     enabling unqualified symbol resolution with network symbol      ***
***     server shares in the symbol path may cause the debugger to      ***
***     appear to hang for long periods of time when an incorrect       ***
***     symbol name is typed or the network symbol server is down.      ***
***                                                                     ***
***     For some commands to work properly, your symbol path            ***
***     must point to .pdb files that have full type information.       ***
***                                                                     ***
***     Certain .pdb files (such as the public OS symbols) do not       ***
***     contain the required information.  Contact the group that       ***
***     provided you with these symbols if you need this command to     ***
***     work.                                                           ***
***                                                                     ***
***     Type referenced: nt!KPRCB                                       ***
***                                                                     ***
***************************************************************************
***************************************************************************
***                                                                     ***
***                                                                     ***
***     Either you specified an unqualified symbol, or your debugger    ***
***     doesn't have full symbol information.  Unqualified symbol       ***
***     resolution is turned off by default. Please either specify a    ***
***     fully qualified symbol module!symbolname, or enable resolution  ***
***     of unqualified symbols by typing ".symopt- 100". Note that      ***
***     enabling unqualified symbol resolution with network symbol      ***
***     server shares in the symbol path may cause the debugger to      ***
***     appear to hang for long periods of time when an incorrect       ***
***     symbol name is typed or the network symbol server is down.      ***
***                                                                     ***
***     For some commands to work properly, your symbol path            ***
***     must point to .pdb files that have full type information.       ***
***                                                                     ***
***     Certain .pdb files (such as the public OS symbols) do not       ***
***     contain the required information.  Contact the group that       ***
***     provided you with these symbols if you need this command to     ***
***     work.                                                           ***
***                                                                     ***
***     Type referenced: nt!_KPRCB                                      ***
***                                                                     ***
***************************************************************************
***************************************************************************
***                                                                     ***
***                                                                     ***
***     Either you specified an unqualified symbol, or your debugger    ***
***     doesn't have full symbol information.  Unqualified symbol       ***
***     resolution is turned off by default. Please either specify a    ***
***     fully qualified symbol module!symbolname, or enable resolution  ***
***     of unqualified symbols by typing ".symopt- 100". Note that      ***
***     enabling unqualified symbol resolution with network symbol      ***
***     server shares in the symbol path may cause the debugger to      ***
***     appear to hang for long periods of time when an incorrect       ***
***     symbol name is typed or the network symbol server is down.      ***
```

```
***                                                               ***
***    For some commands to work properly, your symbol path       ***
***    must point to .pdb files that have full type information.   ***
***                                                               ***
***    Certain .pdb files (such as the public OS symbols) do not   ***
***    contain the required information.  Contact the group that   ***
***    provided you with these symbols if you need this command to ***
***    work.                                                       ***
***                                                               ***
***    Type referenced: nt!KPRCB                                   ***
***                                                               ***
*******************************************************************
*******************************************************************
***                                                               ***
***                                                               ***
***    Either you specified an unqualified symbol, or your debugger ***
***    doesn't have full symbol information.  Unqualified symbol   ***
***    resolution is turned off by default. Please either specify a ***
***    fully qualified symbol module!symbolname, or enable resolution ***
***    of unqualified symbols by typing ".symopt- 100". Note that   ***
***    enabling unqualified symbol resolution with network symbol  ***
***    server shares in the symbol path may cause the debugger to  ***
***    appear to hang for long periods of time when an incorrect   ***
***    symbol name is typed or the network symbol server is down.  ***
***                                                               ***
***    For some commands to work properly, your symbol path       ***
***    must point to .pdb files that have full type information.   ***
***                                                               ***
***    Certain .pdb files (such as the public OS symbols) do not   ***
***    contain the required information.  Contact the group that   ***
***    provided you with these symbols if you need this command to ***
***    work.                                                       ***
***                                                               ***
***    Type referenced: nt!_KPRCB                                  ***
***                                                               ***
*******************************************************************
*******************************************************************
***                                                               ***
***                                                               ***
***    Either you specified an unqualified symbol, or your debugger ***
***    doesn't have full symbol information.  Unqualified symbol   ***
***    resolution is turned off by default. Please either specify a ***
***    fully qualified symbol module!symbolname, or enable resolution ***
***    of unqualified symbols by typing ".symopt- 100". Note that   ***
***    enabling unqualified symbol resolution with network symbol  ***
***    server shares in the symbol path may cause the debugger to  ***
***    appear to hang for long periods of time when an incorrect   ***
***    symbol name is typed or the network symbol server is down.  ***
***                                                               ***
***    For some commands to work properly, your symbol path       ***
***    must point to .pdb files that have full type information.   ***
***                                                               ***
***    Certain .pdb files (such as the public OS symbols) do not   ***
***    contain the required information.  Contact the group that   ***
***    provided you with these symbols if you need this command to ***
***    work.                                                       ***
***                                                               ***
***    Type referenced: nt!_KPRCB                                  ***
***                                                               ***
*******************************************************************
```

```
*************************************************************************
***                                                                   ***
***                                                                   ***
***      Either you specified an unqualified symbol, or your debugger ***
***      doesn't have full symbol information.  Unqualified symbol    ***
***      resolution is turned off by default. Please either specify a ***
***      fully qualified symbol module!symbolname, or enable resolution ***
***      of unqualified symbols by typing ".symopt- 100". Note that   ***
***      enabling unqualified symbol resolution with network symbol   ***
***      server shares in the symbol path may cause the debugger to   ***
***      appear to hang for long periods of time when an incorrect    ***
***      symbol name is typed or the network symbol server is down.   ***
***                                                                   ***
***      For some commands to work properly, your symbol path         ***
***      must point to .pdb files that have full type information.    ***
***                                                                   ***
***      Certain .pdb files (such as the public OS symbols) do not    ***
***      contain the required information.  Contact the group that    ***
***      provided you with these symbols if you need this command to  ***
***      work.                                                        ***
***                                                                   ***
***      Type referenced: nt!_KPRCB                                   ***
***                                                                   ***
*************************************************************************
*************************************************************************
***                                                                   ***
***                                                                   ***
***      Either you specified an unqualified symbol, or your debugger ***
***      doesn't have full symbol information.  Unqualified symbol    ***
***      resolution is turned off by default. Please either specify a ***
***      fully qualified symbol module!symbolname, or enable resolution ***
***      of unqualified symbols by typing ".symopt- 100". Note that   ***
***      enabling unqualified symbol resolution with network symbol   ***
***      server shares in the symbol path may cause the debugger to   ***
***      appear to hang for long periods of time when an incorrect    ***
***      symbol name is typed or the network symbol server is down.   ***
***                                                                   ***
***      For some commands to work properly, your symbol path         ***
***      must point to .pdb files that have full type information.    ***
***                                                                   ***
***      Certain .pdb files (such as the public OS symbols) do not    ***
***      contain the required information.  Contact the group that    ***
***      provided you with these symbols if you need this command to  ***
***      work.                                                        ***
***                                                                   ***
***      Type referenced: nt!_KPRCB                                   ***
***                                                                   ***
*************************************************************************
*************************************************************************
* Symbols can not be loaded because symbol path is not initialized. *
*                                                                   *
* The Symbol Path can be set by:                                    *
*   using the _NT_SYMBOL_PATH environment variable.                 *
*   using the -y <symbol_path> argument when starting the debugger. *
*   using .sympath and .sympath+                                    *
*********************************************************************
Probably caused by : csrss.exe

Followup: MachineOwner
---------
```

5. Open a log file:

```
0: kd> .logopen C:\AWMA-Dumps\M5.log
Opened log file 'C:\AWMA-Dumps\M5.log'
```

6. Set up a link to Microsoft symbol server and reload symbols:

```
0: kd> .symfix c:\mss

0: kd> .reload
Loading Kernel Symbols
...............................................................
...............................................................
...........
Loading User Symbols
.................................
Loading unloaded module list
.........Unable to enumerate user-mode unloaded modules, NTSTATUS 0xC0000147
```

7. We switch to the second CPU using **~<n>s** command and check its IDT:

```
0: kd> ~1s

1: kd> k
ChildEBP RetAddr
WARNING: Frame IP not in any known module. Following frames may be wrong.
0018fd8c 7787027f 0xab76be
0018fdf0 76113833 ntdll!NtSecureConnectPort+0xb
0018fe18 00000000 kernel32!BaseThreadInitThunk+0xe
```

It looks like we have a false positive instance of RIP Stack Trace pattern because it disappears as soon as we reload symbols:

```
1: kd> .reload
Loading Kernel Symbols
...............................................................
...............................................................
...........
Loading User Symbols
...
Loading unloaded module list
.........Unable to enumerate user-mode unloaded modules, NTSTATUS 0xC0000147
*** ERROR: Module load completed but symbols could not be loaded for ApplicationE.exe

1: kd> k
ChildEBP RetAddr
WARNING: Stack unwind information not available. Following frames may be wrong.
0018fda8 00ab13fc ApplicationE+0x76be
0018fdf0 76113833 ApplicationE+0x13fc
0018fdfc 7784a9bd kernel32!BaseThreadInitThunk+0xe
0018fe3c 00000000 ntdll!_RtlUserThreadStart+0x23
```

8.　　Let's check CPU 1 IDT:

```
1: kd> !idt

Dumping IDT: 857ee960

eefa51a100000037:    81bb50e8 hal!PicSpuriousService37
eefa51a100000050:    8393aa50 pci!ExpressRootPortMessageRoutine (KINTERRUPT 8393aa00)
eefa51a100000051:    848e37d0 serial!SerialCIsrSw (KINTERRUPT 848e3780)
eefa51a100000052:    83951cd0 pci!ExpressRootPortMessageRoutine (KINTERRUPT 83951c80)
eefa51a100000053:    8395ca50 pci!ExpressRootPortMessageRoutine (KINTERRUPT 8395ca00)
eefa51a100000054:    8399d7d0 pci!ExpressRootPortMessageRoutine (KINTERRUPT 8399d780)
eefa51a100000055:    839ac550 ataport!IdePortInterrupt (KINTERRUPT 839ac500)
eefa51a100000060:    8393acd0 pci!ExpressRootPortMessageRoutine (KINTERRUPT 8393ac80)
eefa51a100000062:    8393a050 pci!ExpressRootPortMessageRoutine (KINTERRUPT 8393a000)
eefa51a100000063:    8395ccd0 pci!ExpressRootPortMessageRoutine (KINTERRUPT 8395cc80)
eefa51a100000064:    8399da50 pci!ExpressRootPortMessageRoutine (KINTERRUPT 8399da00)
eefa51a100000065:    839ac7d0 pci!ExpressRootPortMessageRoutine (KINTERRUPT 839ac780)
eefa51a100000070:    83911050 pci!ExpressRootPortMessageRoutine (KINTERRUPT 83911000)
eefa51a100000071:    848e3a50 i8042prt!I8042MouseInterruptService (KINTERRUPT 848e3a00)
eefa51a100000072:    8393a2d0 pci!ExpressRootPortMessageRoutine (KINTERRUPT 8393a280)
eefa51a100000073:    83951050 pci!ExpressRootPortMessageRoutine (KINTERRUPT 83951000)
eefa51a100000074:    8399dcd0 pci!ExpressRootPortMessageRoutine (KINTERRUPT 8399dc80)
eefa51a100000075:    839aca50 pci!ExpressRootPortMessageRoutine (KINTERRUPT 839aca00)
eefa51a100000076:    8764dcd0 ndis!ndisMiniportIsr (KINTERRUPT 8764dc80)
eefa51a100000080:    839112d0 pci!ExpressRootPortMessageRoutine (KINTERRUPT 83911280)
eefa51a100000081:    848e3cd0 i8042prt!I8042KeyboardInterruptService (KINTERRUPT 848e3c80)
eefa51a100000082:    8393a550 pci!ExpressRootPortMessageRoutine (KINTERRUPT 8393a500)
eefa51a100000083:    839512d0 pci!ExpressRootPortMessageRoutine (KINTERRUPT 83951280)
eefa51a100000084:    8395c050 pci!ExpressRootPortMessageRoutine (KINTERRUPT 8395c000)
eefa51a100000085:    839accd0 pci!ExpressRootPortMessageRoutine (KINTERRUPT 839acc80)
eefa51a100000086:    848e3050 USBPORT!USBPORT_InterruptService (KINTERRUPT 848e3000)
eefa51a100000090:    83911550 pci!ExpressRootPortMessageRoutine (KINTERRUPT 83911500)
eefa51a100000092:    8393a7d0 pci!ExpressRootPortMessageRoutine (KINTERRUPT 8393a780)
eefa51a100000093:    83951550 pci!ExpressRootPortMessageRoutine (KINTERRUPT 83951500)
eefa51a100000094:    8395c2d0 pci!ExpressRootPortMessageRoutine (KINTERRUPT 8395c280)
eefa51a100000095:    8399d050 pci!ExpressRootPortMessageRoutine (KINTERRUPT 8399d000)
eefa51a100000096:    848e32d0 *** ERROR: Symbol file could not be found.  Defaulted to export
symbols for vmci.sys -
vmci!DllUnload+0x552 (KINTERRUPT 848e3280)
                     portcls!KspShellTransferKsIrp+0x2a (KINTERRUPT 8764da00)
                     dxgkrnl!DpiFdoLineInterruptRoutine (KINTERRUPT 8764d500)
eefa51a1000000a0:    839117d0 pci!ExpressRootPortMessageRoutine (KINTERRUPT 83911780)
eefa51a1000000a3:    839517d0 pci!ExpressRootPortMessageRoutine (KINTERRUPT 83951780)
eefa51a1000000a4:    8395c550 pci!ExpressRootPortMessageRoutine (KINTERRUPT 8395c500)
eefa51a1000000a5:    8399d2d0 pci!ExpressRootPortMessageRoutine (KINTERRUPT 8399d280)
eefa51a1000000a6:    839ac050 storport!RaidpAdapterInterruptRoutine (KINTERRUPT 839ac000)
                     USBPORT!USBPORT_InterruptService (KINTERRUPT 8764d780)
eefa51a1000000b0:    83911a50 pci!ExpressRootPortMessageRoutine (KINTERRUPT 83911a00)
eefa51a1000000b1:    83911cd0 acpi!ACPIInterruptServiceRoutine (KINTERRUPT 83911c80)
eefa51a1000000b2:    848e3550 serial!SerialCIsrSw (KINTERRUPT 848e3500)
eefa51a1000000b3:    83951a50 pci!ExpressRootPortMessageRoutine (KINTERRUPT 83951a00)
eefa51a1000000b4:    8395c7d0 pci!ExpressRootPortMessageRoutine (KINTERRUPT 8395c780)
eefa51a1000000b5:    8399d550 pci!ExpressRootPortMessageRoutine (KINTERRUPT 8399d500)
eefa51a1000000b6:    839ac2d0 ataport!IdePortInterrupt (KINTERRUPT 839ac280)
eefa51a1000000c1:    81bb53d8 hal!HalpBroadcastCallService
eefa51a1000000d1:    81ba497c hal!HalpClockInterruptPn
eefa51a1000000df:    81bb51c0 hal!HalpApicRebootService
eefa51a1000000e1:    81bb5934 hal!HalpIpiHandler
eefa51a1000000e3:    81bb56d4 hal!HalpLocalApicErrorService
```

```
eefa51a1000000fd:     81bb5edc hal!HalpProfileInterrupt
eefa51a1000000fe:     81bb6148 hal!HalpPerfInterrupt
eefa51a1000000ff:     87fe9724 E1G60I32!□htoskrnl_NULL_THUNK_DATA
```

Note the last entry ff is different from expected hal and other hardware modules. We check the address of interrupt function:

```
1: kd> u 87fe9724
E1G60I32!□htoskrnl_NULL_THUNK_DATA:
87fe9724 0000               add       byte ptr [eax],al
87fe9726 0000               add       byte ptr [eax],al
87fe9728 0000               add       byte ptr [eax],al
87fe972a 0000               add       byte ptr [eax],al
87fe972c 0000               add       byte ptr [eax],al
87fe972e 0000               add       byte ptr [eax],al
87fe9730 0000               add       byte ptr [eax],al
87fe9732 0000               add       byte ptr [eax],al

1: kd> u
E1G60I32!□htoskrnl_NULL_THUNK_DATA+0x10:
87fe9734 db6ad2             fld       tbyte ptr [edx-2Eh]
87fe9737 44                 inc       esp
87fe9738 0000               add       byte ptr [eax],al
87fe973a 0000               add       byte ptr [eax],al
87fe973c 0200               add       al,byte ptr [eax]
87fe973e 0000               add       byte ptr [eax],al
87fe9740 25000000c0         and       eax,0C0000000h
87fe9745 58                 pop       eax
```

The code seems to be wild and most likely if some code uses this interrupt for communication it will definitely crash the system. The module is itself seems to be normal as it has symbol files be we hypothesize it was modified by malware in order to hide malicious activities under its name but something went wrong with hooking IDT.

9.   We now check SSDT. In order to dump it we need to know its size:

```
1: kd> dps nt!KeServiceDescriptorTable
81931b00    81880624 nt!KiServiceTable
81931b04    00000000
81931b08    0000018e
81931b0c    81880c60 nt!KiArgumentTable
81931b10    00000000
81931b14    00000000
81931b18    00000000
81931b1c    00000000
81931b20    00000021
81931b24    82b85ad0
81931b28    e57a42bd
81931b2c    d6bf94d5
81931b30    00000200
81931b34    82b81910
81931b38    00000000
81931b3c    00000000
81931b40    81880624 nt!KiServiceTable
81931b44    00000000
81931b48    0000018e
81931b4c    81880c60 nt!KiArgumentTable
81931b50    8a9ca000 win32k!W32pServiceTable
81931b54    00000000
```

```
81931b58    00000304
81931b5c    8a9caf20 win32k!W32pArgumentTable
81931b60    82b817a0
81931b64    82b81350
81931b68    82b81630
81931b6c    82b814c0
81931b70    00000000
81931b74    82b811e0
81931b78    00000000
81931b7c    00000000


1: kd> dps nt!KiServiceTable L18e
81880624    819be057 nt!NtAcceptConnectPort
81880628    818657ce nt!NtAccessCheck
8188062c    81a4a707 nt!NtAccessCheckAndAuditAlarm
81880630    81865805 nt!NtAccessCheckByType
81880634    81a4a746 nt!NtAccessCheckByTypeAndAuditAlarm
81880638    81865840 nt!NtAccessCheckByTypeResultList
8188063c    81a4a78f nt!NtAccessCheckByTypeResultListAndAuditAlarm
81880640    81a4a7d8 nt!NtAccessCheckByTypeResultListAndAuditAlarmByHandle
81880644    81a88f47 nt!NtAddAtom
81880648    81a8aff4 nt!NtAddBootEntry
8188064c    81a8c282 nt!NtAddDriverEntry
81880650    81a3eee5 nt!NtAdjustGroupsToken
81880654    81a3eacd nt!NtAdjustPrivilegesToken
81880658    81a1d327 nt!NtAlertResumeThread
8188065c    81a1d2cf nt!NtAlertThread
81880660    81a89390 nt!NtAllocateLocallyUniqueId
81880664    819e743f nt!NtAllocateUserPhysicalPages
81880668    81a88a70 nt!NtAllocateUuids
8188066c    819d531f nt!NtAllocateVirtualMemory
81880670    819c0b37 nt!NtAlpcAcceptConnectPort
81880674    819c62c7 nt!NtAlpcCancelMessage
81880678    819bfe3b nt!NtAlpcConnectPort
8188067c    819bf54b nt!NtAlpcCreatePort
81880680    819c839b nt!NtAlpcCreatePortSection
81880684    819c9cc3 nt!NtAlpcCreateResourceReserve
81880688    819c8637 nt!NtAlpcCreateSectionView
8188068c    819ca27f nt!NtAlpcCreateSecurityContext
81880690    819c853a nt!NtAlpcDeletePortSection
81880694    819c9dfa nt!NtAlpcDeleteResourceReserve
81880698    819c886d nt!NtAlpcDeleteSectionView
8188069c    819ca577 nt!NtAlpcDeleteSecurityContext
818806a0    819cc39b nt!NtAlpcDisconnectPort
818806a4    819ca803 nt!NtAlpcImpersonateClientOfPort
818806a8    819ce107 nt!NtAlpcOpenSenderProcess
818806ac    819ce6b7 nt!NtAlpcOpenSenderThread
818806b0    819cd953 nt!NtAlpcQueryInformation
818806b4    819c70d5 nt!NtAlpcQueryInformationMessage
818806b8    819ca430 nt!NtAlpcRevokeSecurityContext
818806bc    819c615b nt!NtAlpcSendWaitReceivePort
818806c0    819cd48b nt!NtAlpcSetInformation
818806c4    81a9f2f9 nt!NtApphelpCacheControl
818806c8    819d21cb nt!NtAreMappedFilesTheSame
818806cc    81a1f5bb nt!NtAssignProcessToJobObject
818806d0    8188037c nt!NtCallbackReturn
818806d4    8198046c nt!NtRequestDeviceWakeup
818806d8    8198bd6c nt!NtCancelIoFile
818806dc    81879318 nt!NtCancelTimer
818806e0    81a87095 nt!NtClearEvent
```

```
818806e4   819f189c   nt!NtClose
818806e8   81a4acc9   nt!NtCloseObjectAuditAlarm
818806ec   8193cd2b   nt!NtCompactKeys
818806f0   81a4e0c9   nt!NtCompareTokens
818806f4   819be0db   nt!NtCompleteConnectPort
818806f8   8193cfb7   nt!NtCompressKey
818806fc   819be023   nt!NtConnectPort
81880700   818903b8   nt!NtContinue
81880704   819752d2   nt!NtCreateDebugObject
81880708   819ed9df   nt!NtCreateDirectoryObject
8188070c   81a870e8   nt!NtCreateEvent
81880710   81a8fa91   nt!NtCreateEventPair
81880714   8198ec5e   nt!NtCreateFile
81880718   8198b298   nt!NtCreateIoCompletion
8188071c   81a1f339   nt!NtCreateJobObject
81880720   81a2210f   nt!NtCreateJobSet
81880724   81937576   nt!NtCreateKey
81880728   819375d9   nt!NtCreateKeyTransacted
8188072c   8198ed8f   nt!NtCreateMailslotFile
81880730   81a8ff0a   nt!NtCreateMutant
81880734   8198eca1   nt!NtCreateNamedPipeFile
81880738   819fa0b6   nt!NtCreatePrivateNamespace
8188073c   819e37ec   nt!NtCreatePagingFile
81880740   819bdb25   nt!NtCreatePort
81880744   81a123b2   nt!NtCreateProcess
81880748   81a123fd   nt!NtCreateProcessEx
8188074c   81a90403   nt!NtCreateProfile
81880750   819d7703   nt!NtCreateSection
81880754   81a880ff   nt!NtCreateSemaphore
81880758   819efc6b   nt!NtCreateSymbolicLinkObject
8188075c   81a11f31   nt!NtCreateThread
81880760   81a8f6f1   nt!NtCreateTimer
81880764   81a4cced   nt!NtCreateToken
81880768   81a53ac4   nt!NtCreateTransaction
8188076c   81a53dd7   nt!NtOpenTransaction
81880770   81a53fcf   nt!NtQueryInformationTransaction
81880774   81a56472   nt!NtQueryInformationTransactionManager
81880778   81a54e64   nt!NtPrePrepareEnlistment
8188077c   81a54da3   nt!NtPrepareEnlistment
81880780   81a54f25   nt!NtCommitEnlistment
81880784   81a553a9   nt!NtReadOnlyEnlistment
81880788   81a55468   nt!NtRollbackComplete
8188078c   81a54fe6   nt!NtRollbackEnlistment
81880790   81a544cf   nt!NtCommitTransaction
81880794   81a54538   nt!NtRollbackTransaction
81880798   81a55168   nt!NtPrePrepareComplete
8188079c   81a550a7   nt!NtPrepareComplete
818807a0   81a55229   nt!NtCommitComplete
818807a4   81a552ea   nt!NtSinglePhaseReject
818807a8   81a545b5   nt!NtSetInformationTransaction
818807ac   81a56879   nt!NtSetInformationTransactionManager
818807b0   81a55d36   nt!NtSetInformationResourceManager
818807b4   81a55ed0   nt!NtCreateTransactionManager
818807b8   81a560e7   nt!NtOpenTransactionManager
818807bc   81a56356   nt!NtRollforwardTransactionManager
818807c0   81a549c3   nt!NtRecoverEnlistment
818807c4   81a55999   nt!NtRecoverResourceManager
818807c8   81a56417   nt!NtRecoverTransactionManager
818807cc   81a55527   nt!NtCreateResourceManager
818807d0   81a557ed   nt!NtOpenResourceManager
```

```
818807d4    81a559f2  nt!NtGetNotificationResourceManager
818807d8    81a55b07  nt!NtQueryInformationResourceManager
818807dc    81a5470d  nt!NtCreateEnlistment
818807e0    81a547fa  nt!NtOpenEnlistment
818807e4    81a54c06  nt!NtSetInformationEnlistment
818807e8    81a54a1f  nt!NtQueryInformationEnlistment
818807ec    81a89383  nt!NtStartTm
818807f0    819bdb8f  nt!NtCreateWaitablePort
818807f4    81976096  nt!NtDebugActiveProcess
818807f8    819766ec  nt!NtDebugContinue
818807fc    81a90aa5  nt!NtDelayExecution
81880800    81a891fb  nt!NtDeleteAtom
81880804    81a8b027  nt!NtDeleteBootEntry
81880808    81a8c2b3  nt!NtDeleteDriverEntry
8188080c    8198c187  nt!NtDeleteFile
81880810    819379a7  nt!NtDeleteKey
81880814    819fa6aa  nt!NtDeletePrivateNamespace
81880818    81a4adab  nt!NtDeleteObjectAuditAlarm
8188081c    81937c3a  nt!NtDeleteValueKey
81880820    8198ee63  nt!NtDeviceIoControlFile
81880824    81a7a099  nt!NtDisplayString
81880828    819f1fb3  nt!NtDuplicateObject
8188082c    81a3f88b  nt!NtDuplicateToken
81880830    81a8b228  nt!NtEnumerateBootEntries
81880834    81a8c4b2  nt!NtEnumerateDriverEntries
81880838    81937f12  nt!NtEnumerateKey
8188083c    81a8adfb  nt!NtEnumerateSystemEnvironmentValuesEx
81880840    81868f61  nt!NtEnumerateTransactionObject
81880844    81938171  nt!NtEnumerateValueKey
81880848    819e1387  nt!NtExtendSection
8188084c    81a40316  nt!NtFilterToken
81880850    81a890a1  nt!NtFindAtom
81880854    8198c299  nt!NtFlushBuffersFile
81880858    819e84b3  nt!NtFlushInstructionCache
8188085c    819383f0  nt!NtFlushKey
81880860    818cdfab  nt!NtFlushProcessWriteBuffers
81880864    819da8e1  nt!NtFlushVirtualMemory
81880868    819e84a0  nt!NtFlushWriteBuffer
8188086c    819e7b6e  nt!NtFreeUserPhysicalPages
81880870    818beb63  nt!NtFreeVirtualMemory
81880874    818d0683  nt!NtFreezeRegistry
81880878    81869169  nt!NtFreezeTransactions
8188087c    8198ee9f  nt!NtFsControlFile
81880880    81a1a9bf  nt!NtGetContextThread
81880884    81a0dbc7  nt!NtGetDevicePowerState
81880888    81a8610b  nt!NtGetNlsSectionPtr
8188088c    819b9d7a  nt!NtGetPlugPlayEvent
81880890    818e4864  nt!NtGetWriteWatch
81880894    81a4decf  nt!NtImpersonateAnonymousToken
81880898    819be383  nt!NtImpersonateClientOfPort
8188089c    81a22455  nt!NtImpersonateThread
818808a0    81a84da7  nt!NtInitializeNlsFiles
818808a4    8193860d  nt!NtInitializeRegistry
818808a8    81a0d9b8  nt!NtInitiatePowerAction
818808ac    81a21f63  nt!NtIsProcessInJob
818808b0    81a0dbad  nt!NtIsSystemResumeAutomatic
818808b4    819be3b1  nt!NtListenPort
818808b8    81998384  nt!NtLoadDriver
818808bc    8193a414  nt!NtLoadKey
818808c0    8193a43b  nt!NtLoadKey2
```

```
818808c4   8193a467   nt!NtLoadKeyEx
818808c8   8198eedb   nt!NtLockFile
818808cc   81a7a35c   nt!NtLockProductActivationKeys
818808d0   8193d08e   nt!NtLockRegistryKey
818808d4   8181ad7f   nt!NtLockVirtualMemory
818808d8   819ef3b9   nt!NtMakePermanentObject
818808dc   819f18cb   nt!NtMakeTemporaryObject
818808e0   819e67e2   nt!NtMapUserPhysicalPages
818808e4   819e6d4b   nt!NtMapUserPhysicalPagesScatter
818808e8   819d0206   nt!NtMapViewOfSection
818808ec   81a8b1f7   nt!NtModifyBootEntry
818808f0   81a8c483   nt!NtModifyDriverEntry
818808f4   8198fd76   nt!NtNotifyChangeDirectoryFile
818808f8   81938716   nt!NtNotifyChangeKey
818808fc   81938753   nt!NtNotifyChangeMultipleKeys
81880900   819edae3   nt!NtOpenDirectoryObject
81880904   81a87211   nt!NtOpenEvent
81880908   81a8fbc7   nt!NtOpenEventPair
8188090c   819900cb   nt!NtOpenFile
81880910   8198b3a5   nt!NtOpenIoCompletion
81880914   81a1f4f7   nt!NtOpenJobObject
81880918   8193922f   nt!NtOpenKey
8188091c   8193928b   nt!NtOpenKeyTransacted
81880920   81a9000f   nt!NtOpenMutant
81880924   819fa335   nt!NtOpenPrivateNamespace
81880928   81a4a823   nt!NtOpenObjectAuditAlarm
8188092c   81a1385d   nt!NtOpenProcess
81880930   81a40d3c   nt!NtOpenProcessToken
81880934   81a40d61   nt!NtOpenProcessTokenEx
81880938   819da58b   nt!NtOpenSection
8188093c   81a8822b   nt!NtOpenSemaphore
81880940   819e46cf   nt!NtOpenSession
81880944   819efe95   nt!NtOpenSymbolicLinkObject
81880948   81a13bbf   nt!NtOpenThread
8188094c   81a40f2b   nt!NtOpenThreadToken
81880950   81a40f53   nt!NtOpenThreadTokenEx
81880954   81a8f840   nt!NtOpenTimer
81880958   819b9eff   nt!NtPlugPlayControl
8188095c   81a079bc   nt!NtPowerInformation
81880960   81a4fd36   nt!NtPrivilegeCheck
81880964   81a49869   nt!NtPrivilegeObjectAuditAlarm
81880968   81a49aca   nt!NtPrivilegedServiceAuditAlarm
8188096c   819e8767   nt!NtProtectVirtualMemory
81880970   81a872e4   nt!NtPulseEvent
81880974   8198c4b5   nt!NtQueryAttributesFile
81880978   81a8b6d3   nt!NtQueryBootEntryOrder
8188097c   81a8bb27   nt!NtQueryBootOptions
81880980   8187c403   nt!NtQueryDebugFilterState
81880984   81a7ec28   nt!NtQueryDefaultLocale
81880988   81a7efaf   nt!NtQueryDefaultUILanguage
8188098c   8198fd0d   nt!NtQueryDirectoryFile
81880990   819edba2   nt!NtQueryDirectoryObject
81880994   81a8c03b   nt!NtQueryDriverEntryOrder
81880998   81990107   nt!NtQueryEaFile
8188099c   81a873c7   nt!NtQueryEvent
818809a0   8198c657   nt!NtQueryFullAttributesFile
818809a4   81a89228   nt!NtQueryInformationAtom
818809a8   81990cf6   nt!NtQueryInformationFile
818809ac   81a1ff3f   nt!NtQueryInformationJobObject
818809b0   819be429   nt!NtQueryInformationPort
```

```
818809b4    81a14191  nt!NtQueryInformationProcess
818809b8    81a1774b  nt!NtQueryInformationThread
818809bc    81a41198  nt!NtQueryInformationToken
818809c0    81a7ef2b  nt!NtQueryInstallUILanguage
818809c4    81a908f7  nt!NtQueryIntervalProfile
818809c8    8198b47c  nt!NtQueryIoCompletion
818809cc    81939557  nt!NtQueryKey
818809d0    8193be73  nt!NtQueryMultipleValueKey
818809d4    81a900e2  nt!NtQueryMutant
818809d8    819f7c1d  nt!NtQueryObject
818809dc    8193c4e7  nt!NtQueryOpenSubKeys
818809e0    8193c76b  nt!NtQueryOpenSubKeysEx
818809e4    81a909b0  nt!NtQueryPerformanceCounter
818809e8    819920e7  nt!NtQueryQuotaInformationFile
818809ec    819e34f2  nt!NtQuerySection
818809f0    819f470b  nt!NtQuerySecurityObject
818809f4    81a882fe  nt!NtQuerySemaphore
818809f8    819eff54  nt!NtQuerySymbolicLinkObject
818809fc    81a8a223  nt!NtQuerySystemEnvironmentValue
81880a00    81a8a831  nt!NtQuerySystemEnvironmentValueEx
81880a04    889aa114  crashdmp!□htoskrnl_NULL_THUNK_DATA
81880a08    81a7ac06  nt!NtQuerySystemTime
81880a0c    81a8f913  nt!NtQueryTimer
81880a10    81a7aeeb  nt!NtQueryTimerResolution
81880a14    8193985a  nt!NtQueryValueKey
81880a18    819e9273  nt!NtQueryVirtualMemory
81880a1c    8199274e  nt!NtQueryVolumeInformationFile
81880a20    81a1a655  nt!NtQueueApcThread
81880a24    81890400  nt!NtRaiseException
81880a28    81a87cb7  nt!NtRaiseHardError
81880a2c    8199302b  nt!NtReadFile
81880a30    819936b7  nt!NtReadFileScatter
81880a34    819be4e9  nt!NtReadRequestData
81880a38    819d6eee  nt!NtReadVirtualMemory
81880a3c    81a1c3c5  nt!NtRegisterThreadTerminatePort
81880a40    81a9028f  nt!NtReleaseMutant
81880a44    81a88447  nt!NtReleaseSemaphore
81880a48    8198b61b  nt!NtRemoveIoCompletion
81880a4c    819761e1  nt!NtRemoveProcessDebug
81880a50    8193caab  nt!NtRenameKey
81880a54    8193bd46  nt!NtReplaceKey
81880a58    819be5c3  nt!NtReplyPort
81880a5c    819be6c8  nt!NtReplyWaitReceivePort
81880a60    819be6ef  nt!NtReplyWaitReceivePortEx
81880a64    819be92f  nt!NtReplyWaitReplyPort
81880a68    8198046c  nt!NtRequestDeviceWakeup
81880a6c    819be253  nt!NtRequestPort
81880a70    819be31c  nt!NtRequestWaitReplyPort
81880a74    81a0d95b  nt!NtRequestWakeupLatency
81880a78    81a874f7  nt!NtResetEvent
81880a7c    818e5127  nt!NtResetWriteWatch
81880a80    81939bb0  nt!NtRestoreKey
81880a84    81a1d271  nt!NtResumeProcess
81880a88    81a1d130  nt!NtResumeThread
81880a8c    81939ccf  nt!NtSaveKey
81880a90    81939dd6  nt!NtSaveKeyEx
81880a94    81939f21  nt!NtSaveMergedKeys
81880a98    81a579bb  nt!NtSavepointComplete
81880a9c    8198046c  nt!NtRequestDeviceWakeup
81880aa0    81a579bb  nt!NtSavepointComplete
```

```
81880aa4   81a545a1  nt!TmSavepointTransaction
81880aa8   81a579bb  nt!NtSavepointComplete
81880aac   819bdbf9  nt!NtSecureConnectPort
81880ab0   81a8b91a  nt!NtSetBootEntryOrder
81880ab4   81a8be1c  nt!NtSetBootOptions
81880ab8   81a1ac4b  nt!NtSetContextThread
81880abc   81a9a87b  nt!NtSetDebugFilterState
81880ac0   81a88043  nt!NtSetDefaultHardErrorPort
81880ac4   81a7ecaf  nt!NtSetDefaultLocale
81880ac8   81a7f995  nt!NtSetDefaultUILanguage
81880acc   81a8c8bd  nt!NtSetDriverEntryOrder
81880ad0   8199070d  nt!NtSetEaFile
81880ad4   81a875d6  nt!NtSetEvent
81880ad8   81a876bb  nt!NtSetEventBoostPriority
81880adc   81a8fea7  nt!NtSetHighEventPair
81880ae0   81a8fdd9  nt!NtSetHighWaitLowEventPair
81880ae4   8197684d  nt!NtSetInformationDebugObject
81880ae8   81991555  nt!NtSetInformationFile
81880aec   81a20763  nt!NtSetInformationJobObject
81880af0   8193b8e3  nt!NtSetInformationKey
81880af4   819f82e7  nt!NtSetInformationObject
81880af8   81a15c65  nt!NtSetInformationProcess
81880afc   81a183c7  nt!NtSetInformationThread
81880b00   81a5056f  nt!NtSetInformationToken
81880b04   81a908d4  nt!NtSetIntervalProfile
81880b08   8198b5b4  nt!NtSetIoCompletion
81880b0c   81a1eff7  nt!NtSetLdtEntries
81880b10   81a8fe44  nt!NtSetLowEventPair
81880b14   81a8fd6e  nt!NtSetLowWaitHighEventPair
81880b18   81992739  nt!NtSetQuotaInformationFile
81880b1c   819f44f0  nt!NtSetSecurityObject
81880b20   81a8a52f  nt!NtSetSystemEnvironmentValue
81880b24   81a8ab57  nt!NtSetSystemEnvironmentValueEx
81880b28   81a829f3  nt!NtSetSystemInformation
81880b2c   81ac7bb4  nt!NtSetSystemPowerState
81880b30   81a7acaa  nt!NtSetSystemTime
81880b34   81a0d82d  nt!NtSetThreadExecutionState
81880b38   818794bf  nt!NtSetTimer
81880b3c   81a7afca  nt!NtSetTimerResolution
81880b40   81a888eb  nt!NtSetUuidSeed
81880b44   8193a08b  nt!NtSetValueKey
81880b48   81992c2f  nt!NtSetVolumeInformationFile
81880b4c   81a7a057  nt!NtShutdownSystem
81880b50   81847951  nt!NtSignalAndWaitForSingleObject
81880b54   81a90642  nt!NtStartProfile
81880b58   81a90813  nt!NtStopProfile
81880b5c   81a1d213  nt!NtSuspendProcess
81880b60   81a1d047  nt!NtSuspendThread
81880b64   81a90b4f  nt!NtSystemDebugControl
81880b68   81a21670  nt!NtTerminateJobObject
81880b6c   81a1b043  nt!NtTerminateProcess
81880b70   81a1b497  nt!NtTerminateThread
81880b74   81a1d42e  nt!NtTestAlert
81880b78   818d06e7  nt!NtThawRegistry
81880b7c   81869250  nt!NtThawTransactions
81880b80   8186e91b  nt!NtTraceEvent
81880b84   81a6db67  nt!NtTraceControl
81880b88   81a8cacb  nt!NtTranslateFilePath
81880b8c   81998552  nt!NtUnloadDriver
81880b90   8193abd4  nt!NtUnloadKey
```

```
81880b94    8193abf3  nt!NtUnloadKey2
81880b98    8193b219  nt!NtUnloadKeyEx
81880b9c    8198f34f  nt!NtUnlockFile
81880ba0    81815d20  nt!NtUnlockVirtualMemory
81880ba4    819e0bf0  nt!NtUnmapViewOfSection
81880ba8    81a5c76c  nt!NtVdmControl
81880bac    8197642f  nt!NtWaitForDebugEvent
81880bb0    819f514c  nt!NtWaitForMultipleObjects
81880bb4    819f5027  nt!NtWaitForSingleObject
81880bb8    81a8fd05  nt!NtWaitHighEventPair
81880bbc    81a8fc9c  nt!NtWaitLowEventPair
81880bc0    81993c33  nt!NtWriteFile
81880bc4    8199436b  nt!NtWriteFileGather
81880bc8    819be556  nt!NtWriteRequestData
81880bcc    819d701b  nt!NtWriteVirtualMemory
81880bd0    818b59c6  nt!NtYieldExecution
81880bd4    81a90f41  nt!NtCreateKeyedEvent
81880bd8    81a91073  nt!NtOpenKeyedEvent
81880bdc    81a9114d  nt!NtReleaseKeyedEvent
81880be0    81a91434  nt!NtWaitForKeyedEvent
81880be4    81a15902  nt!NtQueryPortInformationProcess
81880be8    81a18eee  nt!NtGetCurrentProcessorNumber
81880bec    819f525b  nt!NtWaitForMultipleObjects32
81880bf0    81a1d964  nt!NtGetNextProcess
81880bf4    81a1dbd1  nt!NtGetNextThread
81880bf8    8198bf27  nt!NtCancelIoFileEx
81880bfc    8198c064  nt!NtCancelSynchronousIoFile
81880c00    8198b7b4  nt!NtRemoveIoCompletionEx
81880c04    81869663  nt!NtRegisterProtocolAddressInformation
81880c08    81869672  nt!NtPullTransaction
81880c0c    818696af  nt!NtMarshallTransaction
81880c10    81869687  nt!NtPropagationComplete
81880c14    8186969b  nt!CcTestControl
81880c18    81a9171b  nt!NtCreateWorkerFactory
81880c1c    81879c2d  nt!NtReleaseWorkerFactoryWorker
81880c20    81879ce4  nt!NtWaitForWorkViaWorkerFactory
81880c24    81879fd7  nt!NtSetInformationWorkerFactory
81880c28    8187a4a7  nt!NtQueryInformationWorkerFactory
81880c2c    8187a72f  nt!NtWorkerFactoryWorkerReady
81880c30    81a919be  nt!NtShutdownWorkerFactory
81880c34    81a23d84  nt!NtCreateThreadEx
81880c38    81a2256f  nt!NtCreateUserProcess
81880c3c    81a7c753  nt!NtQueryLicenseValue
81880c40    81a92b75  nt!NtMapCMFModule
81880c44    81a545a1  nt!TmSavepointTransaction
81880c48    81a9354d  nt!NtIsUILanguageComitted
81880c4c    81a9356f  nt!NtFlushInstallUILanguage
81880c50    81a9317f  nt!NtGetMUIRegistryInfo
81880c54    81a91b88  nt!NtAcquireCMFViewOwnership
81880c58    81a91d4f  nt!NtReleaseCMFViewOwnership
```

Note that one of entries is outside nt module range and point to an address in crashdmp module range.

10.   To navigate drivers and their devices which are represented as objects we can use **!object** command:

```
1: kd> !object \Driver
Object: 8585c218  Type: (82b38d60) Directory
    ObjectHeader: 8585c200 (old version)
    HandleCount: 0  PointerCount: 87
    Directory Object: 858074c0  Name: Driver

    Hash Address  Type        Name
    ---- -------  ----        ----
    00   8395e688 Driver      NDIS
         83eaeaf0 Driver      KSecDD
         87746840 Driver      Beep
    01   84beff38 Driver      mouclass
    03   848ea030 Driver      vm3dmp
         848ae9e0 Driver      kbdclass
    04   876a62c8 Driver      monitor
         8392dec0 Driver      msisadrv
         83932688 Driver      Compbatt
         8760a848 Driver      NDProxy
         87768590 Driver      VgaSave
    05   839d6708 Driver      Ecache
         83933688 Driver      MountMgr
    08   87d59128 Driver      PEAUTH
         83993660 Driver      atapi
         848ec2f0 Driver      vmmouse
    09   83937688 Driver      volmgrx
         879e4030 Driver      VMAUDIO
    10   87753590 Driver      RasAcd
         8776c868 Driver      PSched
    11   87738720 Driver      Win32k
         8780b9b0 Driver      usbuhci
         877858c8 Driver      mouhid
    12   877fa410 Driver      usbhub
         84aa5e38 Driver      tunnel
         848e2e08 Driver      swenum
    13   87cd4458 Driver      HTTP
         848c5b30 Driver      RasPppoe
         8774c3e0 Driver      RDPCDD
         877f3910 Driver      usbccgp
    14   848e2c60 Driver      TermDD
    15   848c5030 Driver      fdc
         848ec4e0 Driver      Rasl2tp
    16   87d48268 Driver      Parvdm
    17   879e6f38 Driver      umbus
         848c06b0 Driver      vmci
    18   87d5b560 Driver      secdrv
         82b41190 Driver      ACPI_HAL
         82b37f00 Driver      WMIxWDM
         8395a688 Driver      CLFS
         843271f8 Driver      crcdisk
         84b1ded0 Driver      Serenum
         848e8e30 Driver      PptpMiniport
         8778c630 Driver      Smb
    19   83e4c1c8 Driver      spldr
    21   87d5e368 Driver      tcpipreg
         839d6610 Driver      agp440
         877f3120 Driver      netbt
    22   848bf5a0 Driver      iScsiPrt
         879e6880 Driver      mssmbios
```

197

```
        8780b578 Driver          cdrom
        8760e988 Driver          RDPENCDD
    23  877d7d98 Driver          tdx
        8397fde8 Driver          rspndr
    24  87d2df00 Driver          mpsdrv
        87745608 Driver          Tcpip
    25  83e50f38 Driver          volsnap
        83931688 Driver          volmgr
        877fcf38 Driver          nsiproxy
    26  87668258 Driver          intelppm
    27  839a5650 Driver          LSI_SCSI
        878078b0 Driver          Wanarpv6
        8396d348 Driver          lltdio
    28  87d55030 Driver          VMMEMCTL
        848e20d8 Driver          usbehci
        87746c28 Driver          Null
        877f74a0 Driver          ws2ifsl
    29  83eae3c0 Driver          disk
        83d7f118 Driver          pci
    30  83e53b10 Driver          partmgr
        848ee488 Driver          NdisWan
        87dfd9e0 Driver          NdisTapi
        87dfd030 Driver          Serial
    31  8488a8e8 Driver          DXGKrnl
    32  838c0188 Driver          Wdf01000
        838c1ba8 Driver          ACPI
    33  82b82b08 Driver          PnpManager
        84bfeb88 Driver          flpydisk
    34  8774b3b0 Driver          vmrawdsk
        877f88d0 Driver          AFD
    35  878da110 Driver          Parport
        879ff500 Driver          E1G60
        8776b030 Driver          HidUsb
    36  83934688 Driver          intelide
        87668378 Driver          CmBatt
        84a0c2f0 Driver          i8042prt

1: kd> !object \Device
Object: 8580f2e0  Type: (82b38d60) Directory
    ObjectHeader: 8580f2c8 (old version)
    HandleCount: 0  PointerCount: 256
    Directory Object: 858074c0  Name: Device

    Hash Address  Type            Name
    ---- -------  ----            ----
     00  83eae9d8 Device          KsecDD
         83960668 Device          Ndis
         8598e918 SymbolicLink    ScsiPort2
         87cccd38 Device          SrvNet
         82b41030 Device          00000032
         87746570 Device          Beep
         82b3e458 Device          00000025
         82b3c430 Device          00000019
     01  8776d980 Device          Netbios
         871072c0 SymbolicLink    ScsiPort3
         82b41d80 Device          00000033
         82b3e198 Device          00000026
     02  82b41ad0 Device          00000034
         8825bfe0 SymbolicLink    Ip
         8392a980 Device          00000040
```

```
        82b3fed0 Device          00000027
03      871ea268 SymbolicLink    {E3FE0F52-6729-43AC-8488-5AC1FB2AE7A9}
        8760e040 Device          Video0
        838c1e38 Device          KeyboardClass0
        82b41850 Device          00000035
        8392a868 Device          00000041
        838c1030 Device          KMDF0
        82b37030 Device          WMIAdminDevice
        82b3fc10 Device          00000028
04      92b235d0 SymbolicLink    MailslotRedirector
        871dc7d8 SymbolicLink    {6EA11ADB-6FEB-425D-A3CB-3CB73F334E62}
        87747030 Device          Video1
        8760a030 Device          NDProxy
        848e2450 Device          KeyboardClass1
        83930510 Device          VolMgrControl
        8392a750 Device          00000042
        82b41468 Device          00000036
        82b3f950 Device          00000029
05      848be8a0 Device          Serial0
        87ccb690 Device          SrvAdmin
        877475d8 Device          Video2
        848d1030 Device          PointerClass0
        88240710 SymbolicLink    Ip6
        84b88028 Device          00000050
        8392a638 Device          00000043
        83da6d50 Device          00000037
        82b3adb0 Device          0000000a
06      84be2258 Device          Video3
        8392d828 Device          00000038
        848de028 Device          USBPDO-0
        848ed648 Device          PointerClass1
        83962778 Device          CompositeBattery
        87665028 Device          00000051
        848a94e0 Device          Serial1
        8392a520 Device          00000044
        82b3ab30 Device          0000000b
07      87781030 Device          NetBT_Tcpip_{0DC6D9AD-70DC-41CE-9798-F71D1A8C899F}
        839da1e8 Device          SpDevice
        82b37be8 Device          WMIDataDevice
        8760c028 Device          USBPDO-1
        876a6ea0 Device          Video4
        87772328 Device          PointerClass2
        8585ec78 SymbolicLink    {6AF476B1-AA92-4BE1-AA1C-49257F765446}
        8392a408 Device          00000045
        839e6210 Device          00000039
        838a7bf0 Device          RawTape
        82b3a8b0 Device          0000000c
08      848ebb90 Device          FloppyPDO0
        8760f030 Device          USBPDO-2
        87dad030 Device          PEAuth
        92b1f758 SymbolicLink    WebDavRedirector
        8392a2f0 Device          00000046
        8776f2d0 Device          PointerClass3
        87783030 Device          00000053
        83912098 Device          NTPNP_PCI0000
        82b3c178 Device          0000001a
        82b3a5f8 Device          0000000d
09      8782e030 Device          USBPDO-3
        87d2d9f8 Device          MPS
        8392b030 Device          00000047
```

```
      8777e030 Device         00000054
      83bab030 Device         NTPNP_PCI0001
      82b3df10 Device         0000001b
      82b3a338 Device         0000000e
10    87753478 Device         RasAcd
      877a53a8 Device         Psched
      870f4620 SymbolicLink   {0DC6D9AD-70DC-41CE-9798-F71D1A8C899F}
      8777ec90 Device         00000055
      8392bf18 Device         00000048
      83bab4c8 Device         NTPNP_PCI0002
      82b3dc90 Device         0000001c
      82b3b030 Device         0000000f
11    877f1f18 Device         DfsClient
      87d4c398 Device         ParallelVdm0
      84a3caa0 Device         ParallelPort0
      877d70a8 Device         Tcp
      8776e030 Device         00000056
      8392b1a0 Device         00000049
      83bc4030 Device         NTPNP_PCI0010
      839e6b98 Device         NTPNP_PCI0003
      82b3da10 Device         0000001d
12    8776f888 Device         00000057
      877bff18 Device         eQoS
      83bc4b98 Device         NTPNP_PCI0011
      82b3f690 Device         0000002a
      82b3d790 Device         0000001e
13    8452d6c0 Device         HarddiskVolume1
      878ea3d0 Device         NDMP1
      92b12350 Directory      Http
      877e7028 Device         00000058
      82b3f3d0 Device         0000002b
      83bc4700 Device         NTPNP_PCI0012
      83da6030 Device         NTPNP_PCI0005
      82b3d4d8 Device         0000001f
14    849f3030 Device         CdRom0
      83da68b8 Device         NTPNP_PCI0006
      839d6ab0 Device         ECacheControl
      877f4178 Device         NDMP2
      84be2b38 Device         00000059
      877fc340 Device         FsWrap
      82b40030 Device         0000002c
      848e2a68 Device         Termdd
      83c4b030 Device         NTPNP_PCI0013
15    859b5d98 Directory      Ide
      8782f030 Device         hgfsInternal
      877f53d0 Device         NDMP3
      877835a8 Device         _HID00000000
      877f6030 Device         RawIp6
      84b1d678 Device         Parallel0
      83babbb0 Device         0000003a
      82b40db0 Device         0000002d
      839ad030 Device         NTPNP_PCI0007
      82b45b98 Device         NTPNP_PCI0020
      83c4bb98 Device         NTPNP_PCI0014
16    848d0408 Device         NDMP4
      8776bd48 Device         _HID00000001
      82b37180 Device         0000003b
      82b40b30 Device         0000002e
      82b45700 Device         NTPNP_PCI0021
      83c4b700 Device         NTPNP_PCI0015
```

```
     839adb28 Device         NTPNP_PCI0008
17   82b831f0 Event          VolumesSafeForWriteAccess
     848f1400 Device         NDMP5
     82b40870 Device         0000002f
     84a2bec8 Device         vmci
     82b46030 Device         NTPNP_PCI0022
     83cfa030 Device         NTPNP_PCI0016
     839ad690 Device         NTPNP_PCI0009
     8390fda0 Device         0000003c
18   848e43d0 Device         NDMP6
     87cc9160 Device         Secdrv
     877503a8 Device         Tcp6
     82b7c700 Device         NTPNP_PCI0030
     82b46b98 Device         NTPNP_PCI0023
     83cfab98 Device         NTPNP_PCI0017
     83a51f18 Device         0000003d
19   879e43d0 Device         NDMP7
     8776b460 Device         NetBt_Wins_Export
     8392cf18 Device         0000004a
     83913030 Device         NTPNP_PCI0031
     82b46700 Device         NTPNP_PCI0024
     83cfa700 Device         NTPNP_PCI0018
     83a51450 Device         0000003e
20   877c4e58 Device         WFP
     8392ce00 Device         0000004b
     83a2c030 Device         0000003f
     83913b98 Device         NTPNP_PCI0032
     82b7b030 Device         NTPNP_PCI0025
     82b45030 Device         NTPNP_PCI0019
21   877e5030 Device         NetbiosSmb
     8392cce8 Device         0000004c
     83913700 Device         NTPNP_PCI0033
     82b7bb98 Device         NTPNP_PCI0026
22   87da8168 Device         0000005a
     839af6b0 Device         0000004d
     83916b98 Device         NTPNP_PCI0040
     83914030 Device         NTPNP_PCI0034
     82b7b700 Device         NTPNP_PCI0027
23   83963858 Device         MountPointManager
     879ec730 Device         rspndr
     877d71c8 Device         Tdx
     8392c2d0 Device         NTPNP_PCI0041
     83914b98 Device         NTPNP_PCI0035
     82b7c030 Device         NTPNP_PCI0028
24   839d5998 Device         RaidPort0
     83e8f7c8 Device         Mup
     87d14098 Device         LanmanServer
     877fce20 Device         Nsi
     87cfd998 Device         Srv2
     8782f798 Device         WANARP
     8392fb98 Device         NTPNP_PCI0042
     8763e030 Device         INTELPRO_{0DC6D9AD-70DC-41CE-9798-F71D1A8C899F}
     848ef030 Device         0000004f
     83914700 Device         NTPNP_PCI0036
     82b7cb98 Device         NTPNP_PCI0029
25   8392f700 Device         NTPNP_PCI0043
     87115a70 SymbolicLink   {54950694-33A2-408C-9E06-ABBEB791E26F}
     877e6830 Device         Udp
     87900800 Device         RaidPort1
     83915030 Device         NTPNP_PCI0037
```

```
26   87103878 Directory       Harddisk0
     8717ebb8 SymbolicLink    NdisWanIp
     877e6378 Device          RawIp
     83930030 Device          NTPNP_PCI0044
     82b37a58 Device          00000001
     839159c8 Device          NTPNP_PCI0038
27   87dfddb8 Device          Floppy0
     83978cc8 Device          lltdio
     8782f620 Device          WANARPV6
     838a7e20 Device          RawDisk
     83916030 Device          NTPNP_PCI0039
     82b37738 Device          00000002
28   848a7028 Device          USBFDO-0
     87d76c30 Device          vmmemctl
     87746b10 Device          Null
     859bb478 SymbolicLink    hgfs
     877f7388 Device          WS2IFSL
     82b3bdb0 Device          00000010
     82b39030 Device          00000003
29   877ad340 Device          NXTIPSEC
     82b39db0 Device          00000004
     848ab028 Device          USBFDO-1
     82b3baf0 Device          00000011
30   87da56e0 Device          AscKmd
     87ccbe20 Device          LanmanDatagramReceiver
     85812ef0 Section         PhysicalMemory
     877e6710 Device          Udp6
     8775f030 Device          NdisWan
     87900698 Device          NdisTapi
     82b3b838 Device          00000012
     82b39b30 Device          00000005
31   92b23470 SymbolicLink    LanmanRedirector
     848c6710 Device          DxgKrnl
     82b3b578 Device          00000013
     82b398b0 Device          00000006
32   877539e0 Device          NamedPipe
     8599feb8 SymbolicLink    FtControl
     82b3d220 Device          00000020
     82b3b2c0 Device          00000014
     82b39630 Device          00000007
33   87747d50 Device          Mailslot
     8717ec68 SymbolicLink    NdisWanIpv6
     82b3ef10 Device          00000021
     82b3cf10 Device          00000015
     82b393b0 Device          00000008
34   877f87b8 Device          Afd
     83959668 Device          FileInfo
     838a7d08 Device          RawCdRom
     82b3ec90 Device          00000022
     82b3cc58 Device          00000016
     82b3a030 Device          00000009
35   877c6f18 Device          WfpAle
     82b405b0 Device          00000030
     859949a0 SymbolicLink    ScsiPort0
     82b3e9d8 Device          00000023
     82b3c9a0 Device          00000017
36   82b40300 Device          00000031
     870bf680 SymbolicLink    ScsiPort1
     82b3e718 Device          00000024
     82b3c6e8 Device          00000018
```

Note that if you find any device suspicious you can get a pointer to its driver object:

```
1: kd> !devobj 877c6f18
Device object (877c6f18) is for:
 WfpAle \Driver\Tcpip DriverObject 87745608
Current Irp 00000000 RefCount 1 Type 00000012 Flags 00000040
Dacl 8824c504 DevExt 00000000 DevObjExt 877c6fd0
ExtensionFlags (0000000000)
Characteristics (0x00000100)  FILE_DEVICE_SECURE_OPEN
Device queue is not busy.

1: kd> dt _DEVICE_OBJECT 877c6f18
ntdll!_DEVICE_OBJECT
   +0x000 Type             : 0n3
   +0x002 Size             : 0xb8
   +0x004 ReferenceCount   : 0n1
   +0x008 DriverObject     : 0x87745608 _DRIVER_OBJECT
   +0x00c NextDevice       : 0x877c4e58 _DEVICE_OBJECT
   +0x010 AttachedDevice   : (null)
   +0x014 CurrentIrp       : (null)
   +0x018 Timer            : (null)
   +0x01c Flags            : 0x40
   +0x020 Characteristics  : 0x100
   +0x024 Vpb              : (null)
   +0x028 DeviceExtension  : (null)
   +0x02c DeviceType       : 0x12
   +0x030 StackSize        : 1 ''
   +0x034 Queue            : <unnamed-tag>
   +0x05c AlignmentRequirement : 0
   +0x060 DeviceQueue      : _KDEVICE_QUEUE
   +0x074 Dpc              : _KDPC
   +0x094 ActiveThreadCount : 0
   +0x098 SecurityDescriptor : 0x8824c4f0 Void
   +0x09c DeviceLock       : _KEVENT
   +0x0ac SectorSize       : 0
   +0x0ae Spare1           : 0
   +0x0b0 DeviceObjectExtension : 0x877c6fd0 _DEVOBJ_EXTENSION
   +0x0b4 Reserved         : (null)

1: kd> !drvobj 0x87745608
Driver object (87745608) is for:
 \Driver\Tcpip
Driver Extension List: (id , addr)

Device Object list:
877bff18  877c6f18  877c4e58  877ad340
877454f0
```

```
1: kd> dt _DRIVER_OBJECT 0x87745608
ntdll!_DRIVER_OBJECT
   +0x000 Type            : 0n4
   +0x002 Size            : 0n168
   +0x004 DeviceObject    : 0x877bff18 _DEVICE_OBJECT
   +0x008 Flags           : 0x12
   +0x00c DriverStart     : 0x88b03000 Void
   +0x010 DriverSize      : 0xd1000
   +0x014 DriverSection   : 0x84b1dce8 Void
   +0x018 DriverExtension : 0x877456b0 _DRIVER_EXTENSION
   +0x01c DriverName      : _UNICODE_STRING "\Driver\Tcpip"
   +0x024 HardwareDatabase : 0x81b02ed8 _UNICODE_STRING
"\REGISTRY\MACHINE\HARDWARE\DESCRIPTION\SYSTEM"
   +0x028 FastIoDispatch  : (null)
   +0x02c DriverInit      : 0x88bc81b9     long  tcpip!GsDriverEntry+0
   +0x030 DriverStartIo   : (null)
   +0x034 DriverUnload    : 0x88bc55b2     void  tcpip!DriverUnload+0
   +0x038 MajorFunction   : [28] 0x88b28e22     long  tcpip!NlDispatchClose+0
```

11.   Suppose we find a suspicious driver object (for example, from its name or from a problem thread which has an IRP in WinDbg output) then we can check its IRP dispatch table:

```
1: kd> !drvobj \Driver\CmBatt 3
Driver object (87668378) is for:
 \Driver\CmBatt
Driver Extension List: (id , addr)

Device Object list:
849e38a0  848c29b8

DriverEntry:    85a399bc     CmBatt!GsDriverEntry
DriverStartIo:  00000000
DriverUnload:   85a38b06     CmBatt!CmBattUnload
AddDevice:      85a38588     CmBatt!CmBattAddDevice

Dispatch routines:
[00] IRP_MJ_CREATE                     85a38b40     CmBatt!CmBattOpenClose
[01] IRP_MJ_CREATE_NAMED_PIPE          8181d171     nt!IopInvalidDeviceRequest
[02] IRP_MJ_CLOSE                      85a38b40     CmBatt!CmBattOpenClose
[03] IRP_MJ_READ                       87fe6226     E1G60I32!EepromRead
[04] IRP_MJ_WRITE                      8181d171     nt!IopInvalidDeviceRequest
[05] IRP_MJ_QUERY_INFORMATION          8181d171     nt!IopInvalidDeviceRequest
[06] IRP_MJ_SET_INFORMATION            8181d171     nt!IopInvalidDeviceRequest
[07] IRP_MJ_QUERY_EA                   8181d171     nt!IopInvalidDeviceRequest
[08] IRP_MJ_SET_EA                     8181d171     nt!IopInvalidDeviceRequest
[09] IRP_MJ_FLUSH_BUFFERS              8181d171     nt!IopInvalidDeviceRequest
[0a] IRP_MJ_QUERY_VOLUME_INFORMATION   8181d171     nt!IopInvalidDeviceRequest
[0b] IRP_MJ_SET_VOLUME_INFORMATION     8181d171     nt!IopInvalidDeviceRequest
[0c] IRP_MJ_DIRECTORY_CONTROL          8181d171     nt!IopInvalidDeviceRequest
[0d] IRP_MJ_FILE_SYSTEM_CONTROL        8181d171     nt!IopInvalidDeviceRequest
[0e] IRP_MJ_DEVICE_CONTROL             85a38bac     CmBatt!CmBattIoctl
[0f] IRP_MJ_INTERNAL_DEVICE_CONTROL    8181d171     nt!IopInvalidDeviceRequest
[10] IRP_MJ_SHUTDOWN                   8181d171     nt!IopInvalidDeviceRequest
[11] IRP_MJ_LOCK_CONTROL               8181d171     nt!IopInvalidDeviceRequest
[12] IRP_MJ_CLEANUP                    8181d171     nt!IopInvalidDeviceRequest
[13] IRP_MJ_CREATE_MAILSLOT            8181d171     nt!IopInvalidDeviceRequest
[14] IRP_MJ_QUERY_SECURITY             8181d171     nt!IopInvalidDeviceRequest
[15] IRP_MJ_SET_SECURITY               8181d171     nt!IopInvalidDeviceRequest
```

```
[16] IRP_MJ_POWER                85a37ef8    CmBatt!CmBattPowerDispatch
[17] IRP_MJ_SYSTEM_CONTROL        85a39492    CmBatt!CmBattSystemControl
[18] IRP_MJ_DEVICE_CHANGE         8181d171    nt!IopInvalidDeviceRequest
[19] IRP_MJ_QUERY_QUOTA           8181d171    nt!IopInvalidDeviceRequest
[1a] IRP_MJ_SET_QUOTA             8181d171    nt!IopInvalidDeviceRequest
[1b] IRP_MJ_PNP                   85a3811c    CmBatt!CmBattPnpDispatch
```

We see that one of entries (IRP_MJ_READ) points to memory outside of the driver module range.

12.   Close the log file:

```
1: kd> .logclose
Closing open log file C:\AWMA-Dumps\M5.log
```

13.   To avoid possible confusion and glitches we recommend exiting WinDbg after each exercise.

If you are presented with this dialog choose No:

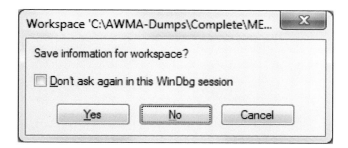

Direct Dump Manipulation

- Malware effects modeling

- Process and complete dumps

- ep <address> value

- .dump /f <file name>

For this dump we used the so called direct dump manipulation (by analogy with a known malware technique called direct kernel object manipulation, DKOM). We just modified some pointers using **e** command variants such as **ep** and saved a copy using **.dump** command. Thus we modeled certain malware effects in memory without spending much time writing actual code that does that.

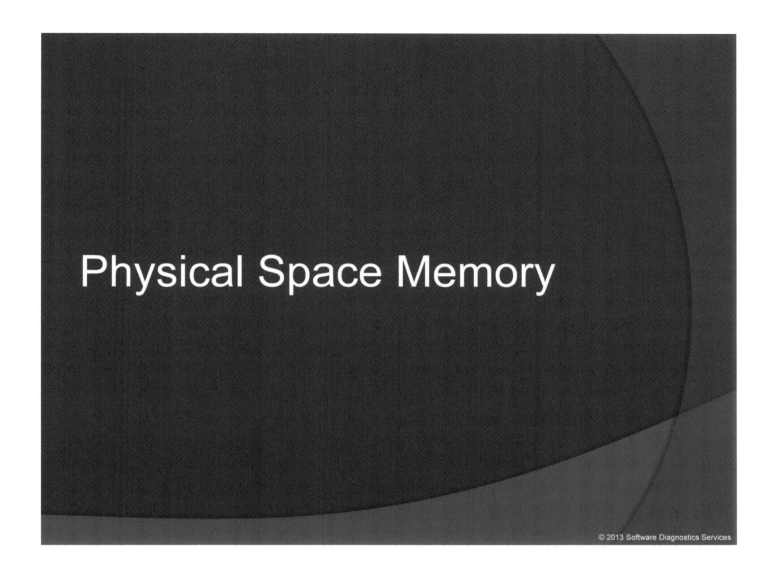

Physical Space Memory

Now we discuss physical memory space. Because we already analyzed a complete memory dump in M4 exercise you won't see much differences in our next exercise.

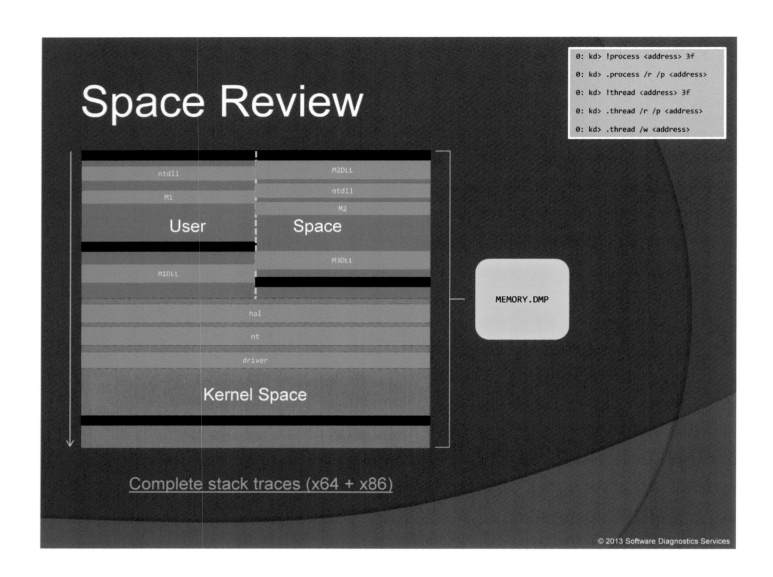

In a physical space (and in a complete memory dump) we have several user spaces but only one kernel space. When we navigate between processes we need to make sure that we change to the correct user space and reload symbols. Also for x64 systems we might have running 32-bit processes and if you use **!process** command like we did previously you won't find 32-bit thread stacks. On this presentation I provided a small WinDbg script that dumps both types of stack traces.

Complete stack traces (x64 + x86)
http://www.dumpanalysis.org/blog/index.php/2010/02/09/complete-stack-traces-from-x64-system/

Exercise M6

- **Goal:** Navigate processes in a complete memory dump, check x64 SSDT entries, check process and thread tokens, discover hidden processes and drivers, check IRP stacks

- **Patterns:** Deviant Token, Hidden Process, Hidden Module, Stack Trace Collection (I/O)

- \AWMA-Dumps\Exercise-M6.pdf

Now we come back to our 64-bit dump we analyzed in exercise M4.

Goal: Navigate processes in a complete memory dump; check x64 SSDT entries; check process and thread tokens; discover hidden processes and drivers; check IRP stacks.

Patterns: Deviant Token, Hidden Process, Hidden Module, Stack Trace Collection (I/O)

1.   Launch WinDbg from Windows Kits \ Debugging Tools for Windows (X64) or Debugging Tools for Windows (X86)

2.   Open \AWMA-Dumps\Complete\MEMORY.DMP

3.   If you are presented with this dialog say No:

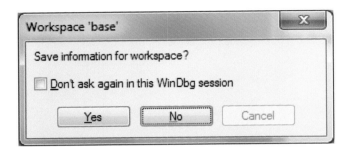

4.   You get the dump file loaded (we skip the output as it should be the same as in exercise M4).

5.   Open a log file:

```
0: kd> .logopen C:\AWMA-Dumps\M6.log
Opened log file 'C:\AWMA-Dumps\M6.log'
```

6.   Set up a link to Microsoft symbol server and reload symbols:

```
0: kd> .symfix c:\mss

0: kd> .reload
Loading Kernel Symbols
...............................................................
...............................................................
.....................
Loading User Symbols
...............................................................
...........
Loading unloaded module list
...................................................................
```

7.   First we check SSDT to see if there is any difference compared to x86 32-bit version:

```
0: kd> dps nt!KeServiceDescriptorTable
fffff802`b3ddf900  fffff802`b3afef00 nt!KiServiceTable
fffff802`b3ddf908  00000000`00000000
fffff802`b3ddf910  00000000`000001ad
fffff802`b3ddf918  fffff802`b3affc6c nt!KiArgumentTable
fffff802`b3ddf920  00000000`00000000
fffff802`b3ddf928  00000000`00000000
fffff802`b3ddf930  00000000`00000000
fffff802`b3ddf938  00000000`00000000
fffff802`b3ddf940  fffff802`b3afef00 nt!KiServiceTable
fffff802`b3ddf948  00000000`00000000
fffff802`b3ddf950  00000000`000001ad
fffff802`b3ddf958  fffff802`b3affc6c nt!KiArgumentTable
fffff802`b3ddf960  fffff960`0014ee00 win32k!W32pServiceTable
fffff802`b3ddf968  00000000`00000000
fffff802`b3ddf970  00000000`000003da
fffff802`b3ddf978  fffff960`001510b4 win32k!W32pArgumentTable
```

However, it looks like it is either encrypted or compacted:

```
0: kd> dps nt!KiServiceTable
fffff802`b3afef00  04fe7c00`ffeb9f00
fffff802`b3afef08  ffff5b00`03cae400
fffff802`b3afef10  03e9d306`03705805
fffff802`b3afef18  03b0c801`03eaea05
fffff802`b3afef20  03f42e40`03567900
fffff802`b3afef28  0369c600`0395fe40
fffff802`b3afef30  03cf3b00`03d1ef00
fffff802`b3afef38  036f3301`0356c601
fffff802`b3afef40  0392d802`03c44c00
fffff802`b3afef48  03a05e40`03686000
fffff802`b3afef50  037a7402`037ea001
fffff802`b3afef58  03b86601`03fa0602
fffff802`b3afef60  0317ce05`03078101
fffff802`b3afef68  03926e03`03b12900
fffff802`b3afef70  04f7abc0`00757300
fffff802`b3afef78  037b4201`03cafa00
```

Search on Internet gives some algorithms but most of them do not work on all entries. The closest one I found that works on all entries is described here:

http://kitrap08.blogspot.ie/2010/11/ssdt-x64.html

But the article is in Russian so I show you the algorithm on the 4th entry (index 3):

```
; Get the DWORD entry

0: kd> ? dwo(nt!KiServiceTable+4*3)
Evaluate expression: 4294925056 = 00000000`ffff5b00

; if negative sign extend

0: kd> ? 00000000`ffff5b00 or ffffffff`00000000
Evaluate expression: -42240 = ffffffff`ffff5b00
```

```
; Right arithmetic shift by 4 bits (sign extended)

0: kd> ? (ffffffff`ffff5b00 >>> 4)
Evaluate expression: -2640 = ffffffff`fffff5b0

; Add to nt!KiServiceTable address

0: kd> ? nt!KiServiceTable + ffffffff`fffff5b0
Evaluate expression: -8784488438608 = fffff802`b3afe4b0

0: kd> ln fffff802`b3afe4b0
(fffff802`b3afe4b0)   nt!NtCallbackReturn   |   (fffff802`b3afe610)   nt!DbgBreakPoint
Exact matches:
    nt!NtCallbackReturn (<no parameter info>)

0: kd> u fffff802`b3afe4b0
nt!NtCallbackReturn:
fffff802`b3afe4b0 654c8b1c2588010000 mov   r11,qword ptr gs:[188h]
fffff802`b3afe4b9 4d8b5328           mov   r10,qword ptr [r11+28h]
fffff802`b3afe4bd 4d8b4a20           mov   r9,qword ptr [r10+20h]
fffff802`b3afe4c1 4d85c9             test  r9,r9
fffff802`b3afe4c4 0f841e010000       je    nt!NtCallbackReturn+0x138 (fffff802`b3afe5e8)
fffff802`b3afe4ca 418bc0             mov   eax,r8d
fffff802`b3afe4cd 498b99d8000000     mov   rbx,qword ptr [r9+0D8h]
fffff802`b3afe4d4 48890b             mov   qword ptr [rbx],rcx
```

8.   Now we find out notepad process address from the output of **!process 0 3f** command (exercise M4) and make it current:

```
0: kd> .process /r /p fffffa8001e0f740
Implicit process is now fffffa80`01e0f740
Loading User Symbols
.......................
```

Let's now check its module load address, dump PE header and check IAT:

```
0: kd> lm m notepad
start               end                 module name
000007f6`54c30000 000007f6`54c70000   notepad    (deferred)

0: kd> !dh 000007f6`54c30000

File Type: EXECUTABLE IMAGE
FILE HEADER VALUES
    8664 machine (X64)
       6 number of sections
501099BC time date stamp Thu Jul 26 02:13:32 2012

       0 file pointer to symbol table
       0 number of symbols
      F0 size of optional header
      22 characteristics
            Executable
            App can handle >2gb addresses

OPTIONAL HEADER VALUES
     20B magic #
   10.10 linker version
   1D400 size of code
   1F200 size of initialized data
```

```
       0 size of uninitialized data
    5A40 address of entry point
    1000 base of code
         ----- new -----
000007f654c30000 image base
    1000 section alignment
     200 file alignment
       2 subsystem (Windows GUI)
    6.02 operating system version
    6.02 image version
    6.02 subsystem version
   40000 size of image
     400 size of headers
   3DB82 checksum
0000000000080000 size of stack reserve
0000000000011000 size of stack commit
0000000000100000 size of heap reserve
0000000000001000 size of heap commit
    8160 DLL characteristics
         High entropy VA supported
         Dynamic base
         NX compatible
         Terminal server aware
       0 [       0] address [size] of Export Directory
   23738 [     118] address [size] of Import Directory
   25000 [   19AE8] address [size] of Resource Directory
   22000 [     678] address [size] of Exception Directory
       0 [       0] address [size] of Security Directory
   3F000 [     128] address [size] of Base Relocation Directory
   1DAA0 [      38] address [size] of Debug Directory
       0 [       0] address [size] of Description Directory
       0 [       0] address [size] of Special Directory
       0 [       0] address [size] of Thread Storage Directory
   1DA30 [      70] address [size] of Load Configuration Directory
       0 [       0] address [size] of Bound Import Directory
   23000 [     738] address [size] of Import Address Table Directory
       0 [       0] address [size] of Delay Import Directory
       0 [       0] address [size] of COR20 Header Directory
       0 [       0] address [size] of Reserved Directory


SECTION HEADER #1
   .text name
   1D390 virtual size
    1000 virtual address
   1D400 size of raw data
     400 file pointer to raw data
       0 file pointer to relocation table
       0 file pointer to line numbers
       0 number of relocations
       0 number of line numbers
60000020 flags
         Code
         (no align specified)
         Execute Read


Debug Directories(2)
       Type      Size    Address   Pointer
       cv        24      1dadc     1cedc    Format: RSDS, guid, 2, notepad.pdb
```

213

```
       (    10)       4       1dad8     1ced8

SECTION HEADER #2
   .data name
    2AEC virtual size
   1F000 virtual address
    1A00 size of raw data
   1D800 file pointer to raw data
       0 file pointer to relocation table
       0 file pointer to line numbers
       0 number of relocations
       0 number of line numbers
C0000040 flags
         Initialized Data
         (no align specified)
         Read Write

SECTION HEADER #3
   .pdata name
     678 virtual size
   22000 virtual address
     800 size of raw data
   1F200 file pointer to raw data
       0 file pointer to relocation table
       0 file pointer to line numbers
       0 number of relocations
       0 number of line numbers
40000040 flags
         Initialized Data
         (no align specified)
         Read Only

SECTION HEADER #4
   .idata name
    1E30 virtual size
   23000 virtual address
    2000 size of raw data
   1FA00 file pointer to raw data
       0 file pointer to relocation table
       0 file pointer to line numbers
       0 number of relocations
       0 number of line numbers
40000040 flags
         Initialized Data
         (no align specified)
         Read Only

SECTION HEADER #5
   .rsrc name
   19AE8 virtual size
   25000 virtual address
   19C00 size of raw data
   21A00 file pointer to raw data
       0 file pointer to relocation table
       0 file pointer to line numbers
       0 number of relocations
       0 number of line numbers
40000040 flags
         Initialized Data
         (no align specified)
```

                 Read Only

SECTION HEADER #6
   .reloc name
        128 virtual size
      3F000 virtual address
        200 size of raw data
      3B600 file pointer to raw data
          0 file pointer to relocation table
          0 file pointer to line numbers
          0 number of relocations
          0 number of line numbers
   42000040 flags
            Initialized Data
            Discardable
            (no align specified)
            Read Only

0: kd> dps 000007f6`54c30000+23000 L738/8
000007f6`54c53000  000007fe`f78d13f0 ADVAPI32!RegQueryValueExWStub
000007f6`54c53008  000007fe`f78d1fb0 ADVAPI32!RegCreateKeyW
000007f6`54c53010  000007fe`f78d13b0 ADVAPI32!RegCloseKeyStub
000007f6`54c53018  000007fe`f78d13d0 ADVAPI32!RegOpenKeyExWStub
000007f6`54c53020  000007fe`f78d15c0 ADVAPI32!IsTextUnicode
000007f6`54c53028  000007fe`f78d1d50 ADVAPI32!RegSetValueExWStub
000007f6`54c53030  00000000`00000000
000007f6`54c53038  000007fe`f6047150 KERNEL32!FindNLSStringStub
000007f6`54c53040  000007fe`f6012fb0 KERNEL32!GlobalAllocStub
000007f6`54c53048  000007fe`f60133e0 KERNEL32!GetLocalTimeStub
000007f6`54c53050  000007fe`f6035660 KERNEL32!GetDateFormatWStub
000007f6`54c53058  000007fe`f604d420 KERNEL32!GetTimeFormatWStub
000007f6`54c53060  000007fe`f6035330 KERNEL32!GlobalLock
000007f6`54c53068  000007fe`f60352e0 KERNEL32!GlobalUnlock
000007f6`54c53070  000007fe`f60119fc KERNEL32!GetUserDefaultUILanguageStub
000007f6`54c53078  000007fe`f60113c0 KERNEL32!UnmapViewOfFileStub
000007f6`54c53080  000007fe`f6012ff0 KERNEL32!LocalReAllocStub
000007f6`54c53088  000007fe`f6011c90 KERNEL32!MultiByteToWideCharStub
000007f6`54c53090  000007fe`f6011d70 KERNEL32!MapViewOfFileStub
000007f6`54c53098  000007fe`f6013030 KERNEL32!CreateFileMappingWStub
000007f6`54c530a0  000007fe`f6011d8c KERNEL32!GetFileInformationByHandle
000007f6`54c530a8  000007fe`f60356f8 KERNEL32!SetEndOfFile
000007f6`54c530b0  000007fe`f60135e0 KERNEL32!DeleteFileW
000007f6`54c530b8  000007fe`f6013500 KERNEL32!GetACPStub
000007f6`54c530c0  000007fe`f6012e78 KERNEL32!WriteFile
000007f6`54c530c8  000007fe`f60114f0 KERNEL32!SetLastErrorStub
000007f6`54c530d0  000007fe`f6012d20 KERNEL32!WideCharToMultiByteStub
000007f6`54c530d8  000007fe`f60114e0 KERNEL32!GetLastErrorStub
000007f6`54c530e0  000007fe`f601cd30 KERNEL32!LocalSize
000007f6`54c530e8  000007fe`f6013430 KERNEL32!GetFullPathNameW
000007f6`54c530f0  000007fe`f606be44 KERNEL32!FoldStringWStub
000007f6`54c530f8  000007fe`f6013010 KERNEL32!LocalUnlockStub
000007f6`54c53100  000007fe`f6013000 KERNEL32!LocalLockStub
000007f6`54c53108  000007fe`f6014018 KERNEL32!FormatMessageWStub
000007f6`54c53110  000007fe`f6012db8 KERNEL32!FindClose
000007f6`54c53118  000007fe`f6012dc4 KERNEL32!FindFirstFileW
000007f6`54c53120  000007fe`f6011c30 KERNEL32!lstrcmpWStub
000007f6`54c53128  000007fe`f6011410 KERNEL32!GetCurrentProcessId
000007f6`54c53130  000007fe`f6012d80 KERNEL32!GetModuleHandleExWStub
000007f6`54c53138  000007fe`f6011ad8 KERNEL32!GetTickCount64Stub
000007f6`54c53140  000007fe`f601396c KERNEL32!HeapSetInformationStub

```
000007f6`54c53148    000007fe`f601397c    KERNEL32!GetCommandLineWStub
000007f6`54c53150    000007fe`f6011510    KERNEL32!lstrlenWStub
000007f6`54c53158    000007fe`f6011dac    KERNEL32!CreateThreadStub
000007f6`54c53160    000007fe`f6014870    KERNEL32!FreeLibraryAndExitThreadStub
000007f6`54c53168    000007fe`f6011cf0    KERNEL32!GetModuleFileNameWStub
000007f6`54c53170    000007fe`f6011d30    KERNEL32!GetProcAddressStub
000007f6`54c53178    000007fe`f6011360    KERNEL32!GetProcessHeapStub
000007f6`54c53180    000007fe`f6011260    KERNEL32!HeapFreeStub
000007f6`54c53188    000007fe`f6012ebc    KERNEL32!LoadLibraryExWStub
000007f6`54c53190    000007fe`f7ec5670    ntdll!RtlAllocateHeap
000007f6`54c53198    000007fe`f6011b98    KERNEL32!FreeLibraryStub
000007f6`54c531a0    000007fe`f6011a20    KERNEL32!MulDiv
000007f6`54c531a8    000007fe`f6013368    KERNEL32!GetLocaleInfoWStub
000007f6`54c531b0    000007fe`f6012f80    KERNEL32!GlobalFreeStub
000007f6`54c531b8    000007fe`f6011350    KERNEL32!LocalAllocStub
000007f6`54c531c0    000007fe`f601152c    KERNEL32!CloseHandle
000007f6`54c531c8    000007fe`f6012e60    KERNEL32!ReadFile
000007f6`54c531d0    000007fe`f6012e54    KERNEL32!CreateFileW
000007f6`54c531d8    000007fe`f6011230    KERNEL32!GetTickCountStub
000007f6`54c531e0    000007fe`f60135b8    KERNEL32!SetErrorModeStub
000007f6`54c531e8    000007fe`f60123c0    KERNEL32!lstrcmpiWStub
000007f6`54c531f0    000007fe`f6011340    KERNEL32!LocalFreeStub
000007f6`54c531f8    000007fe`f6011010    KERNEL32!SleepStub
000007f6`54c53200    000007fe`f6012b90    KERNEL32!GetStartupInfoWStub
000007f6`54c53208    000007fe`f606b774    KERNEL32!UnhandledExceptionFilterStub
000007f6`54c53210    000007fe`f6012be4    KERNEL32!SetUnhandledExceptionFilterStub
000007f6`54c53218    000007fe`f60113b0    KERNEL32!GetCurrentProcess
000007f6`54c53220    000007fe`f6013900    KERNEL32!TerminateProcessStub
000007f6`54c53228    000007fe`f6011c00    KERNEL32!GetModuleHandleWStub
000007f6`54c53230    000007fe`f6011390    KERNEL32!QueryPerformanceCounterStub
000007f6`54c53238    000007fe`f6011250    KERNEL32!GetCurrentThreadId
000007f6`54c53240    000007fe`f6011550    KERNEL32!GetSystemTimeAsFileTimeStub
000007f6`54c53248    00000000`00000000
000007f6`54c53250    000007fe`f58322a8    GDI32!CreateDCW
000007f6`54c53258    000007fe`f583ef88    GDI32!StartPage
000007f6`54c53260    000007fe`f588e094    GDI32!StartDocW
000007f6`54c53268    000007fe`f588e010    GDI32!SetAbortProc
000007f6`54c53270    000007fe`f5812f80    GDI32!DeleteDC
000007f6`54c53278    000007fe`f5840940    GDI32!EndDoc
000007f6`54c53280    000007fe`f588ef20    GDI32!AbortDoc
000007f6`54c53288    000007fe`f588e7d4    GDI32!EndPage
000007f6`54c53290    000007fe`f5814330    GDI32!GetTextMetricsW
000007f6`54c53298    000007fe`f58129a0    GDI32!SetBkMode
000007f6`54c532a0    000007fe`f5813af0    GDI32!LPtoDP
000007f6`54c532a8    000007fe`f5836a20    GDI32!SetWindowExtEx
000007f6`54c532b0    000007fe`f5841db0    GDI32!SetViewportExtEx
000007f6`54c532b8    000007fe`f5835554    GDI32!SetMapMode
000007f6`54c532c0    000007fe`f5822efc    GDI32!GetTextExtentPoint32W
000007f6`54c532c8    000007fe`f5850360    GDI32!TextOutW
000007f6`54c532d0    000007fe`f5832c50    GDI32!EnumFontsW
000007f6`54c532d8    000007fe`f5823324    GDI32!GetTextFaceW
000007f6`54c532e0    000007fe`f58124b0    GDI32!SelectObject
000007f6`54c532e8    000007fe`f5811520    GDI32!DeleteObject
000007f6`54c532f0    000007fe`f5821bbc    GDI32!CreateFontIndirectW
000007f6`54c532f8    000007fe`f5812c00    GDI32!GetDeviceCaps
000007f6`54c53300    00000000`00000000
000007f6`54c53308    000007fe`f56ca750    USER32!NtUserGetWindowPlacement
000007f6`54c53310    000007fe`f56cb510    USER32!CharUpperWStub
000007f6`54c53318    000007fe`f56d7420    USER32!NtUserGetSystemMenu
000007f6`54c53320    000007fe`f56d2590    USER32!LoadAcceleratorsW
```

```
000007f6`54c53328    000007fe`f56c8b10 USER32!SetWindowLongW
000007f6`54c53330    000007fe`f56cb260 USER32!RegisterWindowMessageW
000007f6`54c53338    000007fe`f56cad70 USER32!LoadCursorW
000007f6`54c53340    000007fe`f56cc5b0 USER32!CreateWindowExW
000007f6`54c53348    000007fe`f56d3660 USER32!NtUserSetWindowPlacement
000007f6`54c53350    000007fe`f56cb610 USER32!LoadImageW
000007f6`54c53358    000007fe`f56cc8d0 USER32!RegisterClassExW
000007f6`54c53360    000007fe`f56ed1d0 USER32!SetScrollPos
000007f6`54c53368    000007fe`f56c4a20 USER32!NtUserInvalidateRect
000007f6`54c53370    000007fe`f56cb530 USER32!UpdateWindow
000007f6`54c53378    000007fe`f56cea80 USER32!GetWindowTextLengthW
000007f6`54c53380    000007fe`f56c4ed0 USER32!GetWindowLongW
000007f6`54c53388    000007fe`f56c10c0 USER32!PeekMessageW
000007f6`54c53390    000007fe`f56ca030 USER32!GetWindowTextW
000007f6`54c53398    000007fe`f56ce600 USER32!EnableWindow
000007f6`54c533a0    000007fe`f56ddae0 USER32!CreateDialogParamW
000007f6`54c533a8    000007fe`f56cea20 USER32!DrawTextExW
000007f6`54c533b0    000007fe`f56c48a0 USER32!GetParent
000007f6`54c533b8    000007fe`f5708a28 USER32!ChildWindowFromPoint
000007f6`54c533c0    000007fe`f56cdbc0 USER32!ScreenToClient
000007f6`54c533c8    000007fe`f56c3570 USER32!GetCursorPos
000007f6`54c533d0    000007fe`f56e1f50 USER32!WinHelpW
000007f6`54c533d8    000007fe`f56cde60 USER32!GetDlgCtrlID
000007f6`54c533e0    000007fe`f56eb070 USER32!SendDlgItemMessageW
000007f6`54c533e8    000007fe`f56ebb00 USER32!EndDialog
000007f6`54c533f0    000007fe`f56eb960 USER32!GetDlgItemTextW
000007f6`54c533f8    000007fe`f56ec2f0 USER32!SetDlgItemTextW
000007f6`54c53400    000007fe`f56ed830 USER32!NtUserCloseClipboard
000007f6`54c53408    000007fe`f56ef3e0 USER32!NtUserIsClipboardFormatAvailable
000007f6`54c53410    000007fe`f56ed850 USER32!OpenClipboard
000007f6`54c53418    000007fe`f56ed430 USER32!GetMenuState
000007f6`54c53420    000007fe`f56c7430 USER32!SetWindowTextW
000007f6`54c53428    000007fe`f56ce030 USER32!NtUserUnhookWinEvent
000007f6`54c53430    000007fe`f56c1520 USER32!DispatchMessageW
000007f6`54c53438    000007fe`f56c11c0 USER32!TranslateMessage
000007f6`54c53440    000007fe`f56c1fa0 USER32!TranslateAcceleratorW
000007f6`54c53448    000007fe`f56d5f50 USER32!IsDialogMessageW
000007f6`54c53450    000007fe`f56c1ed0 USER32!GetMessageW
000007f6`54c53458    000007fe`f56d2f70 USER32!SetWinEventHook
000007f6`54c53460    000007fe`f56cb830 USER32!CharNextWStub
000007f6`54c53468    000007fe`f56c2090 USER32!GetKeyboardLayout
000007f6`54c53470    000007fe`f56c3410 USER32!NtUserGetForegroundWindow
000007f6`54c53478    000007fe`f56ec8a0 USER32!MessageBeep
000007f6`54c53480    000007fe`f56ce050 USER32!PostQuitMessage
000007f6`54c53488    000007fe`f56cbbc0 USER32!IsIconic
000007f6`54c53490    000007fe`f7ec1ac9 ntdll!NtdllDefWindowProc_W
000007f6`54c53498    000007fe`f56c5280 USER32!LoadStringW
000007f6`54c534a0    000007fe`f56d4f80 USER32!NtUserSetActiveWindow
000007f6`54c534a8    000007fe`f56cdd70 USER32!NtUserSetCursor
000007f6`54c534b0    000007fe`f56c3d10 USER32!ReleaseDC
000007f6`54c534b8    000007fe`f56c3d40 USER32!NtUserGetDC
000007f6`54c534c0    000007fe`f56d4ae0 USER32!NtUserShowWindow
000007f6`54c534c8    000007fe`f56c4b50 USER32!GetClientRect
000007f6`54c534d0    000007fe`f56ed9e0 USER32!CheckMenuItem
000007f6`54c534d8    000007fe`f5730720 USER32!MessageBoxW
000007f6`54c534e0    000007fe`f56c3400 USER32!GetFocus
000007f6`54c534e8    000007fe`f56cc870 USER32!LoadIconW
000007f6`54c534f0    000007fe`f56ebb80 USER32!DialogBoxParamW
000007f6`54c534f8    000007fe`f56c86c0 USER32!NtUserSetFocus
000007f6`54c53500    000007fe`f56efdd0 USER32!GetSubMenu
```

```
000007f6`54c53508    000007fe`f56ed940 USER32!EnableMenuItem
000007f6`54c53510    000007fe`f56ef330 USER32!GetMenu
000007f6`54c53518    000007fe`f56c24a0 USER32!PostMessageW
000007f6`54c53520    000007fe`f56cded0 USER32!NtUserMoveWindow
000007f6`54c53528    000007fe`f56c4760 USER32!SendMessageW
000007f6`54c53530    000007fe`f56c3540 USER32!NtUserDestroyWindow
000007f6`54c53538    00000000`00000000
000007f6`54c53540    000007fe`f78239c0 msvcrt!iswctype
000007f6`54c53548    000007fe`f78249a0 msvcrt!strchr
000007f6`54c53550    000007fe`f7821100 msvcrt!memcpy
000007f6`54c53558    000007fe`f7827420 msvcrt!wtol
000007f6`54c53560    000007fe`f78234b0 msvcrt!vsnwprintf
000007f6`54c53568    000007fe`f7870ad0 msvcrt!terminate
000007f6`54c53570    000007fe`f787fefc msvcrt!XcptFilter
000007f6`54c53578    000007fe`f78877e4 msvcrt!amsg_exit
000007f6`54c53580    000007fe`f7828cc8 msvcrt!_getmainargs
000007f6`54c53588    000007fe`f78277a0 msvcrt!_set_app_type
000007f6`54c53590    000007fe`f782615c msvcrt!exit
000007f6`54c53598    000007fe`f7821060 msvcrt!memset
000007f6`54c535a0    000007fe`f78af0e4 msvcrt!commode
000007f6`54c535a8    000007fe`f78af0e0 msvcrt!fmode
000007f6`54c535b0    000007fe`f78ae858 msvcrt!acmdln
000007f6`54c535b8    000007fe`f7ee4f5c ntdll!_C_specific_handler
000007f6`54c535c0    000007fe`f7823cd0 msvcrt!initterm
000007f6`54c535c8    000007fe`f78a0214 msvcrt!_setusermatherr
000007f6`54c535d0    000007fe`f7828ae8 msvcrt!ismbblead
000007f6`54c535d8    000007fe`f782f75c msvcrt!cexit
000007f6`54c535e0    000007fe`f7887790 msvcrt!exit
000007f6`54c535e8    00000000`00000000
000007f6`54c535f0    000007fe`f7a3a6f0 COMDLG32!GetSaveFileNameW
000007f6`54c535f8    000007fe`f7a50170 COMDLG32!FindTextW
000007f6`54c53600    000007fe`f7a5da60 COMDLG32!PageSetupDlgW
000007f6`54c53608    000007fe`f7a54be8 COMDLG32!ChooseFontW
000007f6`54c53610    000007fe`f7a21cc0 COMDLG32!GetFileTitleW
000007f6`54c53618    000007fe`f7a6cc0c COMDLG32!PrintDlgExW
000007f6`54c53620    000007fe`f7a4f360 COMDLG32!GetOpenFileNameW
000007f6`54c53628    000007fe`f7a46d04 COMDLG32!CommDlgExtendedError
000007f6`54c53630    000007fe`f7a50148 COMDLG32!ReplaceTextW
000007f6`54c53638    00000000`00000000
000007f6`54c53640    000007fe`f68f1d14 SHELL32!ShellAboutW
000007f6`54c53648    000007fe`f67d47dc SHELL32!DragFinish
000007f6`54c53650    000007fe`f65e58d0 SHELL32!SHCreateItemFromParsingName
000007f6`54c53658    000007fe`f65dbcf0 SHELL32!SHAddToRecentDocs
000007f6`54c53660    000007fe`f67d4814 SHELL32!DragQueryFileW
000007f6`54c53668    000007fe`f67194cc SHELL32!DragAcceptFiles
000007f6`54c53670    00000000`00000000
000007f6`54c53678    000007fe`eb5f3e60 WINSPOOL!OpenPrinterW
000007f6`54c53680    000007fe`eb5f3660 WINSPOOL!ClosePrinter
000007f6`54c53688    000007fe`eb5f5230 WINSPOOL!GetPrinterDriverW
000007f6`54c53690    00000000`00000000
000007f6`54c53698    000007fe`f7b31130 combase!CoTaskMemFree
000007f6`54c536a0    000007fe`f7b31180 combase!CoTaskMemAlloc
000007f6`54c536a8    000007fe`f7b42100 combase!CoCreateInstance
000007f6`54c536b0    000007fe`f7b37c20 combase!CoInitializeEx
000007f6`54c536b8    000007fe`f7b37460 combase!CoUninitialize
000007f6`54c536c0    00000000`00000000
000007f6`54c536c8    000007fe`f7ad1070 SHLWAPI!SHStrDupWStub
000007f6`54c536d0    000007fe`f7ad6200 SHLWAPI!PathIsFileSpecWStub
000007f6`54c536d8    00000000`00000000
000007f6`54c536e0    000007fe`f2791740 COMCTL32!CreateStatusWindowW
```

```
000007f6`54c536e8   000007fe`f280ad28 COMCTL32!TaskDialogIndirect
000007f6`54c536f0   00000000`00000000
000007f6`54c536f8   000007fe`f5501780 OLEAUT32!SysAllocString
000007f6`54c53700   000007fe`f5501220 OLEAUT32!SysFreeString
000007f6`54c53708   00000000`00000000
000007f6`54c53710   000007fe`f7f0dd48 ntdll!RtlVirtualUnwind
000007f6`54c53718   000007fe`f7ee43e0 ntdll!RtlLookupFunctionEntry
000007f6`54c53720   000007fe`f7ec4d10 ntdll!RtlCaptureContext
000007f6`54c53728   000007fe`f7f3da10 ntdll!WinSqmAddToStream
000007f6`54c53730   00000000`00000000
```

9.   Now we check notepad process token (**!token** command) and whether it has impersonating threads:

```
0: kd> !process fffffa8001e0f740 3f
PROCESS fffffa8001e0f740
    SessionId: 2  Cid: 0d7c    Peb: 7f65412f000  ParentCid: 0c78
    DirBase: 0e165000  ObjectTable: fffff8a00055ff00  HandleCount: <Data Not Accessible>
    Image: notepad.exe
    VadRoot fffffa80038c6d30 Vads 55 Clone 0 Private 228. Modified 4. Locked 0.
    DeviceMap fffff8a000290b20
    Token                             fffff8a0018dc8c0
    ElapsedTime                       00:05:13.216
    UserTime                          00:00:00.000
    KernelTime                        00:00:00.000
    QuotaPoolUsage[PagedPool]         191120
    QuotaPoolUsage[NonPagedPool]      6912
    Working Set Sizes (now,min,max)   (1311, 50, 345) (5244KB, 200KB, 1380KB)
    PeakWorkingSetSize                1311
    VirtualSize                       93 Mb
    PeakVirtualSize                   97 Mb
    PageFaultCount                    1348
    MemoryPriority                    BACKGROUND
    BasePriority                      8
    CommitCharge                      315
    Job                               fffffa8003e3ea30

    PEB at 000007f65412f000
    InheritedAddressSpace:     No
    ReadImageFileExecOptions:  No
    BeingDebugged:             No
    ImageBaseAddress:          000007f654c30000
    Ldr                        000007fef7ff88a0
    Ldr.Initialized:           Yes
    Ldr.InInitializationOrderModuleList: 000000554ff41a10 . 000000554ff48cb0
    Ldr.InLoadOrderModuleList:           000000554ff41b70 . 000000554ff48c90
    Ldr.InMemoryOrderModuleList:         000000554ff41b80 . 000000554ff48ca0
                    Base TimeStamp                     Module
            7f654c30000 501099bc Jul 26 02:13:32 2012 C:\WINDOWS\system32\notepad.exe
            7fef7ec0000 505ab405 Sep 20 07:13:25 2012 C:\WINDOWS\SYSTEM32\ntdll.dll
            7fef6010000 5010a83a Jul 26 03:15:22 2012 C:\WINDOWS\system32\KERNEL32.DLL
            7fef4fd0000 5010ab2d Jul 26 03:27:57 2012 C:\WINDOWS\system32\KERNELBASE.dll
            7fef78d0000 5010a732 Jul 26 03:10:58 2012 C:\WINDOWS\system32\ADVAPI32.dll
            7fef5810000 50108b7f Jul 26 01:12:47 2012 C:\WINDOWS\system32\GDI32.dll
            7fef56c0000 505a9a92 Sep 20 05:24:50 2012 C:\WINDOWS\system32\USER32.dll
            7fef7820000 5010ac20 Jul 26 03:32:00 2012 C:\WINDOWS\system32\msvcrt.dll
            7fef7a20000 50108ed8 Jul 26 01:27:04 2012 C:\WINDOWS\system32\COMDLG32.dll
            7fef6520000 507635b5 Oct 11 03:57:57 2012 C:\WINDOWS\system32\SHELL32.dll
            7feeb5f0000 501081fa Jul 26 00:32:10 2012 C:\WINDOWS\system32\WINSPOOL.DRV
```

```
            7fef5340000 50108270 Jul 26 00:34:08 2012 C:\WINDOWS\system32\ole32.dll
            7fef7ad0000 501080dd Jul 26 00:27:25 2012 C:\WINDOWS\system32\SHLWAPI.dll
            7fef2760000 501084f0 Jul 26 00:44:48 2012
C:\WINDOWS\WinSxS\amd64_microsoft.windows.common-
controls_6595b64144ccf1df_6.0.9200.16384_none_418c2a697189c07f\COMCTL32.dll
            7fef5500000 50108a1d Jul 26 01:06:53 2012 C:\WINDOWS\system32\OLEAUT32.dll
            7fef55d0000 50108a41 Jul 26 01:07:29 2012 C:\WINDOWS\SYSTEM32\sechost.dll
            7fef5be0000 50108bb9 Jul 26 01:13:45 2012 C:\WINDOWS\system32\RPCRT4.dll
            7fef7b30000 505a9af2 Sep 20 05:26:26 2012 C:\WINDOWS\SYSTEM32\combase.dll
            7fef2ed0000 505a97e0 Sep 20 05:13:20 2012 C:\WINDOWS\system32\SHCORE.DLL
            7fef54c0000 501088ce Jul 26 01:01:18 2012 C:\WINDOWS\system32\IMM32.DLL
            7fef5d20000 50108881 Jul 26 01:00:01 2012 C:\WINDOWS\system32\MSCTF.dll
            7fef4c30000 5010ab50 Jul 26 03:28:32 2012 C:\WINDOWS\system32\CRYPTBASE.dll
            7fef4bd0000 50108a4c Jul 26 01:07:40 2012 C:\WINDOWS\system32\bcryptPrimitives.dll
            7fef3c80000 505a9614 Sep 20 05:05:40 2012 C:\WINDOWS\system32\uxtheme.dll
            7fef2a10000 5010894e Jul 26 01:03:26 2012 C:\WINDOWS\system32\dwmapi.dll
    SubSystemData:      0000000000000000
    ProcessHeap:        000000554ff40000
    ProcessParameters: 000000554ff411e0
    CurrentDirectory:   'C:\WINDOWS\system32\'
    WindowTitle:    'C:\WINDOWS\system32\notepad.exe'
    ImageFile:      'C:\WINDOWS\system32\notepad.exe'
    CommandLine:    '"C:\WINDOWS\system32\notepad.exe" '
    DllPath:        '< Name not readable >'
    Environment:    000000554ff40860
        ALLUSERSPROFILE=C:\ProgramData
        APPDATA=C:\Users\Dmitry\AppData\Roaming
        CommonProgramFiles=C:\Program Files\Common Files
        CommonProgramFiles(x86)=C:\Program Files (x86)\Common Files
        CommonProgramW6432=C:\Program Files\Common Files
        COMPUTERNAME=MACAIR1
        ComSpec=C:\WINDOWS\system32\cmd.exe
        FP_NO_HOST_CHECK=NO
        HOMEDRIVE=C:
        HOMEPATH=\Users\Dmitry
        LOCALAPPDATA=C:\Users\Dmitry\AppData\Local
        LOGONSERVER=\\MicrosoftAccount
        NUMBER_OF_PROCESSORS=2
        OS=Windows_NT

Path=C:\WINDOWS\system32;C:\WINDOWS;C:\WINDOWS\System32\Wbem;C:\WINDOWS\System32\WindowsPowerSh
ell\v1.0\
        PATHEXT=.COM;.EXE;.BAT;.CMD;.VBS;.VBE;.JS;.JSE;.WSF;.WSH;.MSC
        PROCESSOR_ARCHITECTURE=AMD64
        PROCESSOR_IDENTIFIER=Intel64 Family 6 Model 15 Stepping 11, GenuineIntel
        PROCESSOR_LEVEL=6
        PROCESSOR_REVISION=0f0b
        ProgramData=C:\ProgramData
        ProgramFiles=C:\Program Files
        ProgramFiles(x86)=C:\Program Files (x86)
        ProgramW6432=C:\Program Files
        PSModulePath=C:\WINDOWS\system32\WindowsPowerShell\v1.0\Modules\
        PUBLIC=C:\Users\Public
        SystemDrive=C:
        SystemRoot=C:\WINDOWS
        TEMP=C:\Users\Dmitry\AppData\Local\Temp
        TMP=C:\Users\Dmitry\AppData\Local\Temp
        USERDOMAIN=MACAIR1
        USERDOMAIN_ROAMINGPROFILE=MACAIR1
        USERNAME=Dmitry
```

```
        USERPROFILE=C:\Users\Dmitry
        windir=C:\WINDOWS


          THREAD fffffa8001ec4b00  Cid 0d7c.0bc4  Teb: 000007f65412d000 Win32Thread:
fffff90104165010 WAIT: (WrUserRequest) UserMode Non-Alertable
            fffffa8003808f20  SynchronizationEvent
          Not impersonating
          DeviceMap                 fffff8a000290b20
          Owning Process            fffffa8001e0f740     Image:         notepad.exe
          Attached Process          N/A            Image:         N/A
          Wait Start TickCount      15741108       Ticks: 20 (0:00:00:00.312)
          Context Switch Count      2411           IdealProcessor: 0
          UserTime                  00:00:00.000
          KernelTime                00:00:00.046
          Win32 Start Address notepad!WinMainCRTStartup (0x000007f654c35a40)
          Stack Init fffff88015856dd0 Current fffff880158565f0
          Base fffff88015857000 Limit fffff88015851000 Call 0
          Priority 10 BasePriority 8 UnusualBoost 0 ForegroundBoost 2 IoPriority 2 PagePriority 5
          Child-SP          RetAddr           Call Site
          fffff880`15856630 fffff802`b3b2d99c nt!KiSwapContext+0x76
          fffff880`15856770 fffff802`b3b29c1f nt!KiCommitThreadWait+0x23c
          fffff880`15856830 fffff802`b3b2943e nt!KeWaitForSingleObject+0x1cf
          fffff880`158568c0 fffff960`00153e07 nt!KeWaitForMultipleObjects+0x2ce
          fffff880`15856970 fffff960`00154765 win32k!xxxRealSleepThread+0x2c7
          fffff880`15856a40 fffff960`00152e99 win32k!xxxSleepThread+0xc5
          fffff880`15856a90 fffff960`001545f3 win32k!xxxRealInternalGetMessage+0x629
          fffff880`15856bb0 fffff802`b3b02d53 win32k!NtUserGetMessage+0x83
          fffff880`15856c40 000007fe`f56c1eba nt!KiSystemServiceCopyEnd+0x13 (TrapFrame @
fffff880`15856c40)
          00000055`4fdbf918 000007fe`f56c1ef5 USER32!NtUserGetMessage+0xa
          00000055`4fdbf920 000007f6`54c31064 USER32!GetMessageW+0x25
          00000055`4fdbf950 000007f6`54c3133d notepad!WinMain+0x178
          00000055`4fdbf9d0 000007fe`f601167e notepad!StringCchLengthW+0x315
          00000055`4fdbfa90 000007fe`f7ee3501 KERNEL32!BaseThreadInitThunk+0x1a
          00000055`4fdbfac0 00000000`00000000 ntdll!RtlUserThreadStart+0x1d

0: kd> !token fffff8a0018dc8c0
_TOKEN fffff8a0018dc8c0
TS Session ID: 0x2
User: S-1-5-21-1611807509-3540313852-1071111378-1001
User Groups:
 00 S-1-16-8192
    Attributes - GroupIntegrity GroupIntegrityEnabled
 01 S-1-1-0
    Attributes - Mandatory Default Enabled
 02 S-1-5-21-1611807509-3540313852-1071111378-1002
    Attributes - Mandatory Default Enabled
 03 S-1-5-32-544
    Attributes - DenyOnly
 04 S-1-5-32-545
    Attributes - Mandatory Default Enabled
 05 S-1-5-4
    Attributes - Mandatory Default Enabled
 06 S-1-2-1
    Attributes - Mandatory Default Enabled
 07 S-1-5-11
    Attributes - Mandatory Default Enabled
 08 S-1-5-15
    Attributes - Mandatory Default Enabled
```

```
 09 S-1-11-96-3623454863-58364-18864-2661722203-1597581903-1397600407-1841757693-3687432443-
3003626526-223860046
    Attributes - Mandatory Default Enabled
 10 S-1-5-5-0-847879
    Attributes - Mandatory Default Enabled LogonId
 11 S-1-2-0
    Attributes - Mandatory Default Enabled
 12 S-1-5-64-32
    Attributes - Mandatory Default Enabled
Primary Group: S-1-5-21-1611807509-3540313852-1071111378-1001
Privs:
 19 0x000000013 SeShutdownPrivilege              Attributes -
 23 0x000000017 SeChangeNotifyPrivilege          Attributes - Enabled Default
 25 0x000000019 SeUndockPrivilege                Attributes -
 33 0x000000021 SeIncreaseWorkingSetPrivilege    Attributes -
 34 0x000000022 SeTimeZonePrivilege              Attributes -
Authentication ID:         (0,cf0c8)
Impersonation Level:       Anonymous
TokenType:                 Primary
Source: User32             TokenFlags: 0x2a00 ( Token in use )
Token ID: 12bd79           ParentToken ID: cf0cb
Modified ID:               (0, cf0d4)
RestrictedSidCount: 0      RestrictedSids: 0000000000000000
OriginatingLogonSession: 3e7
PackageSid: (null)
CapabilityCount: 0      Capabilities: 0000000000000000
LowboxNumberEntry: 0000000000000000
```

10.   To check for hidden processes and drivers we can dump all kernel pool entries having *Proc* and *Driv* tags (**!poolfind** command) and then find out any discrepancy with active process list (**!process 0 0**), for example.

```
0: kd> !poolfind Proc

Scanning large pool allocation table for Tag: Proc (fffffa8003c00000 : fffffa8003d80000)


Searching NonPaged pool (fffffa80017a1000 : fffffa80f0a00000) for Tag: Proc

*fffffa800182e410 size:    700 previous size:    80  (Allocated) Proc
*fffffa80019726c0 size:    720 previous size:   190  (Free)      Proc
*fffffa8001c4b000 size:    720 previous size:     0  (Allocated) Proc
*fffffa8001d078e0 size:    720 previous size:   490  (Allocated) Proc
*fffffa8001d544f0 size:    720 previous size:   240  (Allocated) Proc
*fffffa8001e0f6e0 size:    720 previous size:   120  (Allocated) Proc
*fffffa8001e998e0 size:    720 previous size:    a0  (Free)      Proc
*fffffa8001f41350 size:    720 previous size:   150  (Allocated) Proc
*fffffa8001f4b8e0 size:    720 previous size:   8e0  (Allocated) Proc
*fffffa8001f7b730 size:    720 previous size:   120  (Allocated) Proc
*fffffa8001fe88e0 size:    720 previous size:    d0  (Allocated) Proc
*fffffa800200e000 size:    720 previous size:     0  (Allocated) Proc
*fffffa80020b0000 size:    720 previous size:     0  (Allocated) Proc
*fffffa800210 98e0 size:    720 previous size:    20  (Allocated) Proc
*fffffa800218b8e0 size:    720 previous size:    50  (Free)      Proc
*fffffa80021b7000 size:    c00 previous size:     0  (Free)      Proc
*fffffa80027728e0 size:    720 previous size:    90  (Allocated) Proc
*fffffa8002cb28e0 size:    720 previous size:    90  (Allocated) Proc
*fffffa8002cc28e0 size:    720 previous size:    e0  (Allocated) Proc
*fffffa8002cf7160 size:    720 previous size:    40  (Allocated) Proc
*fffffa8002d5d8e0 size:    720 previous size:    90  (Allocated) Proc
```

```
*fffffa8002d6c4e0 size:    720 previous size:     50  (Allocated) Proc
*fffffa8002d740f0 size:    720 previous size:     50  (Allocated) Proc
*fffffa8002d78490 size:    700 previous size:     30  (Allocated) Proc
*fffffa8002e6b160 size:    720 previous size:     20  (Allocated) Proc
*fffffa8002e7b8e0 size:    720 previous size:    560  (Allocated) Proc
*fffffa800305c6b0 size:    720 previous size:     90  (Allocated) Proc
*fffffa80030a64e0 size:    720 previous size:     50  (Allocated) Proc
*fffffa80033bb8e0 size:    720 previous size:     50  (Allocated) Proc
*fffffa80033c3000 size:    720 previous size:      0  (Allocated) Proc
*fffffa80036948e0 size:    720 previous size:     90  (Allocated) Proc
*fffffa80037404e0 size:    720 previous size:     90  (Allocated) Proc
*fffffa80037634e0 size:    720 previous size:     80  (Allocated) Proc
*fffffa800379c8e0 size:    720 previous size:     c0  (Allocated) Proc
*fffffa80037ae8e0 size:    720 previous size:     50  (Allocated) Proc
*fffffa80037e98e0 size:    720 previous size:     90  (Allocated) Proc
*fffffa80038168e0 size:    720 previous size:    1e0  (Allocated) Proc
*fffffa80038798e0 size:    720 previous size:     80  (Allocated) Proc
*fffffa80038e68e0 size:    720 previous size:    200  (Allocated) Proc
*fffffa800392c4e0 size:    720 previous size:     90  (Allocated) Proc
*fffffa80039a98e0 size:    720 previous size:    130  (Allocated) Proc
*fffffa8003b50400 size:    720 previous size:     30  (Allocated) Proc
*fffffa8003d8f000 size:    720 previous size:      0  (Allocated) Proc
*fffffa8003ed3590 size:    720 previous size:     d0  (Allocated) Proc
*fffffa8003eec8e0 size:    720 previous size:     50  (Allocated) Proc
*fffffa8003fea360 size:    720 previous size:     80  (Allocated) Proc
*fffffa80041458e0 size:    720 previous size:     a0  (Allocated) Proc
*fffffa800417d8e0 size:    720 previous size:    300  (Allocated) Proc

0: kd> !poolfind Driv

Scanning large pool allocation table for Tag: Driv (fffffa8003c00000 : fffffa8003d80000)

*fffffa80017e9c90 size:     30 previous size:     10  (Allocated) Driv
*fffffa8002ca61e0 size:    200 previous size:    120  (Allocated) Driv
*fffffa8002dc26f0 size:     30 previous size:     20  (Allocated) Driv
*fffffa8002dc2720 size:    200 previous size:     30  (Allocated) Driv
*fffffa80025fa310 size:    200 previous size:     70  (Allocated) Driv

Searching NonPaged pool (fffffa80017a1000 : fffffa80f0a00000) for Tag: Driv

*fffffa80017ff5a0 size:    200 previous size:     50  (Allocated) Driv
*fffffa8001804e00 size:    200 previous size:     30  (Allocated) Driv
*fffffa800180d1b0 size:    200 previous size:     30  (Allocated) Driv
*fffffa800180e4e0 size:     30 previous size:     60  (Allocated) Driv
*fffffa80018195d0 size:    200 previous size:     b0  (Allocated) Driv
*fffffa800181f0f0 size:     30 previous size:     f0  (Allocated) Driv
*fffffa80018378c0 size:    200 previous size:     20  (Allocated) Driv
*fffffa8001841d80 size:    200 previous size:     40  (Allocated) Driv
*fffffa800184f240 size:    200 previous size:     20  (Allocated) Driv
*fffffa8001858380 size:    200 previous size:    380  (Allocated) Driv
*fffffa8001905c60 size:    200 previous size:    190  (Allocated) Driv
*fffffa800199a190 size:     30 previous size:    190  (Allocated) Driv
*fffffa80019ba380 size:    200 previous size:    380  (Allocated) Driv
*fffffa80019d46c0 size:     30 previous size:     10  (Allocated) Driv
*fffffa80019d8750 size:    200 previous size:    220  (Allocated) Driv
*fffffa80019df4b0 size:    200 previous size:    1d0  (Allocated) Driv
*fffffa80019e4120 size:    200 previous size:    120  (Allocated) Driv
*fffffa80019f08e0 size:     30 previous size:     60  (Allocated) Driv
*fffffa80019f1240 size:    200 previous size:     40  (Allocated) Driv
*fffffa80019f6bf0 size:    200 previous size:    220  (Allocated) Driv
```

```
*fffffa80019f9a40 size:    30 previous size:    60  (Allocated) Driv
*fffffa80019f9ce0 size:   200 previous size:   190  (Allocated) Driv
*fffffa80019fa860 size:   200 previous size:   190  (Allocated) Driv
*fffffa80019faf90 size:    70 previous size:    30  (Allocated) Driv
*fffffa80019fb830 size:   200 previous size:    80  (Allocated) Driv
*fffffa80019fc5a0 size:   200 previous size:   190  (Allocated) Driv
*fffffa80019fcd10 size:   200 previous size:   190  (Allocated) Driv
*fffffa80019fd000 size:   200 previous size:     0  (Allocated) Driv
*fffffa800249ee00 size:   200 previous size:    30  (Allocated) Driv
*fffffa800249fdb0 size:    50 previous size:   100  (Allocated) Driv
*fffffa800249fe00 size:   200 previous size:    50  (Allocated) Driv
*fffffa80024a1220 size:   200 previous size:   100  (Allocated) Driv
*fffffa80024a2090 size:    30 previous size:    30  (Allocated) Driv
*fffffa80024a2ad0 size:   200 previous size:    30  (Allocated) Driv
*fffffa80024a53d0 size:   200 previous size:    80  (Allocated) Driv
*fffffa80024af970 size:   200 previous size:    60  (Allocated) Driv
*fffffa80024e81a0 size:   200 previous size:    b0  (Allocated) Driv
*fffffa80024f5e00 size:   200 previous size:   220  (Allocated) Driv
*fffffa80024f6670 size:   200 previous size:    20  (Allocated) Driv
*fffffa80024f6a80 size:   200 previous size:    30  (Allocated) Driv
*fffffa80024f7000 size:   200 previous size:     0  (Allocated) Driv
*fffffa80024f74e0 size:   200 previous size:    d0  (Allocated) Driv
*fffffa80024fb550 size:   200 previous size:    30  (Allocated) Driv
*fffffa80024fb9c0 size:   200 previous size:    30  (Allocated) Driv
*fffffa80024fe3a0 size:   200 previous size:    40  (Allocated) Driv
*fffffa80024fe8a0 size:   200 previous size:   220  (Allocated) Driv
*fffffa80025e2e00 size:   200 previous size:    10  (Allocated) Driv
*fffffa80025e3c70 size:   200 previous size:   100  (Allocated) Driv
*fffffa80025e48c0 size:   200 previous size:    20  (Allocated) Driv
*fffffa80025e4e00 size:   200 previous size:   240  (Allocated) Driv
*fffffa80025ea000 size:   920 previous size:     0  (Allocated) Driv
*fffffa80025eb000 size:   bf0 previous size:     0  (Allocated) Driv
*fffffa80026378c0 size:   200 previous size:   220  (Allocated) Driv
*fffffa800263a590 size:   3b0 previous size:   190  (Allocated) Driv
*fffffa800263aad0 size:   200 previous size:   190  (Allocated) Driv
*fffffa8002749cb0 size:   350 previous size:   160  (Allocated) Driv
*fffffa8002791000 size:   200 previous size:     0  (Allocated) Driv
*fffffa8002c48600 size:   200 previous size:   120  (Allocated) Driv
*fffffa8002c4d530 size:   200 previous size:    60  (Allocated) Driv
*fffffa8002c59000 size:   200 previous size:     0  (Allocated) Driv
*fffffa8002c5d000 size:   200 previous size:     0  (Allocated) Driv
*fffffa8002c5e8b0 size:   200 previous size:   160  (Allocated) Driv
*fffffa8002c603e0 size:   200 previous size:   3e0  (Allocated) Driv
*fffffa8002c60a00 size:   200 previous size:   160  (Allocated) Driv
*fffffa8002c6dcb0 size:   350 previous size:    90  (Allocated) Driv
*fffffa8002c875f0 size:   200 previous size:   220  (Allocated) Driv
*fffffa8002c897e0 size:   200 previous size:    10  (Allocated) Driv
*fffffa8002c9a000 size:   200 previous size:     0  (Allocated) Driv
*fffffa8002cac3d0 size:   200 previous size:    10  (Allocated) Driv
*fffffa8002caf700 size:   200 previous size:    10  (Allocated) Driv
*fffffa8002d545e0 size:    30 previous size:    20  (Allocated) Driv
*fffffa8002d77120 size:    30 previous size:   120  (Allocated) Driv
*fffffa8002d7cc20 size:   200 previous size:    f0  (Allocated) Driv
*fffffa8002d7f700 size:    30 previous size:    20  (Allocated) Driv
*fffffa8002d84000 size:   470 previous size:     0  (Allocated) Driv
*fffffa8002d8d420 size:   200 previous size:   110  (Allocated) Driv
*fffffa8002d91b70 size:   200 previous size:   130  (Allocated) Driv
*fffffa8002d925f0 size:   200 previous size:    30  (Allocated) Driv
*fffffa8002d928b0 size:   200 previous size:    70  (Allocated) Driv
*fffffa8002d945f0 size:   200 previous size:   220  (Allocated) Driv
```

```
*fffffa8002d94e00 size:    200 previous size:     80  (Allocated) Driv
*fffffa8002d965f0 size:    200 previous size:    120  (Allocated) Driv
*fffffa8002d9d000 size:    470 previous size:      0  (Allocated) Driv
*fffffa8002da0b90 size:    470 previous size:    3b0  (Allocated) Driv
*fffffa8002da15f0 size:    200 previous size:    190  (Allocated) Driv
*fffffa8002da4000 size:    470 previous size:      0  (Allocated) Driv
*fffffa8002db15f0 size:    200 previous size:    190  (Allocated) Driv
*fffffa8002db19f0 size:    200 previous size:    190  (Allocated) Driv
*fffffa8002db8430 size:    200 previous size:     30  (Allocated) Driv
*fffffa8002dc3000 size:    200 previous size:      0  (Allocated) Driv
*fffffa8002dc85f0 size:    200 previous size:    120  (Allocated) Driv
*fffffa8002dcae00 size:    200 previous size:    190  (Allocated) Driv
*fffffa8002dcc820 size:     30 previous size:    150  (Allocated) Driv
*fffffa8002dcc8c0 size:    200 previous size:     60  (Allocated) Driv
*fffffa8002dcce00 size:    200 previous size:    160  (Allocated) Driv
*fffffa8002dd05e0 size:    200 previous size:    1d0  (Allocated) Driv
*fffffa8002dd25f0 size:    200 previous size:    160  (Allocated) Driv
*fffffa8002dd67c0 size:    200 previous size:     40  (Allocated) Driv
*fffffa8002ddc840 size:     30 previous size:     40  (Allocated) Driv
*fffffa8002ddc8b0 size:    350 previous size:     40  (Allocated) Driv
*fffffa8002ded4e0 size:    200 previous size:    120  (Allocated) Driv
*fffffa8002df3120 size:     30 previous size:     20  (Allocated) Driv
*fffffa8002dff5e0 size:    200 previous size:     80  (Allocated) Driv
*fffffa8002dffae0 size:    220 previous size:     50  (Allocated) Driv
*fffffa8002e6d160 size:    200 previous size:     30  (Allocated) Driv
*fffffa8002e72550 size:    480 previous size:     c0  (Allocated) Driv
*fffffa8002e75000 size:    200 previous size:      0  (Allocated) Driv
*fffffa8002e79000 size:    200 previous size:      0  (Allocated) Driv
*fffffa8002e82270 size:    200 previous size:     10  (Allocated) Driv
*fffffa8002e9f000 size:    470 previous size:      0  (Allocated) Driv
*fffffa8002ea9000 size:    200 previous size:      0  (Allocated) Driv
*fffffa8002eaf2e0 size:    200 previous size:     e0  (Allocated) Driv
*fffffa8002ebb000 size:    200 previous size:      0  (Allocated) Driv
*fffffa8002ec0000 size:    470 previous size:      0  (Allocated) Driv
*fffffa8002ec1de0 size:    150 previous size:    160  (Allocated) Driv
*fffffa8002ecb000 size:    200 previous size:      0  (Allocated) Driv
*fffffa8002ecb6f0 size:     30 previous size:    300  (Allocated) Driv
*fffffa8002ece000 size:    470 previous size:      0  (Allocated) Driv
*fffffa8002ed32b0 size:    200 previous size:     60  (Allocated) Driv
*fffffa8002ee5870 size:    200 previous size:     a0  (Allocated) Driv
*fffffa8002ef0000 size:    200 previous size:      0  (Allocated) Driv
*fffffa8002f00500 size:    200 previous size:     f0  (Allocated) Driv
*fffffa80030a2e00 size:    200 previous size:     f0  (Allocated) Driv
*fffffa80031b0790 size:    470 previous size:     20  (Allocated) Driv
*fffffa80031c4770 size:    200 previous size:     40  (Allocated) Driv
*fffffa80031fe950 size:    200 previous size:     d0  (Allocated) Driv
*fffffa80031ff000 size:     90 previous size:      0  (Allocated) Driv
*fffffa800320c360 size:    200 previous size:     30  (Allocated) Driv
*fffffa8003217270 size:    200 previous size:    120  (Allocated) Driv
*fffffa8003226e00 size:    200 previous size:     60  (Allocated) Driv
*fffffa800324d9f0 size:    200 previous size:    190  (Allocated) Driv
*fffffa80032a0e00 size:    200 previous size:     50  (Allocated) Driv
*fffffa80032aa270 size:    150 previous size:     60  (Allocated) Driv
*fffffa80032ac340 size:     f0 previous size:     10  (Allocated) Driv
*fffffa80032b36e0 size:    200 previous size:    120  (Allocated) Driv
*fffffa8003653c00 size:    200 previous size:     c0  (Allocated) Driv
*fffffa8003744200 size:    200 previous size:     80  (Allocated) Driv
*fffffa80038bd000 size:    200 previous size:      0  (Allocated) Driv
*fffffa80038d1cc0 size:    200 previous size:     80  (Allocated) Driv
*fffffa80039035f0 size:    200 previous size:     d0  (Allocated) Driv
```

```
*fffffa800392a890 size:   200 previous size:    60  (Allocated) Driv
*fffffa800397bb20 size:   200 previous size:   2c0  (Allocated) Driv
*fffffa80039a2880 size:   200 previous size:    90  (Allocated) Driv
*fffffa80039b28b0 size:   200 previous size:    c0  (Allocated) Driv
*fffffa80039bae00 size:   200 previous size:    c0  (Allocated) Driv
*fffffa80039bc000 size:   470 previous size:     0  (Allocated) Driv
*fffffa80039c8000 size:   200 previous size:     0  (Allocated) Driv
*fffffa8003b54440 size:   200 previous size:   150  (Allocated) Driv
*fffffa8003b54920 size:   200 previous size:   150  (Allocated) Driv
*fffffa8003b54e00 size:   200 previous size:   150  (Allocated) Driv
*fffffa8003b55380 size:   200 previous size:    c0  (Allocated) Driv
*fffffa8003b59580 size:   200 previous size:    20  (Allocated) Driv
*fffffa8003b61e00 size:   200 previous size:   150  (Allocated) Driv
*fffffa8003b78000 size:   200 previous size:     0  (Allocated) Driv
*fffffa8003b7de00 size:   200 previous size:   190  (Allocated) Driv
*fffffa8003d9f800 size:    30 previous size:    90  (Allocated) Driv
*fffffa8003fcf810 size:   200 previous size:    10  (Allocated) Driv
```

Let's check the last *Proc* entry:

```
0: kd> dc fffffa800417d8e0
fffffa80`0417d8e0  02720030 636f7250 c12c04f1 42d60064  0.r.Proc..,.d..B
fffffa80`0417d8f0  00001000 00000688 00000048 fffff802  ........H.......
fffffa80`0417d900  b3d121c0 fffff802 00000000 00000000  .!..............
fffffa80`0417d910  002ffd7d 00000000 0000000c 00000000  }./.............
fffffa80`0417d920  00000000 00000000 00080007 00000000  ................
fffffa80`0417d930  b3d121c0 fffff802 000050ed fffff8a0  .!.......P......
fffffa80`0417d940  00b20003 00000000 0203b320 fffffa80  ........ .......
fffffa80`0417d950  037e07d0 fffffa80 0417d958 fffffa80  ..~.....X.......
```

```
0: kd> !process fffffa80`0417d940 0
PROCESS fffffa800417d940
    SessionId: 2  Cid: 0a28    Peb: 7f66fc54000  ParentCid: 0a3c
    DirBase: 6d36d000  ObjectTable: fffff8a00192a600  HandleCount: <Data Not Accessible>
    Image: winlogon.exe
```

Note that another approach is to dump all handles of Process type from System process:

```
0: kd> !process 0 0
**** NT ACTIVE PROCESS DUMP ****
PROCESS fffffa800182e480
    SessionId: none  Cid: 0004    Peb: 00000000  ParentCid: 0000
    DirBase: 00187000  ObjectTable: fffff8a000003000  HandleCount: <Data Not Accessible>
    Image: System
```

[…]

```
0: kd> !handle 0 3 fffffa800182e480 Process

Searching for handles of type Process

PROCESS fffffa800182e480
    SessionId: none  Cid: 0004    Peb: 00000000  ParentCid: 0000
    DirBase: 00187000  ObjectTable: fffff8a000003000  HandleCount: <Data Not Accessible>
    Image: System

Kernel handle Error reading handle count.
```

```
0004: Object: ffffffa800182e480  GrantedAccess: 001fffff Entry: fffff8a000006010
Object: ffffffa800182e480  Type: (ffffffa8001825670) Process
    ObjectHeader: ffffffa800182e450 (new version)
        HandleCount: 6  PointerCount: 1835102


00c0: Object: ffffffa8002d78500  GrantedAccess: 0000002a Entry: fffff8a000006300
Object: ffffffa8002d78500  Type: (ffffffa8001825670) Process
    ObjectHeader: ffffffa8002d784d0 (new version)
        HandleCount: 1  PointerCount: 523890


[…]


14f8: Object: ffffffa8002cb2940  GrantedAccess: 0000002a Entry: fffff8a007f163e0
Object: ffffffa8002cb2940  Type: (ffffffa8001825670) Process
    ObjectHeader: ffffffa8002cb2910 (new version)
        HandleCount: 11  PointerCount: 2359105


1550: Object: ffffffa8004145940  GrantedAccess: 0000002a Entry: fffff8a007f16540
Object: ffffffa8004145940  Type: (ffffffa8001825670) Process
    ObjectHeader: ffffffa8004145910 (new version)
        HandleCount: 8  PointerCount: 2097247


15b4: Object: ffffffa8001d54580  GrantedAccess: 0000002a Entry: fffff8a007f166d0
Object: ffffffa8001d54580  Type: (ffffffa8001825670) Process
    ObjectHeader: ffffffa8001d54550 (new version)
        HandleCount: 4  PointerCount: 1310496



0: kd> !process ffffffa8001d54580 0
PROCESS ffffffa8001d54580
    SessionId: 0  Cid: 0f98    Peb: 7f76acaa000  ParentCid: 0220
    DirBase: 18acb000  ObjectTable: fffff8a0022e3980  HandleCount: <Data Not Accessible>
    Image: msiexec.exe
```

11.   And finally we check I/O stack traces for all IRPs (verbose form of **!irpfind** command):

```
0: kd> !irpfind -v

[…]

ffffffa80040696c0: Irp is active with 6 stacks 3 is current (= 0xffffffa8004069820)
 No Mdl: No System Buffer: Thread 00000000:  Irp stack trace.
     cmd  flg cl Device   File     Completion-Context
 [  0, 0]   0  0 00000000 00000000 00000000-00000000

                    Args: 00000000 00000000 00000000 00000000
 [  0, 0]   0  0 00000000 00000000 00000000-00000000

                    Args: 00000000 00000000 00000000 00000000
>[ 16, 0]   0  1 ffffffa8002f35050 00000000 00000000-00000000    pending
            \Driver\usbuhci
                    Args: 00000005 00000000 00000000 00000000
 [ 16, 0]   0 e0 ffffffa8002ee0c50 00000000 00000000-00000000
            \Driver\ACPI
                    Args: 00000005 00000000 00000000 00000000
 [ 16, 0]   0 e1 ffffffa8002f39050 00000000 fffff802b3ba42a8-ffffffa8002e95f00 Success Error Cancel pending
            \Driver\usbhub nt!PopRequestCompletion
                    Args: 00000005 00000000 00000000 00000000
 [  0, 0]   0  0 00000000 00000000 00000000-ffffffa8002e95f00

[…]
```

If any entry is suspicious you can check its Device and File fields using **!devobj** and **!fileobj** commands.

12.   Close the log file:

```
0: kd> .logclose
Closing open log file C:\AWMA-Dumps\M6.log
```

13.   To avoid possible confusion and glitches we recommend exiting WinDbg after each exercise.

If you are presented with this dialog choose No:

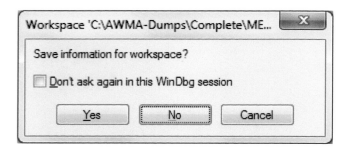

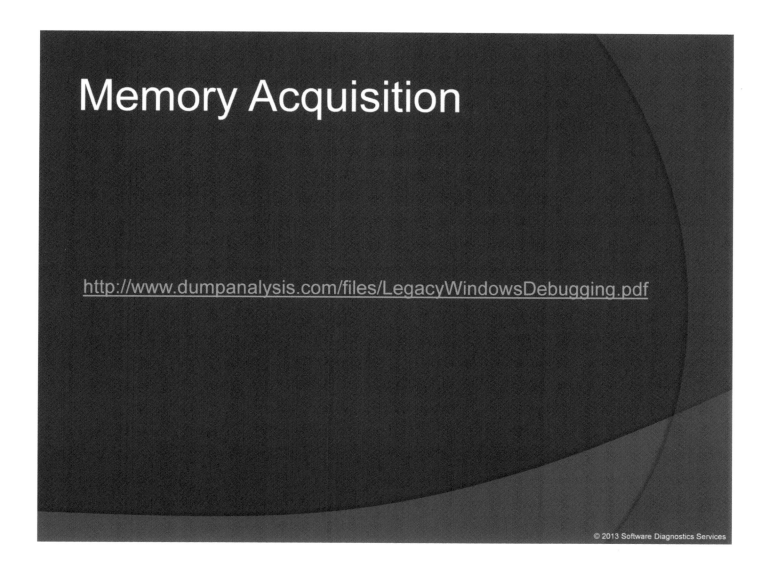

Here I provide a link to a PDF file. Just look at Special Topics slides and I also plan add more methods there.

http://www.dumpanalysis.com/files/LegacyWindowsDebugging.pdf

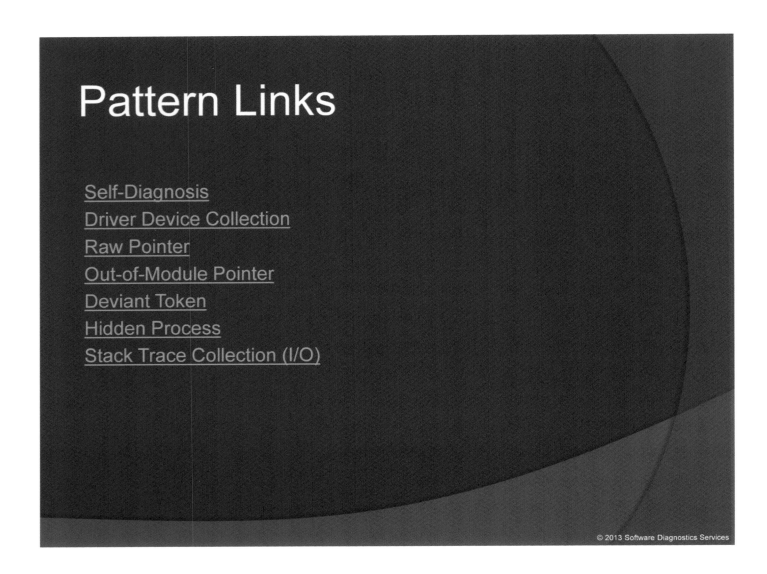

Pattern Links

Self-Diagnosis
Driver Device Collection
Raw Pointer
Out-of-Module Pointer
Deviant Token
Hidden Process
Stack Trace Collection (I/O)

Here are links to descriptions of patterns we found in our last 3 exercises.

Self-Diagnosis
http://www.dumpanalysis.org/blog/index.php/2011/04/26/crash-dump-analysis-patterns-part-69b/

Driver Device Collection
http://www.dumpanalysis.org/blog/index.php/2013/01/20/malware-analysis-patterns-part-10/

Raw Pointer
http://www.dumpanalysis.org/blog/index.php/2013/02/09/malware-analysis-patterns-part-22/

Out-of-Module Pointer

http://www.dumpanalysis.org/blog/index.php/2013/02/10/malware-analysis-patterns-part-23/

Deviant Token

http://www.dumpanalysis.org/blog/index.php/2012/12/31/crash-dump-analysis-patterns-part-191/

Hidden Process

http://www.dumpanalysis.org/blog/index.php/2012/11/13/crash-dump-analysis-patterns-part-186/

Stack Trace Collection (I/O)

http://www.dumpanalysis.org/blog/index.php/2012/01/11/crash-dump-analysis-patterns-part-27d/

Resources

- WinDbg Help / WinDbg.org (quick links)
- DumpAnalysis.org
- The Rootkit Arsenal (2nd edition)
- Windows Internals, 6th ed.
- Windows Debugging: Practical Foundations
- x64 Windows Debugging: Practical Foundations
- Memory Dump Analysis Anthology (Volumes 1 – 6)

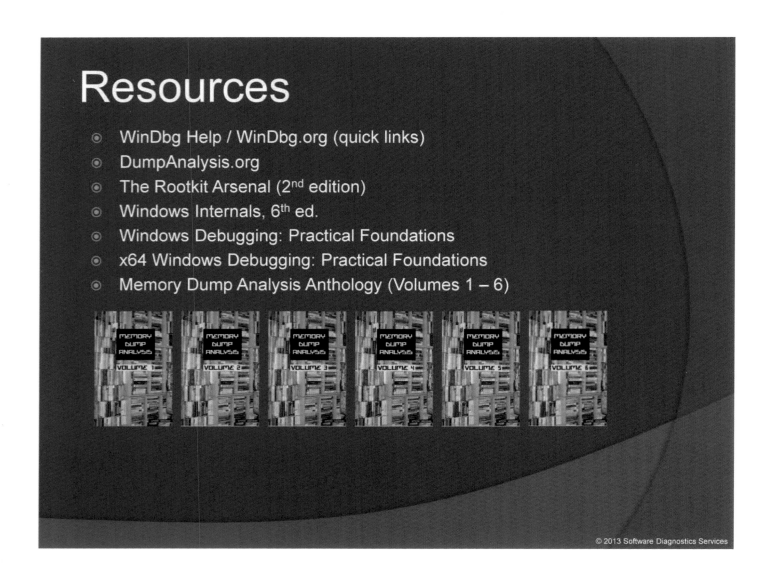

A few notes about references. The Rootkit Arsenal book is very useful as it discusses the very opposite of what we were doing. If you need basics of assembly language for both 32-bit and 64-bit systems such as function calls, their prologues and epilogues, parameter passing then you can find 2 Windows Debugging books from Practical Foundations series useful.